Walk Europe

Activity Series

Also available:
National Parks Europe

On the internet:
www.activityseries.com

Ažvinčiai forest, Abelines Gård, Agri Bavenhøj, Ahtari region, Aiguilles Rouges Nature Reserve, Aladaglar Mountains, Alentejo, Algarve, Allgäu Alps, Almindingen, Alpine Pass Route, Alto Adige, Ammarnas, Ammergebirge, Art Lover's Tour of Eastern Tuscany, Angel's Pastures, Aradena gorge, Arctic Circle, Arezzo, Armagh, Around Chamonix, Åsbyrgi canyon, Augstenberg Walk, Aukštaitija National Park, Austvågøya, Avebury, Áyios Nikolaos, Badacsony, Balaton Uplands National Park, Balcons de la Méditerranée, Ballons des Vosges Regional Nature Park, Banská Bystrica, Bardsey island, Baske Oštarije, Bay of Trieste, Beautiful Caves, Belianske Tatry, Ben Nevis, Ben Rinnes, Benbrack, Berliner Spitze, Bernese Oberland, Besançon, Beyşehir lake, Birdoswald, Blansky les, Bled, Bledne Skały, Boat O' Brig, Boda, Boggle Hole, Bohemian Paradise, Bolt Head, Bolzen, Bonagual castle, Bonne river, Bork Havn, Bornholm, Borris, Börzsöny hills, Bosco-Gurin, Bosjökloster, Bouillon castle, Boulby potash mine, Boyne valley, Bran castle, Brijuni National Park, Broumov Walls, Bruges, Bucegi massif, Buda hills, Burdenerhal hills, Burg Rabenstein, Burgenweg, Cader Idris, Caherdaniel, Cairn Damh, Cambrian Way, Camino Real, Cangas de Onis, Capanna Cava, Cape St Vincent, Caragh lake, Cares gorge, Carlaveyron, Carlingford lough, Carnic Alps, Carrick-on-Suir, Castiglione di Sicilia, Castle of Peace, Castlebar, Castro Marim Reserve, Cave Hill, Celikbuyduran, Central Alps, Central Swiss Alps, Cerknica lake, Cesky Krumlov, Český raj, Champex, Château de Prieur, Chiusi della Verna monastery, Chocholowska valley, Chopok, Church of Panagia Forviotrissa of Asinou, Cicarija mountains, Cime du Gelas, Cimonega range, Cirque de Gavarnie, Clwydian hills, Clynnog Fawr, Coastal walks in Finistere, Cockburnspath, Col de Côte Belle, Col de Romeion, Col de St-Pierre, Conic Hill, Cote d'Azur, County Donegal, County Mayo, Covadonga National Park, Crickhowell, Cromdale hills, Csucs Hill, Curral das Freiras, Czestochowa, Czech Greenways, Dammusi pass, Danube Bend, Daverdisse, De Panne, Dedegul, Deister Forest Park, Demanovska dolina, Denmark's Sunrise Island, Der Süden Sudtirols, Derryquin castle, Désert en Valjouffrey, Dettifoss waterfall, Deutsche Alpenstrasse, Devil's Cave, Die Frankische Schweiz, Diekirch, Disko Bay, Dolomiti Bellunesi National Park, Domogled mountain, Donja Spilja, Drawa National Park, Dublin, Duje river, Dune and Polder Way, Eğirdir lake, Eccles Cairn, Echternach, Egloffstein, Eiger, Eildon peaks, Eksharad, Ellemandsbjerget, Emsland, Engelsmanplaat, Ensko lake, Entraigues plain, Esztergom, Eysturoy, Fazana Channel, Fagaras mountains, Faroe Islands, Fisherman's Way, Śrbské Pleso, Fivemiletown, Flaschenberg, Fluelen, Forggensee, Formazza, Fourneau St-Michel, Foxford Way, Freedom Cave, French Cornwall Coast, Fridaythorpe, Friesenweg, From Riga to Cape Kolka, Frutigland, Funchal, Garmisch-Partenkirchen, Garrotxa, Gdansk, Giant's Causeway, Glacier des Bossons, Glarner Alps, Glasgow, Glen Coe, Glendalough, Gorna Spilja, Gorski Kotar, Gory Stolowe National Park, Gory Złote, Graiguenamanagh, Grand Balcon Sud trail, Grindelwald, Grindelwaldgletscher, Grosse Scheidegg, Grosser Moseler, Grüntensee, Guadiana river, Gwyrtheyrn valley, Haarlem, Hadrian's Wall Path, Hall of Mirrors, Hallein Bad Durrnberg, Hammero island, Hammershus Slot, Hangman Point, Hartland Point, Haute Randonnée Pyreneene, Haute Route, Hay Bluff, Hegyestü, Heidiland, Hel peninsula, Helgenæs, Helligdomsklipperne, Helmsley castle, Hemavan Mountain Park, Hergest ridge, Het Zwin Nature Reserve, Highland High Way, Hiking in the Black Forest, Hirviharju ridge, Hljodaklettar, Hohtürli, Holmatungur, Holmsland Klit, Hook of Holland, Hornisgrinde, Hosingen, Húsavik, Icknield Way, Ilomantsi, Imvrós Gorge, Ioannina, Istria, Cres and Risnjak, Ivinghoe Beacon, Jurmala, Jedburgh abbey, Jelenia Gora, Jičin, Jokulsa Canyon National Park, Jungfrau, Juuma, Juuma, Kas, Kaitumjaure lake, Kåli basin, Karawanken Alps, Karelian Circuit, Kärnten, Katwijk aan See, Kemeri National Park, Kerloas-en-Plouarzel, Kiagtuut Sermiat, King Ludwig's Trail, Kingussie, Kirkjubøur, Kis Balaton, Klaralven river, Klausenpass, Koivusuo Nature Park, Koksijde, Koloska valley, Kopské Sedlo, Krivaň, Kuusamo-Sallo road, Kykkos monastery, La Moselle, La Roche-en-Ardenne, Lac Labarre, Ladakalnis Hill, Lago del Mis, Lahemaa National Park, Lahnhöhenwege, Lake Balaton, Lake Como, Lake Dhrakólimni, Lake Iseo, Lake Kanieris, Lake Lucerne, Land of the Thousand Ponds, Las Alpujarras, Lascaux cave, Le Bouchet St-Nicholas, Le Coeur du Bon Pays, Le Grand Capelet, Le Monastier-sur-Gazeille, Lechtal valley, Lefka Ori, Legnica Field, Les Ardennes, Les Eyzies, Les Houches, Les Terres Rouges, Letterfrack, Lindisfarne, Linnansaari National Park, Little Bear Trail, Little Hell, Lizard's Point, Llandovery, Llyn peninsula, Loch Trool, Lomnicky štit, Lot-et-Garonne, Lough Erne, Lough Neagh, Lycian Way, Lysefjordbreen glacier, Maamturks, Madeira's levadas, Maeterlinck path, Magistrala, Malmö, Mantova, Marathasa valley, Marburg, Mattmarksee reservoir, Mawdach estuary, Mediterranean Sea, Melintaou, Mer de Glace, Merry Maidens, Metéora monasteries, Mikkeli, Milford Haven, Mittelweg, Moesgård museum, Moldoveanu, Molène archipelago, Mols Bjerge, Moltke tower, Monadhliath mountains, Monflanquin, Mont Blanc, Montagnes Noires, Monte Faié, Monte Falterona, Monte Perdido, Moskenesøy, Mount Pakhnes, Mount Pisivic, Mourne mountains, Moutoulas, Mt Barla, Mt Demirlazik, Mt Olympus, Mt Pizzicco, Mt Sleza, Mt Vallazza, Mud walking on the Wadden Sea, Mulhacén, Mullerthal, Nanortalik, Narva castle, National Blue Trail, Neideck tower, Nephin mountain, Newport Sands, Nidaros, Nine Stones, Nizké Tatry, Nockberge National Park, Nömmeveski, Nordrhein-Westphalen, Nørre Lyngvig lighthouse, North East Bohemia, Northern Aquitaine, Northern Limestone Alps, Notranjska, Oberammergau, Oberpfalzweg, Obwalden, Ogrodzieniec castle, Ohn river, Ojcow National Park, Ordesa National Park, Orlické hory, Ortler-Cevedale glaciers, Ortlergruppe range, Osmotherley, Osnabruck, Osterhorn mountains, Österlen Path, Ötztaler Alps, Paklenica National Park, Paluse, Palava hills, Paldiski, Panoramaweg, Panoramique du Mercantour, Paradise hills, Parc National des Pyrénées, Parco delle Groane, Parco delle Orobie Bergamasche, Path of Lighthouses, Patvinsuo National Park, Pavinpolku Trail, Pembrokeshire Coast Path National Trail, Pen-yr-Afr, Pennine Alps, Pforzheim, Pian di Crest, Piani Eterni, Piatra Craiului, Pico de Aneto, Pico do Ariero, Pico Ruivo, Pilgrims' Way, Pivka river, Planica, Po river ralley, Poland's Baltic Coast, Pollino National Park, Pomeranian Lakelands, Pontassieve, Poqueira gorge, Porth Yslaig, Postojna Basin and Cerknica, Pratomagno ridge, Praz-sur-Arly, Predjama castle, Premosello-Malesco traverse, Premuzic's path, Puffin Land, Pulpit Rock, Pustertal, Qaqortoq, Raganello gorge, Ragginger lakes, Rannoch Moor, Ransby, Rauris valley, Refsvatn lake, Reichenbach falls, Rheidol valley, Rhône-Alpes, Ribčev Laz, Richetlipass, Ridge to Ridge Path, Riga, Rijeka mountain traverse, Ringkabing fjord, Rio Arazas, Rio Formosa National Park, Ritten plateau, Rožanski kukovi, Romantische Strasse, Römerstrasse, Rond Vlaanderen, Rothaargebirge Nature Park, Rovinj, Rufina, Rura Integral de los Tres Mil, Rütli meadows, Słowinski National Park, Saimaa Lakelands, Salzburg, Salzkammergut, Samaria Gorge, Samina valley, San Gotthard pass, Sansepolcro, Saone valley, Sarek National Park, Savilahti Church, Savonlinna, Savoy Alps, Schiermonnikoog, Schlißkopf, Schloss Linderhof, Schwarzwald, Scott's View, Scottish Borders, Seelisberg cliffs, Semois river, Serra Caldeirão, Serra de Monchique, Serra Dolcedorme, Settrington Beacon, Shropshire Union canal, Sidyma, Sierra Nevada, Sila forests, Silesia and the Sudeten mountains, Silsbury Hill, Simmental, Skåne and the Skåncleden, Slitere Nature Reserve, Slettåa waterfall, Soča valley, Solvere Slott, Sophienhohle, Southern Carpathians, Southern Regions of Luxembourg, Speilsalen cave, Sperrin mountains, St Cuthbert's Way, St Dogmaels, St-Hubert, Staniceva koca, Stavanger, Stein torrent, Steinwald, Stelvio National Park, Stenshuvud National Park, Stirovacá valley, Stonehenge, Stora Sjöfallet National Park, Strata Florida, Strumble Head, Stuba waterfall, Studalsvatnet lake, Sugarloaf mountain, Szczecin Bay, Trebońsko wetlands, Tábor, Tahtali Dag, Tain Way, Taitaja's Trail, Tallinn, Taormina, Tarnon gorge, Tarra valley, Tarraios river, Tasiilaq, Tatry National Park, Tauernsee, Taurus mountains, Telč, Terschelling, Texel, The Arnoweg, The Bear Trail, The Bear's Ring Trail, The Beara Way, The Cleveland Way, The foothills of Mount Etna, The Franche-Comte, The Great Walser Route, The Julian Alps, The Kerry Way, The Kungsleden, The Lahn Valley, The North Estonian Glint, The North-West Passage, The Offa's Dyke Path, The Padjelantaleden, The Picos de Europa, The Pirkan Taival, The Pyrenees, The Ridgeway, The South Leinster Way, The South West Coast Path, The Southern Upland Way, The Speyside Way, The Stevenson Trail and the Cevennes, The Swiss Path, The Transardennaise, The Ulster Way, The Upper Palatinate, The Valbonnais, The West Highland Way, The Western Way, The Wicklow Way, The Wolds Way, Thor's Harbour, Ticino, Tihany peninsula, Tollymore Forest Park, Torc waterfall, Tour du Mont Blanc, Tour du Pays du Mont Blanc, Trail of the Eagles' Nests, Transylvanian Alps, Trekking 700, Trescolmen pass, Trelvez, Trezien lighthouse, Triangle, Triesen, Trimontium, Trollheimen, Troodos mountains, Trosky, Turkey's Lakeland, Twin Law Cairns, Tyne valley, Uffington castle, Ukkusissaq, Ukojas lake, Ulupinar, Upper Swabian Baroque Highway, Upper Theodul glacier, Urra moor, Urrieles massif, Vaduz, Vågakallen, Vaganski, Vaisoluokta, Val d'Ossola, Val Pogallo, Valentia island, Valgejogi river, Valle de Ordesa, Valley of Marvels, Valley of the Flowers, Valley of the Seven Castles, Valley of Triglav Lakes, Vallon-du-Bérard, Varmland and The Pilgrims' Way, Velebit, Veleta, Velika Kapela, Vestmanna bird cliffs, Vézere valley, Vibo Valentia, Vierwaldstättersee, Vindolanda, Virgin Island, Virihaure lake, Visegrad, Vlaamse Banken, Vosges mountains, Voyvale Tatry, Waldnaab river, Walking along the Dutch Coast, Walking amongst Slovakia's mountains, Walking and hiking in Liechtenstein, Walking in Calabria, Walking in Carinthia, Walking in Greenland, Walking in Lombardy, Walking in Ryfylke-Setesdalsheicne, Walking in the Alpes-Maritimes, Walking in the Austrian Tirol, Walking in the Franconian Switzerland, Walking in the Pindhos Mountains, Walking in the Southern Dolomites, Walking in the Südtirol, Walking in Val Grande National Park, Walking on the Lofoten Islands, Walltown Crags, Wanlockhead, Wayland's Smithy, Welshpool, Weser-Ems, West-Vlaanderen, Westhoek, Westweg, Wetzlar, Whin Sills, White Mountains of Western Crete, White Sands, Wieliczka salt mine, Wierzchowska Hill cave, Windischeschenbach, Wittekindsweg, Wolin National Park, Woman Hill, Wörthersee, Wrocław, Wye valley, Yedigöller, Zbojnicka chalet, Zeimena river, Zillertaler Hohestrasse, Zsigmondy Spitze.

Series editor
Mark Hancox

Editorial team
Stephen Bird, Olivia Dickinson, Emma Gilliland,
Sarah Johnson, Aoibhe O'Shea, Toner Quinn,
Julia Sandford

Information co-ordination
Alison Compton

Design
ENDAT Design

Production
Suzy Gillespie, Mhairi Dawson

• Front cover image:
Le Lac Blanc de Polset, vue vers le Col du Soufre
Used with the permission of Parc National de la
Vanoise. Photographer – Christophe Gotti.

• Printed by Tipolitografia Petruzzi Corrado of
Perugia, Italy.

ACTIVITY SERIES

Activity Series guides are different from other travel
books. Intended to be read and enjoyed at the creative
stage of choosing a holiday, each title provides a
stimulating overview of a particular environment or
activity across a wide geographical area.

Walk Europe offers a snapshot of possible destinations
across the whole continent, from the windswept Faroe
Islands to the warmth of the Turkish coast.

■ Clear and engaging text
Written in a lively style, the text acts as an introduction
to an area covering the landscape, flora and fauna,
selected walking routes, outdoor activities, history,
culture and the best time to go.

■ Vivid pictures
The colour pictures are bold, attractive, dramatic
and intriguing. Each one helps bring the walk and
surrounding region to life.

■ Illustrative maps
Each entry has a simple illustrative map that helps
to locate places and features included in the text.
A smaller map places the walk within the country.

●	Village / town / city
★	Place of interest
- - - -	International border
———	Regional boundary
- - - -	National park boundary
· · · · · ·	Walking route
———	River
⌒	Lake
♦	Forest
ѵ ѵ	Marsh
⟋\	Mountain
⟋⟍	Small mountain / big hill
⌒	Hill

■ Contact information
The contact information, both at the start of each section
and at the end of each entry, is the ideal stepping stone
for finding out more about a particular area. Postal,
phone, fax and electronic address details are provided for
tourism authorities and other relevant organisations.

CONTENTS

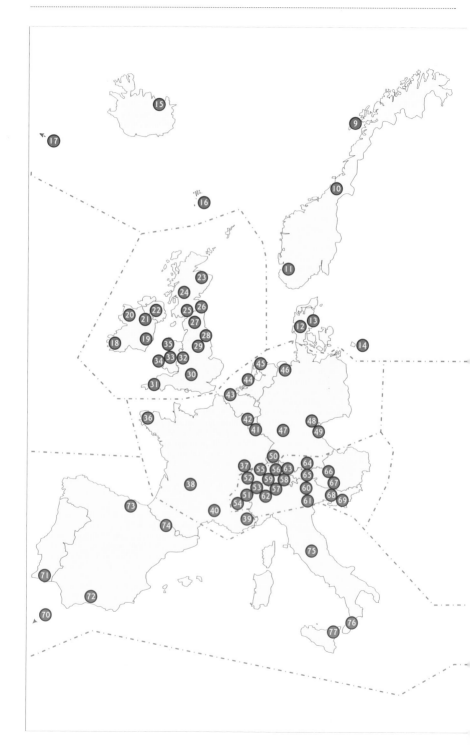

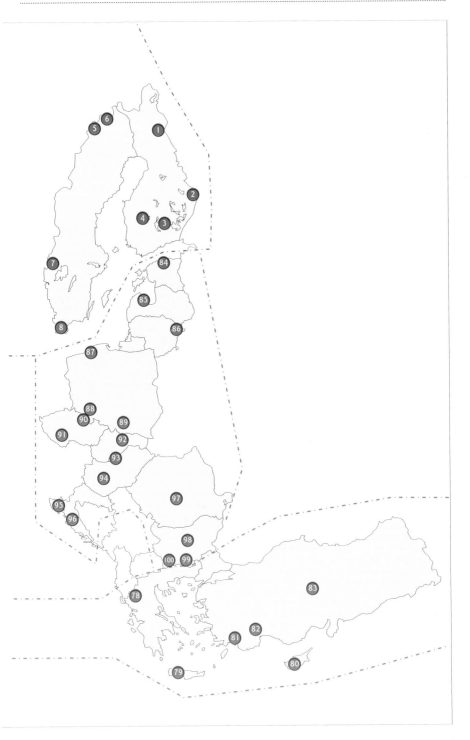

i CONTACT INFORMATION

Danish Tourist Board
55 Sloane Street
London SW1X 9SY
Tel: 020 7259 5959
Fax: 020 7259 5955
E-mail: dtb.london@dt.dk
Web: www.dtb.dt.dk

The Faroe Islands Tourist Board
Gongin
PO Box 118
FO-110 Tórshavn
Faroe Islands
Tel: (00 298) 316055
Fax: (00 298) 310858
E-mail: tourist@tourist.fo
Web: www.tourist.fo

Finnish Tourist Board
30-35 Pall Mall
London SW1Y 5LP

Tel: 020 7839 4048
Fax: 020 7321 0696
E-mail: Mek.Lon@mek.fi
Web: www.mek.fi

Greenland Tourism
PO Box 1139
Pilestraede 52
DK 1010 Copenhagen K
Denmark
Tel: (00 45) 3369 3200
Fax: (00 45) 3393 3883
E-mail: greenfo@inet.uni2.dk
Web: www.greenland-guide.gl

Icelandair
172 Tottenham Court Road
London W1P 0LY
Tel: 020 7874 1000
Fax: 020 7387 5711
E-mail: london@icelandair.is
Web: www.icelandair.is

Norwegian Tourist Board
5th Floor, Charles House
5 Regent Street (Lower)
London SW1Y 4LR
Tel: 020 7839 2650
Fax: 020 7839 6014
E-mail: infouk@ntr.no
Web: www.visitnorway.com

Swedish Travel & Tourism Council
11 Montagu Place
London W1H 2AL
Tel: 020 7870 5600 (information)
01476 578811 (brochures)
Fax: 020 7724 5872
E-mail: info@swetourism.org.uk
Web: www.visit-sweden.com

 **FINLAND**

The Bear's Ring Trail

The Bear's Ring Trail, known in Finnish as the Karhunkierros, has been an established favourite among hikers for over forty years.

A section of the Kiutaköngäs falls

Totalling approximately 90km, the Bear's Ring Trail winds through the Kuusamo region of eastern Finland, just south of the Arctic Circle. Two-thirds of the trail is inside the boundaries of Oulanka National Park, linking some of its most renowned beauty spots and offering a real diversity of landscapes. In places, meadows and sandbanks overlook the tranquil river, its violent rapids hidden around the next bend. Elsewhere, peatland wilderness, heaths and coniferous forests stretch for miles in every direction.

Although the trail can be completed in three to four days, the rugged terrain is difficult in places, and most walkers prefer to enjoy the spectacular scenery at a more leisurely pace. There are a number of variations on the main route, and frequent cabins and campsites allow it to be broken down into shorter sections.

Oulanka

Oulanka's marshes, forests, rivers and heaths are a haven for a number of rare plants, birds and animals. The harshness of the Arctic winter is tempered by humid sea winds brought by the Gulf Stream, encouraging luxuriant vegetation unusual for such a northerly region. Such conditions enable hardy northern tree species such as spruce and pine to thrive on shady or damp rockfaces, while southern plants – wild strawberry, sedge and campion – grow on warm, sunny slopes.

Winters are harsher and snowier than in southern Finland, with temperatures below freezing from mid October until the end of April, with an average January temperature of -16°C. However, although summers are short, they can also be spectacular – July averages 15°C, and 30°C has been recorded in exceptional years. The best time for walking is June and July, although the weather is always unpredictable.

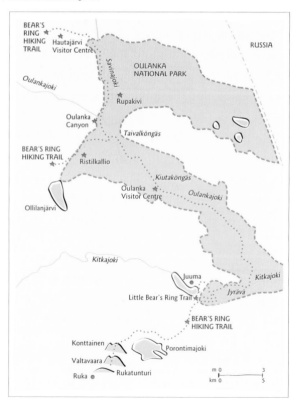

Beginning the trail

The trail avoids the pine swamps and spruce forests of the northern section of the park, winding instead along the Oulanka river and its tributaries – the Kitkajoki, Savinajoki, Maaninkajoki and Aventojoki. *Joki* means 'river' or 'stream' in Finnish. The river valleys are notable for their steep banks carved into the gravelly river bed, in places resembling canyons flanked by rugged cliffs. The way is clearly marked with signs and daubs of orange paint on trees.

Despite its name, the route is not circular. However, the starting and finishing points can be linked by the Kuusamo–Salla road, with regular buses on weekdays. The trail begins at Hautajärvi Nature Cabin, a few kilometres away from the northern boundary of the national park. Hautajärvi is open daily from spring to autumn. Walkers can prime themselves in the upcoming landscapes by visiting the exhibitions on different bog types, flora and fauna, geology and local history.

Rivers and waterfalls

Following the Savinajoki south, the trail passes Rupakivi, a strangely shaped rock standing in the water. The valley deepens until it reaches Lake Savilampi, where the Savinajoki and Oulankajoki join. The latter must be crossed here by suspension bridge, the first of many, offering a view of Oulanka canyon to the west.

At the Taivalköngäs falls, a few kilometres downstream, the waters rush down into two main channels. The view of the falls is worth the exhilaration of standing on one of the precarious suspension bridges as they swing with the force of the water and the gusts of wind. Further down the river are the Kiutaköngäs falls. 600m long, with a horizontal drop of 100m, the surging river crashes dramatically into the deep pool below. These falls were created when the river, running over a confluence of hard quartzite and soft dolomite, eroded the softer rock to form a steep precipice. The striking rusty brown colour of the falls' rocks intensifies its visual effect.

A narrow suspension bridge across one of the rushing rivers

The south of Oulanka

Once these treats have been savoured, it is time to press on along the river until the Oulankajoki begins to twist so violently that in places it has cut itself off to leave crescent-shaped oxbow lakes as evidence of its original path. From here the Bear's Ring Trail leads towards Lake Kulmakkojärvi and the Kitkajoki, a river valley that deepens until it reaches the beautiful Jyrävä falls. A cabin here overlooks the waterfall and the pool beneath it, offering a memorable place to stay for the night, and the experience of eating breakfast while watching the sun glint on foaming waters.

Nearby is Myllykoski, an idyllic restored mill, and the picturesque village of Juuma, representing a brief return to civilisation before the final push. This is also the site of the Little Bear's Ring Trail, which follows a 9km circular route from Juuma, passing Myllykoski mill and the Jyrävä rapids before continuing round Lake Jyrävänjärvi back to Juuma. Although short, the trail is demanding in places, but combines the torrents, valleys and quiet rivers that can be found on a larger scale along the full route.

Rukatunturi

The southernmost section of the trail follows the Porontimajoki, with more old mills dotted along its shores. Despite the tranquillity of the spot, it is too soon to relax, as hikers must first tackle a row of hills which provides an opportunity to admire the view. The route ends at Rukatunturi Fell (493m), at the ski resort of Ruka. Hikers can reward themselves for completing the trail by descending the fell on Finland's longest summer toboggan slope, which, at 1,001m, is perhaps no less tiring than the long trek behind them.

$\boxed{i}$ CONTACT INFORMATION

Oulanka Visitor Centre
Liikasenvaarantie 132
FIN-93999 Kuusamo
Finland
Tel: (00 358) 205 646850
Fax: (00 358) 205 646851
E-mail: oulanka@metsa.fi

Kuusamo Tourist Office
Karhuntassu
Torangintaival 2
FIN-93600 Kuusamo
Finland
Tel: (00 358) 8 850 2910
Fax: (00 358) 8 850 2901
E-mail: info@kuusamo.fi

FINLAND

The Karelian Circuit

Bordering Russia, boasting a rich heritage and a memorable landscape, North Karelia captivates and fascinates in equal measures.

The Karelian Circuit, or Karjalan Keirros, is the longest circular hiking route in Finland. Covering over 1,000km, it is broken into eleven smaller sections around the province of North Karelia. The trail crosses four national parks and numerous conservation areas, passing forested hills, lakes and marshes. This versatile route is suitable for hiking, riding, skiing, cycling or even canoeing.

A distinctive culture

The Ilomantsi region in North Karelia is further east than St Petersburg and contains the easternmost point in the European Union. North Karelia shares 300km of its border with Russia, and its name, pronounced 'kar-yela', is derived from Russian. A unique cultural identity has been forged from the fusion of east and west. Yet this has been hard won, shaped by the pressures of climate, religion and war.

The glacial influence

Nature was the first conqueror, shaping the region over millions of years. Eskers and moraine ridges are a spectacular reminder of the retreating ice sheet, while calm lakes reside in huge kettle holes, formed when blocks of ice carved basins into the rock. Hills are relicts of hard rocks, eroded more slowly than softer rock around them.

The religious influence

In the last thousand years, however, the greatest influence on the area has been political. North Karelia's vulnerable position has always made it a pawn in the ongoing power struggles of neighbouring countries. In the 12th century, the Russian Orthodox church converted the inhabitants of Karelia. Subsequent wars devastated the province until 1617, when Swedish rule brought peace but also imposed Lutheran beliefs upon the people. The largely Orthodox population fled, to be replaced by Finnish Lutherans, lured by tax relief and exemption from military service. Slowly, however, the Orthodox Karelians returned, particularly to Ilomantsi which today is a vibrant mix of both cultures.

The territorial influence

Over the years, Karelia was split into Finnish and Russian sections, each trying to claim back the other half. The bloodiest battles occurred during the Winter War of 1939–40 and the Continuation War that followed it. Trenches and tank barriers remain throughout North Karelia, as if to reinforce today's peace and beauty. Ilomantsi is proud of its survival and of its name – whether *ila* is derived from the word for happiness or from local associations with St Elias, it signifies the strength of the town and of North Karelia as a whole.

The inhabitants' influence

Far from being a wilderness, people have made their living on the land for centuries. Farms and fishing villages were once common on the shores of lakes. Log floating was a traditional activity, transporting timber down-river towards towns such as Eno, Joensuu or St Petersburg. Canals were built in the 1870s and by 1947, 3,000 log floaters were working in North Karelia. It was often dangerous work – many people were killed in the rapids of the Saramojoki river which now entertain canoeists. But after power plants were built on the river in the 1960s, log floating became difficult and stopped within just fifteen years. Sawmills and foresters' huts still line rivers as a memorial to this lost trade.

Trails in Ilomantsi

When exploring the Karelian Circuit, the town of Ilomantsi is worth visiting for its mixture of Lutheran and Orthodox culture. The church of St Elias is the largest wooden Orthodox church in Finland, while the Lutheran church is famous for its striking wall paintings.

Taitaja's Trail, the oldest in North Karelia, begins in Finland's smallest national park, Petkeljärvi, winding along picturesque watercourses for 37km. The Pavinpolku Trail is 80km long, ending in Patvinsuo National Park which covers 1,000 sq km, characterised by its precious peatlands and untamed wilderness. It is home to lynx, brown bears, wolves and also, it is said, to the Devil, who lives in a cave under an enormous glacial boulder called Marinkivi. More reassuringly, there is a great diversity of birds including kestrels, goshawks, cranes, Siberian jays and orioles.

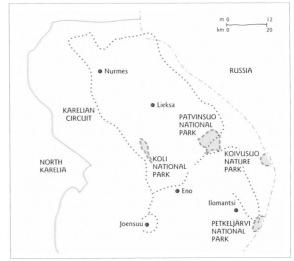

The Jaama Trail

The Jaama Trail is a 47km circuit around North Karelia's capital Joensuu, taking in natural and cultural points of interest. Traditionally a town of merchants and artisans, Joensuu nestles idyllically between lakes and leafy groves. Its university is active in the study of Karelian history and ecology. The highlight of the trail is the university's botanical garden, boasting more than 1,000 species and surrounded by an arboretum.

Trails in the Koli area

Koli National Park is the starting point for the Herajärvi and the Kilinpolku trails. Beautiful hill scenery includes Ukko-Koli, the highest peak in southern Finland. This typical Karelian landscape has inspired writers, artists and composers such as Jean Sibelius, whose *Finlandia* is world-renowned. Until the 18th century, however, the area was associated with witchcraft, with only the brave or foolhardy settling there. This reputation has perhaps contributed to the profuse calypso, helleborine, orchid and lady's-slipper lining the brooks.

Trails in the Lieksa area

Perhaps the most representative part of the Karelian Circuit is the Bear's Trail (not to be confused with the Bear's Ring Trail in northern Finland) which totals 133km. Following the Russian border, it incorporates many of the characteristic features of North Karelia including ridges, swamps, forests and lakes, as well as the relics of war. The path follows the canoeing route at the unharnessed Ruunaa rapids, so that sore feet may be replaced with tired arms. Birds, ducks and swans lend the trail a vibrant life, a constant reminder of nature's bounty even in a turbulent world.

[i] CONTACT INFORMATION

Lieksa Tourist Service Ltd
Pielisentie 7
FIN-81700 Lieksa
Tel: (00 358) 13 520 2400
Fax: (00 358) 13 526 438
E-mail: matkailu@lieksa.fi
Web: www.lieksa.fi/
lieksa/english.htm

Ilomantsi Tourist Services Ltd
Mantsintie 8
FIN-82900 Ilomantsi
Finland
Tel: (00 358) 13 881707
Fax: (00 358) 13 883270
E-mail: ilomantsin.
matkailu@co.inet.fi
Web: www.travel.fi/
int/Ilomantsin.htm

The versatile route can be walked, cycled or skied

 **FINLAND**

Saimaa

Saimaa is Europe's biggest lake district, with the Great Saimaa lake system itself covering 4,400 sq km, boasting a shoreline of 14,850km and harbouring approximately 13,710 islands.

In Finland's Saimaa lake district, nature trails and historical curiosities abound, while well-signposted canoe routes enable the quiet waters to offer endless opportunities for combining walking with boating.

The Saimaa seal

Sharp-eyed visitors may catch a glimpse of an endangered Saimaa ringed seal basking on sun-warmed rocks. The seal is found only in the Saimaa region, having adapted itself to a freshwater habitat after becoming stranded in the lakes at the end of the last Ice Age.

Although the seals can live for thirty years, most do not die of old age. In the past, they were hunted almost to extinction for their leather, fat and meat, and although this practice has been outlawed, modern hazards abound. Motorised boats disrupt the seals' breeding patterns, while pollution, fishing and shoreline building mean that fewer than 200 of these endearing creatures remain. Lake users can demonstrate their support for the plight of the seals by purchasing a special 'Saimaa seal' sticker for their boat or canoe.

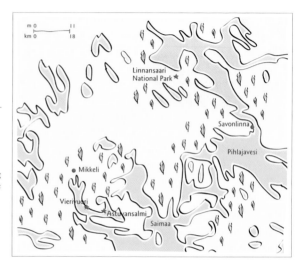

The sticker entitles the bearer to use the 220 waste disposal points dotted around the lakes which are also identified with the seal logo and run by the 'Keep the Islands Clean' organisation. In this way, the rare Saimaa seal has become both the symbol of a precarious ecosystem and the representative of the drive towards its preservation.

Linnansaari National Park

Lakelands all over Finland have been damaged by building developments over recent years. Linnansaari National Park was established in 1956 to preserve the characteristic inland archipelago scenery, flora, heritage sites and habitat of the Saimaa seal. The national park covers a 40km long

The 'Grand Boat Race of Sulkava'

The forested islets of the Saimaa lakelands

section of the Lake Haukivesi region of Great Saimaa, incorporating 130 islands larger than a hectare, as well as innumerable smaller islets. Accessible only by boat, the total surface area is 37 sq km, although the great expanses of water are not included as part of the national park.

Some islands are just heaps of stone or gravel ridges, while some of the larger ones are strewn with inhospitable boulders, sheer cliff-faces jutting out of the water. Here, the barren rock is clothed only in lichen and stunted Scots pine. Other islands, however, boast inviting sandy beaches and support lush vegetation, rich in herbs and shrubs. A typical woodland may include birch, alder, pine, aspen and lime trees, with hares, moose or badgers wandering across the fertile soil below the trees. Ornithologists are in their element here – Linnansaari teems with water birds of all varieties, including the rare osprey.

The best way to explore the park is to hire a boat and camp for a few days. There are hiking paths and nature trails on the main island, whilst those inclined towards social history can visit Linnansaari croft. Established in the 1850s and inhabited for over one hundred years, it is representative of the island crofts that were popular from the 17th century. With their little fields and farmyards, tenants enjoyed a certain independence from demanding landlords, a peace that can be replicated today in the isolation of the watery landscape.

Mikkeli

The lush lakelands have been inhabited since the Stone Age. The Astuvansalmi Nature Trail leads to the biggest set of rock paintings in Scandinavia, where sixty paintings cover a 15m area and date back 4,000 years. Just across Lake Yövesi are the Vierivuori rock paintings. These fragmentary pictures of people, elks and boats cover the steep cliff-face, but are now visible only from water.

Although Iron Age cemeteries also dot the area, the town itself only began to develop in the 15th century when it was named after St Michael, who is said to have stayed in the region. In 1838, Czar Nicholas I of Russia rather optimistically declared Mikkeli a city, apparently unconcerned that only sixty three people lived there at the time. But today, Mikkeli is the lively provincial capital with a

population of over 40,000. Its neat streets are built on a grid system centring around the the red Neo-Gothic cathedral. An adjacent square is dominated by the Naisvuori tower, a former water tower that offers a panoramic vantage point for viewing the lakes and forests surrounding Mikkeli. Standing on the edge of the town is the oldest building in this part of Finland, the stone sacristy of Savilahti church, built in 1320.

Urpola Nature Centre is located near the town centre. As well as offering exhibitions on the flora, fauna, waters and geology of the area, it is the site of the oldest wooden building in Mikkeli, Urpola manor, which is associated with the wars that raged here at the end of the 18th century when Sweden and Russia fought for the territory. Other nature reserves in the vicinity of Mikkeli are suitable for walkers, botanists and bird-watchers.

Savonlinna

Savonlinna is built on a chain of islands on the Great Saimaa lake, its many sections divided by narrow straits. The town was a spa resort in the 19th century and remains one of the most popular holiday centres in Finland. It is perhaps best known for its international opera festival which attracts 100,000 people every July. Savonlinna also claims to host the largest regatta in the world, the 'Grand Boat Race of Sulkava', which attracts 8,000 participants every year.

Another attraction is Olavinlinna, a medieval castle, which affords lofty views from the rocks of Kyrönsalmi Island. Nearby is Rauhalinna villa, built by a general as a silver wedding gift to his wife and now a restaurant. Its intricate wood carvings and romantic name (The Castle of Peace) provide a perfect setting for relaxing after a hard day's activity.

[i] CONTACT INFORMATION

Mikkeli District Tourist Service,
Hallituskatu 3a,
FIN-50100 Mikkeli
Finland
Tel: (00 358) 15 151 490
Fax: (00 358) 15 151 625
E-mail: msmry.hr@kolumbus.fi
Web: www.travel.fi/Mikkeli

FINLAND

The Pirkan Taival

The Pirkan Taival winds for 330km through the unspoilt rural heart of southern Finland, immersing the walker in the timeless tranquillity of the Finnish countryside.

The Pirkan Taival covers eight municipalities and passes countless lakes and nature reserves. From Ähtäri, the path proceeds through Kuru, Ruovesi, Virrat, Keuruu, Parkano, Ikaalinen and Kihniö. More a network of paths than a single trail, the route is marked with red circles or triangles, and by a bear logo in urban areas. Huts, campsites and cooking areas are located regularly along the path, so that the long stretches between settlements are not quite as inhospitable as they might seem.

Helvetinjärvi National Park

Southern sections of the trail are rich in conservation areas, marshlands and maintained woodlands. Helvetinjärvi National Park is a rugged forest wilderness, riven with ancient river gorges. These relics of a turbulent past now form a spectacular present, with sheer rocky walls towering above fjord-like valleys, and rolling tree-covered slopes alternating with boulder-strewn cliffs. The drama culminates with a descent into Hell's Canyon, a cleft which seems to epitomise the wild, untamed atmosphere of the national park. Yet hell is contrasted with the paradise of Lake Helvetinjärvi's calm waters, which lap gently on the white sandy beaches of the shore.

Seitseminen National Park

Seitseminen is one of the most famous and most popular of Finland's national parks, hosting over 35,000 visitors every year. Founded in 1982, its 420 sq km abound with the gravel ridges, coniferous forests and lakeside bogs typical of southern Finland. Known as the Suomenselkä watershed region, this distinctive landscape was formed at the end of the last Ice Age. A huge glacier, which had moulded the land as it travelled south, began to melt, depositing ridges of sand and gravel to form eskers. The Seitsemisharju and Hirviharju ridges are very striking examples of this phenomenon. Even today, the ground remains damp and fertile, encouraging a diversity of plants and animals.

Poetry in motion

As if to demonstrate the region's close relationship with its scenery, some sections of the trail are associated with the Finnish national poet Johan Ludwig Runeberg. As the Finnish equivalent of English Romantic poets such as Wordsworth, Runeberg's simple lyricism stems from his love of rustic life and the heroic legends of Finnish folk tradition.

He spent the summer of 1825 in the Ruovesi area, and the Poet's Spring, Runbergin Lähde, is said to have been an inspiration for his work. Now a conservation area, the spring remains a niche of natural beauty to stimulate the weary hiker.

One of Runeberg's best known works is *The Tales of Ensign Stål*, the first song of which, *Vårt Land* (Our Country), is now the Finnish national anthem although ironically, like other Finnish authors of his day, Runeberg wrote in Swedish. Walkers of a literary persuasion can visit Ensign Stål's cabin in Kuru, where his adventures are re-enacted in the summer months. Those seeking visual rather than mental stimulation can travel the Poet's Way on the steamboat *SS Tarjanne*, which sails from Tampere to Virrat via Ruovesi and back throughout the summer.

ℹ CONTACT INFORMATION

Green Heart Nature Tourism Project
FIN-34800 Virrat
Finland
Tel: (00 358) 3485 111
Fax: (00 358) 3485 1612
E-mail: virrat@virrat.fi
Web: www.virrat.fi/greenheart

The Padjelantaleden

Passing through a variety of landscapes, from river valleys and rocky slopes to meadows and moors, the open fells provide a sense of freedom that is rarely found in other parts of Europe.

Although overshadowed by the more famous Kungsleden, those who have walked the Padjelantaleden testify to the appeal of its remoteness: some points are 40km from the road. The trail stretches for about 150km south-east from Ritjem or Vaisoluokta to the village of Kvikkjokk. Padjelantaleden means 'highland trail' but while it covers a diverse, often mountainous, landscape, there are no sudden changes in elevation and the path is suitable for most hikers. Much of the route is within Padjelanta National Park, but one 500m stretch also crosses both Sarek and Stora Sjöfallet National Parks. Small huts (*stugor*) appear every 10 to 20km for walkers who do not wish to carry heavy camping equipment. The communal bedrooms are crowded in the summer, but this is often a good excuse to make new friends. At some points, the Padjelantaleden meets the Kungsleden and other long-distance trails. The national parks offer their own marked hiking paths but walkers should avoid Sarek National Park, a primitive trackless wilderness in which it is easy to get lost.

Time to go

The path is marked with orange-painted cairns and sticks which are buried in snowy weather. In June, melting snow swells the streams, making them difficult to cross. Although there are boardwalks and suspension bridges, these protect the environment from the walker, not vice versa. The best time to walk the Padjelantaleden is in July and August, when temperatures top 20°C and darkness never truly falls. However, the weather can change suddenly to fog and heavy rain. More irritatingly, the summer swarms with midges which gather in valleys and near water. Mosquito repellent is many walkers' most valued equipment and as midges cannot survive at higher altitudes, their presence in the lowlands provides an impetus for tackling the more arduous slopes.

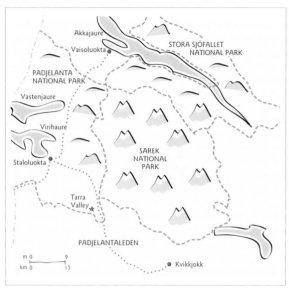

Padjelanta National Park

Covering about 5,200 sq km, Sarek, Padjelanta and Stora Sjöfallet National Parks constitute Europe's largest protected area and are a UNESCO world heritage site. Padjelanta is a vast plateau interspersed with gentle mountains and lakes. Situated 50km above the Arctic Circle, this is no barren polar landscape: over 400 plant species grow here, which is unusual for a northern mountain region almost entirely above the tree line. While the larger plants are dwarfish arctic birches, marshlands and river valleys nurture luxuriant vegetation including rare orchids, sandwort, cinquefoil and yellow gentian. The Tarra valley, near the park's border with Sarek, is particularly lush, benefiting from the shelter of the cliffs, the rushing waters and the rich soils. Yet it is not until the path nears Kvikkjokk that a thin coniferous fir forest begins to grow. Animals and birds also thrive in this apparently harsh region as well as about 25,000 reindeer, owned by the indigenous Sami.

Sami and Staloluokta

About 10% of Sweden's Sami population still herd reindeer in Lapland. The colourful Sami culture is always evident but should not be romanticised. Conditions in the Arctic Circle can be harsh, and snowmobiles, helicopters and radios have markedly improved life. The Padjelantaleden passes a number of Sami summer settlements, notably Staloluokta where several trails meet. It is the biggest village on the route and visitors are often tempted to rest here, lured by the beach, sauna, and arctic char which is baked or smoked and eaten with unleavened Lapp bread – a treat for those who have been living on camping food for several days.

[i] CONTACT INFORMATION

Swedish Travel & Tourism
11 Montagu Place
London W1H 2AL
Tel: 020 7870 5600
Fax: 020 7724 5872
Web: www.visit-sweden.com

The Kungsleden

Experienced walkers agree that they have not truly hiked in Sweden until they complete the Kungsleden. Devotees return year after year as if lured by the irresistible challenge of the wilderness.

Lapporten in summer moonlight

The Kungsleden is Sweden's most famous long-distance skiing and walking trail. About 450km long, it can be divided into several shorter sections. Stretching through Lapland, from Abisko in the north to Hamavan in the south, it is mostly well marked and punctuated by cabins. Originally, the trail was about half its current length but when the northern railway was built at the end of the 19th century, improved accessibility encouraged the STF (Swedish Touring Club) to extend the path.

The trail's special character

Initially named *Kungsvägen* – Royal Road, implying its importance as a national treasure – the route has attracted crowds of walkers since the 1930s. Passing through several national parks and a huge nature reserve, the trail cleaves glacial valleys ranging from the narrow, rocky canyons to wide, flat plains. Valley floors may be scored with brooks, widening into rivers spanned by precarious hanging bridges.

The mountains that tower on either side are part of the Caledonian folding system that forms the backbone of Scandinavia. Their snow-capped peaks jut into the sky, contrasting with the mottled colours of the grassy plains and mysterious forests. Huge boulders and smaller ridges of gritty moraine are evidence of an even colder time, when glaciers enveloped the land. It is a pristine wilderness that is rarely experienced even in the Alps. Few other places in Europe seem so utterly untouched by the modern world.

Facilities

The STF-run cabins offer a bed for the night as well as, in many cases, provisions and a sauna. Camping gear can therefore be left at home, although a lightened rucksack may not seem such a good idea when there is a sudden spell of bad weather and nowhere to shelter from the storm. The cabins also have a tendency to become crowded during the holiday season and although nobody is ever turned away, nothing

quite matches the peace and privacy of a tent perched beside a tumbling stream. However, the Kungsleden requires careful preparation and an awareness of the immensity of the wilderness it penetrates. The weather, particularly at higher altitudes, is likely to be unpredictable, while this southern part of Sweden is also notoriously expensive.

Yet novice hikers should not be discouraged. Regular Kungsleden walkers and cabin hosts are usually on hand to offer advice, and the companionship and fireside stories of fellow enthusiasts is always reassuring. In fact, very few people complete the entire trek in one attempt, preferring to take it in smaller stages so that time can be devoted to enjoying the scenery, returning another year to explore a new part of the trail. Buses, ferries and helicopters often prove invaluable. Whilst allowing for a sudden change of plans, these alternative forms of transport reveal facets of Lapland not usually seen by hikers.

The midnight sun

The region is beautiful in different ways according to the changing seasons. In winter and early spring, when deep snow makes the path impossible to follow on foot, hikers are replaced by skiers who often practice the telemark method, a traditional downhill technique using cross-country skis.

The popularity of the route makes it difficult to become lost except in the very worst weather – the path is marked not only by distinctive red crosses on posts but also by the tracks of others. By May, streams are fed by the melting snow and the ground can be boggy. Most people find that June to September is the best time to undertake the walk, when the midnight sun glints on the alpine flowers and, later, when the landscape turns golden in the clear autumn light. Temperatures hover around freezing point for most of the year and are unlikely to top 10°C even in high summer.

While it is possible to walk for days without a hint of sunshine, rain clouds that fill one valley may be absent in another. As long as hikers are prepared for sudden changes in weather conditions, these unpredictable elements may be regarded as part of the area's charm.

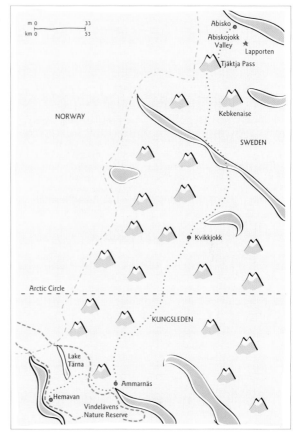

The view towards Lapporten

Nature

Despite the region's apparent desolation, there are many species of plants and wildlife to be found if the time is taken to look for them. Small alpine flowers such as purple saxifrage and moss campion grow close to the ground, while higher up, lichen and small mountain bushes carpet the rock. Trees grow in protected corners, most notably the dwarf willows that are typical of the low alpine zone. Small mammals and birds of prey are likely companions, and larger animals are represented by reindeer and the occasional elk.

Abisko and Lapporten

The first and by far the most popular section of the trail stretches for 86km between Abisko and Kebnekaise. Abisko Tourist Station, to the north of Abisko National Park, welcomes 12,000 visitors each year. A large wooden arch and the first of the red crosses herald the start of the path, leading to a track so well maintained that it seems to be more of a road. Out of the realm of day-trippers, however, it is soon possible to be

accompanied only by the reindeer that are herded nearby. Winding through the splendid Abiskojokk valley, gentle mountains and beech forests rise on either side of the trail to the Kungsleden's highest point. The Tjäktja pass (1,105m) provides wonderful views of the national park and the Norwegian mountains beyond.

However, if visitors had to choose just one sight to remember, many would pick Lapporten. The most distinctive and most photographed natural landmark in Sweden, Lapporten is a glacial U-shaped valley between the mountains of Tjuonatjåkka and Nissotjårro. It is known as 'the gateway to Lapland'.

Kebnekaise

The double peak of Kebnekaise is an unmissable landmark. While not technically part of the Kungsleden, many walkers cannot resist the opportunity of tackling its slopes. Its southern peak rises to 2,117m, making it not only the highest mountain in Sweden but also, being 90 km north of the Arctic Circle, the highest northerly point in the world.

It is said that a tenth of Sweden can be seen from the top, although as it is often obscured by clouds, this claim usually goes unchallenged. Kebnekaise was first conquered by Charles Rabot in 1883 but today tourists and experienced climbers alike enjoy its challenge, affectionately referring to the mountain as 'Keb'.

The central sections

The central sections are the least frequented of the route and are therefore often regarded as the most attractive. This is where the true wilderness can be found. Between Kvikkjokk and Ammarnäs, there are no STF-run cabins at all and at times the path even disappears. Rivers and lakes here must be forded.

The landscape slowly becomes more fertile as the route continues southwards and the Arctic Circle is left behind, yielding some of the most beautiful scenery on the trail. The valley and lake of Kaitumjaure is a particular treat whilst an extra day taken to climb the cliff-like Skierfe mountain is well worth the views of the shifting Rapadalen delta.

Lapporten, with Abisko Tourist Station in the foreground

Vindelälvens Reserve

Covering an area greater than Luxembourg, the diverse terrain of Vindelälvens includes heather-covered moors, rushing waterfalls, dense woodland and, most notably, the archipelago of Lake Tärna. The channels of this deep fishing lake are linked by a series of wooden bridges that successfully blend the natural with the man-made. Spectacular scenery is present right to the end of the trail, from the U-shaped valley called Syterskal with its sheer sides, to the fine vistas afforded on the final slopes, far above the tree line. The final descent can be made by cable-car, although it is also pleasant to savour the last few birch covered kilometres of the Kungsleden before returning to everyday life.

Hemavan

The trail ends at the village of Hemavan which crouches in a narrow valley between two mountain ranges. Although hardly a metropolis, the attractions here may appear overwhelming after so many days in the wilderness. Hemavan Mountain Park boasts a ten storey golden tower, along with the Sinneriket museum, 'The World of the Senses', which presents the history of the region through multimedia formats.

Hemavan's botanical gardens are adjacent to the park and are the most northerly botanical gardens in the world, displaying 400 species of flowering alpine plants in their natural surroundings. It claims a threefold purpose: to make alpine flora accessible to the public, to be a genetic bank of such species and to be a place of inspiration. After experiencing the wonders of the Kungsleden, most visitors surely will have had sufficient inspiration to last until their inevitable return.

ℹ CONTACT INFORMATION

Kiruna Lappland Tourist Board
Box 113
S-981 22 Kiruna
Sweden
Tel: (00 46) 980 18880
Fax: (00 46) 980 18286
E-mail: lappland@kiruna.se

Swedish Travel & Tourism
11 Montagu Place
London W1H 2AL
Tel: 020 7870 5600
Fax: 020 7724 5872
E-mail: info@swetourism.org.uk
Web: www.visit-sweden.com

Värmland and the Pilgrims' Way

The popular image of Värmland is a mix of history and legend. A county rich in folklore, it is a place of gentle hills, dense forests and over 10,000 lakes and ponds, skirted by many long hiking trails.

Despite its many charms, Värmland has always been sparsely populated, the local economy traditionally centring around small farming communities. Värmland's rich cultural tradition has sprung from the great variety of people who passed through the region, especially traders, pilgrims, and visitors from nearby Norway.

As long ago as the 16th century, the north-western forests attracted Finnish immigrants who practised the 'slash and burn' method of agriculture, producing abundant harvests from rye grown in the ashes. Some 'Finnish forest' settlements still survive in the hills, including well-preserved 17th century farms and smokehouses.

The Pilgrims' Way

The Pilgrims' Way follows the winding Klaräleven river valley northwards beside Route 62. The path was used by medieval pilgrims who travelled from Hammarö to the tomb of St Olof at Trondheim in Norway, passing through Forshaga, Munkfors, Norra Råda, Ekshärad, Norra Ny,

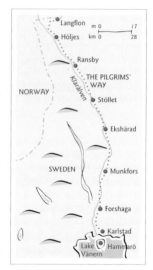

Höljes and Långflon. Place names along the road are reminders of its long history – Munkfors, for instance, means 'monks' stream', a resting place for holy men on their long trek to salvation.

St Olof

Olof is the Swedish name for Olaf II, also known as Olaf Haraldsson or Olaf the Fat. Born in Norway, he spent his youth as a Viking pirate until becoming a Christian. After winning Norway back from the Swedes and Danes, he declared himself king and began to convert his subjects by force. His harshness did not make him very popular and he was exiled then subsequently killed as he tried to battle his way back into power. However, his brutal reputation was soon forgotten when it was reported that after a year his body had still not decomposed.

A shrine and then a chapel were built at his tomb which, after further reported miracles, was expanded to become the cathedral of Nidaros (now Trondheim), a great pilgrimage centre attracting the faithful from all over Scandinavia. Remembered today for unifying Norway through Christianity, St Olof is the country's patron saint, whilst several Swedish churches are named in his honour.

The Ostrā Bron over the Klarälven river

Karlstad

The Pilgrims' Way begins on Hammerö, a peaceful island boasting sandy beaches, golf courses and hiking paths and a churchyard containing stone circles dating back to the Iron Age. The island is linked by two bridges to the mainland and Karlstad, the capital of Värmland.

Karlstad is and has been an important commercial centre since the Middle Ages. Strategically situated on the northern shore of Lake Vänern, it is the point from which all roads seem to lead, although, as one of the European Union's 'car-free cities', these roads often take the form of footpaths. In the centre of the town, cars must give way to pedestrians, bikes and buses, greatly contributing to the harbour's low-key atmosphere.

With more sunlight hours than anywhere else in Sweden, Karlstad is pleasant for summer walking. Its rich history is evident in its 19th century architecture, its statues, and in features such as the Osträ Bron which, with its graceful arches, is the longest stone bridge in Sweden. The Museum of Värmland at Karlstad was opened in 1998, with attractions including 'The Square' – a meeting point dominated by a monolithic sculpture incorporating Värmland's natural materials – slate, wood and water. In fact, Värmland is brimming with museums, covering every element of the region's unique identity.

Floating on the Klarälven

The Klarälven

Klarälven, meaning 'clear', is the longest river in Sweden, running right through Värmland until it reaches Karlstad harbour. The old practice of log rafting which continued on the river until 1991 is commemorated at Dyvelston. Today, timber is less romantically transported by road but small wooden rafts can be made by tourists who wish to spend their holiday drifting slowly down the river. The first ironworks in the region were situated in the valley of Klarälven and the ruins of smelting-houses can still be seen along the Pilgrims' Way.

Ekshärad and Stöllet

As the Pilgrims' Way winds further north, the mountains become higher whilst roads and villages are fewer and more widely spaced. Now small settlements are more significant and are well supplied with facilities such as shops, hotels and bus links.

Ekshärad is famous for its 16th century church, clad in red tiles and containing cloths that date back to the 13th century. The churchyard features about 400 medieval wrought iron crosses. The old church square and a folklore park are nearby. Each summer, Ekshärad hosts a 'Pilgrim Festival' in full medieval style, complete with jousting, crafts, drama, music, dancing and banqueting. This coincides with *Olsok*, the Olof mass, held on St Olof's Day, 29th July.

Another interesting church is found in Stöllet, a small village situated on a peninsula formed by a river bend. Built in 1764, Norra Ny Kyrke is covered in distinctive timber slats and is famous for its portrait of St Olof, a relic from 13th century pilgrimages.

Ransby

The Swedish section of the path ends near Höljes, which may be a relief to walkers who are daunted by the sudden steep inclines and ski slopes. The highlight of the journey, however, can be found halfway between Stöllet and Höljes. A giant tapestry depicting the history of the Pilgrims' Way was made for Trondheim's millennium anniversary in 1997 and is displayed at the Hunting and Fishing Museum in the town of Ransby.

i CONTACT INFORMATION

Värmland Tourist Information
Tage Erlandergatan 10 B
SE-652 20 Karlstad
Sweden
Tel: (00 46) 54 222550
Fax: (00 46) 54 101622
Web: www.varmland.org

Karlstad Tourist Board
Carlstad Conference Centre
SE-651 84 Karlstad
Sweden
Tel: (00 46) 54 222140
Fax: (00 46) 54 222141
E-mail: tourist@karlstad.se

Skåne and the Skåneleden

*Skåne's network of paths offers endless opportunities to
explore the lovely scenery and fascinating heritage of
Sweden's most southerly county.*

The ancient name for Skåne was
Scandinawio, leading some historians
to suggest that it was the home of
the first Scandinavians. Until 1658,
Skåne was part of Denmark, and a
rough translation of Scandinawio
might be 'dangerous land beside the
water'. Indeed, as a result of its
location on the southernmost tip of
Sweden, Skåne is closer in character
to the picturesque rural communities
of Denmark or Norway than to the
untamed wilderness of Swedish
Lapland. The region might be peaceful
now, but it has been the site of
countless battles and a deep-rooted
sense of history pervades the area.

Footpaths are well signposted

The Skåne region

Skåne boasts so many different types
of landscape that it is often known as
'Scandinavia in miniature'. The north-
east corner of Skåne is still a virtually
unspoilt wilderness of beech and pine
forests, in contrast to the rolling hills
and fertile plains of the far south and
the sandy beaches of the eastern
coast. Oases of beauty can be found
in the region's many nature reserves
or by the sudden discovery of a shady
valley, ancient remains or a glistening
lake. The region is also noted for its
gastronomy. The *smörgåsbord* is said
to have originated here and can be
enjoyed in its most authentic form at
local restaurants or wayside inns.

Palaces and gardens

Skåne is notable for its numerous
castles, manor houses and gardens, a
phenomenon more typical of western
Scandinavia. Near to Helsingborg is
Sofiero Slott, a unique palace built in
1865 that became the summer
residence of the Swedish royal family.
Inside, each room is decorated in a
different style, authentically reflecting
the palace's changing interiors over
more than a hundred years. It is the
gardens, however, that attract most
visitors, boasting not only skilful
landscaping but also one of Europe's
largest collections of rhododendrons.

Other buildings open to the public
include the 12th century Bosjökloster,
which was established as a convent
as early as 1080 but became a manor
house after the Reformation. Visitors
can stroll in the courtyard or the herb
and rose gardens. To the east is
Glimmingehus, near Simrishamn, a
500 year old fortress regarded as the
best preserved in Scandinavia.

Skåneleden

The comparatively flat land and mild
climate of Skåne make it ideal for
undemanding rambling. About 900km
of footpaths, collectively known as
the Skåneleden, form a network
across the region and allow walkers
to experience the diversity of nature
and culture that Skåne has to offer.

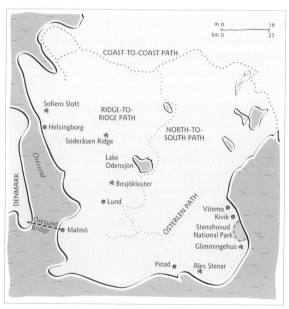

The Skåneleden is divided into four main sections: the Coast to Coast Path; the North to South Path; the Ridge to Ridge Path; and the Österlen Path that follows the coast and flatlands in the south-east. The well-marked trails have frequent cabins, toilets and drinking water, and every year attract over 70,000 people to walk at least a part of the Skåneleden.

The Ridge to Ridge Path

The Ridge to Ridge Path (Ås till Åsleden) follows the line of the spectacular Söderåsen ridge, with its steep ravines, thick woodland, water meadows and streams. One canyon, Skäralid, is almost 100m deep with vertical rocky sides. This lovely nature reserve is filled with deciduous woodland that bursts into leaf in early summer. The cool damp air of the valley floors encourages certain types of moss, fern and lichen usually found only in northern Sweden.

As always there are stories linked with the landscape. One tale concerns the sea king Grim, who built a castle high on the Söderåsen ridge. When a monastery was built on the plains below, he was so annoyed at this challenge to his power that he and his warriors planned to destroy it. However, a burning cross descended from heaven, splitting the ridge apart and swallowing Grim's blasphemous castle into the earth. An angel who had witnessed these events began to cry for the lost souls. The tears formed a spring in the broken rock and created a lake where the castle had once been.

The Österlen Path

The term Österlen traditionally refers to the flat countryside to the east of Ystad. The light in this part of Skåne has a special quality that inspires poets and painters, but also cheers walkers on their way. The open, fertile fields and mild climate contribute to the region's success as an agricultural area, whilst fishing and fruit growing are also common activities.

Ystad's cobbled streets retain a layout unchanged since medieval times. The town still exudes a respectability that was no doubt useful when it was thriving on the spoils of smuggling. Today, the dunes are more likely to shelter an unusual plant than hide a barrel, but perhaps this past influenced the rumour that the Pive Spring further up the coast was alcoholic. Why else do the flowers bloom so profusely?

The Österlenleden follows a circular route near many of these attractions, along the coast and inland towards the picturesque Brösarp hills. The path meanders along trickling streams before plunging into fine beech forests. Out by the sea, it passes through fishing hamlets such as Vitemo and Kivik, where pastel-coloured houses are tightly packed together for protection against storms.

Stenshuvud National Park

Just south of Kivik, the Österlenleden reaches Stenshuvud National Park. The rocky cliff after which the park is named rises nearly 100m from the sea, providing a useful landmark to sailors and memorable views for those who prefer to keep their feet on land.

Literally meaning 'stone head', the cliff is an outcrop of a hard volcanic rock which has not been worn away as quickly as the softer rock around it. Erosion has created a dramatic coastline to the east, with jagged rocks and rubble terraces running parallel to the beach. To the south the scenery is more gentle, as heaths and meadows seem to stretch forever across the sandflats.

ⓘ CONTACT INFORMATION

Skåne Tourist Information
Skiffervägen 34
SE-224 78 Lund
Sweden
Tel: (00 46) 46 124350
Fax: (00 46) 46 122372
Web-site: www.skanetur.se

Bosjökloster – from convent to manor house to museum

 **NORWAY**

The Lofoten Islands

*Off the coast of Bodø, north of the Arctic Circle, the island chain
of Lofoten rises out of the sea like a giant looming wall.*

Stretching from Værøy and Røst in the west to Austvågøya in the east, the Lofoten islands form an arm of fragmented land reaching from the mainland into the Norwegian Sea. Narrow strips of shoreline, dotted with the colourful wooden cottages of small fishing hamlets, separate the sea from distinctive craggy pinnacles which characterise the interior of these islands. Due to its remoteness, Lofoten does not receive the same number of tourists as more southern parts of Norway and so offers outdoor enthusiasts a welcome opportunity to get away from the crowds.

Although found on the same latitude as Greenland and Alaska, the Lofoten islands are warmed by the Gulf Stream. Nevertheless, summers this far north are short but intense. In addition, their exposed position in the Norwegian Sea means that the Lofoten islands must contend with a changeable climate that is at times cold and rainy, with snow from November to April.

In the summer months, there is practically continuous daylight, with corresponding months of near total darkness during the winter. On clear summer days, the whole disc of the midnight sun can be seen in June and July, and between November and February walkers can sometimes see the northern lights or Aurora Borealis.

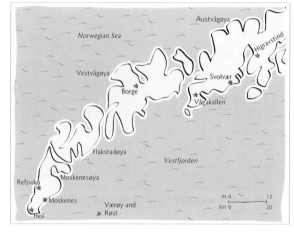

The islands' origins

The mountains of Lofoten are up to 3.5 billion years old, shaped by the effect of the ice which covered the area during past ice ages. Lofoten was at the very edge of the gigantic ice sheet that covered the whole of Scandinavia. A peculiarity of the islands are their lakes which, in relation to surface area, are among the world's deepest. At Moskenes, the Studalsvatnet is 127m deep and reaches 50m below sea level. Several of these lakes previously formed parts of fjords, and have been found to contain fossilised saltwater.

Fishing communities

People have lived on the Lofoten islands for over 3,000 years, and fishing has been one of the mainstays of life here. Each little cluster of houses is surrounded by the characteristic wooden frames on which thousands of arctic cod are hung out to dry. The resulting *stokkfisk* is a Lofoten speciality and has been preserved in this way since Viking times.

Whale watching

Although elk thrive on Austvågøy, there are few large wild mammals on the Lofoten islands, but smaller animals like mink, otter, snow weasel, stoat and fox are all present. There are seabirds in abundance, including puffins and cormorants, and in autumn and winter Lofoten plays host to the world's largest population of white-tailed eagles. For those wishing to experience more of the marine life of Lofoten, whale safaris are a popular choice, especially as sightings are practically guaranteed. June brings a blaze of colours as alpine flowers and orchids bloom. In autumn there are rich pickings of blueberries and mountain cranberries.

Walks in Lofoten

Although the local tourist board provides detailed route descriptions, it is worth noting that some of the trails may be only partially marked, and slippery rocks and steep climbs can turn an otherwise easy trail into a challenging hike. Nevertheless, good hiking and climbing routes lead up to many of the islands' peaks.

The wildest of these may be found on Austvågøya, home to Higravstind, Lofoten's highest mountain at 1,146m. Vågakallen, at 942m, is the most well-known summit, but also the most difficult to climb. Another famed pinnacle is the two-pronged Geita (the Goat), near Svolvaer harbour.

Moskenesøy

Moskenesøy is the southernmost of the Lofoten islands. The sea surrounding the island is rich in fish, mammals and seabirds. The sea swallow, a relation of the albatross, breeds on Moskenesøy in autumn.

At the very tip of this island, nestling in a natural harbour, is the abandoned hamlet of Hell. Only the foundations are now left of Hell's houses, but it was a thriving farming and fishing community up until the 1940s. The beach at Hell is now the starting point of a beautiful walking trail which leads up to the large Hellsegga plateau, 600m above sea level. This is where the inhabitants of Hell would

hold their midsummer feasts and bonfires. The view from Hellsegga spans the open ocean in the west and the whole string of islands stretching towards the mainland in the east.

i CONTACT INFORMATION

Nordland Tourist Board
Postboks 434
8001 Bodø
Norway
Tel: (00 47) 75 545200
Fax: (00 47) 75 545210
E-mail: nordland@nordland
reiseliv.no
Web: www.nordlandreiseliv.no

Lofoten Touring Association
Postboks 90
8370 Leknes
Norway

Trollheimen

*With its fairytale scenery, Trollheimen, the Home of Trolls,
lives up to its name by constantly stimulating the imagination.*

Trollheimen's varied landscape – from lush valleys to alpine peaks, from ancient pine forests to stretches of marshland and lakes – sets it apart from the country's other reserves.

This was the first mountainous area in Norway to be released from the grip of the last Ice Age, and archaeological finds from as long as 9,000 years ago indicate that this is where early Norwegians found their reindeer hunting-grounds. Several large, walled animal traps, most of them dating from the age of the Vikings up to the time of the bubonic plague in the 14th century, can still be seen. Though now an established area for nature preservation, Trollheimen is still used for the herding of around 2,500 farmed reindeer, their owners competing with the hill farmers for the rights to use summer pasture within the reserve.

Over a brief period in the 1960s and 70s, dams and hydroelectric power stations were developed in the area, until campaigning by conservationists finally resulted in the 1987 decision to make the large, still untouched parts of Trollheimen a protected nature reserve.

The Hall of Mirrors

Geological time

Over the last 2 million years glacial activity has shaped the landscape, resulting in a marked division between Trollheimen's mountains. Glacial arms and meltwater torrents have created open U-shaped valleys in the east, and narrower V-shaped valleys in the west. Giant boulders broken loose by frost have crashed down into the chasms to form a harshly beautiful landscape.
The western gneiss peaks are high and craggy; their eastern counterparts are composed of softer slate and

limestone, more easily broken down to provide a rich, fertile soil. One of the remarkable relicts from this period is Litjhelvetet (Little Hell), beneath the peak of Trollhetta, where a glacier has gouged a deep hollow. The little lake, now filled with clear water, is called Trolløyet (the Troll's Eye).

Trolls and the like

Sheep and cows find rich summer pasture on the hills but walkers may also spot less familiar beasts such as wolverine, lynx, arctic fox and otter. Unfortunately trolls appear to be

The Norwegian Mountain Touring Association's cabin at Gjevilvassdalen

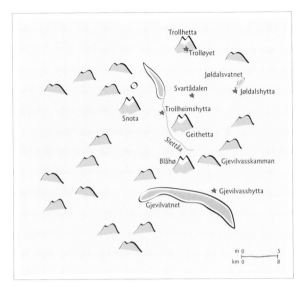

extinct. Brown bears and wolves used to roam the fells in the 19th century, but more recent sightings have been unconfirmed. The area is of particular interest to botanists, with sub-species of mountain poppy and dandelion which cannot be found anywhere else. Certain species have survived here since before the last Ice Age, growing on peaks which escaped the glaciers' ruthless progress.

Trails around Trollheimen

Trollheimen affords countless opportunities for walkers, with marked and unmarked routes ranging from leisurely strolls through the valleys to challenging hikes up to the peaks. Shelter is provided by the Norwegian Mountain Touring Association, varying from simple log cabins to chalets. Built in the late 1800s, many of the cabins are now listed buildings, their weathered timber and turfed roofs blending into the surrounding landscape.

One of the classic walking trails in Trollheimen is Trekanten (the Triangle), established in the 1920s. The trail winds through some of Trollheimen's most stunning scenery, taking in the mountains of Blåhø and Gjevilvasskamman, and passing Slettåa's spectacular waterfall. From Trollheimshytta, many walkers leave the path to spend a day climbing Snota. At 1,668m, Snota is not the highest mountain in the reserve, but is considered by many to offer the most rewarding views. Rejoining the way towards Jøldalshytta, there are several alternative tracks to choose from: the shortest walk goes through the pine forest of Svartådalen, where one of the trees is estimated to be 490 years old. More dramatic routes cross the Geithetta to the south of Svartådalen, or traverse the three peaks of Trollhetta to the north.

The Hall of Mirrors

Visiting Trollheimen in the early autumn, especially after a warm summer, may provide an opportunity to enter Speilsalen and Blåsalen (the Hall of Mirrors and the Blue Hall) – two caves in the glacier at Svarttjernet, connected by a tunnel which runs from one end of the glacier to the other. The caves were discovered by a goatherd in 1919, who upon entering Speilsalen found that the sunlight streaming through the entrance made the cave sparkle and shine as if made from crystal. His fellow villagers did not believe him until the icy 'gate' to the cave opened again eleven years later.

[i] CONTACT INFORMATION

Trondheim Tourist Information
Munkegt. 64
7011 Trondheim
Norway
Tel: (00 47) 73 924200
Fax: (00 47) 73 924201
Web: www.nvg.unit.no/tt/

Trollheimen Information Office
6657 Rindal
Norway
Tel: (00 47) 71 665681

The Gjevilvass valley

NORWAY

Ryfylke-Setesdalsheiene

*With its diverse and fascinating landscapes, Ryfylke-Setesdalsheiene
can satisfy both the leisurely walker and the serious hiker.*

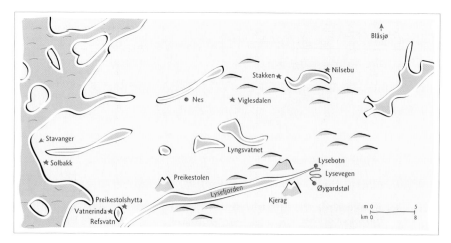

Ryfylke-Setesdalsheiene, in the far
south-west of Norway, boasts a
unique combination of mountains,
moors and fjords. Here it is possible
to encounter landscapes so widely
varied in their nature that they seem
to belong to completely different parts
of the world. From narrow, deep
fjords, 1,000m cliffs rise sharply to
lush fields where sheep and goats
graze among hill-farm settlements.

The northern part of the territory
stretches towards the edge of
Hardangervidda National Park,
whereas the south and east are
dominated by moors, lakes and
woodland. In the west, countless
islands and fjords make up the ragged
coastline. Although there are long
trails and steep climbs for those who
want a challenge, Ryfylke is also one
of Norway's richest areas for gentle,
idyllic routes suitable for families.

Preikestolen

Preikestolen – the Pulpit rock – is a
dramatic and well-known landmark at
Lysefjorden. The sheer cliff-face of this
giant granite shelf formation plunges
600m into the clear waters of the
fjord below. The panoramic view from
the top is truly spectacular, but
should be reserved for those with a
good head for heights. The rock itself
is sharp-angled as if sliced with a
knife, with a wide crack created when
the Lysefjordbreen glacier melted
10,000 years ago and the enormous
pressure on the granite was lifted.
A footpath is cut to the Preikestolen
plateau and although only 3km in
length, it takes one and a half hours
to climb the rocky and winding track.

On the path to Trodla Tysdal

Walking in Ryfylke

Whilst most visitors to Ryfylke will
make time for a look at Preikestolen,
the more adventurous walker should
take full advantage of the extensive
network of other routes in the area.
Preikestolhytta, a turf-roofed timber
cabin, provides a good starting point
for a cluster of varied walks nearby.

An easily walked trail leads to
Vatnerinda, where large walls of
mossy boulders are set in the hills
above the Refsvatn lake. Local legend
claims that trolls built the dykes, but
they are in fact geological relics from
the time when Lysefjorden was filled
with glacial ice.

Those seeking a longer and more
challenging walk may choose to
follow the trail starting at Nes and
ending up at Lysebotn at the
innermost corner of Lysefjorden.
The trail calls at Viglesdalen, Stakken
and Nilsebu, where there are
opportunities to eat and stay
overnight. The route takes around
three days and explores a varied
cross-section of the Ryfylke landscape
passing long-abandoned hill-farms,
winding through fertile valleys and
over rocky moors.

Preikestolen – the Pulpit rock

Further inland is Blåsjø, one of Norway's largest artificial lakes. The lake is the most important site for Norway's generation of hydroelectric power, and the dams holding the waters back are impressive. It is open for visitors from July to September, but a long walking trail marked with cairns follows the eastern side of the lake and can be enjoyed at any time of year, on foot or skis.

The climate of Ryfylke is mild and humid with cool summers and snowy winters, making late spring or early autumn the best time to visit for those keen to avoid the crowds.

Ancient animal traps can be seen along the way, as well as signs of habitation from 8,000 years ago. The trail winds up to the majestically craggy shores of Lysefjorden, from where tired walkers can rest their legs on a boat cruise along the narrow fjord back towards the coast. The Lysevegen road from Lysebotn (closed during winter), with its twenty seven dizzying hairpin bends, leads up to Øygardstøl. This is a good starting point for climbing Kjerag, the highest mountain in the Lysefjord area.

Stavanger and surrounds

Stavanger is the nearest city to Ryfylke-Setesdalsheiene and is well worth a visit. Despite its booming offshore industry, Stavanger has retained the atmosphere of a bustling port, with a predominance of 18th century wooden buildings. A short journey from Stavanger brings those interested in prehistoric culture to the 3,000 year old petroglyphs at Solbakk – ancient stone carvings of ships and figures from an early settlement.

i CONTACT INFORMATION

Destination Ryfylke
4130 Hjelmeland
Norway
Tel: (00 47) 51 759510
Fax: (00 47) 51 750783
E-mail: info@ryfylke.com
Web: www.ryfylke.com

**Stavanger Turistforening /
Stavanger Mountain Touring
Association**
Postboks 239
4001 Stavanger
Norway
Tel: (00 47) 51 840200
Fax: (00 47) 51 840214

Lysebotn and the Lysevegen road

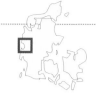

Ringkøbing Fjord

A circuit around Ringkøbing fjord on the West Jutland coast encompasses a mosaic of typically Danish countryside, ranging from sea, dunes and estuaries to heaths, meadows and woodland.

The West Jutland coast is famed as much for its windswept cliffs and violent waves as it is for its clean, white sandy beaches. The total distance around Ringkøbing fjord is 105km, but there are plenty of interesting shorter routes. The path along Holmsland Klit, in particular, crams in a wealth of natural and social history.

Ringkøbing fjord

At 40km long, and over 10km wide, Ringkøbing fjord is the largest fjord in Denmark, although it is mostly less than a metre deep. The action of wind and waves over time elongated a sandy bar or spit, Holmsland Klit, until it separated the fjord from the sea. It now stretches from the former island of Holmsland in the north to Nymindegab in the south.

The fjord is known as windsurfing heaven, its shallow waters and sheltered position making it particularly suitable for beginners. Slightly breezier than elsewhere, Bork Havn is a small town on the southern shore that has become a trendy windsurfing base. Equipment is available for hire in all the main towns. The fjord is also safe for swimming. However, for warmth and excitement, it may be preferable to use one of the indoor pools which are equipped with slides and saunas. Holmsland Klit is also a popular horse-riding and cycling area.

A small harbour in Ringkøbing fjord

Holmsland Klit

Today, Holmsland Klit is so stable that it supports a number of farms and campsites, and even the town of Hvide Sande. Rich agricultural land flanks the path that runs along the causeway, interspersed with planted woodland and the occasional marsh.

The entire area is the property of the state, and subject to protection orders. However, the sand-dunes themselves are constantly shifted by the wind. Lyme grass, galea and spruce hedges have been planted in an attempt to slow their migration. Even some of the 20m cliffs have been moved by the western wind across the spit towards Ringkøbing fjord. Whilst cliffs facing the coast shine white with sand, cliffs further to the

east are grey, covered with lichen and grasses, and spotted with yellow burnet roses. Amber is often found washed up on the beaches after storms, and is used by local artists to make jewellery and ornaments. Reeds are still gathered in the winter for thatching roofs. In previous centuries, reeds were also used to make coffins, which were launched across the fjord as the dead journeyed to the after-life.

Birds thrive in this coastal environment, with hundreds of species coming to breed here in the summer. Geese, ducks, curlew, golden plover and lapwings are all common, as are the herons which fish in the shallows all year. Tipperne, a nature reserve on the fjord's southern tip, provides migratory birds with a place to rest, and offers ornithologists a place to observe them.

Around Ringkøbing

In this region, the human influence is just as enticing to the visitor as the natural landscape. The largest wind farm in Europe is situated at Lem, to the east of the fjord. Wartime concrete bunkers line the beaches, whilst ancient burial mounds are scattered throughout Holmsland. For those who tire of the countryside, Ringkøbing is one of the best-preserved market towns in Denmark.

This traditional building is now a museum

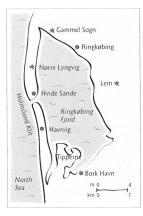

The older buildings are fine examples of traditional West Jutland architecture. Constructed using timber collected from the coast, painted red, and thatched with reeds from the fjord, most of the houses are only a storey high and are very capable of withstanding the rigours of the sea wind.

Ringkøbing Hotel, dating from 1600, was the only two storey building in the town for 200 years. Today, lively cafés and bars join the hotel and its resident jazz band as the focal points of the marketplace.

Nørre Lyngvig

Nørre Lyngvig lighthouse, on the northern section of Holmsland Klit, is still in full working order after nearly one hundred years. Standing on a 17m cliff, the lighthouse itself is 36m high and summer visitors with the energy to climb the stairs are rewarded by a spectacular view of the spit and the fjord beyond it.

Nearby are a number of 19th century farmsteads and Nørre Lyngvig church. Before it was built in 1869, villagers had to sail 10km across the fjord to worship at Gammel Sogn church on Holmsland, where recent restoration work has revealed a series of 11th century Romanesque murals.

Hvide Sande

The town of Hvide Sande (White Sands) lies at the break about halfway along Holmsland Klit, linking the fjord with the sea. A huge lock and sluice gate controls not only the flow of the sea but also the salt content of the waters, maintaining their brackish nature (neither salt nor fresh). Hvide Sande grew up next to the lock after its completion in 1931, and is now a thriving fishing centre and home to 3,500 people.

Havrvig

The small village of Havrvig takes its name from an inlet formed when the fjord was still open to the sea. On the seaward side of the road, a series of red wooden towers stand to attention. Called *båker*, they were constructed in 1880 to assist in navigation. An old rescue station in Havrvig was responsible for saving the lives of sixty four sailors during its time of operation and is now open to visitors. Behind it, the track along which horses drew the lifeboat is a cycle and footpath, running between the pines that grow in the sandy soil.

ⓘ CONTACT INFORMATION

West Jutland Tourist Board
Torevet 5
DK-6830 Nørre-Nebel
Denmark
Tel: (00 45) 75 287400
Fax: (00 45) 75 288676
E-mail: tgv@tgv.dk
Web: www.tgv.dk

Holmsland Klit Tourist Office
'Fiskeriets Hus'
Nørregade 2B
DK-6960 Hvide Sande
Denmark
Tel: (00 45) 97 311866
Fax: (00 45) 97 312880
E-mail: turistinformation@ hvidesande.dk

Ringkøbing fjord is a haven for windsurfers

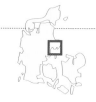

Mols Bjerge

Nestling on a peninsula in east Jutland, nowhere in the vicinity of Mols Bjerge is far from the sea. Shaped by nature, the legacy of man has been most influential, from the Stone Age to Viking times and beyond.

Mols Bjerge should be translated as 'The Mountains of Mols', but sensibly, for an area less than 200m above sea level, they are more usually described as 'hills'. In common with most of Denmark's hilly areas, Mols Bjerge were created in the Ice Age. A sand and gravel moraine was squeezed up between two tongues of ice, and left riven with valleys when the ice melted. The seabed has risen since the Stone Age, so that the hills soar like cliffs from shoreline plateaux.

The highest hill, Agri Bavenhøj, is just 137m tall. Trehøj (Three Hills) is a close second, but its height has been aided by humans, being part of a network of fourteen Bronze Age burial mounds. The spirits of dead sailors were believed to stand sentry at their elevated posts, protecting the bay from invasion.

The natural landscape

Their presence no doubt contributed to the peace of the farming communities in the region. For centuries the oak woods on the hills were cleared for agriculture. Yet the dry, sandy soils and uneven ground left fields exhausted after only a few years, forcing farmers to abandon them to scrubland and fell more trees to create new farmland. By 1688, this 'slash and burn' method had left only three small woods intact. The largest of these, Skovbjerg, is now grazed by cattle, but part of it remains in its natural state and is a thriving habitat for many species that grow among the great oaks. After an unsuccessful attempt to plant coniferous trees, it is hoped that the park will return to deciduous forest within 300 years.

Mols Bjerge may be compared with Hyllested Bjerge, which is slightly further north. Here, the trees are more varied, and include Scots pine, willow and beeches, which are all unusual in this part of Denmark.

Walking in the hills

A hugely popular area with walkers, the profusion of tracks and paths is not as disorientating as might be expected, as the National Forest and Nature Agency has provided information points at regular intervals. The challenge of following a steep path upwards is amply rewarded by panoramic views of the coastline.

Helgenæs

To the south of Mols Bjerge, a narrow stretch of land connects the peninsula of Helgenæs to the mainland. This is known as Dragsmur, a name that may be derived from the words *drage* (to pull) and *mur* (wall). It is thought that the Vikings, unwilling to waste time sailing around Helgenæs, would drag their boats over the 'wall' instead. Locals like to describe Helgenæs as the geographical and spiritual heart of Denmark and a circuit of the peninsula reveals rich cultural roots. When Lake Vænge Sø was drained in the early 20th century, the remains of Stone Age dwellings were found on its banks. Another village, of Viking origin, has been excavated near Ellemandsbjerget, a hill where offerings were made to appease the gods. Helgenæs Præstgård, near the village of Stødov, hosts an exhibition on Helgenæs in the Viking Age, featuring a replica blacksmith's pit house. The hull of a Viking ship stands opposite the Friluftgård farm, leading to a track that passes carved figures from Norse mythology.

Ebeltoft

Across the bay is Ebeltoft, which was granted its charter 700 years ago and remains a charming harbour town, little changed since the Middle Ages. Its winding, cobbled streets are lined with hollyhocks in the summertime, enhancing the pretty timber-frame houses. The town hall has the unusual distinction of being the smallest in Europe, possibly even in the world. Yet this is not Ebeltoft's only claim to fame. As well as being the site of the first modern public baths, it also provides a dry dock for the longest wooden frigate. The 72m *Frigatten Jylland* has been restored to its full 19th century glory and is one of Ebeltoft's major attractions.

A glass museum is housed in an old Customs and Excise house on the coast road. It is really more of an art gallery, exhibiting spectacular examples of contemporary glasswork from all over the world. Glass-blowers often demonstrate their skills in the museum garden. For music lovers, the 'Midsummer Rock' festival features a host of popular Danish rock bands.

As a counterpoint to this, the 'Den Klassike' festival brings orchestral music into daily life by holding concerts at unconventional venues such as the *Frigatten Jylland* and in the Mols Bjerge themselves.

Moesgård museum

Those looking for a more challenging urban environment can drive around the coast to Denmark's second city, Århus, where the lively social scene offers a sudden return to the present. Yet just 5km south of the city, the Moesgård Museum of Prehistory houses the oldest attractions of all. Here lies Grauballe Man, murdered and thrown into a bog 2,000 years ago, his body preserved by the peat. It is rewarding to follow the 'Ancient Path' in the museum's grounds, passing through fields, groves and a prehistoric landscape full of Stone Age structures that have been brought to

Moesgård from all over the country. The Monument Park features tombs and burial chambers, while Tustrup temple dates back to 2,500 BC. A Viking town has been reconstructed on the basis of archaeological evidence.

It is perhaps inevitable that here, in this region devoted to living history, that Vikings return every summer to celebrate the 'Viking Moot'. They may only be actors, but in the heady atmosphere of the festival, it is easy to imagine that Viking ships are landing on Danish shores once more.

🛈 CONTACT INFORMATION

Ebeltoft & Mols Tourist Board
Strandvejan 2
8400 Ebeltoft
Denmark
Tel: (00 45) 86 341400
Fax: (00 45) 86 340528
E-mail: ebeltoft@post6.tele.dk
Web: www.ebeltoftturist.dk

The hills of Mols

Bornholm

*For hills and valleys, meadows and woodland, charming harbours,
picturesque villages, peace and tranquillity and, most of all, for beauty
and relaxation, Bornholm converts the clichés into a walkers' paradise.*

Bornholm is closer to Germany,
Poland and Sweden than it is to the
rest of Denmark. Situated in the Baltic
Sea, the island is six hours by ferry or
an hour and a half by plane from
Copenhagen. No point on Bornholm
is more than 40km from any other,
and it covers an area similar to that of
Paris, about 587 sq km. Many of the
island's 45,000 residents claim that
its cultural heritage is just as rich.

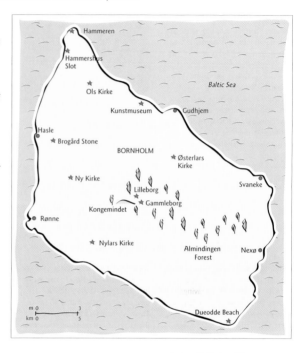

The Pearl of the Baltic

Bornholm is often described as
'Scandinavia in a nutshell'. After God
created Scandinavia, so the legend
goes, he gathered up the fragments of
all its most beautiful features and
threw them into the Baltic Sea.
Nicknames appear to have been
thrown at the island in a similar way.
It is variously called 'The Island of
Contrasts', 'The Mediterranean in
Scandinavia', 'Nightingale Island',
'Denmark's Sunrise Island' and 'The
Pearl of the Baltic Sea'. These names
indicate the variety and abundance of
attractions: the north coast is rocky
and wild, while broad, sandy beaches
stretch around the south of the island
(Dueodde sand is believed to be the
finest in the world). There are more
forests than elsewhere in Denmark,
and the mild climate encourages the
growth of plants uncommon in the
Baltic region, such as figs, almonds
and cherry trees, rare ferns and blue,
white and yellow wood anemones.

Seasonal variety

Bornholm has more sunshine and less
rain than anywhere else in Denmark,
its summer often stretching long into
September. It is therefore a pleasant
walking destination at any time of
year. The towns are at their most
bustling in July and August, with the
countryside a constant haven of
peace. Fewer facilities are available in
the winter, but Bornholm's
attractions do not depend on the
season and it is never uncomfortably
cold or dangerously icy.

The artistic legacy

Bornholm is renowned for its
extraordinary light, and its royal blue
sky, a result of the sea's reflection
and the strong winds that clear
clouds and pollution to leave air pure
and translucent. Artists have gained
inspiration from the island for
centuries and there are said to be
more art galleries than bakeries in
northern Bornholm. Art is not limited
to painting – glass-blowers, cabinet
makers, wood turners, weavers, gold
and silversmiths, sculptors, jewellers,
knife makers and potters may be seen
in the sixty or so workshops around
the island. A number of museums are
devoted to these artistic traditions,
such as Hjorths Fabrik in Rønne
which is a working ceramics museum
covering 300 years of the craft.
The Kunstmuseum near Gudhjem is
itself a testament to local artistic and
architectural skill. Built in 1993, it is

perched on Helligdomsklipperne
(Sanctuary Rocks) and built on three
levels from natural materials such as
granite, sandstone, wood and zinc.
Inside, a Mediterranean-style 'street'
is roofed in glass, the old Sanctuary
Spring trickling through its centre.

A turbulent history

Bornholm's present tranquillity belies
its turbulent past. Hampered by a
strategically important position,
Bornholm has constantly struggled to
defend itself from invasion, plundering
pirates and the medieval struggle
between royal and religious forces.
In 1658, after a period of Swedish
occupation, a group of revolutionaries
shot their dictator and handed
Bornholm over to the Danish king.
Despite finding itself under German
and then Russian control in the
Second World War, Bornholm has
remained part of Denmark ever since.

The only signs of this tempestuous past are numerous ramparts, fortified buildings, and the pride of Bornholm's inhabitants. This deeply-rooted affection for the island and its heritage is shown in the enthusiastically-run museums and immaculate houses. Although the natives of Bornhom are eager to share their island with visitors, the passage of tourists is carefully controlled so that the number of outsiders never more than doubles the number of residents. This, of course, also benefits the tourists themselves, as towns remain lively rather than busy, and countryside always offers solitude to those that search for it.

A visible history

Bornholm might be 40km from the mainland, but firelighting stones suggest that it was inhabited 10,000 years ago. Every generation has left its mark, with Stone Age passage graves and dolmens, cairns and cremation pits, more than 200 Iron Age monoliths, Viking runic stones and the ruins of buildings from later centuries. In north Bornholm, Bronze Age barrows and rock engravings seem to be everywhere. The largest group is on Madsebakke near Sandvig, where ships, feet, circles, sunwheels and cup depressions have been scratched into the rock. Occurring only in fertile regions, such engravings

Walking through one of Bornholm's beech woods

are associated with placating the gods of farming. 12th century runic stones in coastal areas are inscribed to the memory of fathers, sons and wives. The best known of these is the Brogård stone (or Klemsensker Stone No. 3), which has been re-erected to the east of Hasle. A spiral inscription suggests the close family ties of the

Vikings: 'Svenger had this stone erected for his father Toste and for his brother Alvlak and for his mother and sisters' – although the women are not of sufficient status to be named. Bornholm museum in Rønne tells the story of these monuments, but walkers will encounter prehistoric relics beside almost any path.

Nyker round church

DENMARK

A view over the red roofs of Gudhjem

Walking on Bornholm

Bornholm is associated more with cycling than walking, with 200km of cycle routes that follow old rescue paths, railway tracks and side roads. However, well-marked hiking trails are everywhere and the hilly, often rocky terrain makes two feet more practical than two wheels in many places. Although coastal paths wind all the way round the island, it would be a wasted opportunity not to explore the hills and woods of the central regions. Regular buses from every town make most areas easily accessible. Almindingen and Hammeren in particular are attractive and rewarding for all levels of walkers.

Walking in Almindingen

At 24 sq km, Almindingen is the third largest forest in Denmark. It is also the site of many of Bornholm's most interesting features and hilliest ground, with bedrock exposed in places through the thin topsoil. In the damp lowlands, walkers are serenaded by the croaking of rare green tree frogs from the marshes. To the west, a lookout tower on the island's highest point, Kongemindet (162m), offers some impressive views. A path at the foot of the hill can be followed around a small lake to Lilleborg's rocky knoll. This royal castle was destroyed in 1259, and evidence of its sudden demise, such as burnt timber

The ruins of Hammershus castle

and crossbow arrows, remains today. Nearby Gamleborg was constructed as a refuge from attack in AD 800 and expanded with each invasion. An archeological site has been excavated in the vicinity, complete with execution mound and cairns containing human remains.

The magnificent Paradisbakkerne (Paradise hills) are to the east of Almindingen. Although they are privately owned, there are plenty of footpaths to choose from. Rocky outcrops and valleys are lush with heather and forests. Rare plants such as anemones can also be found here. The hills contain a 'rocking stone', a giant erratic boulder weighing more than 40 tonnes, brought by a glacier in the Ice Age.

was founded in 1250 by the Archbishop of Lund to protect the property of the dioceses against the Crown. Expanded over four centuries, it fell into disuse and was pillaged for building materials. Now subject to a conservation order, it is the largest ruined fort in Scandinavia. To walk here is to appreciate one of the most beautiful footpaths in Denmark, with lakes, valleys, marshes, woods and history squeezed into a tiny area.

Rønne and other towns

In Bornholm, buildings are just as attractive as the countryside. Towns have sprung up around natural harbours and display a captivating charm. Narrow, cobbled streets slope down to the sea, lined with colourful

The round churches

Four unusual round churches have almost become synonymous with Bornholm. Whitewashed, with distinctive black conical roofs, they date back to the 1100s. It is thought that, as well as places of worship, they were designed as strongholds, with defensive walls more than a metre thick. Two or three storeys high, the upper level may have been used as a shooting gallery. There is evidence, too, that the churches stored supplies for locals and passing armies. One theory suggests that the churches were built by the Knights Templar on their way to the Crusades. This would explain the strange mix of Romanesque and Middle Eastern architecture. Two of the churches feature 13th century frescoes depicting Bible scenes.

Smokehouses and cuisine

Also typical of Bornholm is the smokehouse, where herring is cured to become 'gold from the sea'. Here, fish are gutted, dried in the wind and smoked in a chimney. Apparently, Bornholmers learnt this technique from Scottish soldiers stationed on the nearby island of Christiansø. Once there were more than fifty smokehouses, but now they are found mainly in the major towns and are of historical interest only.

The famous white sands of Dueodde beach

Walking near Hammeren

Hammeren (The Hammer) is a steep granite crag rising above the Baltic and separated from the rest of Bornholm by a deep rift valley. Grazed bare in the 1860s, the fertile, rocky heath is covered in heather and more than fifty varieties of trees and shrubs including oak, hornbeam, birch, alder, hazel and beech. Nearby, Hammershus Slot (*Slot* means castle) perches on a cliff above the pretty Slotslyngen woods. Hammershus Slot

half-timbered houses and hollyhocks. When Rønne and Nexø, the two largest towns, were bombed in the Second World War, Sweden donated 300 of their unique wooden houses which are still cared for today. Nexø is also the only town in Bornholm to use sandstone as its main building material, giving a softer look than the granite used elsewhere. Gudhjem, with its red tiled roofs, is famed for its Mediterranean atmosphere, with fig trees, mulberries and grapevines growing in gardens around the town.

Often, visitors are invited to try these local delicacies. 'Sun Over Gudhjem', for example, is smoked herring served with sea salt, radishes and chives, topped with an onion ring and a raw egg yolk. Experts say that this is particularly delicious when served with a glass of strong Danish beer. Alternatively, salt-fried herring is eaten on dark rye bread with beetroot and hot mustard, the perfect way to end an exhausting day's walk.

ⓘ CONTACT INFORMATION

Bornholm Welcome Centre
Ndr. Kystvej 3
Dk-3700 Rønne
Bornholm
Tel: (00 45) 7023 2077
Fax: (00 45) 5695 9568
E-mail: velkomst@tourist
bornhom.dk
Web: www.bornhominfo.dk

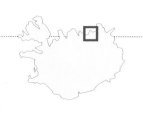

Walking in Jökulsá Canyon National Park

For waterfalls and canyons, woods and rock formations, one of the most fascinating walks in Iceland winds through Jökulsá Canyon National Park.

Arguments over the location of Iceland's best walking area are almost as endless as the hiking opportunities themselves. One serious contender is the Dettifoss to Ásbyrgi trail in Jökulsá Canyon National Park which follows the course of the Jökulsá á Fjöllum river from the Dettifoss waterfall to Ásbyrgi canyon.
Passing through gorges and beside spectacular landmarks, the hike is steep and strenuous in places, but is not difficult for reasonably fit walkers and the scenery more than makes up for the physical challenge.

Jökulsá canyon

The Icelandic name for this national park is Jökulsárgljúfur, which means 'glacial river canyon'. Established in 1973, the park's total area is now 150 sq km, extending for 35km from Dettifoss at its southern end. The diverse vegetation ranges from dwarf trees and scrubby heath to lush grasses and exuberant woodland.

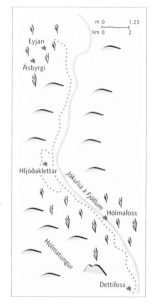

At the heart of the park is the river Jökulsá á Fjöllum, which can be translated as 'glacial river of the mountains', a reference to its source in the Vatnajökull icecap. Although its name implies purity, the river's waters are nearly always darkened with debris so that even the foaming waterfalls often appear to be black with sediment. The Jökulsá canyon itself is the largest in Iceland. Formed by extensive glacial flooding, it is 30km long, half a kilometre wide and up to 100m deep in places.

Dettifoss

Dettifoss, the most powerful waterfall in Europe, is situated at the south of Jökulsá canyon. The first indication of its presence are the rainbows that hover over the valley. The sound of roaring waters too is unmistakable, while the smell of the fresh, damp air tantalises the senses until finally the falls themselves emerge from the valley. At 44m high, Dettifoss is not the biggest of Iceland's waterfalls,

but, uniquely, it handles an average of 500 cubic metres of water every second. On hot summer days, the water thundering over the cliff can be three times that amount, as volcanic activity or warm weather causes melting under the Vatnajökull icecap from which the river Jökulsá á Fjöllum originates. Despite its understandable popularity, Dettifoss is difficult to reach. The path leading to it can be muddy and strewn with rocks and visitors are advised to stay on the marked trail, as the cliff edges have a tendency to give way. The lack of safety barriers has allowed Dettifoss to remain unspoilt, unlike other large waterfalls such as Niagara falls, to which Dettifoss is often compared. It has been saved from another unpleasant fate by the nature of its rocks. In the 1970s, plans to construct a hydroelectric power station were dropped when its basaltic strata was found to be too permeable. Although the waterfall is now protected by the park, the threat of damming remains.

Hólmatungur

Continuing north, the trail suddenly reaches the soft green oasis of Hólmatungur, where springs and waterfalls feed astonishingly verdant vegetation. However, one old legend suggests that sustenance is not as abundant here as it seems to be. According to the story, a widow and her neighbours fled to Hólmatungur to escape bubonic plague. Although they brought plentiful provisions, they were soon faced with starvation. In desperation, the people murdered a shepherd with the intention of eating him but the widow, a large woman, persuaded her companions to return to the lowlands. Whether her anxiety was for the morals of the villagers or for the protection of her life remains open to question. Walkers should remember this story when setting out on the hike and come well prepared.

Hljóðaklettar

Crossing over the Hólmá river, the pretty Hólmáfoss waterfall tumbles down onto the moraine below. Passing over the moors, the path descends to Vesturdalur, dominated by towering cliffs, where several trails encourage exploration of the area. Most notable here are the unusual basalt formations called Hljóðaklettar, or 'whispering cliffs'. These are a group of crater plugs formed by

cooled lava and then eroded to form echoing caves, bizarrely shaped arches and purple columns resembling lions, elephants, spirals, trolls or any other shape the imagination brings to mind.

Ásbyrgi

The goal of the walk is Ásbyrgi, a wide curved canyon formed, it is said, by the hoofprint of Óðinn's eight-legged horse. A more likely explanation is that catastrophic glacial flooding carved a canyon 1km wide and 4km long into young basaltic lava flows over only three days. Alternatively, it is the remains of a valley carved thousands of years ago by Jökulsá á Fjöllum which has subsequently changed course.

To the visitor exploring it, Ásbyrgi resembles an imposing fort on a rolling plain protected on three sides by steep rocky walls. The cliffs rise to 100m in places, while the mouth of Ásbyrgi is divided by an outcrop of the same height. This is called Eyjan and from the top there are views of the woodland that grows in the protection of the cliff walls. The trees are a mixture of willow, larch, fir and birch. A small but pretty pool called Botnstjörn, at the head of Ásbyrgi, was probably gouged out under a waterfall that has long since disappeared. The steep walls overlooking the pool are home to a

large colony of fulmars. It isn't wise to come too close to the nests, as fulmar chicks have a tendency to vomit on intruders, and the showers at the nearby campsite are expensive.

Húsavík

The picturesque fishing town of Húsavík is about 35km to the west of Jökulsá canyon. According to ancient records, it was the first Norse wintering site to be settled. Today, it is a base for those who wish to see Iceland's seventeen species of whale.

Whale watching

ℹ CONTACT INFORMATION

Iceland Travel Group Ltd
Lágmúli 4
PO Box 8650
128 Reykjavik
Iceland
Tel: (00 354) 569 9300
Web: www.iceland-travel.is

The Faroe Islands

Stark and rugged, the Faroe Islands challenge walkers to seek out ever more beautiful landscapes, to climb above the clouds and look down on rocky cliffs and the tumult of the sea far below.

Scattered like a solitary arrowhead between Scotland and Iceland, the eighteen islands of the Faroes have been designated as 'a self-governing community within the kingdom of Denmark'. With a population of about 45,000, there are twice as many sheep on the islands than people (*faroes* means 'sheep'), but the Faroese have nevertheless developed a strong sense of individualism, speaking their own language and retaining an awareness of the legends and traditions that shaped the lives of their ancestors. With more than 1,100km of coastline, fishing remains the principal industry.

Weather permitting

It is the weather that really controls the islands. Moderated by the Gulf Stream, temperatures rarely drop below freezing, even in winter, but conditions are always unpredictable. With rain likely to fall 280 days a year, a fine morning could be followed by torrential hailstorms. 'Weather permitting' is possibly the most common Faroese phrase. Whilst this should be no reason to avoid setting out on a hike, it is important to take precautions that might be neglected in less dramatic countries. Because weather conditions fluctuate throughout the year, the Faroes are very suitable for 'off-peak' walking.

Walking in the Faroe Islands

All the islands have much to see: Kalsoy, where villages are linked by tunnels; Sandoy's black basalt sand dunes; the rocking stones of Eysturoy; and the diverse peaty farmland of Suðeroy. The beauties of the islands can only be fully appreciated by hiking around them.

Most paths originate from the days before paved roads, and much of the more rugged scenery is accessible only on foot. There are footpaths on all the islands, some marked with cairns which function as inland lighthouses to aid walkers' navigation when shifting fogs descend.

Tórshavn

Tórshavn, on the largest island of Streymoy, is one of the smallest capital cities in the world, and is home to about 16,000 people. Situated in the centre of the island group, it is an excellent base for walking holidays. The town is named 'Thor's Harbour' after the Norse god of thunder, wind and natural disasters. Worshipped by the Faroese before the arrival of Christianity, Thor was associated with the triumph of the common man and a readiness to defend the islands from foreign invaders. Today, however, Tórshavn is

a peaceful town, a maze of lanes and narrow passages, with colourful wooden houses jumbled over the hillside, some dating from the 16th century. There are a number of museums and, notably, the parks and gardens contain the only trees in the Faroes. A walk on the Tinganes peninsula beside the town is generally thought to be enough to endear every visitor to the Faroes.

Kirkjubøur

Tórshavn was once the site of the Viking *Thing*, or Parliament, and an easy walk over the mountain to Kirkjubøur reveals that the area has long been the cultural and religious heart of the Faroes. Here, on the southern tip of Streymoy, are the ruins of the St Magnus cathedral, built in the Gothic style in medieval times, but never finished.

Two more historical churches are nearby, as well as Roykstovan, a 900 year old farmhouse that has been home to more than sixteen generations of the same family. It is of split-log construction, made from timber believed to have drifted over from Norway. Traditional houses like this can be seen throughout the islands, with stone walls facing the prevailing wind, wooden walls sealed with tar, and a turf roof to retain the heat.

Islands of birds

The island of Nólsoy protects Tórshavn from the worst of the elements, and has the largest colony of storm petrels in the world. These can only be seen at night, when they return from the sea to feed their young in their underground nests. Over 3.5 million birds are thought to nest in the Faroes. Vestmanna bird cliffs in northern Streymoy is the best-known breeding site, its towering cliffs teeming with fulmars, puffins, kittiwakes, razorbills and guillemots.

Mykines and Vágar

Mykines is a small island to the far west of the cluster. Its single village, reached by a hundred steps from the jetty, has only eighteen inhabitants. Walkers can visit a number of local features, such as Steinskógurin (the Stone forest) or Lundaland (Puffin land), an islet connected to Mykines by a bridge over a deep ravine.

Vágar is the island beside Mykines. The picturesque farming village of Gásadalur has no roads or shops, or even any regular boat links. Mail and supplies are still carried over the mountain from Bøur three times a week. The fantastic scenery, however, is well worth the effort of following the steep path.

A large hollow near the village is known as Risaporith (the Giant's footstep), and is evidence of the fight between two giants who lived on Vágar and Mykines long ago.

The Vágar giant lost the battle and, in order to keep his life, promised to give the inhabitants of Mykines a piece of driftwood, a bottle-nosed whale and a visit by a rare bird every year. When people complained that the driftwood was bent, and that the whale was ugly, these gifts did not arrive the following year. Since then, locals have refused to say anything bad about their remaining gift, the gannet, which nests nowhere else in the Faroes.

Chain dances

Locals and visitors are entertained by the profusion of orchestras, musical groups, choirs, art exhibitions and plays that make up the lively artistic culture of the Faroes. Over 70,000 verses of the traditional epic ballads, *kvæðir*, are still remembered, principally when sung during a chain dance. Once common throughout Scandinavia, chain dances exist in their original form only in the Faroes. Participants link arms, chanting the sagas, endlessly repeating the chorus and rhythmically dancing the steps, which change according to the mood of the narrative.

i CONTACT INFORMATION

The Faroe Islands Tourist Board
Gongin
PO Box 118
FO-110 Tórshavn
Faroe Islands
Tel: (00 298) 316055
Fax: (00 298) 310858
E-mail: tourist@tourist.fo
Web: www.tourist.fo

Kunningarstovan, Tórshavn (Tórshavn Tourist Office)
N. Finsens gøta 13
PO Box 379
FO-110 Tórshavn
Faroe Islands
Tel: (00 298) 315788
Fax: (00 298) 316831

Faroese culture is rooted in maritime tradition

Walking in Greenland

Greenland has some of the most spectacular scenery on Earth and any hiker willing to undertake its challenges will be richly rewarded.

In an attempt to encourage settlers on the newly discovered island, the 10th century outlaw Eric the Red gave Greenland its attractive but misleading name. The Inuit, however, call it *Kalaallit Nunaat*, Land of the People. Yet this name is also ironic – with a population of just 55,000, it is one of the few places in Europe where walkers will miss the crowds.

A unique culture

After a thousand years of successive colonisation by the Norse, Canadians, Icelanders and finally the Danish, Greenland was granted home rule in 1979. Denmark, however, still influences much of Greenland's government and culture. Nearly everybody speaks Danish as a second language, while Denmark's financial support is partly responsible for the modern society that many visitors are surprised to encounter. Subsistence seal and whale hunting remains an important part of the Inuit culture but most other jobs are typical of those in Western Europe. The people of Greenland are famously friendly, polite and quiet. In a country where 1.8 million sq km of the land area lies beneath an ice sheet up to 3,000m thick and where the winter climate can be unimaginably harsh, the Greenlanders' ability to retain their good humour is quite an achievement. The growing tourist industry is welcomed as an opportunity to show their beautiful country and fascinating culture to those who have made the effort to travel there.

The seasons

Although the climate is generally milder in the south, temperatures may still dip below -20°C in the winter. Despite the windchill factor, the dryness of the air can make temperatures more pleasant than they sound, with periods of winter calm accompanied by blue skies and bright sunshine. Winter is, of course, the longest season with up to three months of continual darkness in the far north. Even when days lengthen, summer does not truly arrive until the ice-breaking ships cut their way through the northern harbours in early July. Summer is brief yet intense, with a plethora of flowers bursting into an otherwise barren landscape. Temperatures may reach about 18°C, but visitors should be prepared for both snowstorms and heatwaves. Flaming autumn colours light up the land until the end of September, when there is a period of clear air and stable weather until the snows begin again.

The midnight sun

darkness never truly falls, allowing them to follow their body clocks, eating and sleeping when they wish to. Many visitors fall hopelessly in love with the country, and it becomes an addiction that makes the rest of the world seem bland in comparison.

Plants and wildlife

There are virtually no trees in Greenland and vegetation only grows to any real degree in southern damp, sheltered areas. Flowers tend to be small and colourful, with dandelions, buttercups, gentian, saxifrage, arctic poppy, camomile and harebell all cheering summer walkers on their way. The national flower is the rosebay willow herb, whose large violet petals have inspired many other names, including the dwarf fireweed, broad-leafed willow herb, French willow or *niviarsiat* in Greenlandic, which means 'young maidens'.

Tundra plants such as mountain lichen, sedges, grasses and mosses are less immediately impressive, but vegetation is sufficiently diverse to encourage a range of birds that has specially adapted to the harsh climate. In all, about fifty species nest in Greenland including many types of seabird as well as snow bunting, redpoll and Lapland bunting. It may be possible to catch a glimpse of an arctic fox, a lemming or a hare – as a general rule, their coats are whiter the closer they are to the icecap. Larger mammals consist mainly of musk oxen and reindeer, although polar bears are known to breed in the north and are occasionally trapped on an iceberg floating south. One of the main attractions for nature lovers, however, is the array of sealife. In addition to walruses basking on the rocks, a cruise around the coast may reveal porpoise, narwhal and the white beluga as well as ringed, bearded, spotted, hooded and harp seals. Further out to sea, whale species include pilot, fin, sei, humpback, minke and orca.

Walking in Greenland

Despite its huge area, very little of Greenland is inhabitable. Only the coastal areas are free of inland ice, and this is where the people of Greenland choose to live. The entire north-east section of the country is a national park, closed to the general public. Therefore, only the western and south-eastern coastal areas are accessible, and even then Greenland is not for the casual walker. There are few proper hiking paths, with most routes following dogsled or hunting trails. Even the marked paths traverse steep scree slopes, boulders, glaciers or boggy ground and often require the fording of fast-flowing rivers. Only one or two routes are supplied with overnight cabins or other facilities, and camping is essential. However, comfort is willingly sacrificed for the spectacular scenery and enveloping sense of nature that dominates the wilderness. The harshness of the terrain encourages many walkers to arrive around midsummer, when

Southern Greenland

As the country's agricultural centre, this is the area that puts the 'green' into 'Greenland', with cultivated fields and the largest wood on the island.

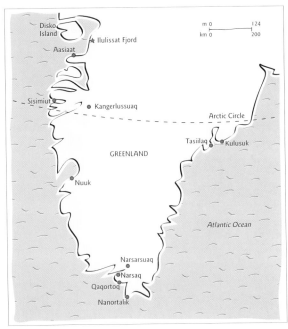

However, the coast is often whiter than some more northerly regions due to field ice (floating sheets of ice formed from sea water) blocking the bays during the summer. From a hiker's point of view, farmers' roads make southern Greenland far more accessible than elsewhere. Its position also encouraged the first settlers, and the region is dotted with the remains of Norse monuments, farmhouses, monasteries and churches. Of the many pleasant walking areas here, Narsarsuaq is perhaps the best, with local attractions that include the Valley of the Flowers, the beautiful Skov and Eiriks fjords, Mount Igdlerfik and Kiagtuut Sermiat, a spur of inland ice. The views of rugged mountains, dry valleys, glistening lakes and gravel ridges are unforgettable.

Traditional turf house

Nanortalik and Narsaq

Greenland's southernmost community, Nanortalik is relatively unspoilt and welcoming. The sharp granite mountains that surround the town tempt the hiker to explore the region further. Alternatively, the pretty town of Narsaq provides the start or end point of the Qassiarsuk to Narsaq trek, a popular route despite inadequate marking in its northern sections. As with other walks in Greenland, the hills, valleys and lakes that border the path are spectacular beyond description.

Qaqortoq

Qaqortoq is famous for both the friendliness of its people and the beauty of its colourful houses which perch precariously on the rocky

mountainside. It is crammed with fascinating historic buildings, constructed from stone and wood, including a replica of a traditional turf house. A museum displays Norse and Inuit artefacts, while the Qaqortoq also boasts the only fountain in Greenland, which sits proudly in the historic town square. Another notable feature is the 'Stone and Man' project, where Scandinavian artists have been commissioned to create sculptures from the granite that dominates the town. Turning a corner may reveal a new surprise, a chiselled face perhaps, or a relief panel.

Day hikes can be made to the well-preserved Viking church and village ruins of Hvalsey; to Igaliku, which combines Norse history with wonderful scenery; or to the inviting hot springs of Uunartoq Island.

Central Greenland

Warmed by the currents, this is one of the mildest areas of Greenland and the main towns are free of ice all year. Nuuk, the capital of Greenland, is located here and, with a population of 13,000, it is a major fishing town with all the trappings of a modern city including traffic, nightlife and public transport. Although, like many of Greenland's larger towns, it has been disfigured by ugly blocks of flats, its older parts retain a certain charm and the Katuaq (Drum) cultural centre offers art exhibitions, a theatre, museum, concerts and Greenland's only cinema. The surroundings are fairly mountainous, but there are a number of rewarding hiking trails. A trek to the twin peaks of Ukkusissaq or through Paradisdalen (Paradise valley) is particularly recommended.

Ruins from the Norse period

Nuuk in central Greenland

Kangerlussuaq

To the north, just above the Arctic Circle, is Kangerlussuaq, the site of an international airport. Unusually for Greenland, it is situated inland, at the end of a 170km long fjord also called Kangerlussuaq (meaning 'big fjord') and is notable for the extremity of its climate. Temperatures in the winter can fall to -50°C but a summer temperature of +28°C is not unusual, so walkers in the area must be prepared for any kind of weather. There are several interesting hikes here through a varied scenery ranging from active glaciers to lush valleys to barren plains, with herds of caribou and musk oxen a likely highlight.

Kangerlussuaq is also the starting point for a popular long distance trail, which stretches for 150km to Sisimiut. The main route is surprisingly well marked and there are even a few overnight cabins and a shop or two along the way. Many hikers recommend this as their favourite route of all time, passing as it does through spectacular mountain scenery and breathtaking lake chains, although the boggy ground and changeable weather is just as memorable. After ten to fifteen days, walkers arrive in the lovely town of Sisimiut, Greenland's second largest settlement away from Nuuk. The old harbour, well served by ferries, is particularly worth a visit, as is the arch made from a whale's jawbone, and the blue and red churches.

Disko Bay

Disko Bay, 560km north of Nuuk, has many attractions, not least its name. It is the southernmost extent of the pack ice in winter, and is the location of the world's most prolific calving glacier at Ilulissat fjord. A calving glacier flows and splinters to create icebergs, or calf ice, and the Ilulissat glacier travels at 30m a day.
The resulting icebergs often become trapped in the narrow channel before breaking up or floating off into the Atlantic. The charmingly haphazard town of Ilulissat itself provides a base for excursions to the glacier while the area's popularity has contributed to a number of marked hiking trails in the vicinity. Options include the five Vandosøen lakes, the eerie lake and desolate peak of Akinnaq, or the ancient settlement of Sermermiut.

Those searching for greater isolation can hike through the high basalt mountains of Disko Island, a wilderness measuring 120km in every direction. Much of the island, however, is inaccessible, dominated by almost vertical cliffs that tower above the unusually rich and tangled vegetation. Even rare orchids may be discovered beside a spring.
The southern part of Disko Bay is calmer, with flat rocks and small islands forming a gentle archipelago beside the college town of Aasiaat. The Nuussuaq peninsula with its beautiful green lake is another good hiking area.

Eastern Greenland

The culture of the south-eastern coast of Greenland is markedly different to that of the west coast. The dialect is almost unintelligible even to west Greenlanders, while the first modern European settlers did not arrive until the late 19th century and exerted only a limited influence on the area. Despite its isolation in relation to the rest of Greenland, its proximity to Iceland has made it a developed tourist region. Daytrippers enjoy handicrafts and the traditional drum dance which is similar to that of the Faroe Islands. In addition to the popular town of Kulusuk, the main town is Tasiilaq, a picturesque cluster of houses sheltered by mountains. The hiking possibilities through peaks and valleys are considerable.

ℹ CONTACT INFORMATION

Greenland Tourism
PO Box 1552
Hans Egedesvej 29
DK-3900 Nuuk
Greenland
Tel: (00 299) 228 88
Fax: (00 299) 228 77
E-mail: tourism@greennet.gl

Greenland Tourism
PO Box 1139
Pilestraede 52
DK-1010 Copenhagen K
Denmark
Tel: (00 45) 3313 6975
Fax: (00 45) 3393 3883
E-mail: greenfo@inet.uni-c.dk
Web: www.greenland-guide.gl

i CONTACT INFORMATION

Britain Visitor Centre
1 Regent Street
London SW1Y 4XT
Tel: 020 8846 9000
E-mail: enquirydesk@bta.org.uk
Web: www.visitbritain.com

Irish Tourist Board
150 New Bond Street
London W1Y 0AQ
Tel: 020 7493 3201
Fax: 020 7493 9065
Web: www.ireland.ie

Northern Ireland Tourist Board
59 North Street
Belfast BT1 1NB
Tel: 028 9024 6609
Fax: 028 9031 2424
E-mail: general.enquiries.
nitb@nics.gov.uk
Web: www.ni-tourism.com

Scottish Tourist Board
23 Ravelston Terrace
Edinburgh EH4 3TP
Tel: 0131 332 2433
Fax: 0131 315 4545
Web: www.visitscotland.com

Wales Tourist Board
Brunel House
2 Fitzalan Road
Cardiff CF24 0UY
Tel: 029 2049 9909
Fax: 029 2048 5031
E-mail: info@tourism.wales.gov.uk
Web: www.visitwales.com

IRELAND

The Kerry Way and the Beara Way

The five peninsulas in the far south-west are known as the fingers of Ireland, and the Kerry Way and the Beara Way trace the edges of two of them.

The counties of Kerry and Cork are very popular with holidaymakers, offering fishing, sailing, diving, windsurfing, golf, tennis and riding. As well as these activities two waymarked routes explore the very fingertips of the country, washed by the Atlantic Ocean and shaded by MacGillycuddy's Reeks, the highest mountains in Ireland. The coastline and the hilly regions were sculpted in the last Ice Age, but the Gulf Stream ensures the climate is always mild, with sub-tropical flowers growing in the higher regions.

Shifting seasons

As the climate is consistently gentle with warm sea breezes, walking along the ways can be enjoyable at any time of year, although not necessarily in all weathers. The sea offers ever changing views, shifting in colour with the seasons and making its presence known further inland through the loughs and rivers that decorate the peninsulas. To tackle the 400 or so kilometres of the combined paths takes three weeks; the best chance of fine weather for this length of time is in spring or summer. However, sections of the routes can be walked on their own, and the reliability of fine weather is less pertinent when shorter stretches are tackled.

Killarney National Park

Covering 214km in total, the Kerry Way begins in Killarney National Park and then takes a circular route around Iveragh peninsula, known as the 'Ring of Kerry'. The path stays beneath MacGillycuddy's Reeks, so that the walking is never very mountainous, following old droving paths and green roads. The tracks the trail follows are higher than the tarmac road, so the views of the coast, sea, hills and low-lying lush land are rewarding. From Killarney town, on the north-east border of the park, the route skirts Lough Leane and Muckross lake, to reach Torc Mountain and the magnificent Torc waterfall, from where there are views of Killarney valley. The park itself offers nature trails, gardens and manor houses for visitors to enjoy, such as Muckross House.

Once onto the old Kenmare road, though still within the park, the Kerry Way divides – walkers can go south to Kenmare town, or north-west to the foothills of MacGillycuddy's Reeks. The latter path sneaks to the south of Carrauntuohill, the highest of the peaks. Ladies' View, just within the park, offers a last lingering vista of Killarney, with the Gap of Dunloe, within sight to the north-east, dividing Macgillycuddy's Reeks from the Purple Mountain.

Coastal views

With the high peaks to the right of the path, the Kerry Way heads out of the Black valley, north-west towards Caragh lake, along a river of the same name. Both are famous for their good salmon fishing. At Glencar the landscape records legends and fables from the *Fianna*, the army of the High Kings of Ireland. Continuing to Glenbeigh, the coast draws nearer, and there are views of Dingle Bay.

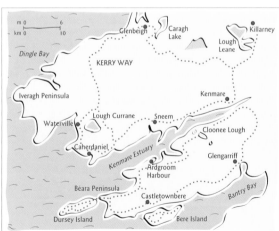

Valentia Island, at the end of Iveragh peninsula, is joined to the mainland by a bridge. To cross the bridge is a diversion from the route, but gives unspoilt views over the Atlantic Ocean. Alternatively, the bridge and island can be seen at various points from the way. Along the westerly coast to Waterville, there are many old churches and monasteries, the first of which is at Killinane.

Up the river estuary

Caherdaniel, further along the coast from Waterville, can be bypassed by walking around the north-eastern shores of Lough Currane. If not, the route keeps the lough on its left and Ballinskelligs Bay on its right, and arrives at Caherdaniel via Derrynane. At the latter village, the house of Daniel O'Connell, the famous Irish nationalist, has been made into a museum about his life and work. Further east, Staigue stone fort, dating from 1000 BC, lies beneath Eagle's Hill on the southern side of the peninsula. The fort is reflected in the 'Pyramids' sculpture at the church in Sneem, the last village before Kenmare.

The penultimate stretch of the Kerry Way winds along the estuary of Kenmare river, in summer decorated with bright red fuchsias. The castles of Derryquin and Dromore act as markers along the route. Kenmare itself is a 'heritage town', neatly planned out in the late 18th century. Iron mining used to be the main industry, but as elsewhere tourism is now central to the local economy.

The Beara peninsula

Once onto the Beara peninsula, the far westerly coast beckons again. As this route is also circular, the Kenmare estuary can be explored from the other side, viewing the Kerry Way from across the water. However, for variety, and to make the sea breezes and views more rewarding, it is possible first to travel further inland across the peninsula to Glengarriff. The route stays on the back roads that will have become familiar from the Kerry Way, passing Dromoughty lake and through the village of Bonane. The village of Glengarriff looks out on to Bantry Bay, and Garinish Island nestles in its harbour.

Westerly islands

The Beara Way heads towards Castletownbere, along a medieval track which became a major coach route in the 18th century. The route follows the bog roads in the forest, but then finds a well-worn gap between Gowlbeg and Sugarloaf mountains, among the Magannagan loughs.

From the foothills of Hungry Hill, made famous by Daphne du Maurier's novel of the same name, the trail drops down towards Park Lough. Bere Island is offshore from Castletownbere, and the route can be extended by walking around the island. Sights include a Martello tower and a central standing stone.

Back to Kenmare

The northerly side of the peninsula, along which the Beara Way runs parallel to the Kerry Way, is dotted with loughs, inlets and stone circles, giving the area a timeless character. At Ardgroom harbour the route moves from Cork into Kerry, passing the standing stones at Cashelkeelty, before following the curve of the jagged coastline. The views across the loughs contrast peacefully with the ubiquitous coastal scenes, while the stone circle near Dromoughty lake reminds visitors of the ancient inhabitants of this south-westerly promontory. The Beara Way then wends its way gently back to Kenmare.

ⓘ CONTACT INFORMATION

Cork Kerry Tourism
Grand Parade
Cork
Ireland
Tel: (00 353) 21 273251
Fax: (00 353) 21 273504

Killarney Tourist Office
Beech Road
Killarney
Co. Kerry
Ireland
Tel: (00 353) 64 31633
Fax: (00 353) 64 34506

Oifig Fáilte (Tourist office)
Town Hall
Skibbereen
Co. Kerry
Ireland
Tel: (00 353) 28 21766
Fax: (00 353) 28 21353

Walking the Kerry Way

The Wicklow Way and the South Leinster Way

*Walking amongst green valleys and grey and purple mountains,
this combined route offers a great variety of sights in a
fertile corner of Ireland.*

The course of the Wicklow Way leads into the South Leinster Way at Clonegal and Kildavin. The two paths mark the first section of a trail, made up of four connecting waymarked routes, that stretches from the outskirts of Dublin towards the Kerry peninsula in the south-west. At the end of the South Leinster Way, at Carrick-on-Suir, is the East Munster Way, which goes on to link up with the Blackwater Way.

The landscape in south-east Ireland varies from lush valleys to open mountains, and from quiet riverbanks to steep forest roads. The two routes together total 230km, with the Wicklow Way the longer at 130km. Walkers can begin and end their journey anywhere along the trail, and the many villages make convenient starting and stopping points.

Walking on the Wicklow Way

Seasonal walking

The summer months are obviously popular for walking, but other times of the year can be particularly savoured, especially as there will be fewer people around. Bluebells among the woodland in spring, together with new green shoots and buds, and the magnificent colour changes of the leaves in autumn, are all worth seeing.

Spring (May) and autumn (October) have been affirmed as being excellent times for enjoying the Wicklow Way by the two walking festivals based in the Wicklow mountains. Both offer a weekend of walks of 15km or 20km, either following the official trail or exploring the mountains further west.

The Wicklow Way

Beginning in Marley Park in the suburbs of Dublin, the Wicklow Way climbs along the east side of the granite bulk of the Wicklow mountains, looking into the valleys and glens of Glendalough and Glenmalure, and then down into low lying farmland on the border between

County Wicklow and County Carlow. The city footways of the outskirts of Dublin contrast with the steep paths among the hills, which in turn contrast with the winding lanes through the woods. Once on top of the mountains, there are breathtaking views across to the coast in the east – on a clear day Snowdonia in Wales can be seen – and into the softer green lands to the west.

The way skirts the very eastern boundary of the Wicklow Mountains National Park, only venturing further into the body of the park at Glendalough valley. Here, a ruined monastery and two loughs remind visitors of past settlements, despite the wilderness of the landscape now. Along the way, other sites of historical interest include the Rathgall stronghold, once the stone-walled residence of the kings of Leinster, and Aghowle church, which has a mysterious cupboard known as the Mill of Purgatory.

The South Leinster Way

Once the county border is crossed from Wicklow to Carlow, the South

Leinster Way begins at Kildavin. The trail continues through the agricultural land that undulates from the southern foothills of the Wicklow mountains to the slopes of Mount Leinster. Here, purple heather calms the rugged landscape and from the Nine Stones there are views south to Brandon Hill and across to the Barrow valley. The descent down from the hill takes walkers into Borris, a picturesque hamlet which has retained the feel of traditional village life.

The Barrow valley, an area made fertile and lush by one of the Three Sisters of Ireland (the rivers Barrow, Suir and Nore), is peaceful to explore. The South Leinster Way follows the towpath of the River Barrow, and walkers will find themselves alongside the barges and boats that cruise the shady waterways in the summer.

At Graiguenamanagh, Carlow is left behind for Kilkenny, though at this point the counties are only divided by a bridge across a river. Brandon Hill rises between Graiguenamanagh and Inistioge, the next village on the route. The hill offers alternative views of now familiar landmarks – the Nore and Barrow rivers, the Blackstairs mountains and the Barrow valley. At Inistioge, the Augustinian priory and St Columcille's well are both worth visiting, each having their own histories and legends.

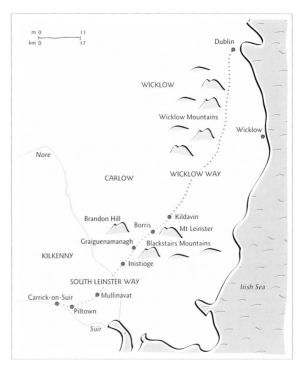

The Wicklow Way

The forest roads continue between Inistioge and Mullinavat, with some hilly walking as well as easier strolls alongside the River Nore. The last part of the way crosses the Blackwater river to Piltown, where an unfinished octagonal building marks the edge of the town. The building, known as the 'sham castle' was built in memory of Lord Bessborough's son, who was believed to have died in the Napoleonic wars. However, as he returned home alive, the monument was abandoned and never completed.

Dublin and Carrick-on-Suir

The city of Dublin and the small town of Carrick-on-Suir, at either end of the two trails, are both ideal for resting or rejuvenating after walking, or building up strength before tackling the route.

At Carrick-on-Suir, Ormond castle, by the River Suir, is a magnificent Elizabethan manor house that records life from the 16th century in Ireland. The house is architecturally significant as it was built in the contemporary domestic style, but was still fortified,

due to the wars between England and Ireland. Other sights open to visitors include a heritage centre and three churches, as well as the park, the town clock and the Old Bridge, dating from the 15th century, all of which record the history of Carrick.

Dublin is well known for its brilliant nightlife, and excellent pubs and cafés. There are plenty of museums and theatres to visit, particularly The Municipal Gallery of Modern Art and The Abbey and Peacock theatres, which show plays by Irish playwrights.

CONTACT INFORMATION

Wicklow Mountains National Park
Glendalough
Co. Wicklow
Ireland
Tel: (00 353) 404 45338
Fax: (00 353) 404 45306

South East Tourism
41 The Quay
Waterford
Ireland
Tel: (00 353) 51 875823
Fax: (00 353) 51 877388

The Western Way

This trail captures the essence of western Ireland, from panoramic sea views to boggy green land and ruined abbeys, exploring the two counties of Galway and Mayo.

Beginning in western Galway, near Oughterard on the shores of Lough Corrib, the Western Way wends north-west through Connemara, and then continues towards the northern tip of the Mayo peninsula. The way covers 170km in total, ending just east of Ballina. If walkers are keen to extend the route, part of the Foxford Way links in, leading nearer to Lough Conn and the town of Castlebar. The Castlebar Walking Festival, held every June or July for four days, makes a good excuse to visit the region.

In Connemara, the landscape is dominated by mountains, such as the Twelve Bens and the Maamturks. However, the walking itself is of a medium grade, so visitors get to enjoy the view of the high ground rather than tackle any strenuous climbing. Coastal views dominate much of the route, from the fjord at Killary, to the fishing off Clew Bay, and on to the puffin holes at Downpatrick Head.

Warming currents

The western seaboard of Ireland is washed by the Atlantic Ocean and warmed by the Gulf Stream, making the region quite wet yet never too hot

Rosserk friary

or too cold. April to October is the most popular time of year for walking, as the climate is slightly more dependable in spring and summer, and this westerly region has a high number of daylight hours. In County Mayo much of the route follows the old bog roads, and the wetness underfoot, however sunny it is, will be a reminder of the characteristic Irish peatland.

Galway and Connemara

The Western Way in County Galway is dominated by Lough Corrib and Connemara National Park. The lough, the largest in the Republic, flows into an estuary in Galway Bay and is very good for salmon and trout fishing. Aughanure castle, near Oughterard, is a 15th century tower house which offers panoramic views of the lough.

Connemara National Park is to the north-west of the lough, and to reach it the Western Way travels upstream of the River Joyce, before climbing to a mountain pass. The Twelve Bens, or Na Beanna Beola, are named after the mythical giant Beola, and several of the peaks fall within the boundaries of the park. A detour from the trail enables walkers to explore the area, which offers excellent hikes in its own right. The visitor centre is open from April to mid October, though the park itself is open all year round.

The Western Way leaves Connemara and County Galway at Killary harbour, the only Irish fjord. This narrow 16km inlet was carved by a glacier to a depth of thirteen fathoms, and is now a peaceful waterway enhanced by the

Killala harbour

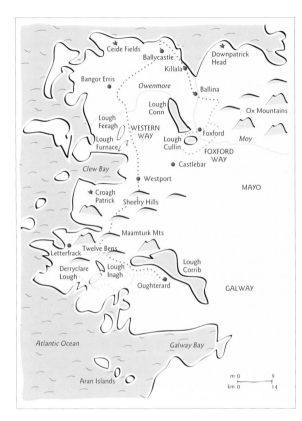

was pushed through the rocks to make a hole, and took a piece of the headland with him, which is now the Doonbristy stack of rocks.

From Killala to Ballina, along the estuary of the River Moy, three ruined abbeys record the religious struggles between Protestants and Catholics. Rathfran is a 13th century Dominican abbey, Moyne dates from the 15th century and Rosserk is a Franciscan friary. At Ballina, walkers have completed most of the Western Way, though for the enthusiastic, there is an option of continuing east to Lough Talt and the official finish.

The Foxford Way

This 86km trail leads from near Lough Talt to the town of Foxford, in the shadow of the Ox Mountains to the east and Nephin Mountain in the west. It loops around Lough Cullin, as well as following the southerly edge of Lough Conn. The scenery in the east of County Mayo is as unspoilt and beautiful as that of the west, with the atmosphere of the loughs contrasting to the coastal views.

Castlebar Walking Festival

The Portwest Castlebar International Four Days' Walks has been established for over thirty years. As a member of the International Marching League, it is one of the biggest walking festivals, and participants come from over thirty countries. Walks include road routes of 10, 20 or 40km, as well as cross-country rambles of 30km over the nearby surrounding countryside.

Aasleagh falls at its head. It is possible to contain the Western Way within County Galway, so that instead of continuing north into Mayo, steps are retraced east and then south, skirting Lough Derryclare on the west and walking close to the coast and the islands.

Moyne abbey

Mayo

Once into Mayo, the route winds its way northwards from Killary and Leenan through the Sheefry hills to Croagh Patrick. This mountain is named after Ireland's patron saint as there is a legend that he fasted on its summit for forty days. A small modern chapel perched on the peak commemorates St Patrick, and offers clear views of glacial Clew Bay with its tear drop islands.

In the north-east of Mayo, legends continue with Doonfeeney graveyard near the quiet village of Ballycastle and Poulnachantinny puffin hole off Downpatrick Head. Fairies are said to frequent the ring fort near the graveyard, perhaps because of the ancient standing stone among the graves. The puffin hole is claimed to have been formed during a fight between St Patrick and the Devil: St Patrick hit the Devil so hard he

ℹ️ CONTACT INFORMATION

Ireland West Tourism
Aras Fáilte
Victoria Place
Eyre Square
Galway
Ireland
Tel: (00 353) 91 563081
Fax: (00 353) 91 565201

Portwest Castlebar International Four Days' Walks Office
New Antrim Street
Castlebar
Co. Mayo
Ireland
Tel & Fax: (00 353) 94 24102
E-mail: ccc@anu.ie

The North-West Passage

This long distance touring route through the Republic and Northern Ireland gives walkers an intimate and varied portrait of both rural and urban life.

The North-West Passage stretches from Dublin on the east coast of the Republic of Ireland, through the westerly counties of Northern Ireland and on to County Donegal in the far north-west. The route is designed as much for motorists as walkers and is signposted along main roads, so for quiet touring it is best not always to follow it exactly. Designed for exploring both countries, walkers will get most out of the trail by using it as a guide to short walks in the region.

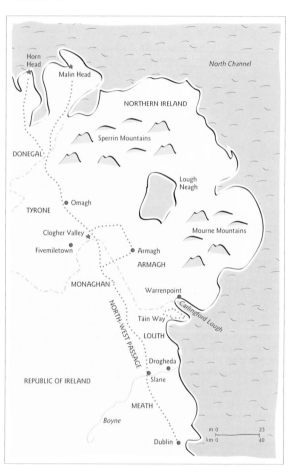

Dublin

In Dublin, at the beginning of the North-West Passage, there are many self-guided walking trails which show visitors the delights of the city. There are also organised walks that bring alive the literary and political past of the capital. The Georgian Trail and the Old City Trail are two of the former walks detailed in guidebooks.

The Georgian Trail explores the once fashionable Georgian streets south of the River Liffey, where none of the front doors or railing patterns are the same as another. The Old City Trail begins at the old Parliament building near Trinity College, and leads to the grand buildings that housed the decision-makers who have influenced Dublin's – and Ireland's – history. Walks around Dublin can be as short or as long as visitors choose, as there are plenty of pubs and parks to rest in, or monuments and museums to waylay walkers' interest.

The Boyne valley

From Dublin the path heads into County Meath, before arriving at County Louth and the River Boyne. In the lush and green valley of the Boyne is the site of the famous Battle of the Boyne, where William of Orange defeated James II, and ensured a Protestant monarchy for Great Britain and Ireland. The site can be reached on a trail in the Townley Hall wood, between the towns of Slane

and Drogheda. The walk is only about 3km, but within the wood there are nature trails and forest tracks which can extend the outing. There is also a very peaceful track between Slane and Drogheda along the towpath of the old Navan to Drogheda canal.

The Táin Way

The Táin Way circles the Cooley peninsula in the north of County Louth, before the North-West Passage moves across the border into

Northern Ireland. At 30km, this walk is the longest on the route, and offers breathtaking views from the Cooley mountains across Carlingford lough to the mountains of Mourne, and towards Warrenpoint. The way is named after the Táin Saga, which tells the tale of Queen Maeve of Connacht and the Bull of Cooley. The queen divided the country and sparked heroic fights when she tried to obtain the Brown Bull of Cooley in order to outdo her husband, who had the White-horned Bull from Connacht.

The start of the walk – the River Liffey in Dublin

Armagh

From the Cooley peninsula, travellers can choose to go through County Monaghan and enter Northern Ireland via County Tyrone, or go straight over the border into County Armagh. The main attraction of the latter is Armagh city, known as the Christian capital of Ireland. St Patrick built his first stone church at Armagh in the 5th century, when it was being established as the ecclesiastical centre of the country. The city skyline is dominated by the two cathedrals, one Protestant and the other Catholic, each on its own hill. The Pilgrim's Path takes walkers around the sites, revealing examples of medieval and Georgian architecture.

The Clogher valley

The Clogher valley lies close to the border in County Tyrone. The area is often associated with the 19th century novelist William Carleton, who lived in the valley and set his stories there. Some of his work, which often documented the hardships of the Irish peasantry, is in the archives at the library at Fivemiletown.

The 9km of the Carleton Trail are dotted with landmarks from Carleton's novels or places associated with him. The area is attractive for its sense of rural isolation. The path is signposted, and information panels tell walkers about points of interest along the way.

The Sperrin mountains

As the passage continues north-west it reaches the Ulster Way, the longest waymarked route in Ireland. Near Omagh, walkers can tread just a few kilometres of the Ulster Way, following the Gortin Burn Walk. This ramble explores the Sperrins, following a stream through the mountains, via the Gortin gap, into Gortin Glen Forest Park.

Glenveagh National Park

The last part of the journey is back in the Republic in County Donegal. There is a short nature trail in the north-east of the 140 sq km Glenveagh National Park, and rangers organise guided walks in the summer months. For longer walks, the Derryveagh mountains are good for hiking, and give fine views of Lough Veagh and the park's woodland. From Glenveagh, the far northern coast of Donegal is within reach, at either Malin Head or Horn Head.

i CONTACT INFORMATION

The North-West Passage
1 Market Street
Omagh
Co. Tyrone BT78 1EE
Northern Ireland
Tel: 01662 250033

The Boyne valley at Ardmulchan in County Meath

The Ulster Way

This meandering circular route explores many of the rural areas of Northern Ireland, sometimes tasting the salty air of the coast and sometimes the clear air of the rivers, loughs and farming land.

The Ulster Way covers over 900km and is the only long distance waymarked path in Northern Ireland. Looping its way around the country, it sticks close to the coast on the eastern side but curves away from the border with the Republic of Ireland in the south and the west. As it takes over a month to walk the Ulster Way in its entirety, it is best to tackle sections in a day, weekend or week.

All points of the compass

As it often rains in Northern Ireland, and no part of the region is more than half an hour by road from the sea, the overall climate is characterised by its moistness. However, this does produce a lush and green landscape. This colourful fertility embraces not only the misty mountains, rocky cliff tops and ancient woodlands, but also the banks of the loughs and the grounds of the castles and country parks.

The circular route of the Ulster Way ensures that all the different landscapes can be experienced, and that the discerning walker can choose between a coastal exploration, a mountain trek, the tranquillity of a lough, the beauty of untouched rural areas, or even the grim splendour of the docks and gantries near Belfast.

Cruising on Lough Erne by Carrickreagh in Fermanagh

The Mournes – south-east

When approaching the Mourne mountains from the north-east, Slieve Donard, Northern Ireland's highest peak, greets the walker. A climb up its 850m gives a view of the surrounding mountains, nearby Carlingford lough and the Irish Sea.

Mourne Wall, which has enclosed the Silent Valley since it was dammed in the 1920s, encroaches onto the mountain. The Castles, which are rock towers, and the Diamond Rocks, part of the mountainous terrain, can also be conquered. To the south-west is

Rostrevor forest, part of which is a nature reserve, which offers even clearer views of Carlingford lough. Narrow Water castle, a tower house dating from 1560, is upstream holding a strategic position on a river bend.

Tollymore Forest Park is a welcome refuge for walkers arriving from the south-west. The stately avenue of cedars, which marks the entrance to the park, contrasts to the wildness of the mountains. For those not as keen to stride the peaks of the Ulster Way, a walk along the banks of the River Shimna is tranquil and fascinating. Exotic trees dot the forest park, whilst bridges, grottoes, caves and follies are glimpsed along the river.

Lough Erne – west

This waterway is made up of two separate loughs linked by tributaries and pools. Upper and Lower Lough Erne have 154 islands dotted throughout them, supporting birds and wildflowers. Swans, terns, scoters, sandpipers, nightjars and garden warblers nest in the lower lough, whilst herons and great crested grebes frequent the upper reaches. The little islands, some of which have peculiar Christian or pagan monuments, such as the 12th century round tower on Devenish Island, can be visited on one of the many cruising boats.

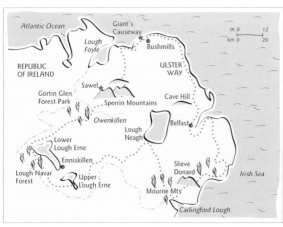

Pony trekking on Newcastle beach

The Sperrin mountains

The peaty Sperrin mountains are dotted with streams and lanes, and the terrain high on their peaks is excellent for walking. The Ulster Way leads from Gortin Glen Forest Park in the south-west, over the mountains and down into Roe valley. Sawel, the highest summit of the range, is off the marked way, but from its top there are views of Lough Neagh to the east, the Foyle estuary to the north and the Mourne mountains away down to the south-east.

The foothills of the Sperrins are fertile, with the Owenkillew river feeding the surrounding countryside. Higher up the terrain is more barren, the grazing sheep contributing to the lack of vegetation. To the east of the mountains are the Beaghmore megaliths which date from the Bronze Age. These seven ceremonial stone circles record the time of the Neolithic inhabitants of the area.

Giant's Causeway – north

Spreading into the Atlantic on the north coast, the Giant's Causeway is made up of over 40,000 basalt columns, formed from cooling lava. The columns are incredibly geometric, most of them being hexagonal in shape, belying their natural origins. Indeed, the myth of Finn McCool building the causeway so that his lover could travel to Ireland from the Outer Hebrides seems as believable an explanation as the volcanic eruptions of millions of years ago.

Two ruined castles, Dunluce to the west and Dunsverick to the east, romantically frame the causeway, and commemorate the 16th century MacDonnells and the ancient kingdom of Dalraida respectively. At Portbraddan, to the east, is Ireland's tiniest church, only 12 feet by 6¹/₂ feet, whilst the town of Bushmills, just off the waymarked path, is home

to the world's oldest legal whiskey distillery. These monuments are attractions in themselves, but the coastal walking and cliff top views make this part of the Ulster Way particularly rewarding.

Belfast – east

The Ulster Way passes around the outskirts of Belfast, and the city is worth visiting for its Victorian and Edwardian architecture, as well as its various museums and entertainments. The city can be a good base for exploring the east of the country, perhaps alternating walking and sightseeing. Nearby there are excellent views of the sea lough, valleys and rolling countryside from Cave Hill, as well as routes along canal towpaths.

ⓘ CONTACT INFORMATION

Northern Ireland Tourist Board
59 North Street
Belfast
BT1 1NB
Tel: 028 9024 6609

Hiking on the Mournes, County Down

SCOTLAND

The Speyside Way

Trying to keep up with the Spey river isn't easy. This long distance footpath does its best, uncovering some of Scotland's railway and whisky distillery history along the way.

In the Monadhliath mountains, at the heart of the Scottish Highlands, is little Loch Spey, the humble source of the river of the same name. From this remote tarn a stream of water travels down, through Kingussie and Aviemore, past the Cairngorm mountains, up through Craigellachie, and into the North Sea 157km away.

Propelled by three tributaries – the Fiddich, Lossie and Dullan – the Spey reaches speeds unsurpassed by other rivers in Britain, weaving its way north to Spey Bay, where its force continually changes the size and shape of its estuary. The Speyside Way, as its name suggests, eventually hopes to shadow this journey, at least from Aviemore to Spey Bay. In its present state, however, it reaches from the North Sea coast down to Tomintoul, a distance of 58km.

Water for the whisky

Considering the proximity of the Spey river, it perhaps isn't at all odd that Speyside is a land of distilleries. Very few of them, however, use the Spey for water – or its main tributaries – preferring instead to use the adjacent springs and rivulets. The distilling is also partly responsible for the railway history in the Speyside area. Defunct for years, the railway tracks have recently found new life. Built in the mid 1800s, they were integrated into the Speyside Way in the 1980s.

South from Spey Bay

Tugnet, at Spey Bay, is a long way from Loch Spey, but there is a practical reason for starting at what is essentially the end of the river and heading upstream. As the terrain is generally flatter from Tugnet to Ballindalloch, this initial journey acts as an uninhibiting warm-up before meeting the more vigorous hikes of Ben Rinnes and Cairn Daimh.

The fishermen's network of traditional footpaths begins the walk up the Spey. Soon, the presence of Spey Bay's terns, shelduck, gulls and ospreys wanes, to be replaced by red grouse and deer in the woods. From Tugnet through Fochabers to Boat O' Brig the way travels down the east side of the Spey, climbing the hill of Aultderg and taking in an impressive view at Ordiequish of the 'Earth Pillars', weathered red sandstone formations.

Native oak

Scots pine and the downy birch are the characteristic trees of the area, but at Craigellachie walkers encounter some of the native woodlands which once covered all of the Highlands. Today, Craigellachie forest is a beech wood, but indigenous oaks still survive in places and the plants on the ground are more typical of oakland, indicating that many of those trees once thrived here.

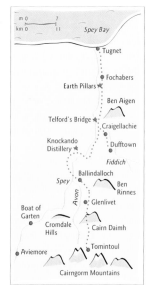

Railway walks

At Craigellachie the Spey is met by the Fiddich, a river that leads wayfarers away from the Spey on an expedition to Dufftown in the south-east. This railway walk is shrouded in wildflowers and is the perfect springboard to experience the Fiddich valley and the remains of 13th century Balvenie castle. The track was originally laid in the middle of the 19th century to serve the Glenfiddich distillery, when the town itself was still only young. It was founded by James Duff in 1817 to relieve unemployment following the Napoleonic wars.

Dufftown and Craigellachie, as well as Ballindalloch further south, were all once served by the Great North of Scotland Railway Company which established the rail infrastructure in the area. The Strathspey railway line, opened in 1863, ran from Boat of Garten to Dufftown to serve the local distilleries, and the two rail walks from Craigellachie retrace part of that

The landscape of Glenlivet

Telford's bridge at Craigellachie

route. The lines were closed in the 1960s owing to lack of use, but walkers can still enjoy remnants of the old train stations along the way, from where Scotch whisky was transported all over Britain and abroad.

Telford's bridge

Craigellachie has also benefited from the engineering genius of Scotsman Thomas Telford (1757-1834). The engineer, who is famed for building the roads, bridges, churches and harbours which opened up the

The Osprey sculpture at Tugnet

north of Scotland, built a bridge in 1814 at Craigellachie. Up until 1974, when another was built downstream, Telford's bridge carried the main town traffic across the Spey.

High spirits

Although the railways are gone, whisky distilling continues to thrive in the Speyside area. In fact, there are over forty distilleries here – more than half of the total number in Scotland. One is never far from a distillery in the triangle between Craigellachie, Aberlour and Dufftown and they are consistently found along the railway walk to Ballindalloch, with plenty of them open to visitors.

Last call

The Speyside's rail theme begins to fade after Ballindalloch, as does the association with the Spey, for the route veers away from the river for the 24km stretch to Tomintoul. Passing the gates of Ballindalloch castle, the seat of the Macpherson-Grants in the 16th century, the hilly walk along the River Avon follows 16th and 17th century drove and cart tracks over the Avonside hills into Glenlivet estate. This area has a particularly good reputation for whisky distilling, and, in the past, distilleries from over 40km away often

recruited the Glenlivet name on to their labels. The area subsequently earned the name 'The Longest Glen'.

The final stage of the walk includes a hike up Cairn Daimh, the 'Hill of the Stags'. The ensuing descent traverses a peat land, Feithmusach, before finishing at Tomintoul. Founded by the 4th Duke of Gordon in 1776, Tomintoul is the highest village in the Highlands and offers splendid views of the Cairngorms, the Cromdales, and further west, the future destination of the trail – next stop Aviemore.

ℹ CONTACT INFORMATION

Speyside Way Ranger Service
Boat O' Fiddich
Craigellachie
Banffshire
Tel: 01340 881266

Aberdeen Tourist Information Centre
St Nicholas House
Broad Street
Aberdeen AB10 1DE
Tel: 01224 632727
Fax: 01224 620415
Web: www.agtb.org

The Highlands of Scotland Tourist Board
Peffery House
Strathpeffer
Ross-shire IV14 9HA
Tel: 01997 421160
Fax: 01997 421168
Web: www.host.co.uk

 **SCOTLAND**

The West Highland Way

A popular, rewarding and accessible long distance trail following ancient drove trails and old military roads from the Lowlands into the Highlands.

Loch Lomond

The West Highland Way is one of Scotland's three official long distance footpaths. The route, which is 152km in length, begins at Milngavie on the northern edge of Glasgow and passes along the eastern banks of Loch Lomond before ending in Fort William within easy reach of Ben Nevis. Walking companies, baggage transport facilities and accommodation booking services are all available to reduce planning and eliminate the carrying of heavy rucksacks. There's even an official certificate of completion on offer for those who are interested.

From south to north

The West Highland Way is generally walked from south to north. There is a good reason for this, as the gentler southern portion eases muscles into a rhythm for the demanding northern section. Regular waymarkers and the existence of a well-trodden path, mean walkers will never truly be alone. The Highland Boundary Fault line, which bisects the way towards the southern end of Loch Lomond, is the cause of the obvious change in landscape and habitat that

characterises the walk. The fault marks the division between the rolling, wooded countryside of the central Lowlands and the foreboding peaks and shadowy valleys of the Highlands. Glacial erosion across the boundary line created the area now filled by Loch Lomond.

After the cold and dark of the Scottish winter, the lengthening days of late spring provide more light and drier weather in which to walk. July and August on the other hand are, if anything, a little wetter and there are also the midges to contend with. As the summer ebbs and the insects retreat, September is an opportunity to enjoy the autumnal colours before the long nights draw in.

Golden eagles

The differing habitats created by the dramatic change in geology along the way means that there is a wealth of wildlife to be seen. Have the patience to stop and look, not always easy to do with a well-marked path, and who knows what can be seen. Roe, fallow and red deer roam the woods and the uplands, with feral goats making occasional appearances. In the waters of Loch Lomond, amongst the fifteen species of fish, lurks the powan, a relation of the salmon found in only

Buachaille Etive Mor guards the entrance to Glen Coe

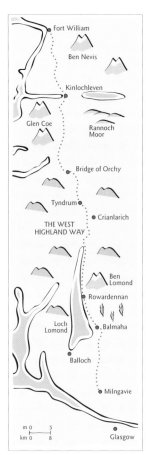

Loch Lomond

Loch Lomond lies across the Highland Boundary Fault line and geology defines the northern and southern portions of the loch. In the last ice age, the spreading ice sheet to the south of the fault was moving over young, soft sandstone and the loch is wide and shallow with many islands rising above the waters. To the north, the glaciers carved their way through harder rock creating narrow valleys. Here the loch is over 180m deep.

The way winds its way up the quiet and secluded eastern shore, skirting the edge of the 300 sq km of the Queen Elizabeth Forest Park and passing through Rowardennan, which is a common starting point for the hike up Ben Lomond (920m), the most southerly of the Munros.

Glen Coe and Rannoch Moor

No part of the route is quite so starkly beautiful as when the way negotiates a path around the expanse of Rannoch Moor and past Buachaille Etive Mor, the looming sentinel at the entrance to the infamous Glen Coe. Rannoch Moor is a magnificent windswept wilderness, penetrated only by a railway line which stands as a testament to Victorian engineering. A treeless tract of peat bog, it is now a Site of Special Scientific Interest. With its twisting valley darkened by sheer mountain sides, Glen Coe can seem an austere place, an appearance appropriately compatible with its historical past as the site for the grisly massacre of the MacDonalds in 1692.

Ben Nevis

At 1,343m Ben Nevis is Britain's highest mountain. An impressive mass, with spectacular and precipitous cliffs on the north-east face, the Ben is a fitting finale for those with sufficient energy. The hike is strenuous and will be busy in season, but when the weather is clear on top – on average only sixty days of the year – walkers are rewarded with panoramic views. Stretching from the Cairngorms in the north-east round to the Western Isles, the vista occasionally includes the flat coastline of Northern Ireland, in the south-west.

The Highland High Way

For those looking for more of a challenge, the unofficial Highland High Way tracks the West Highland Way but takes walkers over all the mountains in between. It includes Ben Lomond, the Black Mount, a traverse of the precipitous Aonach Eagach, a trip across the Mamores and a final ascent of Ben Nevis via the Carn More Dearg arête – at least fourteen Munros for those who are counting.

ℹ CONTACT INFORMATION

**West Highland Way
Ranger Service**
Ionad Nibheis
Glen Nevis
by Fort William
PH33 6PF
Tel: 01397 705922

**Loch Lomond Park
Ranger Service**
Balloch Castle
Balloch G53 8LX
Tel: 01389 758216

two lochs in Scotland. The ultimate reward, however, is the sight of a golden eagle soaring over a peak or across a valley in the distance.

Loch Ossian and Rannoch Moor

SCOTLAND

The Southern Upland Way

A challenging coast to coast route that introduces walkers to the best of nature and wildlife in the hilly south of Scotland.

Open since April 1984, the Southern Upland Way stretches from coast to coast across Scotland. At 340km in length, the trail is renowned as a challenge for even the most dedicated walkers, and can take from ten to twenty days. Beginning at Portpatrick in the west, the way travels north-east to finish at Cockburnspath on the east coast. At Melrose, the path connects with St Cuthbert's Way, another popular Scottish route.

For the less ambitious, however, who would prefer just to sample it, the trail can be broken up into many smaller walks. From Portpatrick to Stranraer is one such popular hike, which surveys the coastal cliffs and heather moors. The journey from Bruce's Stone at Loch Trool to Loch Dee, which takes in oak woodlands and conifer plantations, is another.

In addition to the cliff top walks at either end, the way passes forested lands, lakes, hills and large stretches of moorland, all interspersed with a network of rivers. Where possible, efforts are being made to improve the

Portpatrick harbour – the western end of Southern Upland Way

walker's experience by opening up the splendid views hidden by forest plantations. Although there are no Munros – summits that reach the 3,000ft mark – there are more than eighty peaks over 2,000ft.

Dumfries and Galloway

Commencing at the harbour village of Portpatrick, from where persecuted Covenanters – 17th century Scottish

Presbyterians – sailed to Ireland in search of refuge, the way heads north-east over moorland towards the ruins of Castle Kennedy and the White and Black lochs. It then trails through to New Luce and the Neolithic caves of Kilhern. A long stretch of forested ground, and the impressive Laggangarn standing stones lie between New Luce and Bargrennan. There is also an area of forest after Bargrennan, which lines

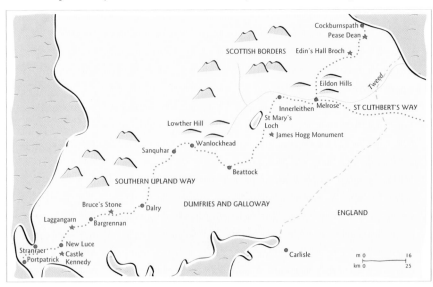

the path up to Loch Trool and Bruce's Stone, commemorating Robert the Bruce's victory against the English there in 1307. The trail then meets Loch Dee and follows the River Dee down to the forested Garroch Glen, and St John's Town of Dalry where the Covenanters began their Pentland rising against the English in 1666.

Turning north, the way heads over Benbrack (580m) to Wanlockhead, reputedly the highest village in Scotland. A further climb follows, up to Lowther Hill (725m), the highest point of the walk, with the path then dropping to a Roman road and Daer reservoir. The last village of the Dumfries and Galloway stretch is Beattock, whose name comes from the Gaelic *battock*, meaning 'land between two burns'.

The Scottish Borders

The Southern Upland Way crosses into the Borders region at Ettrick Head and travels through Ettrick valley. This is James Hogg territory. One of Scotland's favourite literary sons, he was born in Ettrick and worked as a shepherd there for most of his life, yet produced a large amount of acclaimed written work. Crossing the Tweed river three times, the next part of the way heads towards the town of Melrose with its impressive ruined abbey. The penultimate stretch takes the walker over the Twin Law Cairns (447m) to the Iron Age settlement of Edin's Hall Broch. It is an intriguing ancient site, outlining a broch – a type of circular tower which is rare outside Scotland – and its contemporary settlement, built

An old beam engine and miners' cottages at Wanlockhead

inside the walls of an earlier fort. The walk then continues north through Pease Dean, a Scottish Wildlife Trust reserve, to the final destination of Cockburnspath.

Wildlife

The Southern Upland Way is host to a plethora of birds, due particularly to the forests and woodlands found all along the trail. In the coniferous plantations, the stage of the forest's growth influences the species present. The fencing in of young trees deters grazing animals, helping to cultivate cover and food for black grouse, short-eared owls and skylarks. As the trees grow, chaffinches and willow warblers come in while others move on. When the trees are older, they are home to goldcrests, siskins and crossbills.

The gardens of Castle Kennedy, towards the beginning of the walk, are noted as an area for birdlife, as the mixture of trees and water has attracted not only woodland birds but greylag and Canada geese as well. The heather moorland at Wanlockhead is home to a large population of red grouse. Strategic burning creates a mosaic of habitats with different stages of heather growth. The grouse feed on the shoots of the younger heather and nest in the more mature parts that have not been burned for a while.

The hilly terrain is also ideal for grazing animals and Scottish Blackface and Cheviot sheep are a common sight. Friesians and Galloway are the typical cattle but there is also the Belted Galloway, a distinctive local breed. Its 'belt' comes in the shape of a white stripe around its belly.

The barn owl – one of the more secretive inhabitants of southern Scotland

Buzzards are common in the west of the uplands

Flora

The coastal walks at either end of the way are complemented by the pink-flowered sheets of thrift, or sea pink, along the cliff tops. Elsewhere, near the sea, there are the violet-blue flowers of the spring squill. In the summer, the lakes and ponds along the walk are lit up by yellow iris, and water crowfoot with its yellow and white flowers and submerged leaves. The gardens of Castle Kennedy were inspired by French designs and are particularly notable for their displays of rhododendrons and azaleas, and the avenues of trees, some of which would have been unique to the country when first planted.

The Covenanters

On 28th February 1638, Presbyterian Christians signed a national covenant which swore to uphold their forms of worship, against King Charles I's attempts to introduce a liturgy on the English model into Scotland. They became known as the Covenanters.

When Charles II regained the throne after the English Civil War, persecution of the Covenanters intensified. This period after 1660 was called 'The Killing Times'. One of the most severe routings of the Covenanters took place at the Battle of Rullion Green in the Pentland hills, after hundreds of the Presbyterians marched on Edinburgh. There were also dire consequences at Bothwell Bridge in 1670, and at Airds Moss, near Cumnock, in 1680. In 1688 William III relaxed the laws against the Covenanters in an attempt to unite the country. Along the Southern Upland Way there are various memorials to the people who died.

The Ettrick shepherd

Born in 1770 in the parish of Ettrick, James Hogg became shepherd for the Laidlaws of Blackhouse, in the Yarrow valley, at the age of twenty. They were a wealthy family who opened their library to the young man and introduced him to figures such as Walter Scott. This environment prompted him to start writing poetry and, after the death of Robert Burns in 1796, Hogg aspired to be seen as the national poet's successor.

Hogg's oeuvre includes poetry, songs, plays, short stories, essays and journalism – he even ran his own magazine in Edinburgh for a year. Naturally, one of the prominent themes in his work was shepherding, and he even penned a shepherd's guide in 1807 which was subtitled, *A Practical Treatise on the Diseases of Sheep*. Hogg died in 1835 and is buried in the kirkyard at Ettrick.

ⓘ CONTACT INFORMATION

Ranger Services:
Western Section:
Dumfries and Galloway Council
Countryside Ranger Service
Rae Street
Dumfries DG1 2JD
Tel: 01387 260184
E-mail: richardM3@dumgal.gov.uk

Ranger Services:
Eastern Section:
Scottish Borders Council
Countryside Ranger Service
Harestanes Visitor Centre
Ancrum
Jedburgh TD8 6UQ
Tel: 01835 830281
E-mail: mbaker@scotborders.gov.uk

Looking east from Lowther Hill

Oak woodland at Loch Trool

St Cuthbert's Way

This walk is inspired by the life of St Cuthbert, 7th century Bishop of Lindisfarne, teacher of Christianity and performer of miracles.

St Cuthbert's Way is a cross-border trail from Melrose in the Scottish Borders eastwards to Lindisfarne on the coast of Northumbria in England. St Cuthbert's legacy turned the north of England into an important pilgrimage centre in the Middle Ages and the way carries on that tradition. Open since 1996, it is 100km long and connects to the Southern Upland Way at Melrose. It is an historic journey, uncovering many layers of history, and introducing wayfarers to the picturesque Eildon and Cheviot hills, and the River Tweed. As the east of Scotland is generally drier and sunnier than the west, the settled spells from March to June, as well as September and October, are ideal for the walk.

On the final stretch of the way over the sands to Lindisfarne

St Cuthbert's cave

St Cuthbert

The accomplishments of St Cuthbert's life are almost outweighed by the cult status bestowed upon him because of events after his death. Born around the year 634, St Cuthbert was educated by Irish monks at Melrose, before becoming prior at Lindisfarne. At the priory he became renowned for his prophesies and for performing miracles. He subsequently lived in solitude on the island of Inner Farne, interrupted only by pilgrims seeking the benefits of his miraculous powers.

In 684 he returned from Inner Farne to become the Bishop of Lindisfarne, dying only three years later.

Eleven years after his death, his casket was opened and the body was found to be in perfect condition. This lead to his beatification, and an ensuing veneration which surpassed that of his lifetime. In 875, after a second Viking raid on Lindisfarne, the monks were forced to uproot, and, respecting Cuthbert's last wishes, took his body with them to try and find it a peaceful resting place.

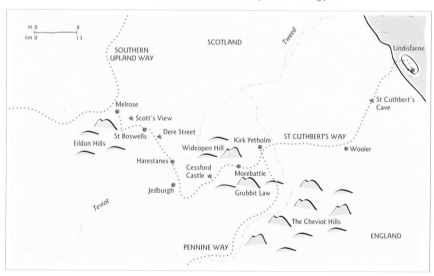

Walking in Tweed-dale

offer a view spanning from the Eildon hills to Yetholm Loch ahead. Situated near the village of Morebattle, and within a few miles of the Cheviot hills, is Cessford castle, the ancient baronial residence of the Kers, one of the 15th and 16th centuries' warring families from the Borders.

A ridge walk takes the path to the village of Kirk Yetholm which was the gypsies' base in Scotland for over 300 years. Between the early 1500s and the death of the last Queen of the Gypsies in 1833, it was where gypsies congregated to appoint a king and queen and hold their coronation. Near the Pennine Way, the path crosses the border into the moorlands of Northumberland National Park.

Holy Island

The first sight of Lindisfarne comes at St Cuthbert's cave. On reaching the coast, the route culminates in a walk across to the island, either by taking the causeway, or the older Pilgrims' Way across the sands which is marked by a series of stakes. Both Lindisfarne's Norman priory, which stands on the site of St Cuthbert's ancient monastery, and the island's castle can be explored.

A series of burials and exhumations finally ended when his body was interred in Durham cathedral in 999. In 1104, however, 418 years after his death, the casket was opened again and the body was found to be still uncorrupted. The last time the casket was opened was in 1827, but only a skeleton covered in decaying robes remained. Although the designs on the garments matched the accounts from 1104, some argued that the real body of St Cuthbert lay elsewhere.

Scott's View

Between Melrose and St Boswells are the heather-covered Eildon peaks, consisting of the Little Hill, the Mid Hill and the North Eildon Hill. Composed of basalt and old red sandstone, the hills are brightened by fragrant yellow gorse in the spring and summer. With peat bogs, resident red grouse and woodland birds, the

hills are a pleasant start to the walk and are relatively easy to climb. There is also plenty of history to explore, from sacred Celtic shroves to the site of a Roman signal station.

Just outside Dryburgh, on a bend above the River Tweed, is a parking spot which is said to be Sir Walter Scott's favourite part of the hills. Folklore recalls that the horses from his funeral procession automatically stopped there on the journey to his grave at Dryburgh abbey, and it has since been called Scott's View.

The Cheviots

The middle part of the journey, from Cessford castle to Wooler, benefits from the constant backdrop of the Cheviot hills. There is also Wideopen Hill and Grubbit Law, which, at 268 and 310m respectively, are some the highest climbs of the journey, and

ⓘ CONTACT INFORMATION

Scottish Borders Tourist Board
Tourist Information Centre
Murrays Green
Jedburgh TD8 6BE
Tel: 01835 863435
Fax: 01835 864099

Scott's View near to Dryburgh

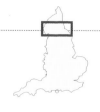

Hadrian's Wall Path

To walk beside Hadrian's Wall is to follow the winding path of history through an evocative landscape that carries the memories of a more turbulent time.

Stretching for about 130km from the Solway Firth to the mouth of the River Tyne, Hadrian's Wall is a designated world heritage site, a reminder of the achievements of a past civilisation. The path beside the wall is being continuously developed so that, from 2002, walkers will be able to follow its entire length. Until then, it is best for circular day walks and enables visitors to explore interesting areas away from the wall itself.

Representing the transition from the southern to the northern landscapes of the British Isles, the scenery ranges from the quiet pastures, gentle slopes and lush woodland of the Tyne valley to the stark border fells and high windswept ridges of Northumberland.

Footbridge over the River Irthing at Willowford

Hadrian and his wall

Hadrian was an empire builder in a different sense to those who had ruled before him. He was the first emperor to give up on the borderlands as a lost cause, deciding instead to consolidate the Roman Empire by constructing fortifications along all its boundaries. He was also interested in civil architecture, and was responsible for some of the most magnificent buildings in Rome including the Athenaeum, the Pantheon and his huge mausoleum, Castel Sant'Angelo. However, the only surviving written evidence that the Emperor Hadrian was responsible for the English wall is in a single sentence of contemporary biography, which states that he 'drew a line along a length of eighty miles to separate barbarians and Romans.' This line marked the northernmost extent of the Roman Empire, stretching across the narrowest part of England from Bowness-on-Solway in the west to Wallsend in the east.

Border politics

The Romans occupied Britain from the 1st century AD to the early 5th century, and spent a lot of their time attempting to subdue tribes from the north. Yet contrary to common belief, Hadrian's Wall has never formed a border between England and Scotland: the two countries as they are known today did not exist when it was built, and most of the English county of Northumberland is north of the wall.

A triumph of engineering

Whether the wall was designed to be an enormous defensive rampart or a military border zone is open to discussion, but it is likely to have fulfilled both roles. There is little evidence of significant battles at the wall, and its principal function was to control the movements of Britons by collecting tolls. Many of the settlements that sprang up to serve the garrisons are still thriving towns.

Hadrian's Wall is a remarkable triumph of engineering. In addition to the wall itself, the Romans developed an entire infrastructure to supply their economic and military needs and to develop the surrounding lands.

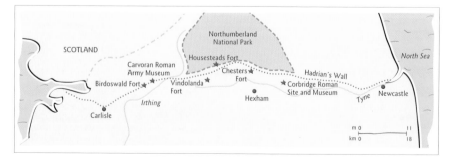

Work began in AD 122 and the wall was finished within six years, but modifications continued until the Romans left Britain to its own devices. Mile castles were added at intervals of one Roman mile (about 1,500m) with two watchtowers placed between each one. At strategic locations every 11km or so along the wall, huge forts capable of housing up to 10,000 soldiers were added.

In places, the wall's stone ramparts were 3m thick and up to 5m high, comparable to the Great Wall of China. However, construction projects have not changed very much over the years, and the pressures of cost and time left many sections far less substantial than originally intended. Over the centuries, the wall was also treated as a source of ready-made building blocks for barns, houses and churches. But great expanses remain, mainly as earthworks, and it is still punctuated by forts and towers which are now museums.

Conserving the wall

That the wall has survived at all is a testament to Roman engineering. However, modern visitors should be aware that this ancient structure is extremely fragile and combine admiration with consideration.

In order to protect buried archaeology and preserve the wall's surroundings, paths are formed from grass sward rather than a hard surface and should be treated with care. The wall is especially vulnerable during the wet winter months, when waterlogged soils and earthworks are at risk from trampling feet. At all times of the year, visitors should follow only the marked paths and avoid walking on the wall itself, keeping dogs on leads and closing gates behind them.

Walking the path

Rather than walking all the way from Carlisle to Newcastle, most visitors explore the shorter circular routes near the most fascinating museums and Roman remains along the wall. Leaflets describing circular paths in both Cumbria and Northumberland can be obtained. A large section of the wall passes through Northumberland National Park which has natural pleasures of its own.

Birdoswald and Carvoran

The first fort along the path from Carlisle is Birdoswald, where all the elements of the Roman frontier system can be viewed in a compact area. Overlooking the Irthing Gorge, it can be reached by an award-winning bridge at Willowford.

Built to blend in with the surrounding historical environment, the bridge is an attraction in itself. Lanercost priory standing near to the fort, was built from stone taken from the wall. Nearby is Carvoran, the Roman army museum, which reconstructs military life using exhibitions and audiovisual shows. Younger visitors can even join up with the Roman army for the day while their parents enjoy the spectacular Walltown Crags section of the wall, which is only a short distance away and offers lovely views towards Scotland.

Vindolanda

Located at Bardon Mill to the south of Hadrian's Wall, on the line of the Stanegate Roman road, excavations continue at the fort and civilian settlement of Vindolanda. Built even before the wall was begun, the fort once housed over 500 soldiers, and today the village around it is one of the most extensive to remain in its original layout. Several unusual Roman artefacts have been found here, including writing tablets containing letters, invitations and shopping lists, as well as textiles, ornaments, armour, boots, pottery and tools that together create a vivid impression of Roman life. Some of these finds are displayed at the site museum. A section of the wall and a turret have been recreated, while replicas of a contemporary temple, house and shop are also on show.

Walltown Crags in Northumberland National Park

the basalt cliffs of the Whin Sill, commands views over open moorlands that were once perfect for defence and are now, in these gentler times, a photographer's dream. This is agreed to be the most dramatic stretch of Hadrian's Wall, offering a vantage point into the rolling hills of Northumberland National Park and across the Tyne valley to the North Pennine moors. Here, the Pennine Way links up with Hadrian's Wall Path, following the wall for 16km.

Chesters Roman fort

Set in a wooded valley, Chesters is another fort which testifies to the skill of Roman plumbing. A bath house beside the River Tyne contains hot and cold rooms, and bath and steam rooms which, if they were still in use, would no doubt be appreciated by today's walkers. Down the road is the historical market town of Hexham, with medieval streets and a thousand year old abbey that seems positively modern in comparison with the Roman remains nearby. The Border History museum tells the story of the infamous 'reivers', bandits who were active in the borderlands before England and Scotland were unified. Other towns and villages nestle in the hills, waiting to be discovered by those willing to open their eyes to the history around them.

Housesteads Roman fort

Housesteads, near the town of Hexham, is the best preserved Roman fort in Britain. Its fine condition is due, ironically, to its occupation by border outlaws at a time when other Roman remains were being plundered for masonry. The fort encompasses facilities for 1,000 men such as military headquarters, commander's lodgings, barracks, granaries and a hospital. The latrines, with their intricate drainage and flushing capabilities, are particularly interesting. The fort's perch, high on

i CONTACT INFORMATION

Hadrian's Wall Path Nat. Trail
c/o Countryside Agency
4th Floor
Warwick House
Grantham Road
Newcastle-upon-Tyne NE2 1QF
Tel: 0191 232 8252
Fax: 0191 222 0185

For circular path leaflets in Northumberland:
Countryside Service
Northumberland County Council
County Hall
Morpeth
Northumberland NE61 2EF
Tel: 01670 533000

For circular path leaflets in Cumbria:
East Cumbria Countryside Project
Warwick Mill
Warwick Bridge
Cumbria CA4 8RR
Tel: 01228 561601

One of the surviving Roman forts along the wall

The Cleveland Way and the Wolds Way

Empty moors, dry-stone walls, warm stone cliffs, crashing seas and sheer limestone escarpments are just some of the colours and textures that greet walkers on these two national trails.

Together the Cleveland Way and the Wolds Way cover over 300km in the north-east of England. The Cleveland Way leads walkers over moors and dales, and then along the coast beside the North Sea. The Wolds Way moves inland, away from where the two trails connect at Filey, exploring the valleys and hills of the Yorkshire Wolds. Throughout the landscape are the remains of old quarrying and mining activities, showing the region's industrial past, and how it was once well-populated and fully employed. The villages that grew up in these times are still picturesquely scattered across the hills and along the cliffs.

The Cleveland Way

The 177km of the Cleveland Way loops across the North York Moors National Park from Helmsley to Saltburn, and then follows the coast south for 80km from Saltburn to Filey. The shorter Tabular Hills Walk, across the southern boundary of the national park, links the two ends of the trail, so that it is possible to complete a circular route. In many places, the way has been routed on the old Yorkshire droving roads, along which farmers would drive their sheep to markets in the south.

The path is accessible to visually impaired or disabled walkers at various points, and there are publications for sale at the visitor centres in the national park which give details of the gradients and difficulty of the walk. The Moorsbus service can take walkers to and from different points of the trail, for those who only wish to tackle part of it.

Helmsley to Osmotherley

At Helmsley, the beginning of the trail is marked by a sculpture carved with the attractions and landmarks along the way. Near to the town, Helmsley castle and Rievaulx abbey, dating from early medieval times, are open to the public, and take visitors back to an

Waves crashing over rocks at Filey Brigg

York Minster

era when monks and kings owned and ruled the land. Heading towards Sutton Bank, the trail reaches the western escarpment of the park. Further west is 'Herriott country', where the vet James Alfred Wight lived, who wrote under the pseudonym James Herriott, and on a clear day there are excellent views of the Vale of York. The White Horse of Kilburn highlights the chalky geology of the landscape, though this horse was carved out in 1857 by a school teacher, not by prehistoric settlers.

Osmotherley to Saltburn

From Osmotherley the trail crosses the Cleveland hills, with views across to Teeside, and the moors and dales below. The hills act as an introduction to the highest and bleakest part of the route, with the trail crossing six moors – with Urra Moor as the highest. Remains of mining for alum, jet and ironstone scar the landscape, whilst stone markers and crosses, set up long ago by monks, reassure walkers on their sometimes lonely trek.

The area around Kildale is known as Captain Cook country as the 18th century explorer was born at nearby Great Ayton. A monument to Cook stands on Easby Moor, and his ships were built at Whitby on the coast. Other attractions are the Esk Valley railway line that continues to run across the north-west corner of the park; the panoramic views from Roseberry Topping, an isolated hill away from the high moors; and Guisborough woods, thick with bluebells and wild garlic in the spring.

Saltburn to Filey

The route starts by following a
section of designated Heritage Coast.
Metal art and sculptures on the cliffs
beyond Saltburn contrast with the
breathtaking sea views. Further along
the coast, Boulby cliff is the highest
promontory on the eastern seaboard
at 203m, while Boulby potash mine is
the deepest in Europe. Staithes and
Whitby are both characterised by
their higgledy-piggledy streets clinging
to the cliffs, seeming dangerously near
the water's edge. Indeed, Kettleness
village slipped into the sea in 1829,
though it has since been rebuilt.

The cliff top walk leads on to Robin
Hood's Bay, before a gentle climb to
Ravenscar on the way to Scarborough.
The trail drops down to sea level at
Boggle Hole and Stoupe Beck, passing
old alum works. The woods of
Hayburn Wyke Nature Reserve are
worth visiting, if only as a respite
from the wild sea breezes that can
dominate the second half of the trail.
Beyond Scarborough, Filey Brigg marks
the end of the Cleveland Way, and
the beginning of the Wolds Way.

Walkers on the Cleveland Way, near Robin Hood's Bay

The Wolds Way

The Wolds Way covers 127km across
the chalk escarpment of the Yorkshire
Wolds, heading west away from the
coast and then south to the Humber
estuary. The walking varies between
the deep valleys formed by the

escarpment, and the high wolds
above. The countryside is dominated
by chalk-loving flora, from wild thyme
to rare orchids, as well as butterflies
and moths that are attracted by the
flowering plants. The ash is the native
tree of the wolds, but sycamore is
now also common, and beech, larch
and yew are frequently found too.
Pheasants and red-legged partridges
are reared on the land, and rabbits,
roe deer and foxes run wild.

Many settlers have left their mark
on the region, be it Roman mosaics,
Saxon village names, Norman
churches or medieval buildings in the
villages. The fields surrounding the
trail are distinctive for their linear and
organised shape, as this part of the
country was one of the first to be
marked out during the parliamentary
enclosures of the late 18th century.

Filey to Fridaythorpe

The trail begins at Filey Brigg, where
the stone by the Brigg is carved with
names and places found along the
Wolds Way to inspire walkers. The
path heads gently south-west, over
Jurassic clays and limestones, passing
many earthworks which date from the
Iron Age and later. The hamlets along
the route have their origins in Anglo-
Saxon and Danish settlements, with
names such as Flixton Wold and
Staxton Brow evoking the Old English
once spoken by the inhabitants.

From the small town of Sherburn, the walk climbs up onto the scarp. Further south, beyond Wintringham, there are clear and wide views to the north of the Vale of Pickering from the high point at Settrington Beacon. On a good day, the North York Moors can be seen beyond the vale, a reminder of how far has been walked.

Fridaythorpe to South Cave

From this mid-point on the trail, the walking is in the high wolds. The porous limestone means the low points, such as Horse Dale or Holm Dale, are often dry valleys. The high ground above Millington offers occasional views of York Minster, although the dales in the middle distance are more frequently seen.

On the way to Market Weighton is Londesborough Wold, remembered in the name of the village, the country house and the landscaped park. From Londesborough there is a short cut to Goodmanham, although Market Weighton is still worth visiting for its original Methodist chapel, where John Wesley preached many times.

Springtime in Hutton le Hole, Ryedale, Yorkshire

The wolds give way to easier walking towards North Newbald. Tumuli dot the landscape, interspersed with a Roman amphitheatre and a medieval granary. The highest point here is High Hunsley Beacon, where there is a television mast above the dry valley of Swin Dale. Views of the Humber estuary allow walkers to set their sights on the end of the trail.

Towards the Humber

From South Cave the wolds begin to fade away, reaching into the estuary lands that spread west from Hull. Welton Wold is one of the last wolds visited, before the Ice Age cliffs that surround the estuary are reached. The disused quarry and the many white pebbles reveal clearly the chalky nature of the escarpment of the Yorkshire and Lincolnshire Wolds. Wading birds act as a reminder that the route is still in the upper reaches of the estuary, but soon walkers pass under a modern contribution to the landscape, the Humber bridge.

The Wolds Way National Trail finishes at Hessle Haven, but the centre of Hull itself is not far away, for train and bus stations.

i CONTACT INFORMATION

**Cleveland Way Project /
Wolds Way Project**
c/o North York Moors National Park
The Old Vicarage
Bondgate
Helmsley
York YO6 5BP
Tel: 01439 770657
Fax: 01439 770691
E-mail: info@northyorkmoors-npa.gov.uk
Web: www.clevelandway.gov.uk
    www.woldsway.gov.uk

Yorkshire Tourist Board
312 Tadcaster Road
York YO24 1GS
E-mail: ytb@ytb.org.uk
Web: www.ytb.org.uk

Silhouette of Lilla Cross against the rising sun, Fylingdales Moor, Scarborough

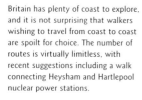
Coast to Coast: The Trans Pennine Trail

Escape from the restrictions of traditional coast to coast routes and try the Trans Pennine Trail, which breaks unwritten walking rules by passing through cities as well as remote countryside.

Britain has plenty of coast to explore, and it is not surprising that walkers wishing to travel from coast to coast are spoilt for choice. The number of routes is virtually limitless, with recent suggestions including a walk connecting Heysham and Hartlepool nuclear power stations.

Wainwright's walk

However, coast to coast walking in England has become synonymous with the route suggested by Alfred Wainwright in 1973. Covering 304km between St Bees in Cumbria and Robin Hood's Bay in North Yorkshire, Wainwright's walk passes through the Lake District, the Yorkshire Dales and the North York Moors. Such spectacular scenery has contributed to its reputation as one of England's greatest, and toughest, routes.

The Trans Pennine Trail

A newer and very different route, the Trans Pennine Trail contrasts sharply and, in many ways, favourably, with Wainwright's walk. The route passes through some of the most heavily populated areas of Britain and in doing so, draws attention to the natural beauties that are surprisingly close to large cities. Progressing along canal towpaths, disused railway tracks, minor roads, forgotten riverside trails and public rights of

way, the path explores landscapes ranging from urban bustle to peaceful meadows and wild moors. By revitalising the industrial past through the use of historical transport links, the Trans Pennine Trail is one of the few long-distance footpaths to present an accurate, small-scale impression of contemporary England.

Coast to coast, the Trans Pennine Trail is 344km long and passes through many of the major towns and cities of northern England, including Liverpool, Warrington, Stockport, Barnsley, Selby and Hull. By contrast, lengthy sections also cut across the Peak District National Park and other protected areas of natural beauty. Additional sections link Chesterfield, Sheffield and Rotherham with Leeds, and Selby with York, taking the total length of the route to 555km.

A community path

Developed to encourage the use of sustainable transport systems, the trail is, in many places, suitable not only for walkers but also for cyclists, horse-riders, wheelchair users and families. The route is popular with nearby residents who wish to use forms of transport other than the car, but co-operation between twenty six local authorities has made it possible to walk the entire trail from Southport on the west coast to Hornsea on the east coast.

The success of the route is a result of communities, councils and other organisations working together to encourage enjoyment of the environment. The 'Friends' of the Trans Pennine Trail, for example, help support the project, as well as producing newsletters and guides. Local schools and youth groups have created artwork, whilst sculptures, landscaping and nature trails provide further points of interest.

Southport

The trail starts – or ends – in Southport, beside the Irish Sea. Once a series of small cockle-fishing settlements and wayside inns, the town grew in the 19th century to become a popular spa resort and a holiday destination for locals, from visiting miners to Lancashire's high sheriff and wealthy mill owners.

The Longdendale section in the Peak District National Park

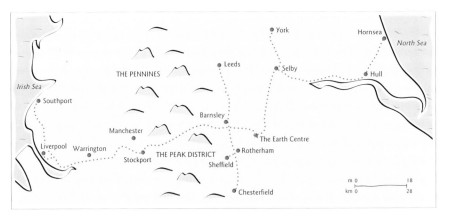

The town's pier was built in 1860 and, at 1,100m in length, remains the second longest in Britain. Victorian influence is evident throughout the town, demonstrated by handsome municipal buildings and parks, and especially by the statue of Queen Victoria herself on the promenade. The surrounding area is attractive walking country, dotted with pretty villages and fields of swaying crops.

The northern cities

Liverpool, Manchester, Sheffield and Hull were among the first cities to grow and prosper as a result of the industrial revolution in the late 18th century. Today, these are modern

cities which have been redeveloped to accentuate their histories. Heritage and sophistication mingle at Albert Dock on the Liverpool waterfront, which also features the Beatles Story museum and Liverpool's Tate gallery. Manchester's Museum of Science and Industry, meanwhile, is located in the world's oldest passenger railway station and exhibitions include the story of the city's textile industry.

Hornsea

At the far end of the route, a 15km disused railway line leads from Hull to the small town of Hornsea on the east coast of Yorkshire. Like Southport, it is a typically English seaside resort

with a well-preserved historical centre. Although most famous for its pottery, the main attraction for walkers and naturalists is Hornsea Mere, a huge freshwater lake situated just a kilometre from the coast. The mere was once about 7km long, but has been reduced in size by drainage and the action of the sea.

The Earth Centre

The ethos of the Trans Pennine Trail is summed up at the Earth Centre, found along the route at Conisbrough in Doncaster's Dearne valley. Sir Walter Scott, exploring the area 150 years ago, declared the rolling hills and rich woodland to be some of the most attractive in England. Subsequent coal mining degraded the region, but the Earth Centre aims to educate and inspire visitors to appreciate their environment.

The emphasis is on sustainable technologies, combining the science of the future with the gentler practices of the past. Outside, there are landscaped thematic gardens and play areas, while inside the futuristic buildings are interactive exhibitions and live entertainment.

The Aire and Calder towing path section at Swillington bridge, Leeds

CONTACT INFORMATION

Trans Pennine Trail Office
c/o Barnsley MBC
Kendray Street
Barnsley
South Yorkshire S70 2TN
Tel: 01226 772574
Fax: 01226 772599

The Ridgeway

History and legend mingle on the Ridgeway to stimulate and divert even the weariest walker.

Dating back 5,000 years or more, the Ridgeway is one of the oldest roads in Europe. It once stretched for 500km from the Dorset coast into deepest Norfolk, and was a drier and more open choice for travellers than paths through the valleys. The Romans ignored the route because it did not link up to any large towns, but part of the Ridgeway's charm today is its apparent remoteness. The modern 137km trail follows the same route, from Avebury in Wiltshire to Ivinghoe in Buckinghamshire.

The Ridgeway

As an officially-designated National Trail, the Ridgeway is well-marked with signs displaying an acorn logo. Diversions and circular day walks are possible along its entire length. While the going can be a little tough in bad weather, the path is enthusiastically maintained by volunteers who also lead guided walks throughout the year. Horses and bicycles can be ridden along the trail between Overton Hill and Streatley, while some stretches of the Ridgeway are also open to motorised traffic.

Two distinct characters

The contrast between the eastern and western halves of the Ridgeway is notable, with the River Thames at Goring providing a natural boundary between two types of scenery. The western half is more isolated, with extensive views far across the chalk grasslands and fields of arable crops. The eastern section is more enclosed and winds along the Chiltern hills through thick beech woods and nature reserves bright with wildflowers.

Chalk habitats

The tradition of farming near the Ridgeway is as old as the road itself and ancient terraced field systems called strip lynchets still dominate many hillsides. The slopes were cut back like enormous steps to provide level surfaces for growing crops. Examples can be seen at Bishopstone and Princes Risborough. Grain fields now dominate the land, although sparse pastures remain in the west. Left to their own devices, hardy downland plants grow close to the thin soil. Some, such as chalk milkwort, clustered bellflower and autumn gentian, grow only on chalk, while several species of orchid also thrive here. Blue, brown and white butterflies dart across the path, and the fields and thickets are alive with songbirds.

Sarsen stones

Scattered sarsen stones are a typical characteristic of chalk landscapes. These hard, pale stones are the remains of a sandstone layer laid down over the chalk thousands of

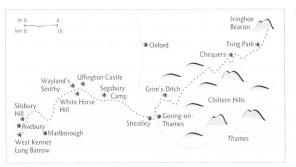

years ago. The softer parts were worn away to leave large exposed slabs that are also known as bridle-stones, druid stones or grey-wethers, because they look like grey sheep from a distance. The stones appear to have been very popular with previous civilisations and are a feature of the ancient monuments that can be seen along the Ridgeway. However many have been broken down over the years to form building blocks.

History

Although the Ridgeway is somewhat isolated, evidence of its past users is more obvious here than in many areas with larger populations. The Stone Age and Bronze Age burial sites that line the entire length of the Ridgeway have been excavated to reveal bones, flint tools, pottery and beads. Perhaps most impressive is West Kennet long chambered barrow, located near to the start of the trail on a prominent chalk ridge. In the 1,000 years after 3600 BC, about forty six burials occurred here, with the chamber marked by a row of large, upright sarsen stones. The barrow has been impressively restored for visitors.

Another interesting example is Wayland's Smithy, a 5,000 year old barrow named after the Saxon smith to the gods. His magic forge is inside the barrow, so the legend goes, and anyone who leaves their horse beside the barrow overnight with a penny on the stone lintel will find it reshod in the morning. Elsewhere, there are Iron Age forts to be explored such as Uffington Castle and Segsbury Camp, or Grim's Ditch, an extensive earthwork constructed for territorial purposes 2,000 years ago.

Avebury

Measuring 427m in diameter and covering an area of more than a square kilometre, Avebury is the largest stone circle in the world. Although nearby Stonehenge tends to steal its limelight, Avebury is just as awe-inspiring in its own way. Both sites probably obtained their sarsen stones from the Marlborough Downs, but unlike Stonehenge, the blocks at Avebury were not smoothed before use and arguably retain a more immediate sense of the prehistoric atmosphere. Originally, ninety eight stones weighing up to 50 tonnes stood on a high bank, enclosing two further circles of thirty stones each. However, only twenty seven stones are still in place, many having been broken up to build Avebury village or buried by locals in the 14th century. The Barber's Stone fell on a man who was moving it for burial and was left

The Ridgeway is signposted along its entire length

where it was. Its name is derived from the discovery of a pair of scissors and a lancet nearby. Another stone, the Devil's Chair, is said to have mystical powers. Running anticlockwise round the stone a hundred times summons the Devil, although onlookers would probably be better advised to summon a doctor.

Silbury Hill

One ceremonial avenue leading out of Avebury still remains. Originally 2.5km long, it is connected to another Neolithic monument called the Sanctuary, on Overton Hill. Like Avebury, it is thought to have had a ritualistic function. Silbury Hill looms nearby, the largest man-made prehistoric mound in Europe. Built 4,600 years ago with simple bone or flint tools, it is nearly 40m to its flat-topped summit. About 248,000 cubic metres of soil was deposited here, an amount equal to the entire population of Britain contributing a bucket's worth each. The hill's purpose is unknown. Perhaps it hides an ornate statue of King Sil himself, or perhaps he is buried there with his golden horse. Perhaps, as some people claim, it was not built at all but is in fact the pile of earth that the

Devil was carrying to drop onto the people of Marlborough before the priests of Avebury dissuaded him.

White horses

To the north is the Vale of White Horse, along which the famous Uffington White Horse has been galloping for perhaps 3,000 years. Huge, fluid lines cut into the white chalk of the hillside suggest the grace and beauty of a horse in motion and, measuring 111m long, it is visible from 30km away. There are many other examples of chalk horses in the region, but most of these are the result of a 19th century horse-carving craze and, being more anatomically correct than the Uffington horse, lack its allure. Walkers with a wish to be granted should stand in the eye of the Uffington horse and spin round three times with their eyes closed. Spinning probably happened quite a lot during the traditional 'scouring festivals', when villagers would gather ostensibly to clean the horse but in reality to drink and be merry. Perhaps this also contributed to the rumour that the horse 'climbs' the hill, although it does move slightly when soil erosion exposes chalk at the top of the carving and grass grows over the lower edges.

The open hills of the western part of the Ridgeway

Chequers and Tring

During the latter part of its route, the Ridgeway passes two estates. The first is Chequers, designated as the Prime Minister's country residence in 1917. Further along, the trail follows King Charles Ride on the southern edge of Tring Park. This is an ancient estate notable for its beautiful 18th century landscaping, including a summerhouse and an obelisk said to be dedicated to Charles II's famous mistress Nell Gwynne. In the 19th century, the eccentric owners of Tring grazed a variety of exotic animals here, including zebras, cassowaries, emus and kangaroos; a very different selection to the rabbits, hares and deer seen along the Ridgeway today. Unfortunately, a main road now slices the park in two, which may not surprise those walkers who have already seen the effects of motorways and ring roads on the countryside beside the Ridgeway.

The end of the trail

The final stretch of the Ridgeway is full of interest, passing a mixture of rolling hills, lush valleys and green fields. The walk ends – or indeed begins – at Ivinghoe Beacon, where the scenery suddenly becomes open again as the land rises. Weary walkers can survey their journey from the top of the hill, where there is another Iron Age fort as well a modern viewing plinth which points out many of the Ridgeway's features.

CONTACT INFORMATION

National Trails Office
Cultural Services
Holton
Oxford OX33 1QQ
Tel: 01865 810224
Fax: 01865 810207
E-mail: mail@rway-tpath.demon.co.uk
Web: www.nationaltrails.gov.uk
/ridgeway/rwayinto.htm

Avebury Tourist Information
The Great Barn
Avebury
Wiltshire SN8 1RF
Tel: 01672 539425
Fax: 01672 539296

Horse-riding and cycling are permitted on certain sections of the trail

 ENGLAND

The South-West Coast Path

*Always busy and almost never ending, this mammoth walk
is addictive for aficionados of the West Country.*

Encompassing virtually the entire
coastline of the south-west peninsula,
the South-West Coast Path is the
longest marked walk in Britain.
Spanning 965km – twice the length of
the Pennine Way – it is easy to be
inhibited by the distance, but no
walker should be put off. This path is
for anyone willing to be seduced by
the famous West Country coast.

The coastal path at Lantic Bay

Even if they do meet streams of
twenty five miles-a-day couples
stomping along the coast, many other
walkers just sample the path, doing
short circular routes that include a
little coastline and some of the inland
countryside. Other visitors make the
path a vocation, undertaking a small
stretch of it each year. Visitors speak
of the enrapturing views, the novelty
of pretty coastal villages, and the
sense of satisfaction from walking a
path so shrouded in history.

Origins

Up until 1856, a daily chore for
coastguards in the south-west was
watching the coastline for smuggling.
As there are so many discrete inlets
and coves they found themselves
taking in every nook and cranny of the
coast. Although patrolling the paths
was eventually taken over by the
Admiralty, the tracks that the
coastguards beat out became more
permanent as inhabitants of the

coastal villages started using them.
The modern South-West Coast Path
is based on those recovered routes
which probably accounts for the
walk's proximity to the cliff edge in
some places, and its generally
meandering course.

High seas and cliffs

The route begins in Minehead, a town
in the north-west corner of Exmoor
National Park. Inland, Exmoor is
gentle moorland, but the coastal area
looking out over the Bristol Channel is
the highest cliff area in England with

an apex of 433m at Hangman point.
Charming harbour villages such as
Lynmouth soften the blow, yet this
little idyll was also once the scene of
tragedy when, in 1952, a torrential
storm wreaked havoc and cost many
lives. Visitors will often be reminded
of the force of the elements along the
path as the wind and rain whip the
sea up into a frenzy. There is a
shipwreck recorded for every furlong
of the Cornish coast.

The tough Cornish coast

Cornwall's coastline, unreservedly
rugged through absorbing the force of
the Atlantic Ocean, makes up 428km
of the entire walk. Its jagged edges
and windswept cliffs, however, far
from making it an inhospitable
stretch, augment its natural beauty.

The first section of path in Cornwall,
reaching from Hartland point to Bude,
is called the 'Iron Coast' due to its
harsh features, but it also has the
best waterfalls of the walk. To avoid
the numerous inlets and caves along
the coast, wayfarers could be forced
to veer inland. However, there are
ferries across most obstructions so
walkers can keep up their momentum.

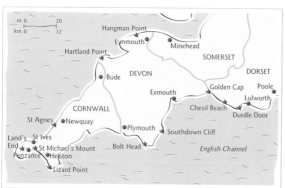

Cornish history

As the path nears the tip of Cornwall, visitors enter the heart of Cornish tin-mining country and St Agnes in particular. Cornwall, like Devon, was once driven by tin extraction, but around St Agnes all that remains are the eerie shells of engine houses from the turn of the 20th century, long redundant since the collapse of the industry.

Further south, the Penwith peninsula has also played an important part in English history. Penzance and Land's End have seen plenty of cultural traffic.

It is an area rich in megaliths, with stone circles such as the Merry Maidens and Boscawen-Un, or the intriguing site of Men an Tol. Towards Lizard point is St Michael's Mount, an island with a magical priory and castle. At 500m offshore, it can be reached by ferry or over a causeway by low tide. The island has some connections to the legend of King Arthur but, in the 11th century, it was given to the monks of Mont St Michel in France.

Around Lizard point

Projecting out to the south, this most southern point of Britain garners effusive testimonies from visitors, forever describing its faraway feel as inspiring. Its seclusion also means that it is home to butterflies, spring flowers and birds not found anywhere else nearby. After this full stop, wayfarers have gone as far out as they can and must begin returning east along the underbelly of the peninsula.

Devon and Dorset

At Plymouth, the walk leaves Cornwall and traverses the Devon coast. With a milder terrain and lush vegetation, the spectacular cliff walks at Bolt head near Salcombe, and the Southdown cliff by Brixham, are particular highlights. The latter also sits at the entrance to the River Dart

which, in the past, was protected from any intruders by chains slung across the water between castles on each pinnacle. The Dart flows northwards, cutting across the rugged tors of Dartmoor National Park.

The Dorset coast, the final leg of the path, is known for its complex geology, the crisp white colours shimmering on bright days. The area is often singled out for its natural chalk formations, not least Durdle Door near Lulworth, a white arch sticking out of the sea, akin to the body of a sea creature. A great pebble barrier bank at Chesil beach stretches from Dorset's Golden Cap towards the Isle of Portland, before this epic path finally bows out at Poole harbour.

i CONTACT INFORMATION

The South-West Way Association
Windlestraw
Penquit
Ermington
Devon PL21 0LU
Tel: 01752 896237
Web: www.swcp.org.uk

Cornwall Tourist Board
Pydar House
Pydar Street
Truro
Cornwall TR1 1EA
Tel: 01872 322900
Fax: 01872 322919
E-mail: tourism@visit.
cornwall.gov.uk

View from Bossington Hill, near Minehead

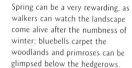

Offa's Dyke

This National Trail portrays the variety of the Welsh countryside. Hill-forts, castles and Georgian towns record the stories of the people who have lived, fought and worked along the Welsh border.

The Offa's Dyke Path winds its way through the border country of the Welsh Marches, hopping from Wales to England and back again. The route, which was established as a National Trail in the early 1970s, is 293km long, stretching from Chepstow in the south to Prestatyn in the north.

Offa's Dyke was an 8th century earthwork, which marked the western frontier of King Offa's Mercian kingdom, from the River Wye in the south to the Dee estuary in the north. The dyke was itself believed to be 130km long and there are frequent occasions along the route when the remains are clear; walkers will often find themselves on what was once an earth embankment up to 2.5m high and 20m wide. The Offa's Dyke Association, based at the Offa's Dyke

Centre at Knighton, halfway along the trail, offers detailed guides and strip maps of the whole route for walkers.

Changing landscapes

The route is often described as 'undulating', offering a variety of terrain to all walkers. There are some flat sections, but for the most part be prepared to climb up and down both gentle and steep hills. The demanding sections are Hatteral Ridge in the Black mountains, the Shropshire hills, and the Clwydian hills in the north.

The weather will be changeable, so in all seasons be ready for rain. May to September are the most popular times for walking the trail, due to the better chance of fine weather, but it is never very crowded at any time of year.

Spring can be a very rewarding, as walkers can watch the landscape come alive after the numbness of winter; bluebells carpet the woodlands and primroses can be glimpsed below the hedgerows.

The path passes through one national park (the Brecon Beacons), three areas of outstanding natural beauty and two environmentally sensitive areas. However, for all these officially protected places, a fair share of the path also finds itself among pasture,

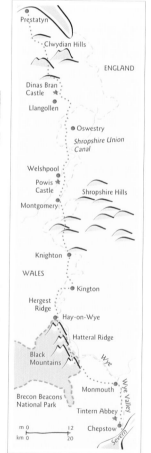

River Wye from Bargain Wood, near Llandogo

Powis castle

Castles and books

An alternative approach to the Offa's Dyke Path is to completely ignore the preponderance of hills and head for the small towns and villages that sit quietly along the route. Many are laden with long histories and are to keen to invite visitors to discover their varied pasts. From these places, small parts of the main path are easily accessible.

At Monmouth, the castle, now in ruins, dates from the birth of Henry V, whilst the town itself was home to a more modern hero, Charles Rolls of the Rolls-Royce car. At Hay-on-Wye a 17th century mansion, referred to as 'the castle', dominates the streets crammed with second-hand bookshops. Near Welshpool is Powis castle, together with a museum about Clive of India, who was associated with the town. Kington records its origins in its name, as Edward the Confessor laid siege to it in 1055. And Oswestry is associated with the detective work of Brother Cadfael, Ellis Peters' medieval monk.

[i] CONTACT INFORMATION

The Offa's Dyke Association
West Street
Knighton
Powys LD7 1EN
Tel: 01547 528753

farmland and grazing sheep. The landscape is dominated by moorland, heath, bracken and gorse, whether in the remote hills or alongside the fields. The River Wye contributes to the lushness of the south, whilst further north two canals, the Llangollen and the Shropshire Union, meander past old mining areas. Hill-forts and castles dot the high ground, highlighting the history of Offa's time, as well as his people's ancestors and descendants.

From the southern valleys

The southern end of the trail takes in the gentleness of the Wye valley, the openness of Hatteral Ridge and the isolation of Hergest Ridge. Gorse and heather colour the slopes with their yellow and purple tones, and among the wooded hills, between Chepstow and Monmouth, bluebells flower. Hay Bluff, in the far north-east corner of the Brecon Beacons offers good views down to Hay-on-Wye.

The Shropshire hills

Before reaching the Shropshire hills, which mark out one of the most strenuous sections of the trail, walkers can stretch their legs along the dyke itself, near to Kington. From Knighton to Churchtown the path steepens, but once the hills have been conquered the way becomes easier, a walk alongside the Shropshire Union Canal offering a gentle, watery respite.

The Clwydian hills

The Pontcysyllte aqueduct between Trefonen and Llandegla cannot be missed, and is worth walking along. It has dominated the skyline since the late 18th century and is a tribute to Thomas Telford's skills. Dinas Bran castle, however, is a reminder of more ancient engineering feats. After a final effort over the Clwydian hills, walkers arrive at Prestatyn. The beach marks the end of the trail, and it is traditional for walkers to paddle immediately in the sea.

Llangollen, north Wales

The Cambrian Way

A journey through the most remote parts of Wales, this route offers a challenge to walkers, but rewards them with stunning views throughout.

The Cambrian Way is not an official waymarked trail in Wales, but it is still one of the best-known long-distance walks in the country. Beginning in Cardiff and ending in Conwy on the north coast, the route takes in two national parks, most of the Welsh mountain ranges, including the peak of Snowdon, and many areas of unspoilt natural beauty.

The 440km of the way have been divided into twenty nine stages by the Cambrian Way Walkers Association (CWWA), each of about 16km each. These stages, when grouped together, form five separate sections which run from south to north. The CWWA also has two other designated walks, one contained within the Brecon Beacons National Park and the other in the remote countryside of the Cambrian Mountains themselves.

In the mountains

Most walkers tackle the Cambrian Way – or parts of it – between Easter and October when the weather is typically British, so be prepared for both rain and sun. In the mountains, whatever the season, the air will be quite cold, and the walking will be affected by the changeable cloud cover. As the trail is not marked, many of the areas it passes through are remote, without roads, so

Pen y Pass near Llanberis, Snowdonia

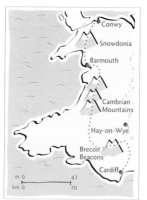

conditions can be strenuous. The CWWA aims to make the arduous terrain more welcoming by breaking it into day-size chunks. However, the walking will usually involve climbing mountains or descending into valleys – there are few gentle respites.

Welsh landscapes

The old industrial areas in the south near Cardiff, together with the abandoned stone quarries and lead mines of the central sections, offer an introduction to Wales' recent working history. The ancient hills, woodlands, waterfalls and mountains offer a record of a more natural and timeless past. The valleys in the south and the Mawddach estuary in the north-west are wooded, contrasting with the heather-covered ridges and empty moors. The coastal views by the seaside town of Barmouth contrast in turn with the lofty mountains of Cader Idris and Snowdonia.

Buzzards, kestrels and ravens follow walkers on their route, whilst in the protected national parks – Brecon Beacons and Snowdonia – lurk polecats and pine martens. Rare birds of prey such as merlins and peregrines inhabit the upper reaches of the Snowdonia massif.

Taf Fechan reservoir, Brecon Beacons

Nant Gwynant, Snowdonia

The Cambrian Mountains

The central section of the Cambrian Way in mid-Wales is the most remote and least known part of the route. However, the CWWA's Five Rivers Trail makes this beautiful section accessible to walkers.

The walk stays resolutely in the Cambrian Mountains over five days, discovering the sources of the Towi, Teifi, Severn, Wye and Rheidol rivers. The scenery is as varied as ever, with ancient woods, rolling moors and calm lakes. There are also monuments such as the chapel at Soar-y-Mynydd, the ruined medieval abbey at Strata Florida and the three-tiered Roman bridge, known as the Devil's Bridge, near Cwmystwyth.

A narrow gauge steam railway takes visitors up to the bridge from the Rheidol valley, but walkers will have the satisfaction of having reached the top under their own power. Towards the end of the walk the views from the summit of Plynlimon take in Cader Idris, the Brecon Beacons, the Snowdonia massif and the Irish Sea.

Snowdonia

After trekking through the bold and harsh Rhinogs, with the sea to the west, the summit of Snowdon and the grandeur of Snowdonia National Park are within grasp. The peak of Snowdon is the highest point in Wales, and the views are as exhilarating and rewarding as the satisfaction of having reached the top. The walks in this northern part of Wales are strenuous, but once the mountains have been scaled walkers are rewarded with the sight of the Edward I's 13th century castle at Conwy, a fitting monument to the end of the Cambrian Way.

ⓘ CONTACT INFORMATION

Brecon Beacons National Park
7 Glamorgan Street
Brecon
Powys LD3 7NP.
Tel: 01874 624437.

Snowdonia National Park
Penrhyndeudraeth
Gwynedd LL48 6LS.
Tel: 01766 770274
Web: www.gwynedd.gov.uk

Capital sights

Although few towns fall along the Cambrian Way, Cardiff and Conwy at either end of the path are worth a visit, together with Hay-on-Wye and numerous other picturesque villages.

Cardiff, as the capital of Wales, offers entertainment and sightseeing. The castle and the cathedral chart the feudal and religious history of the city, whilst the new rugby stadium is a monument to Wales' national sport. Wales is also renowned for its music, and each summer there is a festival for music and theatre, including the Welsh Proms season at St David's Hall. The National Gallery of Wales is also in Cardiff, together with other museums and exhibitions.

Brecon Beacons

The Black to Black Walk organised by the CWWA is contained within the the Brecon Beacons National Park. The trail stretches from the ridge of the Black Mountains in the east, across the Beacons themselves, and on to the Black Mountain in the west. The walk takes in five stages of the Cambrian Way.

The conditions are hilly, but the hard slog up to the summits is rewarded by the breathtaking views of the Wye valley and Carmarthenshire's glacial lakes. The descent into the valleys offers attractive scenery, together with Roman roads and old tramways. The Taff Trail and the Usk Valley Walk are also based within the park.

The Pembrokeshire Coast Path National Trail

The path along the Pembrokeshire coast offers walkers refreshing sea views and breezes, together with a profusion of wildflowers, seabirds and mammals.

The Pembrokeshire Coast Path National Trail was opened in 1971 as Wales' first long-distance route. Most of the trail is within the Pembrokeshire Coast National Park and, as such, is maintained by the park authorities. The trail divides nicely into fourteen sections of between 16 and 20km. To walk the whole length of the trail takes about two weeks, and each summer the park organises a guided walk from Amroth in the south to St Dogmaels in the north. However, it is more common to complete small sections between beaches and towns, either in leisurely rambles or day hikes.

The walking varies from gentle strolls along flat cliff tops to strenuous hikes up steep hills. Early summer is the best time to go as the path is usually at its prettiest, with flowers colouring the ground and the seabirds' nesting season just beginning, However, in any season, the views, weather and landscape still offer much to walkers.

There are at least ten short stretches of the coast path which are accessible to wheelchair users, including an award-winning cliff top access point at Haroldston Chins, near Broad Haven. A wheelchair path has also been specially constructed from Pwll Gwaelod to Cwm-yr-Eglwys, near Dinas Island, east of Fishguard.

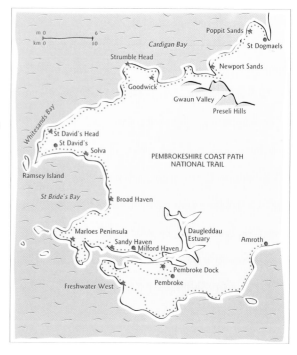

A rainbow of colours

In spring, the flowers carpeting the cliff tops and islands include white scurvy grass, yellow celandine, pink thrift and purple squill. These give way to bluebells, red campion, yellow broom and golden gorse in summer, with dark green fritillary butterflies and common blue butterflies flitting about in the warm air. Purple heather blooms in autumn, together with the gorse which continues into winter. Pembrokeshire lanes are traditionally lined with high hedgebanks, beneath which flourish familiar wildflowers of the British countryside.

From April to August seabirds nest on the coast. White-furred baby seals can be seen in late summer and autumn on secluded rocky beaches. Ramsey Island, off St David's peninsula, is an annual nursery for seals, and can be seen from the cliff path. Seals, porpoises and dolphins often swim close to the shore.

Milford Haven

The area around the Milford Haven tidal estuary, from St Anne's Head to West Angle Bay, offers a walking experience far removed from the cliff top scenery. Most of the path is not within the national park at this point, due to the oil refineries and power station that dominate the landscape. The towns of Pembroke, Pembroke Dock and Milford Haven are all excluded from the park but the trail ploughs on nevertheless.

St David's peninsula

The 48km from Solva to Strumble Head is a popular section of the path. The clean beaches, the views of Ramsey Island and the small 'city' of St David's make this corner of Pembrokeshire very attractive. St David's is worth visiting for its cathedral and ruined Bishop's Palace, as well as its annual Festival of Classical Music in early summer.

i CONTACT INFORMATION

Pembrokeshire Coast National Park
Winch Lane
Haverfordwest
Pembrokeshire SA61 1PY
Tel: 01437 764636
E-mail: pcnp@pembrokeshire coast.org.uk
Web: www.pembrokeshire coast.org.uk

The Pilgrims' Way

*Whether walking for the soul or just for the body, the Pilgrims' Way
explores the little known Llyn peninsula in north Wales.*

The curve of Porth Dinllaen's beach

This 80km route along the north-west coast of the Llyn peninsula follows in the footsteps of medieval pilgrims walking for their salvation. Three pilgrimages from Bangor to Bardsey Island were believed to equal one to Rome, and the route stops at eleven churches, some of which were built especially for the influx of pilgrims. The original monastery established on Bardsey was destroyed by the Saxons in AD 622, but its status as a site of early Christianity in Britain was retained, with the belief that 20,000 saints were buried on the island.

If the route to salvation does not appeal to today's walkers, the way still offers excellent walking and breathtaking views of Wales and the east coast of Ireland. None of the hills are especially strenuous, and the sea mists are the only potential deterrent from a good day's walking. The way is walkable all year round, although few services are open in winter, so it may be best to go in early summer. Accommodation is available in the picturesque Welsh-speaking villages.

The pilgrimage

The first section, along the Menai Strait and towards Clynnog Fawr, is in the shadow of the Snowdonian peaks and the Glyders, with views of Anglesey to the north-west.
Yr Eifl, with the biggest Bronze Age hill-fort in Britain (Tre'r Ceiri), is a short climb from the valley floor.

On a clear day, the Wicklow mountains in Ireland are visible from the Nant Gwyrtheyrn valley, which tumbles down towards the coast away from the hill-fort. The National Language Centre, in the town of Nant Gwyrtheyrn, offers Welsh lessons to passing visitors to help in reading signposts and greeting locals.

From the cathedral at Bangor to St Hywyn's church at Aberdaron, the churches and ancient holy sites along the route are convenient stopping-off places, breaking the way rhythmically each day. Many of the churches are on original sites of Christian worship from the 6th century, though some were restored in the 19th century.

The succession of small coastal towns after Porth Dinllaen offers a welcome sliver of civilisation. Porth Dinllaen itself once competed with Holyhead as the origin of the crossing to Ireland, but now all the towns are no more than sleepy fishing villages. In summer, boats sail daily from Aberdaron to Bardsey Island.

ℹ CONTACT INFORMATION

North Wales Tourism
77 Conwy Road
Colwyn Bay LL29 7LN
Tel: 01492 531731

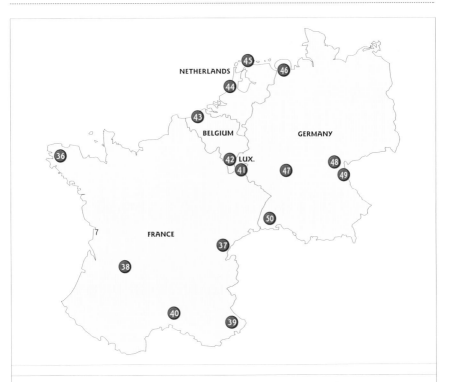

i CONTACT INFORMATION

**Belgian Tourist Office –
Flanders**
31 Pepperstreet
London E14 9RW
Tel: 020 7458 0044
Fax: 020 7458 0045
E-mail: office@flanders-tourism.org
Web: www.visitflanders.com

**Belgian Tourist Office –
Brussels and Ardennes**
255 Marsh Wall
London E14 9FW
Tel: 0800 9545 245
Fax: 020 7531 0393
E-mail: info@belgium-tourism.org
Web: www.belgium-tourism.net

Maison de la France
178 Piccadilly
London W1V 0AL
Tel: 0891 244123
Fax: 020 7493 6594
E-mail: info@mdlf.co.uk
Web: www.franceguide.com

German National Tourist Office
PO Box 2695
London W1A 3TN
Tel: 020 7317 0908
Fax: 020 7995 6129
E-mail: German_National_Tourist_
Office@compuserve.com
Web: www.germany-tourism.de

Luxembourg Tourist Office
122 Regent Street
London W1R 5FE
Tel: 020 7434 2800
Fax: 020 7734 1205
E-mail: tourism@luxembourg.co.uk
Web: www.luxembourg.co.uk

Netherlands Board of Tourism
PO Box 523
London SW1E 6NT
Tel: 0906 871 7777
Fax: 020 7828 7941
E-mail: hollandinfo-uk@nbt.nl
Web: www.holland.com

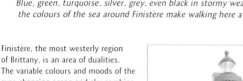

FRANCE

Coastal Walks in Finistère

*Blue, green, turquoise, silver, grey, even black in stormy weather –
the colours of the sea around Finistère make walking here a treat.*

Finistère, the most westerly region of Brittany, is an area of dualities. The variable colours and moods of the ever-changing ocean and sky combine to make the seascape exceptionally beautiful, while the innumerable Neolithic menhirs and dolmens alongside churches, crosses and chapels signify a religious heritage that freely mixes Christian and Celtic roots. Even the linguistic tradition is twofold: Breton is spoken by 250,000 people and actively celebrated in local music and culture, and signs are written both in French and Breton.

Countryside and climate

Although the Arrée range and the Montagnes Noires (the Black Mountains) that spread through the centre of Finistère can reach heights above 300m, the majority of the landscape lies below 100m, offering pleasant walking terrain. The salt air and gentle sea breezes from the Atlantic invigorate and soothe, inspiring visitors to follow one of the walking routes that lead around the magnificent coast. Over 800km of shoreline offers a variety of scenery, from impressively jagged granite headlands where the sea swirls ominously below, to vistas of gorse-overgrown cliff-tops; and from gentle bays, inlets and sand-dunes to busy port towns and villages.

The lighthouse in the abbey at Pointe St-Mathieu

The Path of Lighthouses

The importance of the sea to Finistère is demonstrated by the 111 beacons and lighthouses that are dotted along the coast. Part of the GR 34, a walk of some 100km known as Le Chemin des Phares (the Path of Lighthouses) runs along the cliffs from the famous port of Brest to Portsall. Twenty three of Finistère's lighthouses are used as marking points along this route, including the Pointe de St-Mathieu lighthouse, situated in an old abbey and dating from 1835, and Trézien lighthouse, which marks the meeting

of the Channel with the Atlantic. If the walk is continued a little further north from Portsall, it reaches the highest lighthouse in Europe on L'Ile Vierge (Virgin Island); at 82.5m high, on clear nights the light can be seen from a distance of 50km.

Other curiosities worth visiting along the way include Berthaume fort, a 15th century castle stronghold. Strategically placed on a rock at Plougonvelin, it is a reminder of Brittany's turbulent past when defence against sea invaders was always necessary. In July and August, guided tours take place each night around the floodlit ramparts.

A diversion inland from Trézien to the 12m high menhir at Kerloas-en-Plouarzel is worth the extra trek. From a different period, the ruins of Tremazan castle near Ploudalmézeau at the close of the route are equally as dramatic. Semi-demolished in the 13th century, no one is sure of the origins of the building, but the huge tower that still stands looks like a forbidding Cathar structure. The area nearby suits the castle; the coastline is known as Le Côte Sauvage (the Wild Coast), a name appropriate to the reefs that sprinkle the coast, and the forms of the low cliffs worn into peculiar shapes by centuries of ocean gales and stormy seas.

The harbour of Le Conquet

92

Ouessant and Molène

From Brest or Le Conquet, it is possible to take a boat to the island of Ouessant, the most westerly point in France. Cliffs rise to 60m above the sea, whilst inland grassy heathlands stretch out invitingly. Molène and the smaller islets surrounding it play host to over thirty species of seabird, including puffins and storm petrels, and also shelter one of the few colonies of grey seals and European otters. Since 1988, the archipelago has been designated a UNESCO world biosphere reserve.

Ouessant lighthouse

The French Cornwall Coast

Other sections of the GR 34 introduce the visitor to La Côte de Cornouaille (the French Cornwall coast); from Douarnenez to Lorient, guide books are available for the entire 300km journey. The Sizun cape has more of the stunning Breton cliffs and craggy landscape ideal for scrambling and exploring, especially at its extremity, the Pointe du Raz.

By contrast, Audierne Bay's long wide beaches and dunes have a much calmer, more relaxing atmosphere, although the bay also offers good surfing opportunities. The southern section of the walk is a mix of wooded river bays, ports, beaches, dunes and marshland. Looking inland from the charming river mouth of the Odet at Bénodet, it is possible to see the spires of Quimper cathedral in the distance. The artistic city lies at the junction between the old land and shipping routes so vital to Brittany's economy, and can be a pleasant diversion to a predominantly rural expedition. Further east, the fortified town of Concarneau, France's first fishing port in terms of numbers of fishermen and fish caught, lends itself to exploration. The harbour, the narrow cobbled streets crammed with galleries, shops and crêperies in the old enclosed town, the ramparts, the fishing museum and the beach are all a delight to ramble through.

Themed routes and festivals

Particular themed itineraries created by the local tourist boards aim to show off the regional specialities. La Route des Peintres en Cournouaille (the Artists in Cornwall Trail), gives seven itineraries for following in the footsteps of such artists as Gauguin and Redon, while La Route des Ports de Pêche goes through some of the prettiest fishing ports.

La Route du Cidre (the Cider Trail), goes in search of the home-brewed drink that has a long tradition amongst the idyllic countryside of thatched cottages and apple orchards. In July, the Fête des Pommiers (the Feast of the Apple Trees) takes place at Fouesnant.

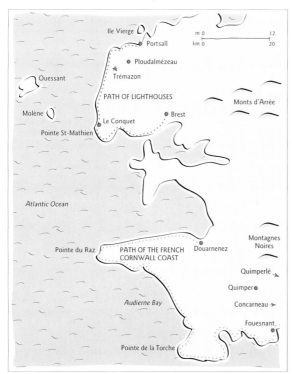

Map labels:
Ile Vierge — Portsall — Ploudalmézeau — Trémazon — Ouessant — PATH OF LIGHTHOUSES — Molène — Le Conquet — Brest — Monts d'Arrée — Pointe St-Mathien — Atlantic Ocean — Pointe du Raz — PATH OF THE FRENCH CORNWALL COAST — Douarnenez — Montagnes Noires — Quimperlé — Quimper — Concarneau — Audierne Bay — Fouesnant — Pointe de la Torche

i **CONTACT INFORMATION**

Finistère Tourist Board
11, rue Théodore Le Hars
BP 1419
29104 Quimper cedex
France
Tel: (00 33) 2 9876 2070
Fax: (00 33) 2 9852 1919
E-mail: finistere.tourisme
@wanadoo.fr

The Franche-Comté

Strength and sweetness mingle in the Franche-Comté, from fortifications and rugged mountains to free-flowing rivers and meadowlands.

The Franche-Comté is a forested land of undulating plains and plateaux lying between Burgundy and Switzerland. The region belonged alternately to German, Spanish and Dutch kingdoms until it gained its independence as the Franche-Comté (Free County). The area finally became part of France in 1678.

Today, the original mix of cultures is echoed by the mix of industry and unspoilt countryside, and the diverse landscapes of the four départements. The Haute-Saône ranges from the foothills of the Vosges to the gentle valleys of the Saône and Ognon; the Territoire-de-Belfort is characterised by military fortifications; and the Doubs and Jura between them offer lakes, rivers, bogs and mountains.

The source of the Lison

Footpaths

Accessibility and moderation are the keynotes of the region. Although the Vosges and Jura mountain ranges can be challenging, the predominant rolling hills and gentle valleys offer relaxing walks with ample opportunity to appreciate the region's cultural, architectural and natural treasures. 7,000km of trackways include short day walks, urban pathways and longer circular trails. Parts of long distance routes also cross the province, such as the GR 59 from the Ballon d'Alsace to Lons-le-Saunier, the E2 in the Jura and Doubs, and the E5 in the Vosges.

Many walks have been designed to incorporate specialities of the region. An 80km trail in the Territoire-de-Belfort links fortified towns; wine and cheese walks in the Jura mingle gastronomy and scenery; and nature walks explore the Doubs peatlands. Well-kept nature trails allow visitors to appreciate local environments, such as the natural peat moors at Frasne and Mouthe, and the lake of Remoray. Yellow iris and crane's bill are amongst the flowers that decorate the scenery, whilst cowslips hide in the woodlands that cover almost half the region.

The southern Vosges

Much of the southern Vosges area of Franche-Comté is covered by the Ballons des Vosges Regional Nature Park, characterised by rounded peaks (*ballons*), rocky inclines and meadows. Here is the extraordinary Land of the Thousand Ponds, a wide plateau covered in small lakes and peat bogs, created when a glacier in the Moselle valley retreated 12,000 years ago. Today birch, pine, gorse and juniper flourish round the crayfish and salmon-filled waters. A 60km trail leads through the countryside, past erratic boulders, rustic stone crosses and villages dating from the Middle Ages. For a treat, stop in Fougerolles to taste the famous local cherry liqueur, *kirsch*.

The Saône valley

'There is a river, the Saône, of incredible gentleness...' wrote Julius Caesar, and the calmness of the river is still matched by the pace of life in the Haute-Saône département. Its charm lies in little things: ruined abbeys, chapels, castles, fountains and peculiar weather-carved rocks all adorn the delicate landscape. Museums give an insight into local customs and glass-blowers in Passavant-la-Rochère demonstrate their skill in the oldest glassworks in France. Old ports such as Port-sur-Saône and Gray remind us that the Saône was once an important trade route; in Gray, a medieval castle, a Gothic basilica and a Renaissance town hall reflect a distinguished past.

The Lion of Belfort

The chapel at Ronchamp

Belfort

Belfort, which lies strategically between the Vosges and Jura massif, was fortified by the military architect Vauban who created an elaborate system of towers, casemates, curtains and counterscarps. The town is also famous for its huge lion statue by the French sculptor Bartholdi, creator of New York's Statue of Liberty. Other architectural delights include the futuristic chapel of Notre-Dame-du-Haut at Ronchamp, built in 1955; St Columba's Abbey in Luxeuil-les-Bains; and the castle in Montbéliard.

Around Besançon

The capital of the region, Besançon, lies within an almost complete loop of the river Doubs. Designated France's first 'green town' in 1990, the city features elegant quayside houses, international classical and jazz festivals, and a citadel perched on the steep hill that guards the town. Designed for Louis XIV in the 17th century, it now holds museums on agriculture, natural history, folk traditions and the Resistance.

Nearly 35km away at Arc-et-Senans, the Royal Saltworks is a UNESCO world heritage site. Created by Claude-Nicolas Ledoux as part of an unfinished 'ideal community', the grandiose neo-classic buildings give an insight into the 18th century architect's visionary ideas.

Lakes and liquors

In the southern part of the region, over eighty natural and artificial lakes create beautiful walking environments. The best-known waters are Saint-Point lake in Doubs, and the Vouglans reservoir in the Jura. The second largest artificial lake in France, Vouglans was created by a hydroelectric dam on the River Ain.

The area is also famous for stronger liquids than water: the Jura vineyards produce the famous *vin jaune* (yellow wine), *vin de paille* (straw wine) and *crémant* (a sparkling wine). Nearby Pontarlier was once famous for its thirty absinthe distilleries; with the banning of the spirit that supposedly inspired numerous French poets and artists, these diversified into producing aniseed and gentian-flavoured apéritifs instead. Walks explore both the vineyards and the cheese-making areas, and there is always the chance of happening upon a local wine, cheese or sausage festival.

ℹ CONTACT INFORMATION

Franche-Comté Tourist Bureau
Le St-Pierre
28, rue de la République
25044 Besançon Cedex
France
Tel: (00 33) 3 8125 0808
Fax: (00 33) 3 8183 3582

North Aquitaine's History

Along the Dordogne and Vézère valleys, paths lead back in time to the contrasting eras of mysterious prehistoric troglodytes and the romance of the Middle Ages.

Between Périgueux in Dordogne and Agen in Lot-et-Garonne there are literally hundreds of reminders of Aquitaine's turbulent medieval history, the stage for years of fighting between the French and English kingdoms and dukedoms. Hilltops are decorated both by bastides, fortified towns from the 13th and 14th centuries, and by castle strongholds. Between the reminders of these wars of the Middle Ages, the landscape extends at times dramatically, with limestone cliffs alongside the Dordogne valley, and at times softly.

Orchards, gentle green hills, and summery yellow soil prompted Stendhal to call Lot-et-Garonne 'the Tuscany of France'. With its balmy climate, the region produces fruit and vegetables which can be sampled in local restaurants. An unhurried walking tour, taking time to soak up the historic atmosphere, is probably the best way to experience the region.

And if the many reminders of struggles for political power become too much, it can be a relief to move onwards to the Vézère valley. Here, in the 'Valley of Man', Europe's richest palaeolithic site includes the Lascaux cave, where beautiful paintings of animals were created long before gunpowder and cannon fire were even dreamt of.

Caves and castles

Although parts of long-distance walking routes such as the GR 6 and GR 36 pass through the region, the wealth of interesting towns, villages and castles perhaps make briefer, localised walks more appealing than strenuous hikes. The average temperature in high summer is over 25°C, again giving an excuse for slower, shorter walks, allowing extra time to loiter in shadowy medieval town streets.

The topo-guides *471 Lot-et-Garonne – Le Pays de l'Agenais* and *DO24 La Dordogne à Pied* offer suggestions for walks throughout the region, while

the walking guide *P474 Pays du Haut-Agenais – Périgord à Pied* describes eighteen routes that link the castles, bastides and forests around Monflanquin. Many of the paths lie close to the Dordogne and Vézère rivers, allowing opportunities for swimming if the weather becomes too warm.

Monflanquin

The bastides in south-west France were new towns built during the Middle Ages, partly as a general movement of urban expansion and partly as a means of fortifying land borders. In return for rights such as markets, house purchase and no

The bastide of Monflanquin

military service, the new citizens had to commit themselves to the upkeep of the town, and defend it in wartime. Each town was planned in a grid fashion, with a market square and the town hall at the centre, which was a move away from the past where the church would have been the focal point of any settlement. Of the hundred or so examples of such towns in this area, particular gems are Monflanquin, Monpazier and Domme.

A French bastide founded by Alphonse of Poitiers in 1252, Monflanquin's central square, with its surrounding houses, is well preserved. The systematic planning was not adjusted for inclines, and the resulting sloped streets can be charming, while efforts have been made to hide such 20th century additions as telephone wires to maintain the character of the town. The *carrerots*, tiny alleys that used to link the main streets but which had

The fertile fields of the Dordogne countryside

frequently been taken over by the people living next to them, have also been re-opened, allowing visitors to wander freely through the town. Monpazier was an English bastide and is a classic example of the architectural style; it was listed as a site of national importance in 1991.

Beynac and Bonaguil

The village of Beynac creeps up a hill from the local river to culminate in an impressive castle that is now famed for its beauty, but was once known by the local peasants as 'Satan's Ark', its barons feared for their excessive cruelty. The 15th century Château de Bonaguil, just north of Fumel, is another splendid example of a medieval fortress. Its ruined towers and bastions stand out in bold contrast to the neighbouring areas.

Prehistory

From Beynac, a longish 19km walk through valleys, woods and maize fields leads to the Vézère valley and the village of Les Eyzies, known as the 'capital of prehistory'. Here, the National Museum of Prehistory is an excellent introduction to the Stone Age sites that abound in the valley's limestone caves, crevasses and stalactite-decorated grottoes. Further north, the Lascaux cave paintings near Montignac have been closed to the public since 1963. However, a faithful reproduction of most of the animal frescoes is on display nearby, in a concrete-covered shell that recreates the atmosphere of the cave.

ⓘ CONTACT INFORMATION

Lot-et-Garonne Tourist Board
4 rue André Chénier
BP 158
47005 Agen Cedex
France
Tel: (00 33) 5 5366 1414
Fax: (00 33) 5 5368 2542

Château de Bonaguil

The Alpes-Maritimes

Majestic mountain scenery, mysterious prehistoric rock carvings and ancient hilltop villages are some of the treats in store for those who venture beyond the glitz and extravagance of the Côte d'Azur.

The beautiful coastline that gave the Côte d'Azur region its name is so well known that the mountainous countryside it borders is often neglected. Yet the exotic architecture, golden beaches and general pizzazz of the French Riviera can seem brash when compared with the stately beauty of the Maritime Alps that rise beyond Monaco, Nice and Cannes.

Nice on the Riviera

The Alpes-Maritimes

From the sun-drenched shoreline of the Riviera to the high peaks of the Cime du Gélas (3,143m) and Le Grand Capelet (2,935m), the Alpes-Maritimes offers breathtaking scenery. The land can be divided roughly into three: the frenetic coast, the quiet and secluded middle country, and the highlands.

In the central middle country, ancient hamlets and villages cling to peaks and rocky spurs, sometimes in seemingly impossible places. Built partly for defence, these close-knit settlements also benefited the feudal lords by keeping the population together and protecting valuable fertile land. Olive plantations cover some of the hillsides, while once-cultivated terraces have been taken over by forest, bearing witness to the depopulation of the interior. Medieval castle and citadel ruins lie here and there, and humble churches or chapels often hide inner riches. From the 14th to the 16th centuries, bright frescoes were painted in churches to teach the scriptures to illiterate peasants. Some of the best remaining examples are found at Notre-Dame de Bon-Coeur in Lucéram, and at Notre-Dame des Fontaines in La Brigue.

Most of the highest mountains are in the Mercantour National Park, which was created in 1979 to protect rare species such as wolves, ibex and bearded vultures. High lakes and alpine meadows create a summer idyll, while in the Vallée des Merveilles (Valley of Marvels) thousands of rock engravings date from the Bronze Age.

Walks for all

Marked trails ensure safe and scenic walks around many of the coastal headlands, such as the Maeterlinck Path on the Cap de Nice, the Tirepoil Way on the Cap d'Antibes, and a tour of the Lérins islands of Cannes.

Day-long inland walks allow some of the back country to be discovered as a break from a lazy beach holiday. It is these inner regions that offer most to the walker. About 4,000km of marked trails are kept up by local councils, which have also installed 3,500 signposts. Each of these has a reference number which can be found on the local walking maps, making it hard to become lost. Paint marks on trees and rocks help to show the correct way – yellow denotes a shorter walk, while red and white is

used for the GR long-distance routes. The regional council also produces two booklets on the middle country and the highlands, each with sixty suggested walks. The routes are described in detail, with advice on maps, the climbs and descents involved, and the level of difficulty. For overnight stays, there are hotels or inns in most of the mountain settlements, along with *gîtes d'étape*, simple, cheap hostels. In the higher mountains, *refuges d'altitude* are mountain huts only reachable by foot.

Long-distance hikes

No fewer than six GR routes cross the region. The GR 4 begins in Grasse and offers three days walking through the Alpes-Maritimes before moving on to the Alpes de Haute Provence. The last section of the Amsterdam–Nice GR 5

St Mary's church by the lake at Breil-sur-Roya

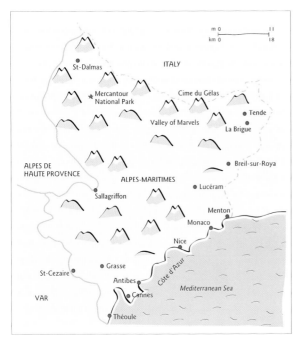

glittering sea. The GR 52 from Tende to Colmars passes along the southern edge of the Mercantour National Park.

Finally, the GR 510, the Sentier des Huit Vallées, follows old tracks that once linked rural hamlets. From Breil-sur-Roya to St-Cézaire, the path enters the Roya, Bévéra, Vésubie, Tinée, Cians, Var, Estéron and Siagne valleys. Little known, the trail is usually deserted, ideal for discovering the perched villages in solitude.

Heat

July and August are far too hot to enjoy hiking and the Riviera will be swarming. May, June and September offer the best walking conditions and fewer crowds. Most walks in the middle country can be undertaken between March and November, some even being suitable all year round.

[i] CONTACT INFORMATION

Côte d'Azur Riviera Tourist Board
55, Promenade des Anglais
BP 1602
06011 Nice
France
Tel: (00 33) 4 9337 7878
Web: www.crt-riviera.fr

Mercantour National Park
23, rue d'Italie
BP 1316
06006 Nice
France
Tel: (00 33) 4 9316 7888

heads south, at times passing through wild mountains, at times through calm scenery and finishing with a plunge down the steep cliffs to Nice. The GR 52 is a four or five day hike from St-Dalmas to Menton that passes over the Boréon peak and the Valley of Marvels before following the Italian border to the coast.

The GR 51, the Balcons de la Méditerranée, and the GR 52, the Panoramique du Mercantour (Mercantour Panorama) offer contrasting scenery. Running along the seaside mountains, the GR 51 gives splendid views over the empty countryside to the north, the urban mass along the coast, and the

The mountain village of St Paul de Vence

 **FRANCE**

The Stevenson Trail and the Cévennes

*A walk in the footsteps of an adventurous writer offers an exciting way
of discovering some of France's untamed and unspoilt countryside.*

While Robert Louis Stevenson's books *Treasure Island* and *Kidnapped* have become classics, few people are aware that the Scottish writer was himself quite an explorer. In 1878, he was staying near Fontainebleau with friends when he met and fell in love with his future wife, Fanny Osborne. When she had to return to America in the autumn, Stevenson's heartache prompted him to seek solitude, and he set off on his own for the south of France. There, he settled for a while at Le Monastier-sur-Gazeille to prepare for a journey across the Cévennes.

The Stevenson Trail

On the 22nd of September, Stevenson left the village accompanied only by a donkey, Modestine, and arrived twelve days and 220km of memorable scenery later in St Jean du Gard. From his journal of the walk, he later published *Travels with a Donkey in the Cévennes*, a work which has since been enjoyed by generations of readers, and inspired in some a desire to follow in the author's footsteps.

Today this route can still be appreciated, with or without a donkey, and indeed it is perhaps one of the best possible introductions to the Cévennes landscape. The trail is now classified as the GR 70, and in 1994 a local organisation called 'Sur le Chemin de R. L. Stevenson'

A bridge over the Tarn river

was formed to help establish it as a recognised itinerary. The organisation's aim is to increase local awareness of the historic way, and encourage anyone involved with tourism to make the walk a rich experience for all those who undertake it. Members include tourist offices, hotels, gites, hostels, restaurants, and even places where donkeys can be hired.

Emulating Stevenson by hiring a donkey can add an extra dimension to a holiday; the gentle animals carry luggage without complaining, and many of the overnight hostels are equipped to shelter them. To make the walking pleasant, it is best to go from April to June, or in the autumn, as July and August can be uncomfortably hot for a long hike.

The Cévennes

The Cévennes are rugged southern foothills of the Massif Central in the Lozère and Gard départements of Languedoc-Roussillon. Bounded by Mont-Lozère in the north and Mont-Aigoual in the south-west, the sparsely populated region is enough to satiate anyone's desire for emptiness and stillness. Steep slopes and vast expanses of untamed countryside cover such a variety of ecosystems that in 1970 much of the area was designated a national park.

The largest of the seven French national parks, the Cévennes' cultural inheritance is almost as impressive as its natural beauty. At Les Bondons on Mont-Lozère, the menhirs are the second finest collection of megalithic standing stones in France. Ruined castles tell tales of a richer past, Roman churches add their simple beauty to the settlements, while abandoned farm buildings and chestnut groves bear witness to a once fruitful land. The hamlets and villages have stone houses with tiled roofs made from local granite, schist or limestone, and the park authority protects the old community buildings such as ovens, mills and forges.

Following the trail

Strictly speaking, Stevenson's walk began to the north of the Cévennes in the Haute-Loire, but the austere landscape is similar throughout. In Le Monastier, where the trail now begins, the sombre Château de Prieur is worth visiting. Now incorporating a museum of local rural life, one room in the castle is dedicated to Stevenson and his journey; a stone tablet honouring the Scot in the marketplace makes a good setting-off point.

From Le Monastier, the route winds its way up through the Haute-Loire into the Lozère region at Langogne, and up, over and through the hills between Le Bleymard, Pont de Montvert, Florac and St Germain de Calberte. Each step of the way has its own particular point of interest. By Goudet, a ridge of rocks has an outline that earned it the name 'rhinoceros', and in nearby Montagnac small caves can be explored. Numerous castles can be seen,

Hiking with a donkey in the Cévennes

such as the ruins of the 12th century Château de Luc that dominate the Allier valley, the Château de Miral with its donjon dating from the 13th century, and the 17th century Château de Florac that houses the Cévennes National Park's ecomuseum.

At the Plan de Fontmort near Cassagnas, an obelisk was erected in 1887 in memory of the Camisards, French Protestants who often sought refuge in the Cévennes during the 17th century Wars of Religion. The medieval Château de St-Germain-de-Calberte would have been impressive enough in Stevenson's time, but now looks even more imposing thanks to its recent restoration by a family of Parisian goldsmiths. An optional climb to the Col de St-Pierre gives a spectacular view over the southern valleys, and down to St Jean du Gard, the end of the walk. Stevenson finished his trek here on 3rd October, staying at the Hôtel l'Oronge which is still open.

Mont-Lozère

One of the most scenic sections of the walk begins at the hamlet of L'Estampe, the starting point of a fairly tough zigzag climb over Le Goulet (1,496m), where the Lot river has its source. After passing through Le Bleymard, with its wonderfully restored town hall, the long haul over Mont-Lozère begins.

The path frequently follows the shepherds' routes to and from the summer pastureland. Large granite needles known as *montjoies* mark the way, while on ancient boundary stones the Maltese cross is engraved, showing the old estates of the medieval Knights of Malta. The trail eventually leads over the Pic du Finiels, at 1,699m the highest point of Mont-Lozère. Walkers will see bright yellow gorse and timid orchids, whilst there is always the chance of spotting a herd of deer or a lone wild boar.

Ecomuseums

In Pont de Montvert, the Mont-Lozère ecomuseum details the history of the land, and points out the most interesting sites. Similar themed museums concentrate on other aspects of local culture, and though not many are on the main trail, they merit a diversion for their insight into the region's character.

The Cévenol museum in Pont-Ravagers has a multitude of photographs to bring the Cévenois people to life, while a butterfly collection and a number of fossil exhibits show the diversity of current and extinct indigenous species. In Molezon, an exhibition in a former *magnanerie* – a silkworm breeding facility – presents the story of the silkworm trade that once had a large impact on the area. And in St-Laurent de Trèves, the town

church houses an exhibition on the 'grallator', a creature from 190 million years ago that left its footprints in the soft limestone surroundings.

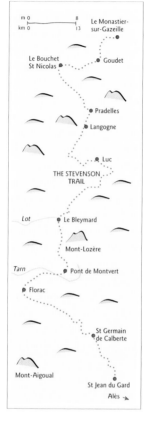

The countryside around La Cham des Bondons

---

[i] CONTACT INFORMATION

'Sur le chemin de R. L. Stevenson' Association
Syndicat d'Initiative
48220 Pont de Montvert
France
Tel & Fax: (00 33) 4 6645 8631

Lozère Tourist Board
14, boulevard Henri-Bourillon
BP 4 - 48001 Mende Cedex
France
Tel: (00 33) 4 6665 0000
Fax: (00 33) 4 6649 2796

Florac Tourist Office
Av. J. Monestier
48400 Florac
France
Tel: (00 33) 4 6645 0114
Fax: (00 33) 4 6645 2580
E-mail: otsi@ville-florac.fr
Web: www.ville-florac.fr

Southern Luxembourg

A literary ramble through the state's capital, a visit to a mine reclaimed by nature, and a stroll through vineyards – all add to Luxembourg's collage of walking delights.

At the heart of southern Luxembourg is the nation's capital, the city of Luxembourg. A centre of European banking and European Union administration, its location gives it perfect access to the four contrasting regions that surround it, and which together make up the lower half of the country. The green valleys of the 'Good Land' are predominantly north of the city; La Moselle in the east is a region of vineyards; in the south are the Red Rocks, the mining source upon which the state's wealth was built; while Mullerthal, the 'Little Switzerland', is in the north-east.

Torchlight parade in the capital city to celebrate the Luxembourg National Holiday

Le Coeur du Bon Pays

Contrasting with the hilly Ardennes of the north, the 'Good Land' of southern Luxembourg is gently rolling countryside, albeit with ample rivers and forests. Its focal point is the city of Luxembourg, but from here the visitor can take in the villages, medieval fortifications and traditional farmsteads of the surrounding rural regions. The vast forests are also perfect terrain for hiking. A good starting point is the town of Mersch, directly above Luxembourg, at the entrance to the Valley of the Seven Castles. The village is host to the

The Romanesque church at Saeul

springs of Hunnebour, the prehistoric caves of the Mamer and Dreibouren, and the remains of a Roman villa. Situated in the centre of a forest, Saeul, with its restored Romanesque church, is equally appealing.

Luxembourg city

The city of Luxembourg is crawling with history and there are walks through the best of it. Unusually the Casemates Tour takes visitors underneath the streets. A 23km network of tunnels, the Casemates were originally a last line of military defence, being capable of sheltering thousands of soldiers and horses. In the 19th century the city's fortress was dismantled, but demolishing the Casemates would have meant destroying part of the town. Instead, the entrances and key connecting galleries were securely plugged.

Another popular walk in the city is the Goethe itinerary. The German writer stayed briefly in Luxembourg-Pfaffenthal in October 1792. He published his impressions in the autobiographical work *The Campaign in France*. The walk retraces the stages of the author's stay via the fish markets, the Goethe memorial, the Promenade de la Corniche and the suburb of Grund.

La Moselle

The Moselle river acts as the Luxembourg–German border south of Mullerthal, and stretches right down to France. This is predominantly a wine growing region and has the festivals to prove it. In Greiveldange in August there is the Léiffrawëschdag, which, although it translates as 'Good Women's Washing Day', is a music, dance and wine festival. Similarly, in Grevenmacher in September, there is a grape festival encompassing music, parades and wine tasting.

Surveying the vineyards is a popular activity. The Domaines de Vinsmoselle co-operative organises a viticulture walk which tours the cellars and vineyards of Wellenstein and Wormeldange. It includes a visit to former wine growers' houses in Wellenstein: 'A Possen' – built in 1617 – and 'Muedulshaus' have both been transformed into wine and folklore museums.

For an alternative route, from the sheltered village of Mertert on the Moselle river, visitors are within easy access of the Moselle gorges and the region's vineyards and forests. There is also an ecological walking tour from Manternach to Mertert, encompassing the local history, flora and fauna.

Walking in the Mullerthal

Mullerthal – La Petite Suisse

Separated from Germany by the River Sûre, the Mullerthal region probably earned its 'Little Switzerland' nickname because of the character of its terrain. Home to curious sandstone rock formations, deep ravines, caves, gorges, waterfalls and castles, the area also boasts an extensive network of footpaths.

The territory is further marked by Ernz Noire and Ernz Blanche, two tributaries of the Sûre which trail into the heart of the region. Between these rivers, and hemmed in by wooded hills, is the town of Beaufort. Complete with Renaissance castle and Neo-Gothic church, it is the ideal starting point for a trek towards the villages of Grundhof or Dillengen in the Sûre valley. Not least, because the journey encompasses some archetypal rock formations and the Hallerbach and Saueracht gorges.

Echternach

Positioned on the banks of the Sûre, Echternach is the main town of the Mullerthal area. The proud host of a 7th century Benedictine abbey and a 15th century town hall, Echternach is also endowed with hundreds of footpaths. They are perfect for exploring the hilly and forested terrain that surrounds the town.

Echternach is also noted for its dance procession, held annually on Whit weekend to honour Luxembourg's only saint, Willibrord, who is credited with bringing Catholicism to the country. Attracting large crowds, the procession moves through the streets with musical accompaniment and pilgrims re-enacting traditional dances. Participants then climb the steps of the church and enter the basilica, to worship where the saint's relics lie.

Les Terres Rouges

In the far south of Luxembourg is the iron ore basin known as Les Terres Rouge – the Red Rocks – a resource which was rediscovered around 1850, subsequently sparking an upturn in the country's economic fortunes. Now no longer in operation, the land has been reclaimed by nature, regaining its untamed look. The tall chimney stacks are still there, as are the iron and steelworks, but today it is a haven of colourful flowers, amphibians, birds and butterflies. Most towns and villages in the Red Rocks region offer a nearby walk that explores the local geology.

Esch-sur-Alzette, the largest town in the area, is known as a commercial centre and for its architectural gems. The nearby rocky landscape is equally charming and dotted with paths and waterfalls. The surrounding region, populated by little towns and villages, also offers plenty for the hiker.

A walk through Dudelange to the south-east, dominated by the typical red rocks, culminates in views from Mount St Jean. At the other side of the mining region is Pétange with its 40km of walking paths, bringing the walker to the scenic valley of Fond-de-Gras at the foot of Titelberg, an ancient Roman hill fortification.

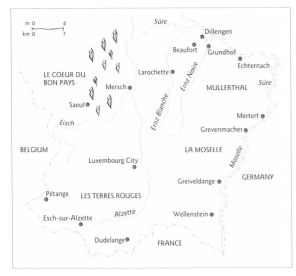

ⓘ CONTACT INFORMATION

Luxembourg National Tourist Office
PO Box 1001
L-1010 Luxembourg
Luxembourg
Tel: (00 352) 42 828210
Fax: (00 352) 42 828238
E-mail: tourism@ont.smtp.etat.lu
Web: www.etat.lu/tourism

BELGIUM

The Transardennaise

A trail that meanders through forests and valleys links castles, medieval and modern history, and the living traditions of the Belgian Ardennes.

Deriving from the Celtic word for 'deep forest', the Ardennes was the name given in ancient times to the enormous forest that stretched between the Rhine and the River Sambre in central Belgium. Today, the dark wooded hills of the Ardennes span three countries: France, Belgium and Luxembourg.

At the very heart of this region, the long-distance walk known as the Transardennaise (the Trans-Ardennes Path) twists through hills and valleys, passing historic fortresses, towns and rustic villages.

The Giant's Tomb near Bouillon

The Transardennaise

Beginning in La Roche-en-Ardenne, the Transardennaise runs via St-Hubert, Nassogne and Daverdisse to its destination in Bouillon. Signposted and well-kept paths pass the Ourthe, Lesse, Lomme and Semois rivers, at times through thick forest, at times through open meadowland.

The 160km path is planned in stages of between 18 and 25km a day, although this can easily be altered to suit individual requirements. Described in G.T.A. (Grande Traversée des Ardennes) guidebooks, the path is marked by yellow and white signs, and can be followed on foot, by bicycle, or even on horseback.

A local tour operator, Europ' Aventure, specialises in offering walking holidays along the route, arranging transport, lodgings, maps and baggage transfer. Their 'Transardennaise Gourmet' is a version of the walk that indulges in the regional gastronomy. A la carte evening meals offer local trout, the *borquin* sausage from St-Hubert, Arville cheeses, Ardennes ham, and *purnalet*, a liqueur from La Roche.

La Roche-en-Ardenne

Perched on the Deister rock, ruins of a 9th century feudal castle overlook the small town known as the 'Pearl of the Ardennes'. The rock was both a Neolithic site and subsequently home to a Roman fort, and the castle ruins now house a museum and exhibition about the excavations.

Below in La Roche-en-Ardenne, local customs, history and nature are celebrated. The Battle of the Bulge Museum takes its name from the battle that was fought around the nearby town of Bastogne. It gives a

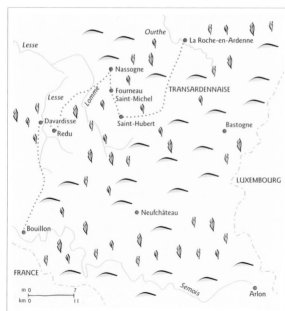

fascinating insight into some of the most important action of the Second World War that took place in the Ardennes. Life-size dummies of soldiers, with military vehicles, documents, photographs and weaponry bring to mind the grim realities of war. On a lighter note, the Pottery and Ardennes Ham Museum offers a chance to see how the local pottery is made, and sample the region's famous ham.

St-Hubert

A good centre for tourist walks through the woods, and the assembly point for hunters, St-Hubert has been called Europe's 'capital of hunting and nature'. During the hunting season – 15th September to 15th January – hikers should observe forest walking regulations, avoiding shoots.

More peaceably, various attractions in the town centre commemorate the life of Pierre-Joseph Redouté, the 'Raphael of the Flowers'. Born in St-Hubert in 1759, Redouté became famous as a botanic artist, developing a stipple technique for his flower prints that permitted subtle variations in the colours. Under Empress Josephine's patronage he became extremely popular and successful. 'La Roseraie', a garden with 400 rose varieties, is a tribute to his memory.

Fourneau St-Michel

About 8km from St-Hubert, a complex of museums on an estate at Fourneau St-Michel presents an overview of Ardennes traditions. An industrial and metallurgical museum in an 18th century ironworks includes a blast furnace, casting bay, bellows hall and forge, and is complemented by tools used by nailmakers, wheelwrights, coopers and blacksmiths.

Another museum is dedicated to the history of the Ardennes forest, while a rebuilt country village displays the rural life of southern Belgium. Farms, thatched cottages, a school and chapel, a public washhouse, and craftsmen's houses have all been reconstructed. Further along the trail, the village of Redu is crammed with twenty bookshops and unsurprisingly is known as the 'book village'.

Bouillon

The most impressive remains of feudalism in Belgium are found at Bouillon castle, where the main path finishes. With origins dating back to the 8th century, the fortified castle still stands proud above the town, recalling its past days of glory. It was from here that Godefroid of Bouillon launched the First Crusade in 1096.

Nearby, the village of Botassart is beautifully positioned amongst the winding bends of the River Semois. The river curls around a succession of densely wooded hills, including the Tombeau du Géant, or 'Giant's Tomb'.

[i] CONTACT INFORMATION

Tourist Federation of Belgian Luxembourg
9 Quai de l'Ourthe
B-6980 La Roche-en-Ardenne
Belgium
Tel: (00 32) 8441 1011
Fax: (00 32) 8441 2439
E-mail: info@ftlb.be
Web: www.ftlb.be

Europ' Aventure
Lic. A. 1660
41 Sprimont
B-6680 Sainte-Ode
Belgium
Tel: (00 32) 6168 8611
Fax: (00 32) 6168 8695
E-mail: d.jusseret@ping.be
Web: www.europaventure.be

On the banks of the Ourthe

BELGIUM

West-Vlaanderen

Sun in summer or pale dune-filled landscapes in winter, but always the haunting calls of birds. The coastal paths of West-Vlaanderen follow the watery line between land and sea.

All of Belgium's coast falls within the northern province of West-Vlaanderen. Bordered in the west by France and to the east by the Netherlands, West-Vlaanderen is best known internationally for its ports – Oostende and Zeebrugge – as well as Brugge (Bruges), the 'Venice of the North'. Within Belgium it is cherished for its 67km of dune-fringed beaches. Once dotted with small fishing villages, the demands of national tourism have transformed the coast into a string of glitzy resorts.

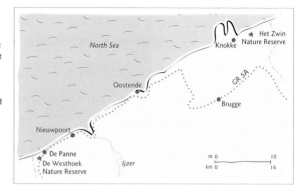

Within this agglomeration there are a surprising number of untouched open spaces. Major nature reserves flank either end of the beach – Westhoek on the French border, Het Zwin on the Dutch – and a number of smaller ones fall between. These, together with long distance and local walking paths, mean that the region's popularity need not hinder its enjoyable exploration on foot.

The long haul

Two long distance footpaths follow the Belgian coast. GR 5A is one of a network of paths running through Belgium, France and Luxembourg which are maintained by volunteers. The paths are marked by distinctive red and white posts, have published route guides and are designed to avoid busy areas, instead following quieter country routes.

GR 5A is known as Rond Vlaanderen, an appropriate name as it completes a circuit of West- and Oost-Vlaanderen in three stages: Oostende to Ronse (200km); Ronse to Antwerpen (155km); Antwerpen to Oostende (200km). Along the coast it runs between Westhoek and Oostende before cutting inland to Brugge.

The second long-distance path, the E9, follows a similar route. Commencing at Bayonne in France, it passes along the Belgian coast before entering the Netherlands.

Currently the route ends in Poland but ultimately it is expected to be extended through the Baltic States to Russia. Both the GR 5A and the E9 give walkers an opportunity to enjoy the beach, the sea, the green reserves beyond the dunes, and the lively resort villages en route.

De Panne

The village of De Panne lies next to the border with France in a shallow basin. The beach is the widest on the coast and boasts one third of all the dunes, a pale undulating expanse topped by golden tussocks. Within these is Westhoek Nature Reserve,

where moss, thyme and burnet grow and small animals such as martens, toads and newts live. Also around De Panne are the smaller reserves of Oosthoek, Cabourg and Calmeynbos, the latter a thickly wooded haven sheltered from the sun with paths leading out onto the beach.

Westhoek is also the name for the corner of Belgium which borders France. Walkers who follow the GR 5A inland will pass through the area, which also has a series of 8km and 10km walking paths suitable for families. An option close to the coast takes in the gentle scenery of the Izenberge, a sandy-soil plateau

Het Zwin Nature Reserve

Before the River Zwin silted up in the 15th century, Brugge was the country's most important port

Sand castles

Koksijde, the first village encountered heading east, calls itself the 'flower-filled seaside resort', and has an annual flower ball and Easter flower market. Its neighbour, Oostduinkerke, was once a fishing village frequented by artists wishing to capture the shifting light over the North Sea. Although it is now a large resort, it is the one place where shrimp are still fished for on horseback.

Between Nieuwpoort and Oostende, the holiday centres of Westende and Middelkerke are dedicated to tourism, offering water sports, casinos and long stretches of beach given over to sunbathers. Middelkerke is one of the few places along the coast where bunkers from the World Wars can still be seen, their concrete remains forming dark hulks in the sand.

Het Zwin

Het Zwin Nature Reserve, the largest and most ecologically important salt marsh in Belgium, extends over the border into the Netherlands. Tides enter the marshes daily along creeks but the River Zwin now only floods completely in spring. The waters of the Zwin are particularly rich in sea-organisms which provide food for flocks of birds. Pink-footed and white-fronted geese arrive in winter, and white storks in summer, while herons and cormorants can be seen all year.

In the north, 1.5km of dunes separate the Zwin from the sea, while the rest of the reserve is encircled by dykes originally built to prevent the sea-arm of the river flooding. The village of Knokke on the edge of the reserve was established when the dykes were being built, but is now the most exclusive of West-Vlaanderen's resorts, with spacious mansions nestling amongst the dunes.

between the Ijzer and the West-Vlaanderen polders. The polders were drained in the 17th century using windmills, which together with First World War cemeteries and monuments, still dot the landscape.

Protected sands

Vlaamse Banken is the name for the lower seashore, shallow waters and submerged sandbanks of the Belgian coast between Oostende and De Panne. Although people work and play within Vlaamse Banken it is protected as an important wetland habitat with huge numbers of wintering birds. Sea ducks and grebes arrive in their thousands, but are prone to disturbance by boats. Measures are being taken to resolve this though, and walkers following the sands can also see great crested grebes and eiders, as well as the darting grey shapes of small waders – usually dunlins or sanderlings.

CONTACT INFORMATION

Vlaanderen Tourist Office
Grasmarkt 61
B-1000 Brussel
Belgium
Tel: (00 32) 2 504 0390
Fax: (00 32) 2 504 0270
E-mail: info@toervl.be
Web: www.toervl.be

Fishing for shrimps on horseback

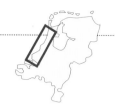

Walking along the Dutch Coast

Walks amongst the Dutch dunes offer the contrasting environments of quiet sandy heathland, bustling seaside resorts and genteel historic towns.

For such a geographically compact country, Holland has a vast 6,000km network of well-marked long-distance footpaths. Maintained by volunteer groups, the walks – known as Lange-Afstand-Wandelpaden, abbreviated to LAW – are marked with the standard continental white and red stripes.

Although most of the guide books that describe the paths are only available in Dutch, the maps included are large-scale and self-explanatory,

whilst a glossary helps decode important information. Two of them make it possible to walk the entire length of the coast between the Hook of Holland and Den Helder, although they can also be used for shorter walks by the sea. Predominantly running through the quiet Dutch dune landscape, paths also pass through fishing villages and popular seaside resorts, and lie within easy reach of both the major bulb fields and Holland's chief cities.

The Visserspad

The Visserspad (Fisherman's Way) is a 100km walk from the Hook of Holland to Haarlem, at times following the old tracks that fishermen would have used between their boats, villages and markets. The dune landscape through which the way runs varies between open sands with marram grass and isolated clumps of thrift, and thickets and meadows overgrown with hawthorn, dog-rose, honeysuckle and gorse.

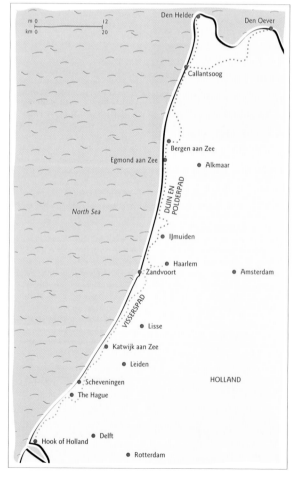

Gently undulating, the dunes can reach heights of 20 or 30m and in between and behind them lie lakes and lagoons. Other characteristic features are the dykes that protect the polders (the land reclaimed from the sea). The track passes through The Hague and its seaside district of Scheveningen, and the resorts of Katwijk aan See, Noordwijk aan See and Zandvoort.

The Hague

The Hague is the seat of Holland's government and home of Queen Beatrix. Its tree-lined avenues lend the city a serene gentility, while an international atmosphere is created by the presence of foreign embassies, global organisations, and such stately buildings as the Peace Palace, home to the International Court of Justice. A visit to Madurodam provides an overview of the whole of Holland – 150 of the country's most famous buildings are reconstructed in this miniature town.

Rotterdam, the largest port in the world, offers an insight into Holland's commercial history, whilst Amsterdam is the country's cultural and historic soul. Of the smaller towns, Delft is the home of the famous Delftware pottery and is the birthplace of Vermeer. Leiden's eleven museums showcase the town's rich cultural heritage and is also within reach of Holland's most famous bulb garden.

The cheese market in Alkmaar

Haarlem

Haarlem is a charming medieval town with St Bavo's late Gothic church as its centrepiece. Old almshouses hidden away in courtyards are a pretty find, whilst the Corrie Ten Boom house commemorates the Haarlem family of the Resistance who helped many Jews escape during the Nazi occupation. The Frans Hals museum is dedicated to the work of the 17th century artist, and the Teylers museum specialises in flower books of the 18th and 19th centuries. In April, away from the serenity of museums, the town comes alive with its annual flower parade.

The Duin en Polderpad

North of Haarlem, the Duin en Polderpad (Dune and Polder Way) stretches either for 139km to finish in Den Helder, or 151km to end in Den Oever. From Zandvoort to Den Helder, bulb fields behind the dunes become a blaze of colour in the spring. The Kennemer Dunes National Park around IJmuiden and the North Holland Dune Reserve near Wijk aan Zee protect some of the most sensitive dunes. Just outside Callantsoog, the Het Zwanenwater Nature Reserve is an oasis of peace, providing a quiet habitat for such birds as spoonbills and grey herons.

Castles, culture and cheese

In Egmond aan de Hoef, the ruins of Duke Lamoraal's castle, destroyed in 1583, remind visitors of Holland's complicated history of foreign wars and occupations, whilst in Egmond-Binnen, the Benedictine monastery dates from the beginning of Europe's Christianisation.

Nearby Bergen, 'the artists' village', saw the birth of the most famous art school in Holland, the Bergen School. Plenty of museums and galleries fill the streets, and in the summer international musicians arrive for the Holland Music Sessions festival. Alkmaar, a small town some 5km inland, has a pretty centre with canals running through it, and is known as the cheese capital of Holland. It is both home to the Dutch Cheese museum, and host to an open-air cheese market every Friday from April to September.

i CONTACT INFORMATION

Stichting Wandelplatform - LAW
Postbus 846
3800 AV Amersfoort
The Netherlands
Tel: (00 31) 33 465 3660
Fax: (00 31) 33 465 4377
E-mail: slaw@wandelnet.nl
Web: www.wandelnet.nl

The flower parade in Haarlem

Mud Walking on the Wadden Sea

A dramatic change from carefully waymarked tracks is offered on the Wadden flats: walkers may find themselves miles from shore or wading waist deep in a gully of mud as they follow their guide.

The Wadden islands stretch like a string of beads along the northern coasts of the Netherlands, Germany and Denmark. There are over fifty islands in the chain, which runs north and east from Den Helder at the tip of North Holland province to Esbjerg on Denmark's west coast.

The Netherlands claims five of the larger islands as well as a spattering of uninhabited islets. The islands form a barrier against the ravages of the North Sea. The Wadden flats, the area between the islands and the mainland, are subsumed by the Wadden Sea at high tide. It is across this expanse of sucking mud and shifting sand that intrepid *wadlopers* may be seen setting out at low tide on an interesting, if dirty, trek over the seabed.

Mud walkers

The Wadden islands

The Wadden islands were formed in the 13th century. At this time, storms caused the North Sea to flood over coastal sandbanks and into the river estuaries, making islands of the sand bars. Archaeological finds date human occupation of the area to the 10th century, but it was after the 13th century that the islands gained strategic status for trade. Farming, fishing and whaling were also important, and it was not until the middle of the 20th century that the tourist industry came to the fore.

Today, a mild sunny climate, extensive sandy beaches and seas warmed by the Gulf Stream make the Wadden islands a favoured Dutch holiday destination. Texel, the largest island, is a short ferry ride from Den Helder, and has comprehensive tourist facilities. Terschelling and Ameland are also relatively developed, whereas Vlieland and Schiermonnikoog are quieter, due mainly to their restrictive policies on cars.

Wadlopen

Described as the 'Dutch equivalent of fell-running', *wadlopen* (mud walking) over the Wadden flats has been taking place for centuries. Historically, crossings occurred in winter when the flats were thickly sheeted in ice, but the increased salinity of the Wadden Sea means it no longer freezes. This has rendered crossings more hazardous. Today, wadlopen should not be undertaken without a guide, and as certain routes can involve mud wading rather than walking – through knee-high and deeper pools – trips are best saved for the warmer months.

Since organised wadlopen began in the 1960s, over 5 million people have taken the plunge and the excursion's popularity is such that it is now necessary to book well in advance. Several tour operators offer guided trips from Friesland and Groningen provinces.

Sea lavender, De Boschplaat Nature Reserve

All the organisations emphasise safety: shifting sands, incoming tides and obscuring mists can combine to make the walks treacherous, but the biggest threat is thunderstorms. In a uniformly flat and featureless landscape, walkers are vulnerable to lightening; trips are cancelled at the least hint of a storm. Recommended footwear is high-lacing boots, as anything else is unlikely to withstand the viscous pull of the mud.

On the flats

An adventure across the Wadden flats promises an unforgettable walking experience. After the safety of the dyke or island has been left behind, hikers may pass through areas of vegetated salt plains or tidal marshes before the muddy sea bottom is reached. From here, the landscape alternates between bare grey flats, riven with channels and mud gullies, and the relative sanctuary of sandbanks.

Near the coast, glasswort, couch grass, sea rocket and thrift grow, while further out only seaweed is likely to be seen. This is the place for birds, and flocks of terns, curlews, oystercatchers and godwits wheel down to feed as the tide retreats. Mallards, teals, eiders and shelducks also inhabit the flats, and in areas where water remains, seals may be seen lolling on sandbanks.

Dirty destinations

Mud walking is strenuous. Official recommendations limit excursions to walkers aged between 12 and 70 who can walk for up to four hours at a

Cycling on Texel

time. However, shorter (and usually cleaner) walks have been developed for less able walkers, often around nature themes. Popular destinations of medium difficulty include Engelsmanplaat, a sand bar between Schiermonnikoog and Ameland, or further to the east, the tiny island of Rottumeroog. Both Rottumeroog and its petite neighbour Rottumerplaat are uninhabited nature reserves.

Island bound

Longer walks lead all the way to Ameland and Schiermonnikoog, and even to Terschelling for the very fit. All these islands are interesting places to rest for a few days. Historically a whaling centre, Ameland's four villages retain their charm with examples of architecture dating from the 15th and 16th centuries. The landscape is one of high dunes and dune lakes, fringed in the north by 27km of white sandy beach. The island's Het Oerd Nature Reserve is home to a diverse collection of plants with over a third of the Netherlands' species found here.

A quieter destination is the island of Schiermonnikoog, which has been designated a national park where cars are not permitted. Cycle and walking tracks lead from the only village on the island, lacing through the dunes, woods and salt meadows. The island's original residents were monks but today the main inhabitants are birds, which thrive in the established woods and bountiful marshes.

To the west, Terschelling is an island of drifting form. Early overuse of the dunes led to unstable sands, and channels separating low-lying sandbanks from the coast were not silted up until the 20th century, when the island gained nearly a third of its territory. 80% of the island is now protected and the Boschplaat is a reserve formed from one of the silt-joined areas. Tides have deposited mud on the flats, where over time, vegetation has taken hold. In summer, the Boschplaat is awash with the perfume of violet-headed sea lavender.

ℹ️ CONTACT INFORMATION

Groningen Tourist Information
VVV Groningen
Ged Kattendiep 6
9711 PN Groningen
The Netherlands
Tel: (00 31) 900 202 3050
Fax: (00 31) 50 313 6358

Friesland Tourist Information
VVV Leeuwarden
Stationsplein 1
8911 AC Leeuwarden
The Netherlands
Tel: (00 31) 900 202 4060
Fax: (00 31) 58 215 3593

Walks in the Weser-Ems Region

Gentle hill paths or walks by slow-moving rivers offer a chance to experience a calmer pace of life amongst a natural landscape of wood, heath and moorland.

In north-west Germany, the Weser and Ems rivers flow gently through Lower Saxony to join the North Sea. Apart from the coastline, which is one of Germany's most popular holiday destinations, the area's predominant mood is one of calm. A flat land, except for the ridge of hills where Nordrhein-Westphalen pushes its way into the south-east corner, the region offers several options for easy, relaxed rambling.

The Wittekindsweg

This 90km walk leads over the ridge of the Wiehengebirge, the gentle range of hills lying between Osnabrück and Porta Westfalica, the point at which the River Weser breaks through the Weser hills to flow into the North German plain. Serving as part of the E11 European long distance route, the path is also the most popular in this part of Germany. Over the last three decades about 83,000 walkers have received a certificate for completing the route, which probably means the

total number of walkers reaches several hundred thousand.

From Osnabrück to Mühlenort, the Wittekindsweg shares its path with two other walks – the Friesenweg and the Pickerweg – and is clearly marked with a white diagonal cross. Once the routes separate at Mühlenort, however, the marking becomes a red and white diagonal line. Walkers who are reasonably fit can expect to complete the walk in three days; the gradients are gradual, with just a few steep exceptions, and the highest point only reaches 320m.

Although generally summers are mild, an old saying of the region is *Rechne mit Regen* – reckon on rain – and there are shelters at various points along the route that offer protection. Perhaps more importantly, most guest houses and restaurants are sympathetic to walkers – even dripping wet, muddy customers can count on a friendly welcome.

Canoeing on the River Ems

Highlights of the path

From Osnabrück, the path leads through the pretty Nette valley, then climbs to the Wittekindsburg, remains of fortifications dating from the 8th century. These are the first of about sixteen such ruins in the hills, named after Wittekind, the patron of this path. An 8th century Saxon leader, Wittekind kept rallying his pagan hordes against the Franks. Defeated regularly, he would retreat for a while to Denmark, and then return with renewed vigour until finally being baptised in 785 and subsequently retiring from the battlefield.

Wittekind's name is given indiscriminately to many local sights such as the ruined strongholds and a hill, the Wittekindsberg. A now-defunct spring, the Wittekindsquelle, is said to have originated from a blow from his horse's hoof.

The undulating and at times wooded hills provide both shelter and views, culminating on the Wittekindsberg. Here, from its 294m lookout platform, the Moltketurm (Moltke tower) offers a wonderful panoramic outlook over the Weser's exit from the hills and across the lowlands to the north.

The Weserweg

For a longer and flatter walk, the 180km Weserweg that links Porta Westfalica with the lively city of Bremen is an excellent alternative. The countryside is one of fertile marshland, given over mainly to agriculture, and broken by few large towns. Marked with a St Andrew's cross and a white 'W' on a black background, the walk wanders through Minden, Nienburg, Verden and Weyhe before arriving in Bremen.

For a rest from walking, boat trips can be taken from Minden to Stolzenau, or even further on to Nienburg. Curiosities along the route include the twisted tower of St Jacob's church in Stolzenau, and the Sachsenhain (Saxon's Grove) north of Verden. It was here that Charlemagne supposedly had 4,500 Saxons executed in 782; the bloody event is commemorated by 4,500 boulders that line the 2km wooded path around the site.

The Emsland

The Emsland, named from the River Ems flowing through it, is a flat landscape of moorland and sandy heath known as *geest*. Decorated with juniper groves, willows and green meadows, it is an ideal area for quiet walking through subtle countryside.

Although the 162km Emsweg path running from Rheine to Leer offers an easy way of traversing the region, it might be preferable to make walking a means of appreciating stillness rather than an energetic end in itself. Numerous walks wind around both banks of the Ems, while in the villages and towns visitors are still treated as guests rather than tourists. A particular treat is the 18th century Schloss Clemenswerth near Sögel.

Built for the Elector and Archbishop of Cologne, Clemens August, the late Baroque hunting lodge has a large central building, a chapel, guest pavilions and a forest park. After substantial restoration, the lodge is now open between April and October as a museum for the Emsland.

i CONTACT INFORMATION

Osnabrück Tourist Office
Krahnstraße 54
49074 Osnabrück
Germany
Tel: (00 49) 541 323 4157
Fax: (00 49) 541 323 4213

Emsland Tourist Office
Ordeniederung 1
49716 Meppen
Germany
Tel: (00 49) 593 144 335
Web: www.emsland.de

The cathedral cities of Osnabrück (above) and Minden mark the start and finish of the Wittekindsweg

The Lahn Valley

*The Deutsches Eck (German Corner) in Koblenz marks the confluence of
the Mosel and the Rhine. A few miles south, the River Lahn slips into the
Rhine with a quiet grace that befits the end of its gentle meanderings.*

The Lahn joining the Rhine at Lahnstein

The River Lahn rises near Netphen
in the Rothaargebirge Nature Park,
a mountain range in southern
Nordrhein-Westfalen. The limpid
green waters of the spring bode well
for the river's journey through Hessen
and Rheinland-Pfalz to the Rhine.
The river flows eastwards until it
meets the River Ohm, where it turns
south, then south-west until joining
the Rhine at Lahnstein. Although the
distance from source to mouth is only
80km as the crow flies, the river itself
takes 245km to complete its journey.

It is easy to understand the reason
for the Lahn's leisure, for it passes
through beautiful scenery decorated
with medieval towns, castles and
water meadows. A particularly lovely
section between Diez and Bad Ems is
characterised by wooded hills clinging
close to the waters. The fact that the
local railway line uses twenty tunnels
hints at the picturesque landscape.

Walking along the Lahn

Three *Lahnhöhenwege*, or Lahn
Highways, offer well-signposted
routes alongside the river. For about
eighty years it has been possible to
walk from Wetzlar to the river mouth
on either side of the Lahn, using trails
that follow the ridges parallel with the
river. At the beginning of the 1990s,
another route from the source to
Wetzlar was created, making it
possible to walk the entire length of
the Lahn. Capital 'L' signs mark the
trails. Although the views over the
valley make the walks well worth the
ups and downs, there is also a cycle
path beside the river that can be used
by walkers who prefer level ground.
As tourist interest in the region has
grown, walking guides for the routes
have been published that describe the
main paths, suggest day stages and
give information on the sights,
transport and practicalities.

Invigoration

Moving from the Lahn's source
Rhinewards, the first two interesting
towns along the way are both
concerned with health. Bad Laasphe
offers the Kneipp cure, while the clear
air of Biedenkopf makes it a state-
approved health resort. Along with
relaxing the body, they also offer
stimulation for the mind. A mycology
museum in Bad Laasphe gives an
insight into the world of fungi, and a
museum in Biedenkopf castle houses
exhibitions on artisanal traditions and
local customs. The castle dominates
the skyline, and the steep climb up to
it is made worthwhile by the view
over the roofs and the valley beyond.
The medieval half-timbered housing in
the old town also makes a simple
town ramble an adventure, as by
looking closely at the craftsmanship
all kinds of curious carvings and
ornamentation are revealed.

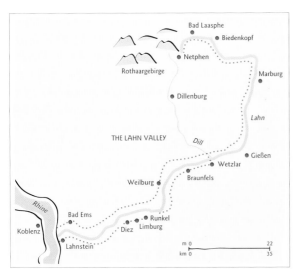

THE LAHN VALLEY

Bad Laasphe
Biedenkopf
Netphen
Rothaargebirge
Marburg
Dillenburg
Lahn
Dill
Gießen
Wetzlar
Weilburg
Braunfels
Rhine
Bad Ems
Runkel
Koblenz
Diez
Limburg
Lahnstein

m 0   22
km 0   35

Learning and life

The next major stops on the route are the university towns of Marburg and Gießen. Marburg's university was founded by Philipp the Magnanimous in 1527, and had the first Protestant religious faculty in Germany. Philipp was the descendant of St Elisabeth, Princess of Thuringia, who built a hospice for the sick and needy here in the 13th century. The splendid Gothic church named after the saint housed her relics until 1539 and the golden shrine that sheltered her bones is still present. Both Marburg and Gießen have bustling markets and cafés giving life to the picturesque streets. In the summer a music festival is held in Gießen, and a town festival occurs in Marburg. Themed walks through the towns are organised by local tourist offices, including a night tour through Marburg that has its own lamplit charm, or a fairytale journey on the trail of the Grimm brothers, who both studied at the university. For those who prefer science, an important chemistry museum is found in Gießen at the laboratory of Justus von Liebig, the 19th century chemist who invented meat extract, and originated nitrogeneous fertilisers.

Goethe and Wetzlar

At Wetzlar, prettily situated at the meeting of the River Dill with the Lahn, the cathedral looms imposingly above the town. A hotch-potch of architectural styles from Romanesque to Baroque, the building betrays a complicated history of wranglings between secular and religious builders and financiers. Much of Wetzlar's importance came from its status as the seat of the Reichskammergericht, the German Supreme Court, for over one hundred years. The court was also responsible for Wetzlar's other overriding theme – Goethe's time here in 1772. Whilst a lawyer for the court, the young man fell hopelessly in love with Charlotte Buff, who was engaged to someone else. From this experience came Goethe's *The Sorrows of Young Werther*, an outpouring of emotion that seems almost comic today, but which had a huge impact on German Romantic literature. Numerous buildings throughout the town commemorating Goethe's stay make it impossible to escape his influence.

The Martinschloß in Lahnstein

Braunfels castle

Beauty and Baroque

Perhaps his expressions of love might be outdated, but Goethe's passion for the countryside around Wetzlar might well be emulated by any visitor. From Wetzlar onwards, an extraordinary collection of medieval and Baroque castles complements the scenery and enchants the eye. Braunfels could be a prototype for a fairytale castle, its battlements visible from afar, while the castle that rises above the Lahn at

Runkel could easily be surrounded by thorn bushes, awaiting the arrival of a knight to wake the sleeping princess. Weilburg's Baroque castle and old town perch on a cliff edge, encircled by a loop in the river, while near Diez, Oranienstein castle is a masterpiece of Baroque floridity. Even Limburg cathedral appears to want to join in the fun; with its seven towers in the late Romanesque style, the church seems to aspire more to mythical than heavenly status.

Bad Ems and Lahnstein

Adding a touch of symmetry to the route, the Lahn way ends as it starts by running through a health resort. Bad Ems' thermal springs date back to Roman times, although it was in the 18th and 19th centuries that kings, poets and composers came to take the waters. If muscles are aching from a walk it is an ideal place to relax, and also to visit the Russian Orthodox church or Germany's oldest casino. Finally, Lahnstein, where the river at last glides into the Rhine, is a quiet town with medieval buildings, towers and ruined walls. A wood around the town is ideal for gentle rambles and, along with Lahneck castle on the hill, makes Lahnstein a fitting end to the Lahn's journey that so beautifully combines culture and nature.

i CONTACT INFORMATION

Lahnstein Tourist Information
56112 Lahnstein
Germany
Tel: (00 49) 2621 914171
Fax: (00 49) 2621 914340
E-mail: TOURIST@Stadt-Lahnstein.de
Web: www.stadt-lahnstein.de

Marburg Tourism
Pilgrimstein 26
35037 Marburg
Germany
Tel: (00 49) 6421 99120
Fax: (00 49) 6421 991212
Web: www.marburg.de

The Lahn flowing through Marburg

The old bridge over the Lahn and the cathedral at Wetzlar

The Franconian Switzerland

Situated in northern Bavaria, the Franconian Switzerland is an enchanting land of dramatic cliffs, mysterious caves, romantic castles, meandering rivers and picturesque villages.

Die Fränkische Schweiz, or the Franconian Switzerland, was given its name by Romantic artists and poets who were captivated by its charm. The entire region is a nature park and over 4,000km of marked footpaths lead through a land of contrasts.

Landscape and nature

The gently rolling hills that characterise the region are scored with deep gorges, punctuated by craggy dolomitic outcrops and have been embellished through the ages by human activity. The dramatic cliffs were used during the Middle Ages as perches for fortified strongholds. Castles and ruins, rising above calm green valleys and orchards, tell of a turbulent past, while homely mills in the valleys capture the power of the rivers. Open farmland is complemented by traditional half-timbered houses.

Numerous marked nature trails and guided walks provide information on the botany, geology and ecology of Franconian Switzerland. The plants found in the region have names almost as beautiful as themselves. The rare *Türkenbund* (turk's cap lily) and *Frauenschuh* (lady's-slipper, an orchid) are two of the hidden wonders. Red and fallow deer, hogs, squirrels and hawks can be glimpsed in the woods, while eagle owls may be heard if not seen. The caves, too, offer much-needed protection for bats.

Changing seasons

The summer should bring plenty of sunshine, but spring and autumn show off the area's nature walks in their best colours. Winter may provide a break from walking to join in southern Germany's Christmas celebrations, such as the *Christkindlesmarkt*, an Advent market in nearby Nürnberg. At Easter the village wells are a sight for sore eyes, each one being extravagantly decorated with brightly-coloured Easter eggs.

The heart of Franconia

The local walking club, the Fränkische-Schweiz-Verein, has worked out a series of adaptable five to seven day walking routes. With such a wealth of footpaths to choose from, it can be hard to know where to start, but one of the suggested walks captures much of Franconia's essence.

Starting and ending in Ebermannstadt, a small town whose treasures include a Baroque lady chapel and a waterwheel dating from 1606, the seven day walk goes through some of the prettiest valleys and towns in Franconian Switzerland. Gößeinstein, Pottenstein and Egloffstein all have a castle to visit, while Gößeinstein also has a beautiful Baroque basilica. In the countryside, the route follows in part the main rivers, the Wiesent, Ailsbach, Püttlach and Trubach, with deviations above the valley to ruins and castles.

Castles

About 170 castles were once strewn across the countryside, although all that remains of many are a few scattered stones. Both the Neideck tower, ancestral home of the mighty Schlüsselberg family, and Streitberg castle on the opposite side of the valley, were destroyed by war during the 16th century. All that is left of the two castles are lonely ruins offering picturesque views of the Wiesent valley below.

Burg Rabenstein

From being a semi-ruin in the 1970s, Burg Rabenstein in the Ailsbach valley has been refurbished to become Europe's centre for the Middle Ages. The complex, which includes an art gallery and museum, hosts spectacular falconry events and jousting contests, with knights in shining armour recreating a chivalric atmosphere.

The castle above Gößeinstein

The ruined Neideck castle above the Wiesent valley

Mysterious caves

Over 1,000 small and large caves lurk beneath the pleasant green surface of the land, waiting to entice passers-by into a realm of mystery. The three best known caves, the Binghöhle, the Sophienhöhle and the Teufelshöhle (Devil's Cave), display amazing stalactitic rock formations. These intricate pagoda-like pillars show nature's craftsmanship at its finest, and the mixing of minerals, soot and clay with the limestone rock has created wonderful colour variations ranging from black to white.

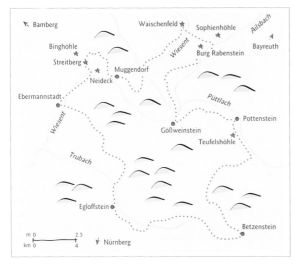

Beer walks

If long hikes begin to pall, the Franconian Switzerland has one more trick up its sleeve. No fewer than seventy two small breweries exist in the area, each producing its own distinctive beer. Special planned walks from brewery to brewery combine attractive landscapes with a chance to taste delicious local drinks. And if beer even loses its pull, there is always the local schnapps. As the biggest sweet cherry-producing area of the EU, and home to apple, pear and plum orchards, virtually every household makes its own schnapps. What better way to keep off the cold in the winter, or perk up the spirits after a long walk?

ⓘ CONTACT INFORMATION

Franconian Switzerland Tourism
Oberes Tor 1
91317 Ebermannstadt
Germany
Tel: (00 49) 9194 797779
Fax: (00 49) 9194 797776
E-mail: tourismus@fraenkische-schweiz.btl.de
Web: www.fraenkische-schweiz.com

The Upper Palatinate

Travel light – the 'Wandern ohne Gepäck' scheme is an ideal to way to ramble through the woods and past the castles of the Oberpfalz.

The Oberpfalz (Upper Palatinate) lies on the north-eastern edge of Bavaria, on the border with the Czech Republic. Within its boundaries nestle three nature parks: Steinwald, the Hessenreuther und Manteler Wald, and the better known Oberpfälzer Wald (Upper Palatinate Forest). Eight major walking routes and numerous local paths run through the region, allowing ample opportunity to roam by lakes and castles, and wander through seemingly endless woodlands.

Mittelpunkt Mitteleuropas

Over 300 million years ago, the original European and African continents crashed together along the line of the Upper Palatinate hills, forming mountains of Himalayan dimensions. Obviously long since worn down by erosion, the hills today offer easy walking terrain with occasional reminders of past activity such as at Parkstein in the Hessenreuther Wald. 'Europe's most beautiful basalt cone' is the remains of a volcano, with strange basalt formations that look like organ pipes. The area is also the main European watershed between the Elbe and the Danube, with wild mountain rivers such as the Fichtelnaab and Waldnaab taking waters from the central European plateau. And just to prove the area's importance, by Hildweinsreuth a granite slab marks the Mittelpunkt Mitteleuropas – the centre of central Europe.

The Oberpfalzweg

Two well-marked parallel paths offer a good introduction to the Oberpfalz. The first half of the Oberpfalzweg (Upper Palatinate Way) runs very close to the open Czech border, allowing walkers to take a day out to visit the spa towns of Karlovy Vary (Karlsbad) and Mariánské Lázně (Marienbad).

The Kappl at the beginning of the Oberpfalzweg

Beginning at the Kappl, a baroque church near Waldsassen, the path runs 220km southwards to its destination in the medieval town of Regensburg. The walk leads first across the Tirschenreuth plateau, an area covered with over 2,000 ponds and lakes, many of which are full of carp or trout as a result of fish farming by Cistercian monks. Thereafter, the path enters the Oberpfälzer Wald, following river valleys or climbing hill tracks. Adjoining both the Bavarian and the Bohemian forests, the woodlands of the Oberpfalz form part of the largest continuous continental forest known as the 'green roof of Europe'. Viewpoints along the walk give panoramas over these huge areas of rolling wooded hills.

Baroque galore

The northern district of the Oberpfalz is known as the Stiftland, meaning monastic land, as part of it was once a monastic endowment. Baroque is very much the predominant ecclesiastical style, and it is always worth stopping for a look inside a church. The Kappl at the starting point of the Oberpfalzweg, and the basilica in nearby Waldsassen, are two local jewels. Dedicated to the Holy Trinity, the 17th century Kappl

The basalt cone at Parkstein

is unique in incorporating three spired sections in one church to represent the Trinity, while the excessively ornate basilica often hosts classical concerts by renowned orchestras.

The Burgenweg

The Burgenweg (Castle Way) links many of the Upper Palatinate castles and stretches for 180km from Marktredwitz in the north to Waldmünchen on the Czech border. Rarely more than 15km away from the Oberpfalzweg, this route has a different emphasis. Sights along the way include the Falkenberg, a 12th century castle perched on granite cliffs above the River Waldnaab, and the ruins of Leuchtenberg, where a festival is held annually from June to August. An alternative to ancient monuments is the Kontinentale Tiefbohrung, where a gigantic drill has reached a depth of over 9,000m into the Earth's crust.

Neustadt a.d. Waldnaab

Crossed by the Burgenweg, Neustadt a.d. Waldnaab is the centre of the porcelain and lead crystal production for which the area is known. There are workshops where glass cutters can be watched shaping the delicate material. Nearby Weiden is home to the International Museum of Ceramics, and also offers many cultural events owing partially to its heritage as the 'Max-Reger-Stadt'. This German composer spent his youth in the town and later composed some of his best-known organ works here; in his memory the 'Weiden Musical Days' take place every three years, but concerts are held in the public parks all through the summer.

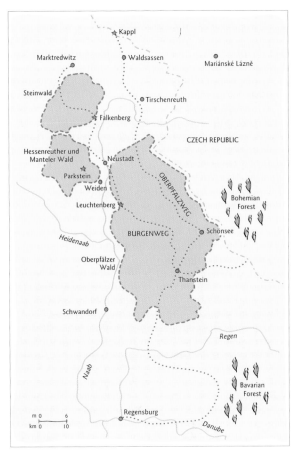

Unburdened walking

The 'Wandern ohne Gepäck' scheme is offered for both the Oberpfalzweg and the Burgenweg, whereby guest houses organise the transport of luggage to walkers' next destination. If people prefer to make a base in one area, rather than follow a linear route, each district within the Oberpfalz has a marked network of local trails with maps available from tourist offices.

A view across to Leuchtenberg

i CONTACT INFORMATION

East Bavaria Tourist Board
Luitpoldstrasse 20
93047 Regensburg
Germany
Tel: (00 49) 941 585390
Fax: (00 49) 941 5853939

Weiden Tourist Office
Altes Rathaus
92637 Weiden i. d. OPf
Germany
Tel: (00 49) 961 19433
Fax: (00 49) 961 416 1403
Email: stadtwen@new-wen.baynet.de

The Black Forest

*The Black Forest, famed for its cakes, cuckoo clocks and Kirschwasser,
also offers an excellent network of well-kept paths.*

Whether from poetic inspiration, or fear of what lurked in the wooded hills, it was the Romans who first gave the Schwarzwald (Black Forest) its name – *silva nigra*. No doubt the ominous overtones once reflected the dangers of the largely unpopulated Black Forest, but today its open highlands, mixed woodlands, spacious green valleys and small towns seem too friendly to merit the title.

Nestling in the extreme south-west corner of Germany in the state of Baden-Württemberg, the Black Forest stretches for about 160km between Pforzheim in the north, and Waldshut in the south. About 60km wide, the long chain of hills is bordered by the Nagold and Neckar valleys to the east, and the Rhine valley to the west. Still overwhelmingly rural, pretty towns such as Offenburg, Baden-Baden, Freudenstadt and Villingen decorate the valleys at the edge of the range.

Landscape and climate

Not quite mountains but too impressive to be mere hills, the Black Forest's rolling highlands were formed during the last Ice Age. The terrain is one of the most popular walking destinations in Europe, with marked trails ranging from short, easy day routes to relatively strenuous long-distance hikes that allow access to all the most beautiful areas.

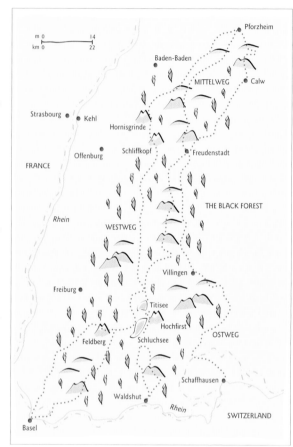

The forests are predominantly fir and pine, but also include deciduous and mixed woodland, the trees providing shelter from the heat of the summer or inclement weather. Much of the land lies at an altitude of over 1,000m, offering both clear air and good views, whilst the valleys between ridges vary from calm green refuges to wild river chasms.

Given that winter brings harsh weather and heavy snowfalls, and high summer swelters at 30°C or more, the best times to explore the region on foot are late spring and early summer, or late summer to early autumn. These seasons also bring gentians, orchids, heart's ease, harebells, and the delicate autumn crocus, along with edible treats such as mushrooms, raspberries, blackberries and chestnuts.

The hiking inheritance

The Black Forest is justified in calling itself the cradle of long distance walking. Germany's oldest walking club, the Schwarzwaldverein, was founded here in 1864 and Europe's first long-distance footpath, the Westweg, was created in 1900. Today the Schwarzwaldverein helps to maintain the Black Forest's intricate web of over 23,000km of waymarked paths, and also campaigns to protect the local environment. Trails are marked with distinctive signs, and paths are traffic-free and surfaced, making the walking generally easy.

Official long distance routes include three north–south high-level paths, shorter circular rambles, wine trails, and west–east tracks across the hills.

High-level routes

The Westweg is the oldest, best known and most popular marked route in Germany. A red diamond on a white background denotes the 280km long path that crosses many of the area's highest summits. In the north, the path goes over the Hornisgrinde (1,163m) and the Schliffkopf (1,055m), and passes by the Mummelsee, the highest of the Black Forest's glacial lakes. In early morning mist, with black pines looming over the dark waters, the myths of ghosts and mermaids that still surround the lake become believable.

The walk covers steep sections of the Kinzig valley, but the ascent is worthwhile for views over the sheer, fissured gorges towards the Rhine, contrasting with much gentler slopes that lead away to the Danube. The final section climbs over the Feldberg (1,493m), before dividing into two paths. The first traverses the Belchen and Blauen summits while the second follows the ridge with the Herzogenhorn and Hochkopf peaks. Both descend to Basel, with glorious views over the Vosges, the Rhine valley and the Alps.

Two further high-level walks, the Mittelweg and Ostweg are both about 240km long, and, like the Westweg, begin in Pforzheim. At first the Mittelweg runs parallel to the Westweg, but after the two ways meet at the Hohlch summit (984m), the Mittelweg continues south to pass through Freudenstadt, location of Germany's largest marketplace. Although the route avoids the highest hills, making do with the Hochfirst (1,190m), it is arguably the most scenic, passing the Titisee and Schluchsee lakes.

The Ostweg crosses more fields and meadows than the other two routes, providing open vistas across the Black Forest and its eastern valleys. Other highlights include beautiful beech woods, the Nagold, Danube and Wutach rivers, and towns such as Calw, birthplace of Hermann Hesse, and medieval Schaffhausen where the walk finishes. This is the quietest of the high-level routes.

Mist over the Black Forest mountains

GERMANY

The 178km Querweg Freiburg–Bodensee leaves Freiburg and climbs to the highland through the Höllental (Hell valley), a dramatic gorge equally matched by the Wutachschlucht that follows. Here, the river rushes through steep cliffs to demonstrate its name – *wut* means 'rage'. When swollen with melted snow in spring, the impressiveness of the waters can make the rest of the journey to Konstanz on the Bodensee (Lake Constance) tame in comparison.

For walkers who prefer flatter ground, the 158km Rheinaue-Weg from Kehl to Basel follows the Rhine valley. It offers a contrasting viewpoint, looking up into the hills rather than down into the valleys. In summer, walkers can sample local delicacies such as fresh asparagus and new wine, as the route passes through many of the region's vineyards.

Hiking without luggage

By far the easiest way to organise a walking holiday in the Black Forest is to take advantage of one of the 'hiking without luggage' schemes, whereby accommodation and walking routes can be arranged before arrival. Planned tours cover all areas of the Black Forest, often using sections of the major pathways, and each route provides insights into the Black Forest's varied culture and geography.

Other major routes

It is impossible to mention all the walks available, but the following are a sample of the options.

The lovely city of Freiburg with its elaborate Gothic cathedral and pretty streams (*Bächle*) that run through the old town's streets is the starting point of the Kandelhohenweg and the Querweg Freiburg–Bodensee walks. The 133km Kandelhohenweg is a north–south path that rises steeply from Freiburg to the most westerly of the high peaks, the Kandel (1,241m). It then travels through wooded hills to the Kinzig valley, over the Mooskopf forest highland and down to Oberkirch in the Rench valley.

A farmhouse in the Black Forest countryside

Mummelsee, a lake near the Hornisgrinde mountain

The Clock Carriers' Trail follows in the footsteps of the door-to-door cuckoo clock salesmen, intrepid travellers who would walk miles on foot in the 18th and 19th centuries to sell the region's famous product.

The Red Deer Trail offers a chance to explore some of the loveliest nature reserves and woodland scenes in the north, while the Feldberg Circular Trail tours the southern region around the Feldberg. Other trails explore the nature and gorges of the southern hills, or visit man-made features such as mills, castles and picturesque historical towns.

Fresh air and food

The region's wines, such as the Kaiserstuhl, Müller-Thurgau and Traminer, are delicious. The Ortenauer Winepath from Baden-Baden to Offenburg wanders through many of the vineyards on the Black Forest's sunny west slopes. Walkers can obtain a pass for areas normally closed during the grape harvest, and enjoy the region's produce in the evening.

The local schnapps can also help liven the spirits. The most popular include *Kirschwasser* (cherry), *Zwetschken* (purple plum), *Mirabelle* (golden

plum) and *Himbeergeist* (raspberry). Other delights include *Spätzle*, a form of egg pasta, particularly tasty served with melted cheese and fried onions; wild mushrooms; schnitzel; and of course, Black Forest gâteau.

CONTACT INFORMATION

Black Forest Information Service
c/o Tourismus Service GmbH
Yorckstrasse 23
79110 Freiburg
Germany
Tel: (00 49) 761 8979 7979
Fax: (0049) 761 8979 7989
Web: www.schwarzwald-tourist-info.de

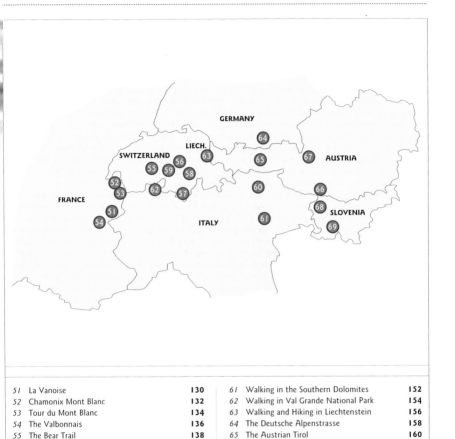

ℹ CONTACT INFORMATION

Austrian National Tourist Office
PO Box 2363
London W1A 2QB
Tel: 020 7629 0461
Fax: 020 7499 6038
E-mail: info@anto.co.uk
Web: http://austria-tourism.at

Maison de la France
178 Piccadilly
London W1V 0AL
Tel: 0891 244123
Fax: 020 7493 6594
E-mail: info@mdlf.co.uk
Web: www.franceguide.com

German National Tourist Office
PO Box 2695
London W1A 3TN

Tel: 020 7317 0908
Fax: 020 7995 6129
E-mail: German_National_Tourist_
Office@compuserve.com
Web: www.germany-tourism.de

Italian State Tourist Board
1 Princes Street
London W1R 8AY
Tel: 020 7408 1254
Fax: 020 7493 6695
E-mail: enitlond@globalnet.co.uk
Web: www.enit.it

Liechtenstein Tourism
Postfach 139
FL-9490 Vaduz
Liechtenstein
Tel: (00 423) 232 1443
Fax: (00 423) 392 1618
E-mail: touristinfo@lie-net.li

Slovenia Pursuits
New Barn Farm
Tadlow Road
Tadlow
Royston SG8 0EP
Tel: 01767 631144
Fax: 01767 631166
E-mail: angela.rennie@virgin.net

Switzerland Travel Centre Ltd
Swiss Centre
Swiss Court
London W1V 8EE
Tel: 0800 100 20030
Fax: 0800 100 20031
E-mail: stc@stlondon.com
Web: www.MySwitzerland.com

La Vanoise

In the crisp heights of the French Alps, the colours, the scale and the vitality of the National Park of La Vanoise are a pleasurable assault on the senses.

Since it was established in 1963, setting out as the first of France's national parks, La Vanoise has maintained a strong tradition of active concern for the natural life of the French Alps. The national park displays nature's finery on a dramatic scale. More than one hundred of its mountains climb to over 3,000m, and 130 spectacular glaciers lie across the slopes. Many of the region's alpine lakes lie high up in La Vanoise.

A central protected area makes it possible for the region's wildlife to be monitored with the utmost attention, whilst a further expanse of protected country lies as a buffer around its periphery. Access here is less restricted, allowing the park to present the natural and cultural heritage of the region.

In spite of its determination to maintain the natural resources of the area, La Vanoise is nevertheless swift to accommodate visitors and seize the educational and economic opportunities that come with them.

An ibex – one of the protected species in the park

Winter and summer

In the winter months, it is alpine sports and skiing opportunities that are the central attraction of the park. The most temperate season however, and therefore a popular time for visitors, is the period from June through to October. The park stretches between the Maurienne and Tarentaise valleys in the Rhône-Alpes département. Here it is sheltered from oceanic rains by the pre-Alps, and in these summer months the weather is kind. It is then that the full scope, colour and richness of the natural heritage of the area is plain to view and most easily accessed.

Endangered species

Amongst the thousand plant species within La Vanoise, sedges, blue thistle, mountain primrose, saxifrage and twinflower are all protected. The park is also home to more familiar flowers and trees. Across its four levels of vegetation – alpine, sub-alpine, mountain and hillside – larch, hook pine, Scots pine, beech, rhododendrons, blueberries, junipers, anemones and edelweiss all thrive.

Although this concentration of plant species is undoubtedly of great natural and scientific significance, it seems to be a glimpse of the animals of the mountains that visitors find particularly satisfying. In many ways, the inhabitants of the crags and the crevices of La Vanoise are its raison d'être. The preservation of a waning population of ibex was the prime reason for the creation of the reserve, and now the park boasts a healthy colony of almost 2,000 of the species. The ibex shares La Vanoise with a further 5,000 chamois, as well as marmots, martens, voles, shrews, badgers, bats, newts and toads.

Of ornithological interest, the park is home to different kinds of owls, woodpeckers, flycatchers, crossbills, sparrows and nutcrackers. There are black grouse, partridges, and twenty pairs of golden eagles. The imposing bearded vulture, which hangs over the valleys with its 2.7m wingspan, has also found its way back into La Vanoise. The bird was driven from the region towards the end of the 19th century amid popular hysteria about unlikely attacks on children and livestock.

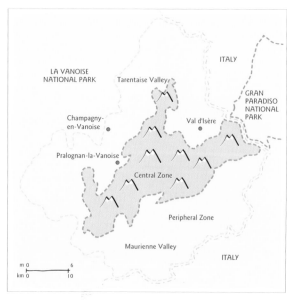

LA VANOISE NATIONAL PARK

ITALY

Tarentaise Valley

GRAN PARADISO NATIONAL PARK

Champagny-en-Vanoise

Val d'Isère

Pralognan-la-Vanoise

Central Zone

Peripheral Zone

Maurienne Valley

ITALY

m 0   6
km 0   10

Androsace helvetica

Hiking in La Vanoise

In spite of the strict preservation of La Vanoise, and the rigid regulations that govern access to it, hiking is encouraged. Both the GR 5 and the GR 55 pass through the park, and over 300km of other well-marked trails climb about the mountains. Following the longer routes is made easier by the forty refuges which are scattered across the park, offering shelter to those planning extended rambles.

Routes can be recommended and refuges reserved by the park wardens. Alternatively, the villages that are situated on the park's perimeter – such as Champagny-en-Vanoise, Pralognan-la-Vanoise or Aussois – are well placed for use as bases from which to embark on day hikes.

Park facilities

Park wardens, of whom there are thirty five working across the valleys of La Vanoise, are able to take visitors with them to play a part in animal counts, bird-watching or botanical investigations – the sort of daily research that feeds back into the more involved scientific study of the area. They also present slide shows and films, and lead guided walks.

A number of visitor centres within the national park offer a thorough information service, selling books for tourists and scientific publications, hosting permanent and temporary exhibitions, and organising activities for children in the summer months. The centres also accommodate study courses and, in some cases, offer laboratory facilities for study parties.

Pockets of heritage

In amongst its wildlife and its natural wealth, La Vanoise is able to direct visitors to many corners of cultural interest: cave paintings, Roman roads and bridges, and medieval churches.

Many of the discreet churches and chapels of Maurienne and Tarentaise have been restored to something of their baroque verve, their sculpted beams and colourful frescoes allowing a glimpse of the cultural surge of the late 16th century Counter Reformation.

In many of the villages a strong pastoral tradition also endures, and in the monumental, civic and religious architecture, idiosyncratic decorative and artistic details are preserved.

Gran Paradiso

Adding to the natural and cultural grandeur of the the park and to its significance as a major reserve, La Vanoise shares a border of 14km with Gran Paradiso in Italy.

In 1856, Victor Emmanuel II of Savoy effectively saved the ibex from extinction when, ironically, he established a royal hunting reserve. In time, this game park became the Gran Paradiso National Park, the first of its kind in Italy. As the ibex population continued to dwindle, disappearing into the hills of La Vanoise across the border, the French also recognised the need to protect the migrating animals. A plan was drawn up to unite the parks across the two zones, and together they constitute one of the largest areas of protected land in Western Europe.

[i] CONTACT INFORMATION

La Vanoise National Park
135 Rue de Docteur Julliand
BP 705
F 73007 Chambéry Cedex
France
Tel: (00 33) 4 7962 3054
Fax: (00 33) 4 7996 3718
Web: www.vanoise.com

A view of the Glacier des Fours

Chamonix Mont Blanc

Whilst the crowds flock to Chamonix Mont Blanc for the big names and the high mountains, a walk in a different direction can open up plenty of paths less travelled.

The town of Chamonix is among the most popular and accessible entry points to the French Alps and has long been a base for those visiting the Mont Blanc massif. Europe's highest summit at 4,807m, Mont Blanc towers behind the Chamonix area: the town itself is the starting point for the Tour du Mont Blanc and the Haute Route to Zermatt, as well as being crossed by the GR 5. In many ways the birthplace of alpine tourism, Chamonix also opens onto a large number of rambles and walks of all grades around the valley and the nearby mountains, glaciers and lakes.

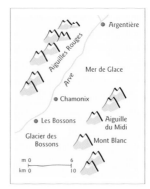

Freedom to choose

The glacial valley of Chamonix cuts deep into the land, and hiking trails can be found up, down and along it. The contours of the valley shape walking routes both for those hoping to scale challenging alpine paths, and for those seeking well-marked, level trails for short excursions. In keeping with this variety, organisations offer all manner of trips, including guided walks, themed routes and *clé en mains* expeditions for the more independent hiker. These programmes allow people to plough on or linger, setting their own pace, whilst luggage is taken ahead. Relaxed series of short walks are another less laboured way of seeing the different faces of Chamonix.

Summertime

Areas above 2,000m are snowbound until July, and the summer months are by far the most hospitable for ramblers unacquainted with extreme conditions. Summer is open season for walking in the Chamonix valley and the weather below the snowline can be warm, although carefully laid plans can occasionally be frustrated by heavy rains. The region of Rhône-Alpes, in which the Chamonix valley lies, is the only part of France where walkers can trek across glaciers all year round, although conditions do vary hugely.

Protecting nature

Over the years the authorities have tried to reconcile the economic and ecological needs of the area. A programme of environmental protection, established to look after the region's flora and fauna, bridges the French, Italian and Swiss areas of

Aiguilles Rouges

Grand Balcon Sud trail

the Éspace Mont Blanc. The benefits of this programme include 350km of footpaths maintained by the Forestry Commission. Around and about the focal point of Chamonix are some 180 sq km of protected land and 380 sq km of nature reserve. The area is also peppered with parks, orchards and botanical gardens which shelter all sorts of plant, bird and wildlife.

Aiguilles Rouges

Set away from the Mont Blanc massif, the Aiguilles Rouges is a smaller range of peaks with a tradition of playing host to mountaineers who are trying to acclimatise before braving the Alps. In addition to its own spectacles, such as the Aiguilles de Belvedere which is situated in the middle of the range, the Aiguilles Rouges offers lots of walks from hikes through alpine vegetation to short jaunts in botanical gardens.

The Aiguilles Rouges Nature Reserve, created in 1972 by local communities, also offers many of the region's more moderate walking opportunities. Located 11km north of Chamonix at the Col des Montets, a visitor centre is open from June to September.

Glacier des Bossons

The village of Les Bossons is set a couple of kilometres away from the centre of Chamonix. Nestled in a large park, it looks out onto Mont Blanc and the Glacier des Bossons, the largest ice-fall in Europe. A popular round-trip hike from Chamonix takes about three hours.

For experienced walkers, or for those looking for wilder landscapes, glacier hiking provides fresh challenges. The glaciers of the Chamonix Mont Blanc region are well-placed for those wishing to make their first steps onto the ice. The advice of guides is widely available for novices, useful as routes often require ropes and crampons.

Grand Balcon Sud trail

The variety of walking routes and terrain allows the Mont Blanc massif to be seen in different lights and from varying perspectives across the Chamonix valley. The western side of the valley has especially fetching views of the mountains. With tramways climbing to its starting point, the Grand Balcon Sud trail runs along this western edge at a height of 2,000m.

Grand Balcon Nord trail

The Grand Balcon Nord trail connects a number of the area's natural attractions. The pinnacle of the Aiguille du Midi is a fine example of how the wilderness of the Alps has been pacified for the public. Almost 12 million people have trodden its heights, by way of the world's longest and highest tramway which climbs to 3,800m in the shadow of Mont Blanc.

The popularity of the Aiguille du Midi has lead to its inclusion in many well-known walking routes. The Grand Balcon Nord trail leads from the halfway stop on the Aiguille de Midi tramway across to the Mer de Glace – the second largest glacier in the Alps, being 14km long, 1,500m wide and 360m thick.

ⓘ CONTACT INFORMATION

Chamonix Mont-Blanc Tourist Office
85 Place du Triangle de L'Amitié
74400 Chamonix Mont-Blanc
France
Tel: (00 33) 4 5053 0024
Fax: (00 33) 4 5053 5890
E-mail: info@chamonix.com
Web: www.chamonix.com

Tour du Mont Blanc

*Whilst the red line on the map seems to show a fixed route around
the massif, the Tour du Mont Blanc offers many more choices.*

The established route of the Tour du
Mont Blanc is a trail of about 200km.
On average, nine to eleven days are
required to complete the circuit.
Registered as one of France's *Sentiers
de Grande Randonnée*, its prestige
leads people to quite different
preconceptions. Either the Tour
du Mont Blanc is thought of as
impregnable, braved only by alpinists,
or it is spoken of in the same breath
as countless other high paths across
Europe, accessible to all.

The commercialisation of the region
and the enduring wilderness of the
Alps mean that neither of these
assumptions is quite true nor wholly
false. The Tour du Mont Blanc does
not have to be a hair-raising assault
on the peak of the mountain, or an
amble through meadows which roll
gently at a safe distance from the
Mont Blanc massif. The lands can be
all things to all people.

Chamonix - the hub of the French Alps

Walking conditions

The usual route of the Tour du Mont
Blanc is quite taxing. The path climbs
at an average gradient of 1:10 through

the seven valleys of the Mont Blanc
massif. At times the trail climbs to
over 2,500m, but for the most part
it stays between 1,500 and 2,000m.
Tidy paved paths can help visitors up
the mountainsides but elsewhere the
trail can become more obscure and
less hospitable. This uncertainty plays
a major part in the attraction of the
route, and over the duration of the
walk glaciers, mountain peaks, chains
of villages, alpine meadows and
barren passes add extra variety.

Visiting the area

In spite of the risk of freak weather,
the summer months are a good time
to consider visiting the mountains.
In the winter, or even in the early
part of the walking season, ice axes,
crampons and some serious walking
experience would probably be
required in the event of bad weather.

Access to the region is no longer
dependent on seasonal conditions.
Chamonix and the Rhône-Alpes
département have been extensively
developed and the area boasts two
international airports, in Lyon and
Geneva. The TGV railway slices from
Paris to Lyon, and more than 1,000km
of motorway crosses the area, leading
drivers easily to the foot of the Alps.

Three cultures

On the usual nine to eleven day walk, the Tour du Mont Blanc crosses, in an anti-clockwise direction, from Les Houches in France to Courmayeur in Italy, through to Champex in the Swiss Alps and back to Les Houches. Switching over three languages, three currencies and three distinct cultures, the tour can appear to have traversed entire nations. For those willing to step off the track and into authentic communities, the bustle of Chamonix in France and the picture postcard outcrops of alpine hamlets in Switzerland supply varied food, accommodation and atmosphere.

Guides

Even without considering alternative routes and approaches to the Tour du Mont Blanc, a wide range of services and facilities can change the face of an excursion. For the less experienced walking party, knowledgeable guides are always available. In Chamonix their work and expertise is highly regarded, and a fête is held in their honour every August. For a more independent alternative, mules can be hired to bear luggage, allowing a little extra freedom to absorb the tremendous panorama that reveals itself along the length of the trail.

Bases

Whilst the Tour du Mont Blanc can be accessed from any number of towns around its circuit, for those intending to begin in the French quarter some choices have to be made. Chamonix,

Walkers leaving Les Drus behind

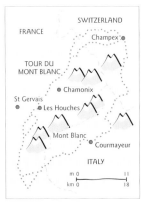

the self-proclaimed capital of the French Alps, has a long tradition of excess, both in its glorious winter sports facilities and its après ski culture. Alternatively, the village of St Gervais is more homely in its scale and approach. Both allow for easy access to Les Houches, the usual starting point for walkers.

Alternatives

The lands of the Tour du Mont Blanc are often presented as an idyll of diverse wildlife, typical alpine scenes and cultural contrasts. In some ways this is a fair representation, but what is increasingly becoming characteristic of the area is the ability of the tourist authorities and tour operator to offer customised packages to visitors. For those stretched for time, brisk routes namecheck the key sites and celebrated passes, peaks, glaciers and cols – the Mer de Glace, Les Drus, the Flegere plateau, Village du Praz. Supervised expeditions are also run for children, activities including hiking, fishing and rafting.

[i] CONTACT INFORMATION

**Chamonix Mont-Blanc
Tourist Office**
85 Place du Triangle de L'Amitié
74400 Chamonix Mont-Blanc
France
Tel: (00 33) 4 5053 0024
Fax: (00 33) 4 5053 5890
E-mail: info@chamonix.com
Web: www.chamonix.com

The Valbonnais

Traditional pathways, national park preservation and nature's clemency come together to make the Valbonnais a fine place to hike.

The Valbonnais is one of the seven districts into which Les Ecrins National Park is divided. The countryside is, therefore, kept under close scrutiny, valued for what it can reveal to science and treasured as a fragile piece of rural heritage. However, this protective outlook does not exclude or indict the walker. In fact, the same wardens who conduct surveys and develop conservation programmes lead parties of ramblers about the region.

Walking holidays in the Valbonnais sit happily with the region's aim to foster good relations between the rural communities and visiting urbanites. Projects have been organised to preserve heritage, to support agriculture, and to encourage the sort of tourism that doesn't trample the lands and lifestyles of a district, but rather wanders through it, appreciating its values.

As the snow melts, ibex return to the high ground

The lay of the land

The Valbonnais is well managed with established routes like the GR 54 and the Tour du Valbonnais passing through or winding about it. There are also trails of other kinds, often starting from public carparks, with information boards cropping up regularly along a lot of the routes.

The landscape is particularly given to short and accessible trails. Footpaths lead effortlessly into areas rich with wildlife. From the valley of the Bonne river, trails cross towards the lake of Vallon where, in the summer months, the ibex emerges to mount the rocky crests of the Grand Renaud. Alongside the ancient paths which connect the small villages, walkers will see alpine pastures coloured with wildflowers.

Canals and waterways

Etched into the plain of Entraigues, canals bring water to fields and gardens. Once, the entire community was dependent upon them but, with the depopulation of the countryside and new technology replacing traditional agricultural practices, the use of the canals declined and they rapidly became neglected. The park authorities have since

The Valbonnais – a panorama

Lac du Valbonnais

Restoration

As the walking routes about the Valbonnais show, much of the rural infrastructure warrants preservation. Kilns, chapels, mills, paths and stone walling are increasingly recognised for their importance. Inventories have been made of artefacts and buildings which make up the heritage of the various communities. Restoration work is now ongoing, and continues to call upon the traditional techniques that are practiced by local artisans.

The Désert en Valjouffrey

Whereas, in some alpine regions, visitors look for wilderness and for a sense of the scale of the natural world, the Valbonnais offers stories of how people have responded to their environment, stubbornly defying the elements to claim and hold on to a measure of land.

A journey along the Bonne river, through the Désert en Valjouffrey, presents, on the one hand, geological spectacles which recount centuries of slipping schist and shale. On the other hand, visitors can see the dry stone walls, banks and channels with which settlers managed their environment: canals irrigate the land and accommodate seasonal floods, whilst hedgerows of ash provide shelter from the winds that tumble along the valleys.

A marmot, resident of the alpine meadows

Notre Dame de la Salette

Many of the walks are also a tour of personal histories, a route through the memories and the beliefs that grow up around a people. By way of Hurtières, it is possible to reach the sacred site of Notre Dame de la Salette, en route to the peak of the Gargas. The site was consecrated in 1846 by the Bishop of Grenoble following the account of the appearance of the Virgin Mary to two young shepherds.

Col de Côte Belle

Before the hiker is drawn along the Tour de l'Oisans, the Col de Côte Belle opens out to present a carpet of flowers sprinkled over the high ground. Alpine asters and other delicate flowers trim the crests in spite of the rocks and the sweeping wind.

A col is a depression, a pass between mountains. Historically, the cols of the area have been meeting places for people from different valleys – a point of communication. To follow these paths today is to enter somewhat into this old pattern. It is to experience something of the land's hospitality, to walk along natural paths and passages, directed by the shape of the land.

organised regular surveys and set up maintenance contracts with farmers to ensure the safeguarding of these waterways. Short trails by their banks proliferate, and level paths, such as the route along the Canal du Beaumont, offer gentle rambling.

Lac Labarre

Water greatly effects how visitors see and appreciate the Valbonnais. Waterfalls are quick to catch the light in the summer months, and throughout the winter the noise of swollen streams is difficult to ignore. In the heights of the land, lakes sit at the feet of the mountains, adding an extra dimension to them. Trout and salmon teem in the waters, and unusual species, such as the alpine triton newt, can also be glimpsed. A small and relatively shallow lake, 8m deep, Lac Labarre is the focal point for an extended walk based on a part of the GR 54 which passes by.

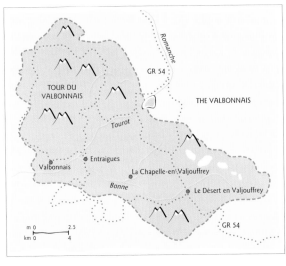

map: TOUR DU VALBONNAIS / THE VALBONNAIS — Romanche, GR 54, Tourot, Valbonnais, Entraigues, Bonne, La Chapelle-en-Valjouffrey, Le Désert en Valjouffrey, GR 54; scale m 0 / 2.5, km 0 / 4

[i] CONTACT INFORMATION

Les Ecrins National Park
Domaine de Charance
F 05000 Gap
France
Tel: (00 33) 4 9240 2010
Fax: (00 33) 4 9252 3834

Valbonnais
Maison du Parc
38740 Entraigues
France
Tel: (00 33) 4 7630 2061
Fax: (00 33) 4 7630 2061

✚ SWITZERLAND

The Bear Trail

A popular trail in the Bernese Oberland incorporates the canton's highlights, as well as its quieter corners.

The Hintere Gasse, or Bear Trail as it is commonly known, runs across the base of the Bernese Oberland in central Switzerland. The region is the source of many of the chocolate box images – of docile belled cows, flowered meadows and alps – which dominate international perceptions of the country. The Bear Trail traverses these picturesque areas but it is foremost an alpine route. High altitudes, steep ascents and inclement or dangerous weather make the itinerary a strenuous one.

Bernese Oberland

The German-speaking Bernese Oberland forms the southern part of Bern canton and is spanned by the Bernese Alps. The varied rocks which form the Alps were once part of a sea floor. Lifted, creased and compacted by movement of the Earth's plates approximately 100 million years ago, they were subsequently shaped by ice ages and the grinding forces of glaciers. Today, the eastern Alps are the highest and most rugged, but the entire range remains heavily glaciated. It is these perpetually frozen peaks, the waterfalls of the glacial gorges, and the fertile alpine meadows which draw hosts of tourists to the Bernese Oberland. The charm is increased by an impressive infrastructure of cable-cars, railways and gondolas.

Grosse Scheidegg

Hintere Gasse

The Bear Trail runs for 122km from Meiringen in the east to Gsteig in the west. It crosses the Haslital, Jungfrau, Frutigland, Simmental and Saanenland regions via eight alpine passes, and is completed over eight days. In places the trail coincides with the Alpine Pass Route which crosses Switzerland from Liechtenstein to France.

The Bernese Oberland has long been popular with walkers and is overrun with trails. As a result there is often a choice of path on any given stretch of the Bear Trail. This may depend upon which waterfall, gorge or village walkers wish to see, but the main destinations en route remain constant. Mountain transport systems enable walkers to truncate the route.

Haslital

Meiringen, where the route begins, lies in the broad Aare valley in Haslital. Before they set out, fans of detective stories should visit the nearby Reichenbach falls where Sherlock Holmes and Moriarty fought to the death. From Meiringen the route heads to the first alpine pass at Grosse Scheidegg. At 1,962m, it is one of the lower passes. This first day provides a taster of what is to come, taking in waterfalls, gorges, and the Hengsterengletscher, a glacier which hangs in icy fingers from the grey face of the Wetterhorn.

Traditional architecture of the Bernese Oberland

Jungfrau

From Grosse Scheidegg the trail leads down through alpine pastures to Grindelwald. The town is a tourist haven, flanked by two massive glaciers, the Unterer and Oberer Grindelwaldgletscher, and overshadowed by the Jungfrau, Eiger and Münch. Walkers can ride in Europe's longest cable-car to the Eiger, take the railway to Europe's highest station at Jungfraujoch, or touch the Oberer glacier in an ice cave. The route from Grindelwald to Kleine Scheidegg, although covering a sizeable climb, is well-trodden.

Kleine Scheidegg is a broad meadow at the base of the Eiger's north face. The face is a legendary ascent for mountaineers, and the meadow provides an excellent view of climbers who come to take the challenge. From Kleine Scheidegg the path heads to the valleys around Lauterbrunnen, meaning 'with many fountains' due to the waterfalls which cascade here. At Stechelberg walkers can head up to spend a night in the Rotstockhütte. At 2,039m this basic mountain hut sits in a basin of rock debris left by water on its way down the Schilthorn.

Frutigland

The first night in Frutigland is also spent at altitude at the Blüemlisalphütte. Perched at 2,834m, the approach to this hut is up a ridge of rock and scree. In bad weather the hut's location can be desolate but on a clear day, encircled by the Blüemlisalp massif with unhindered views through the Hohtürli, it justifies the climb. Hohtürli means 'high doorway' and is the name of the pass which tops the steep descent, under the snout of the Blüemlisalpgletscher, to Öeschinensee lake. Fed by waterfalls, Öeschinensee changes its spectacular colour from azure to emerald depending on the cloud cover. The final stop in Frutigland is at Engstligenalp, an expanse of alpine flowers and pastures on a plateau left by an ancient lake.

Simmental and Saanenland

Once the route passes into the west of the Bernese Oberland, the Alps begin to reduce in size. The Upper Simmental, with its historic spa town of Lenk, is characterised by plateaux and valleys, although waterfalls still abound. From Lenk the path passes through forests, gorges and hamlets to Lauenen. This section's ambling feel is suitable for the end of an arduous route. Lauenen is a small village with a 16th century church and classic regional architecture. Dark wooden houses with overhanging eaves and carved or painted decorations evolved in the Bernese Oberland from the 17th century and the village has a fine 18th century example. Beyond Lauenen, Chrinepass, the last pass of the route, also provides the final views before dropping to Gsteig. The route ends here but the opportunities for walking do not. Both Valais and Vaud canton can be reached from Gsteig, with France and Italy not too far beyond.

i CONTACT INFORMATION

Bernese Oberland Tourism
Jungfraustrasse 38
3800 Interlaken
Switzerland
Tel: (00 41) 33 823 0303
Fax: (00 41) 33 823 0330
E-mail: info@berneroberland.com
Web: www.berneroberland.com

Lauenensee in Gstaad-Saanenland

The Swiss Path

Walking for remembrance but also for pleasure,
on a route in the historical heartland of Switzerland.

Modern Switzerland consists of twenty six cantons representing a process of confederation which began over 700 years ago in central Switzerland, known also as the Swiss 'heartland'. On the 1st of August 1291 the cantons of Uri, Schwyz and Unterwalden pledged a 'Perpetual Union' in favour of self-government and to resist all foreign dominion – in particular the powerful Habsburgs.

The confederation grew as cantons joined progressively, although the process was not always smooth. Over the centuries, religious, economic and political differences, and external factors such as war, lead to schisms and successive constitutions. With time the diverse peoples of the confederacy became known as the Schweizer or Swiss after one of the founder cantons, Schwyz.

Commemoration

In 1991, in commemoration of the 700th anniversary of the original union, the Swiss Path was devised. The path starts at the forest fringed Rütli meadows on the shores of Lake Lucerne where the original pledge was confirmed. Encircling the shores of Lake Uri, Lake Lucerne's southern arm, the path continues for 35km to end in Brunnen in Schwyz. All of Switzerland's cantons assisted in the creation of the path, and a section of it is dedicated to each.

Because of the events which occurred here, this area is very important to the Swiss and the Rütli meadows still form a focus for national celebrations. As a result the Swiss Path is well marked and is easily accessible from various points along its length. There are no especially strenuous sections to the walk and it could be completed in its entirety over two days. Its location on the shores of Lake Lucerne, which itself offers a variety of outdoor activities, means that the Swiss Path is ideal for incorporation into a longer stay or a family holiday.

The legend of William Tell lives on at the Tellkapelle

Lake Lucerne

Lake Lucerne is correctly and locally known as Vierwaldstättersee, meaning the Lake of the Four Forest Cantons. The lake basin was formed when the Reuss glacier receded after the last Ice Age, and consists of several twisted arms. The foothills of the Central Swiss Alps rise from its shores, with the 'real' Alps beginning further south.

Most of the Swiss Path falls within Uri. While the canton's southern area is dominated by glacial rock, around the lake it is fertile and forested. Growth is assisted by Lucerne's reliably mild climate, attributable in part to the föhn winds, which bring warm air from the Mediterranean over the Alps. The winds can be either welcome, by melting the winter snows early in the year, or

Roads and paths cut from the rock face

threatening. At times their force can make the lake hazardous to cross. The people who live in the vicinity of the lake are German-speaking and in addition to tourism are predominantly reliant upon farming for their livelihoods.

Weg der Schweis

The conventional route of the Swiss Path runs from the Rütli meadows on Lake Uri's western shore around its tip to Brunnen in the north-east. From Rütli the path climbs to Seelisberg village, perched on its cliff-top plateau. This is one of the steepest sections of the path and can be bypassed by taking the funicular from nearby Trieb. The Seelisberg cliffs jut into Lake Uri forming a sharp corner between it and the main body of Lake Lucerne.

From Seelisberg the path passes through forests and along high slopes before dropping to Bauen on the lake's shore. This section provides unhindered views of the lake and, further into Uri canton, of the Reuss river and the Alps. Bauen is a pretty village of timbered houses and, due to its sheltered location, a haven for plants from warmer climes. The path continues to Seedorf, close to where the 16th century A Pro castle can be visited. Set in meadows, this compact fortress with its white walls and amber slates, seems too romantic to have once been the stronghold of a knight.

The flatlands from Seedorf to Flüelen form the nature reserve of the Reuss estuary. From Flüelen, visitors can catch one of the steamers which cross the lake. The trip to Lucerne takes approximately three hours but there are several stopping points including

Lake Uri

places along the Swiss Path. Flüelen was historically an important post along the trans-alpine trade routes which traversed the Gotthard massif. In the 19th century extensive works were carried out to open up the route where it ran alongside the lake and the path north to Brunnen now follows these in places.

En route is Tellkapelle, the site where the fictional character William Tell, who has now become a local folk hero, supposedly leapt ashore from a bailiff's boat to save himself. A chapel with 19th century frescoes now depicts the tale. The Swiss Path ends at the town of Brunnen, a resort on a smaller scale than others in the area. Its situation at the corner of Lake Uri makes it a good base for further exploration.

Alternative paths

Other walks within this part of central Switzerland include the Waldstätterweg which circles Lake Lucerne, and the Stern 91 or Étoile 91. The latter is a set of seven commemorative paths starting in differing regions of the country which all converge on the Rütli meadows.

ⓘ CONTACT INFORMATION

Central Switzerland Tourism
Alpenstrasse 1
CH-6002 Lucerne
Switzerland
Tel: (00 41) 41 418 4080
Fax: (00 41) 41 418 4081
E-mail: Info@CentralSwitzerland.ch
Web: www.CentralSwitzerland.ch

SWITZERLAND

The Trekking 700 Route

Based in Switzerland's temperate south, the Trekking 700 provides an accessible 'pass-hopping' route.

Lake Piora in Val Leventina

In 1991, the Swiss celebrated the 700 year anniversary of the confederation of independent cantons which later became Switzerland. As part of the commemoration walking paths were developed throughout the country. The Trekking 700, which stretches across Ticino, is one of these paths and a popular long distance route.

Ticino

Ticino, Switzerland's most southerly canton, is distinct both geographically and culturally from the rest of the country. In the north, the Swiss Alps form a natural border, with access into Ticino via the famous San Gotthard and San Bernardino passes. The Alps decrease in size further south, eventually giving way to the pre-Alps and lakes in Sottoceneri, Ticino's southernmost tip.

Sottoceneri protrudes like a finger into Italy, but all of Ticino has a distinctly Italian flavour as the canton has always been closely affiliated with Lombardy. It was not until the 19th century that Ticino became a canton of the Swiss confederation in its own right. Ticino's enduring and relatively recent links with the south are reflected in its inhabitants, most of whom speak Italian and share Lombardian customs and ways of life.

Although alpine, Ticino's climate is milder than many parts of the country. It experiences a high number of sunshine hours, consistently warm temperatures and a generous level of rainfall. These conditions favour a unique mix of flora, rich in both alpine and mediterranean species. Rural depopulation means that much previously cultivated land is returning to wilderness, making Ticino an ideal location for walking.

Waterfall at Biasca

The Trekking 700

Like many of Switzerland's long distance routes the Trekking 700 is a pass-hopping one. It starts in Mesocco and heads west across Ticino via numerous peaks and valleys to finish at Formazza in Italy. Although the route climbs to over 2,000m on a daily basis, it avoids the highest peaks. This, together with the fact that it can be completed within a week to nine days, has made the route a more popular one than some of the strenuous paths further north.

Mesocco

The walk starts at the village of Mesocco – dominated by the Castello di Mesocco. These beautiful ruins sit high over the Moesa river, which spawns numerous waterfalls as it flows south to join the Ticino river and eventually Lake Maggiore. The path does not follow the river valley but instead climbs north-west out of it to reach the route's first high point of 2,161m at Trescolmen pass.

This section of the route is a series of ascents and descents until after it has traversed l'Alpe della Motta, when walkers can rest for the night at Capanna Cava, a tiny village on the mountain's flank.

The church of Sant Giorgio with its Romanesque tower

Biasca

Biasca is situated in the fertile Ticino river basin at the head of Val Leventina. The valley is one of Ticino's main alpine playgrounds and the villages along its length are bases for skiers, mountaineers and outdoor enthusiasts, as well as those interested in the canton's wealth of Romanesque art and architecture. Biasca was historically an important ecclesiastical and trading town on the route to the San Gotthard pass. Evidence of this history can be admired in San Pietro e Paulo, a 12th century basilica with stunning frescoes.

The path continues from Biasca to the Gagnone pass and the summit of Cima D'Efra. En route it crosses Ticino's wildest country. Scarred by deforestation and soapstone mining, the landscape is slowly reverting to its previous state of harsh peaks, sparse alpine meadows and scrub.

It is scattered with tarns and is a haven for alpine flora. Among the more interesting species are the stemless carline thistle, a plant purported to have saved Roman armies from the plague, and the giant gentian, which also has medicinal properties and, unlike its more common namesake, has large sturdy yellow flowers.

Sonogno and San Carlo

Delicate, blue gentians border the path as it approaches Sonogno. Tucked at a crossroads between valleys, this village is almost entirely built of stone. In the surrounding valley, empty houses are a lonely testament to the depopulation of the area. Attempts are being made to curb the trend by developing crafts and tourism.

After the village the path goes into another cycle of rigorous climbs and descents before levelling briefly as it runs along the Val Bavona. This is a relatively untouched area, despite the depletion of its river by hydroelectric schemes, and the valley's sides are cloaked in forest. Another pretty village, San Carlo is popular with walkers as a cable-car runs from it up into the Cristallina mountains.

From San Carlo, walkers have a choice: a steep but truncated route via beech and larch forests to Pian di Crest; or a circuitous route via the summit of Basòdino and its glacier. The latter will add an extra day to the route but, if the weather is good, gives walkers a panoramic view of the peaks along the Swiss–Italian border. For those not choosing to climb Basòdino, the final day of the Trekking 700 will also be the highest. The crossing to Italy is via the Tamier pass at 2,772m, before the route makes its ultimate descent to end in Val Formazza.

[i] CONTACT INFORMATION

Ticino Tourism
Casella Postale 1441
Via Lugano 12
CH-6501 Bellinzona
Switzerland
Tel: (00 41) 91 825 7056
Fax: (00 41) 91 825 3614
E-mail: ett@www.tourism-ticino.ch
Web: www.tourism-ticino.ch

The San Gotthard pass at the head of Val Leventina

 **SWITZERLAND**

The Great Walser Route

Spanning three cantons and four countries, the path of the Walser migrations poses a modern challenge in an historical context.

Alpine pastures in the Valais High Alps

The Great Walser Route through the southern and eastern cantons of Switzerland follows the history of the Walsers, a nomadic people of Allemanic origin who first migrated into what is now the Valais canton in southern Switzerland around AD 800. A farming people from the Bernese Oberland, the Walsers spoke their own dialect of German, Walsertiitsch. Their migration was via the high passes in the eastern corner of Valais, in an area now known as the Goms.

The daring of their enterprise can be appreciated from the terrain. Heavily glaciated, surrounded by mountains and treacherous passes, covered in snow for much of the year, the Walsers were the first people to farm these high alps. Through innovation, they raised both animals and crops, moving their households into the valleys for the winter.

In Walser society land was passed to a single heir, which lead other members of the family to leave in search of their own land. This took the Walsers deep into the Swiss Alps, to Italy and eastern Switzerland, as far as Austria and Liechtenstein. In each new area, they perpetuated their farming practices, customs and dialect.

The route

The Great Walser Route does not trace the path of the migrations but instead links approximately 150 settlements of Walser origin. The culture can be experienced through museums, architecture, landscape, or in the continued practices of the inhabitants. The route is often high altitude, strenuous and

impassable in winter. For visitors interested in the Walser culture but unable to complete the entire route, sections can be completed from any of the villages it links.

The route is about 300km long and, although mapped and marked, is not always linear. Official guides break the route into thirty four stages, taking a total of four weeks to complete.

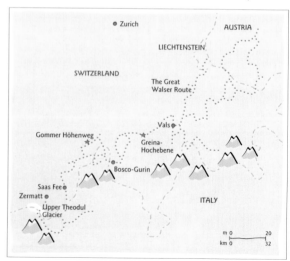

A mountain village in the Goms region of Valais

Starting in Zermatt, the route detours via Italy before crossing the lower part of Valais canton into Ticino canton. The top half of Ticino is traversed via high-level passes before dropping into Graubünden canton. Here the route forks, following the paths of those who chose to stay in their native Switzerland, and those who left.

Valais

From its starting point in Zermatt, the path climbs upwards to the Upper Theodul glacier. Walkers cross the glacial moraine before the path ascends to 3,317m at the Theodul pass. This section of the walk affords stunning views of the Pennine Alps and indicates how rigorous the migrations must have been for the Walsers. However, a cableway is available for today's walkers.

The resort of Saas Fee, which lies on the route once it returns from Italy, is a good base for exploratory walks. The section of the route from Saas Fee to Monte Moro pass and on into Italy takes a full day. Mattmarksee reservoir is an alternative destination. The path to the reservoir is cleared of snow in winter and, once there, visitors can rest at a waterside restaurant.

Ticino

Before leaving Valais, the route takes a loop around the Gommer Höhenweg high on the northern slopes of the Goms. Still sparsely populated, this area displays typical Walser farming methods: small alpine fields irrigated by rock channels or steep slopes where hay was cut. The path dips once more into Italy before entering Ticino over the Guriner Furka, an

original Walser route. Bosco-Gurin, back in Switzerland, is still a Walser village. Perched at over 1,500m on the flanks of the Sonnenhorn, the low cottages of wood and stone are reminiscent of Valais architecture and Walsertiitsch is spoken here.

Graubünden

Another high pass bridges Ticino with neighbouring Graubünden, where the route becomes known as the *senda Gualser* in Romansch dialect. The Walsers were not always made welcome in Graubünden: one area passed a law in 1457 prohibiting land to be held by non-Romansch speakers. Today much of this area forms the Greina-Hochebene, or Plaun la Greina, a nationally protected landscape of high altitude plains and meadows. Greina-Hochebene is only minimally grazed allowing wild plants and flowers to grow in profusion. The nearby Valsertal valley was settled by the Walser in the 13th century, perhaps to take advantage of its natural hot springs. Walkers can enjoy a soak here or visit one of the several lakes for a summer swim.

Beyond the valley walkers must decide which way to go: north to Liechtenstein, east to Austria or south towards the glacier-clad Bernina massif. A decision taken by generations of Walsers before them.

[i] CONTACT INFORMATION

Switzerland Travel Centre Ltd
Swiss Centre
Swiss Court
London W1V 8EE
Tel: 0800 100 200 30
Fax: 0800 100 200 31
E-mail: stc@stlondon.com
Web: www.MySwitzerland.com

The Valais High Alps

The Alpine Pass Route

A passion both for scenery and for alpinism can be indulged on this lengthy route between Switzerland's international borders.

The Alpine Pass Route crosses from Sargans in the east of Switzerland to Montreux in the west and, together with the Haute Route and the tours of Monte Rosa and Mont Blanc, is considered one of Switzerland's classic long-distance walks.

The Alpine Pass Route

The Alpine Pass Route runs right across Switzerland over a distance of approximately 330km, taking in many of the country's most famous high passes. In theory the path can be completed over fifteen days, with a major pass traversed on each. Such an itinerary would involve several long hikes which, combined with the daily differences in altitude, would require walkers to be extremely fit. More commonly, the route is tackled over three to four weeks, or in separate stages over a longer time.

The Glarner Alps

The most popular sections are those within the Bernese Oberland. The path, however, also passes through some of the lesser known eastern and central cantons and is a good means of getting to know these 'peripheral' areas. Due to its nature, the Alpine Pass Route remains inaccessible to all but experienced mountain walkers for much of the year. To ensure that paths are not blocked by snow, it is best tackled from late June to October.

St Gallen

The Alpine Pass Route begins officially in St Gallen canton, although hardened walkers often start further afield, tackling the passes along the Austrian, Liechtenstein and Swiss borders as a warm up. The canton is defined on its eastern side by the broad valley of the Rhine river. It is known for commerce and wine-growing, and has an interesting and well-preserved history, yet it is seldom visited by tourists.

Walkers with time to spare would be well advised to visit the canton's capital, also called St Gallen. The city was founded in AD 612 by Gallus, an Irish monk. His hermitage became a site of pilgrimage, and a Benedictine abbey was built on the site. The *Stift*, or religious district, which surrounds the abbey, is a UNESCO world heritage site. It includes the inspiring *Stiftsbiblithek* (abbey library) where, in the reading room with its gorgeous rococo ornamentation, visitors can view a collection of illuminated manuscripts.

A view of the Stift district in St Gallen

The village of Sargans, where the route proper begins, sits at the base Mount Gonzen. It is promoted locally as 'Heidiland' as the writer Johanna Spyri was supposedly inspired during a holiday to use it as the setting for her famous novels. From Sargans, the walk ambles through vineyards, hamlets and forests before tackling the 2,223m Foopass, which crosses the border from St Gallen to Glarus canton. The track over the pass follows the historic route of the Walser, nomadic farmers from the Bernese Oberland who, from the 9th century, travelled the country in search of land.

Glarus

Glarus is a small canton dominated by the craggy Glarner Alps and the streams which run from them into the River Linth. Although the canton is quite industrial in its flatlands, there is no evidence of this in the alpine areas across which the path meanders. Remaining at altitude, the route zigzags up and down steep valley

sides between the villages of Elm and Linthal. This section of the walk can be demanding as the path is prone to erosion by water and snow. However, walkers will be rewarded with great views towards the Klausenpass, and from May to August the area around the Richetlipass is a blanket of wildflowers. The limestone strata of the Glarner Alps means that blossoms tend to be brightly hued, and species such as flamboyant martagon lilies and orchids can be seen.

Uri

At Klausenpass, another cantonal border is breached as the route leads into Uri. Spreading from the shores of Lake Lucerne, Uri canton is wild and rugged, its harsh rock scarred by glaciers which still cover many of the highest peaks. The canton is fiercely proud of its status as one of the founding members of the original Swiss confederation in 1291. Its cantonal flag is thought to originate from 1231 when the region was

Château de Chillon on Lake Geneva

granted 'imperial freedom' from the Holy Roman Empire. The flag depicts an aurochs, the European bison which once roamed here. The aurochs has a ring through its nose which is said to symbolise the canton's wild nature. The route stays in Uri only long enough to cross the Klausenpass to Altdorf, before heading up and out

The Dents du Midi

again. Just before Altdorf is the village of Bürglen with its two medieval towers, and a chapel marking the reputed birthplace of William Tell.

Obwalden

The Surenenpass is the access point for the pocket of Obwalden canton around Engelberg; it is separated from the rest of Obwalden by an intervening section of Nidwalden canton. This is an untamed area, little affected by development, which acts as an entrance to the apex of the Alps which lies beyond in the Bernese Oberland. The Surenenpass will fulfil even seasoned walkers expectations of an alpine route. It is a long slog in places, the path passing along thin ridges, steep cable-protected ascents and, for much of the year, across extensive snowfields.

Bernese Oberland

From Engelberg, the route passes along the bottom of Nidwalden canton via the Jochpass before dropping to Meiringen in the Bernese Oberland. The Bernese Oberland is home to such defining Swiss landmarks as Grindelwald, the Eiger and the Jungfrau, and it is not surprising that this section of the Alpine Pass Route is well trodden. In most places the path corresponds

with the Bear Trail. The Hohtürli pass at 2,778m is the highest pass on the route yet, despite the altitude, cows are grazed just below here in the brief months when the snow thaws from the pastures. At the end of the summer they are ceremonially herded back down, dressed in their festive best with huge bells slung on brightly decorated yokes. From the pass, the route leads through the scree-covered Bunderchrinde with views back to the Jungfrau, before dropping to the resort of Adelboden, then on through the Hahnenmoospass to Lenk.

Vaud

The entry into Vaud canton in Switzerland's extreme west is via the

The Vaud Alps from above Lake Geneva

Col des Andérets. French-speaking Vaud has its own Alps, with several peaks over 3,000m. High rainfall and lush grassland means that Vaud is dedicated to dairy farming. Not surprisingly, fondue is a characteristic local dish and Vaud is also known for its cold meats – sausages, hams and pâtés. It is also the major producer of Swiss wines, made from grapes grown on the sunny northern shores of Lake Geneva.

Having been dominated by the peaks of the Bernese Oberland for so long, this final section of the route reveals some new horizons. Views from the path are now of Les Diablerets massif, and further afield to the Dents du Midi and the Savoy Alps. As it draws to its end the path becomes easier, dropping into the lower hills of the Vaud pre-Alps, through forest and farmland. From the final pass at Col de Chaude, Lake Geneva comes into view and from there it is not far to Montreux.

ℹ CONTACT INFORMATION

Switzerland Travel Centre Ltd
Swiss Centre
Swiss Court
London W1V 8EE
Tel: 0800 100 200 30
Fax: 0800 100 200 31
E-mail: stc@stlondon.com
Web: www.MySwitzerland.com

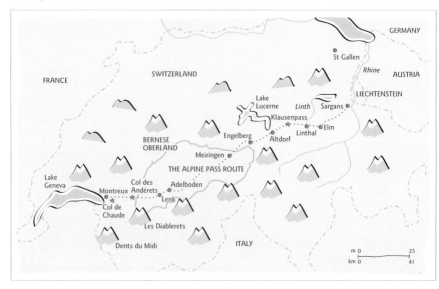

Walking in the Südtirol

Variety characterises Italy's northern province. Its melding of cultures and extensive walking opportunities allow visitors to enjoy both freedom and versatility.

Suspended below the northern border of Italy, the province of Südtirol, or Bolzano, was until recently part of Austria. The province retains its distinctiveness; it is predominantly bilingual and most of its towns are known by at least two names. The ancient Ladin culture and language, which remains in enclaves in the eastern valleys, contributes a third dimension to the province's identity. To add to the linguistic confusion, the area is also known as Alto Adige. Meaning 'tall Adige', the name reflects its location in the mountain basin at the head of the Adige river.

Autumn colours in Südtirol

History

Human history in the area begins about 5,000 years ago with 'Ötzi', a mummified man who was found perfectly preserved in a glacier on the Similaun mountain, where he had been since his death around 3350-3100 BC. During the Bronze Age, the first Rhaetian people, predecessors of the current Ladin population, settled in the area. The Romans arrived in 15 BC and their influence produced the Rhaetian or Ladin language as it is spoken today. In the 7th century the area came under Bavarian rule and in the Middle Ages it was bequeathed to the Austrian Habsburgs.

Other than a decade when it was claimed by Napoleon, the area remained under Austrian rule until it was passed to Italy at the end of the First World War. This arrangement created unrest among the province's Germanic peoples and in 1939 Hitler and Mussolini agreed to allow people to stay in the area as Italian citizens or to emigrate north to become Germans. Many people left but unrest continued, resulting in a series of agreements ceding local autonomy. Today the Südtirol / Bolzano province forms the northern half of the Autonomous Region of Trentino Alto Adige and is distinctly more Germanic in culture than the Italianate southern province of Trentino.

Spice of life

Food, music, art, architecture and customs reflect the three dominant cultures, while distinct areas of geography and land usage give walkers a choice of environments to explore.

Castle Trostburg

Bozen / Bolzano

The province fans out from Bozen / Bolzano. An old market and trading town, its narrow alleys are still lined with gourmet shops, tempting ropes of garlic, chillies and tomatoes hung outside. Mountain ridges and plateaus surround it and are traditional hiking

destinations. Three cable-cars take walkers to over 1,000m if they prefer to miss the initial stiff climb. The Ritten plateau is of particular interest with its sharp-peaked earth pyramids rising in ochre rows and its inns where visitors can try the dark *Weggen* bread or *Knödel*, traditional Tirolean dumplings which come in sweet and savoury varieties.

Der Süden Südtirols

Heading south from Bolzano, visitors will find themselves on the Vineyard Road through Der Süden Südtirols. This area has been famous for its wine since Roman times and is the home of the Gewürztraminer grape. Starting at Bolzano, the intention is to drive from vineyard to vineyard but walking may be the safer option if serious wine sampling is on the agenda. A town such as Tramin / Termeno, which is surrounded by vineyards, makes an ideal starting point, enabling a leisurely stroll to work up a thirst between each stop. This should not be difficult as the local wine, the Traminer Aromatico, is purported to raise the temperature of the blood. If visitors do overheat then Kalterer See / Largo di Caldaro, the alpine area's warmest lake, is close by.

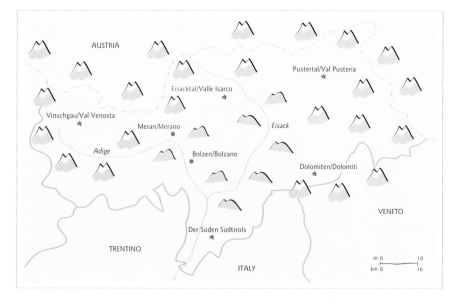

Meran / Merano

To the north is Meran / Merano, the province's main town, which sits in a sub-tropical enclave. Palms, cypress trees and Mediterranean plants grow here, and local valleys contain vineyards and persimmon orchards. An easy path from the hamlet of Dorf Tirol / Tirolo leads to Castel Tirolo. The castle was the last of those belonging to the Counts of Tyrol to pass into Habsburg hands, and gave the region its name. Across the valley, the villages of Vöran / Verano and Mölten / Meltina lie on the slopes of Tschöggelberg. The lanes which spread from them afford views of the Adige.

Schloss Warth at Eppan in Der Süden Südtirols

Eisacktal / Valle Isarco

The Eisacktal / Valle Isarco area encompasses the Wipptal valley with the River Eisack / Isarco flowing at its base and is the traditional trade link between north and south Tirol. Today the Brenner motorway runs along it but walkers may still find seclusion in the many smaller valleys, such as Villnösstal where the Adolf Munkel Path passes the Geisler peaks and the Puez-Geisler Nature Reserve. Upper Wipptal has several peaks exceeding 3,000m and mountain refuges to provide shelter on longer treks, including the Landshuter-Hütte, which straddles the border at 2,693m.

Possibly the best time to walk in this region is autumn, because this is the season of *Törggelen* which involves wandering between villages and farmhouses, calling in to sample their homemade produce. Typically on offer for the hungry walker are *Kasnocken*, *Hauswurst* and *Susser* – cheese dumplings, sausages and new wine.

Pustertal / Val Pusteria

Pustertal / Val Pusteria in the eastern corner of the province harbours contrasting faces of green valleys and bare peaks. The landscape is formed mainly of glaciated primitive rock, with offshoot pockets of dolomite from the main range in the south. It is ideal for walkers who enjoy hiking at altitude, as it is woven with alpine paths and refuges. The most well-known peaks are the Three Turrets, a group of craggy mountains which are popular with climbers. A walk from the Zsigmondy to the Drei Zinnen refuge leads past them. For greener surrounds, walkers can follow the route of the Pustertal ski marathon. Starting at Innichen / San Candido, which is also home of an annual snow sculpturing competition, the course finishes near Olang / Valdaora. An optional extension carries on to Antholz / Anterselva.

The Three Turrets at Pustertal / Val Pusteria

The Dolomites

The Dolomite mountain range provokes images of ragged pearl mountain peaks and intrepid mountaineers. However, the south-eastern corner of the province, which these mountains fringe, also has interesting valleys. Badia, Fassa and Val Gardena are home to the remaining Ladin-speaking communities, preserving not just their language but also their cuisine, dress, housing and legends.

Because of the popularity of the Dolomites as a holiday destination, the facilities for walking are excellent. The peaks themselves are covered in a network of paths, making most areas within them accessible. Alternatively, satisfying hiking is to be had in the Seiser Alm / Alpe di Siusi, a high alpine pastureland extending for 60km in the midst of the mountains, which in summer is speckled with alpine flowers. Paths are well-mapped and signed, making walking possible all year, with many of the refuges remaining open in winter. In summer,

programmes are run for children, enabling them to enjoy excursions in the company of other children and freeing parents to tackle more challenging routes. Alpine guides can be hired to lead hikes which visitors might not wish to tackle alone.

Easier routes include following the redundant Val Gardena railway. Val Gardena is one of the more secluded northern Dolomite valleys, ringed by the peaks of Langkofel, Seceda and Sella. Its railway was built in the First World War to carry supplies but saw more service carrying mountaineers and tourists until 1960. The track runs midway up the mountain slopes, with short tunnels and viaducts, and can be walked all year round.

Vinschgau / Val Venosta

Covering the west of the province, Vinschgau / Val Venosta boasts both high mountains and good weather. With an average of 300 sunny days a year and a higher than usual snow line, the area is ideal for farming apricots and apples. The converse lack

of rain has been been catered for by a network of irrigation channels. These *waale* now form walking routes, with paths following their passage from the mountains to the fields.

The Südtirol / Bolzano section of the Stelvio National Park falls here. It contains the highest peaks in the area in the Ortlergruppe / Ortles-Cevedale mountains, with Ortler the crown at 3,905m. The park contains typical alpine animals, as well as the rarer wood grouse and grey woodpecker. Another animal which visitors may be surprised to meet when walking is the yak: introduced by the mountaineer Reinhold Messner, they have found their new habitat at Sulden / Solda a fine substitute for the Himalayas.

[i] CONTACT INFORMATION

**Südtirol Tourist
Information Service**
Pfarrplatz 11
I-39100 Bozen
Italy
Tel: (00 39) 0471 993808
Fax: (00 39) 0471 993899

ITALY

Walking in the Southern Dolomites

*In the far north-eastern corner of Italy, eagles sweep and soar over the
dramatically carved pinnacles of the Dolomites and the protected
landscape of Dolomiti Bellunesi National Park.*

Bordering the Alps, between the
towns of Trento, Bolzano (Bolzen)
and Cortina d'Ampezzo, and the
Adige and Piave rivers, the distinctive
outline of the Dolomite mountain
range dominates the skyline. Coral
beds forced up from the sea floor over
60 million years ago have since been
shaped into unusual jagged spires by
wind, snow and sun. Fabled amongst
intrepid rock climbers, the sheer
calcite cliff-faces provide a legendary
challenge, whilst hikers and walkers
also enjoy the many walks and trails
of the lower hills and valleys.

Dolomiti Bellunesi

Located along the south-eastern
edges of the Dolomites, the Dolomiti
Bellunesi National Park was formally
established in 1993 and extends over
320 sq km. Its various environments
characterise the park: glassy lakes
reflect mountains, gorges and ravines
which are the source of the many
rivers that flow across the terrain;
wooded evergreen slopes and
deciduous forests contrast with green
pastures swathed in wildflowers in
spring and summer.

One of the main scientific reasons for
the establishment of the park was its
wealth of natural flora. In excess of
1,500 species are endemic to the
region, with specimens such as the
park's symbol, the pretty bell-like
Campanula morettiana, and *Primula
tyrolensis* found in abundance.

The Vette Feltrine

Free from cable-cars and ski resorts,
Dolomiti Bellunesi provides a haven
for walkers. Many of the higher
mountains are inaccessible, whilst
medium and high altitude zones are
scarcely populated. This has meant
that the natural environment has
been preserved for indigenous wildlife.
There are numerous areas where
certain species thrive. For example the
south-west has been famous for its
flora since the 18th century, and the
spectacular Val Falcina in the centre
of the park is particularly favoured as
a hunting ground by birds of prey.

Walking routes

Although there are other Dolomite
mountains taller than those that fall
within the confines of the national
park, Dolomiti Bellunesi's peaks are
still impressive, with La Schiara in
the east, and some of those in the
Cimonega range in the west, reaching
over 2,500m. Interesting geological
formations include karst landscapes
of underground holes and caverns –
some over 900m deep – that are
characteristic of the Piani Eterni
(Eternal plains) plateau. Glacial
features such as scree slopes, cirques
and, in particular, the glacial *buses* –

dark navel-like holes set into the hills
and mountainsides – are evident
around the pyramidal form of
Mt Pavione (2,335m), part of the
Vette Feltrine range in the park's
south-western corner. This area was
least affected by the last period of
glaciation, resulting in a rich
concentration of interesting flora.

The Vette and Mt Pavione

Beginning outside the park, moving
west to east, the Col dei Mich, Croce
d'Aune and the Val de San Martino
are the points where most trails to
Mt Vallazza (2,167m), Mt Pavione
and the Vette Feltrine begin. Steep
paths and ancient mule tracks wind

Sempervium dolomiticum

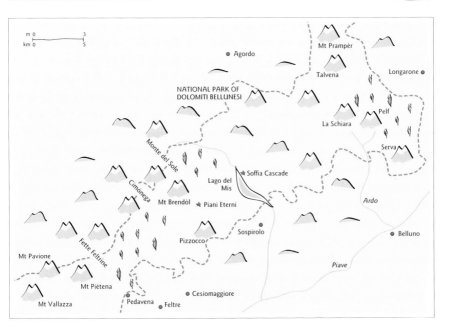

around terraced cultivated plots and wooded areas in the lower zones, with interesting rock formations and a variation in vegetation appearing at higher levels. The Dal Piaz refuge is the base for any excursions into the range, with spectacular scenery along the trails and around the numerous buses. From the village of Aune, the climb up to the Busa de Monsampian is particularly rewarding.

Lower walks suitable for families and children can be found along the Pian d'Avena, between Pedavena and Croce d'Aune. Here there are designated picnic sites as well as a CFS station (official national park wardens), and picturesque villages with disused limekilns and numerous traditional *casere* (cheesemaking huts) scattered throughout.

Also suitable for family expeditions in the spring and summer is the Val de San Martino. Defined by the Stien torrent which rises in the Vette mountains, the path through the lower reaches of the valley passes through a large beech forest and fields of wildflowers. It reaches a fork at over 800m and splits into higher, more difficult routes to Mt Piètena (2,194m) and Mt Ramezza (2,250m).

Monte Pizzon

Lago del Mis

One of the main entrances to the park from the towns of Belluno and Bolzano, the Valle dell'Ardo is as yet quite undeveloped. Walks along the Ardo ravine lead to Refuge 7° Alpini in the hollow of Pis Pilon, and further on to the summits of La Schiara (2,565m) and Pelf (2,502m).

From Sospirolo, steep unmarked paths lead northwards towards Lago del Mis, a vast glassy sheet lying in the southern shadow of Monti del Sole – a stunning landscape of water, land and sky with the Soffia cascade at its northern end. Located in the heart of the park, this man-made lake is surrounded by towering peaks riven with numerous lateral river valleys.

Eagles, falcons and other birds of prey particularly favour the isolated ranges from the Val de Canzoi, through the Piani Eterni (located between Mt Pizzocco, 2,186m, and Mt Brendòl, 2,160m) as far as the jagged summits of Val Falcina and Valle del Mis. Craggy and difficult to access, trails and facilities for walking and hiking are being developed by the local tourist board, which hopefully will not jeopardise the environmental importance of this area.

ⓘ CONTACT INFORMATION

Dolomiti Bellunesi National Park
P.le Zancanaro, 1
32032 Feltre (BL)
Italy
Tel: (00 39) 0439 3328
Fax: (00 39) 0439 332999
E-mail: ente@dolomitipark.it
Web: www.dolomitipark.it

Walking in Val Grande National Park

*Untamed and in places desolate, the Val Grande National Park is
ideal for walkers who enjoy the raw, wild side of nature.*

Located at the top of the Piemonte
region in northern Italy, the Val
Grande National Park covers an area
of 130 sq km. Centred around the
two alpine valleys of Val Pogallo and
Val Grande, the park is surrounded by
mountains. In summer the peaks of
the Pedum range form a harsh dark
barrier to the north, whereas in
winter they are completely blanketed
in snow. Although flanked in the east
by busy Lake Maggiore and in the
west by the Val d'Ossola, a popular
base for walkers, unlike its neighbours
Val Grande remains a wild place.

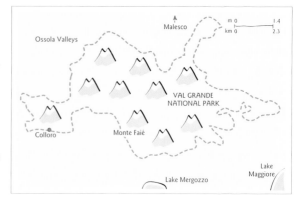

Rough paths, dense vegetation, and
steep and sudden drops mean that
care needs to be exercised. In wet
weather the park can truly become
hazardous, with the southern area in
particular prone to heavy rainfall,
flooding and landslides. However,
standard precautions enable the park
to be enjoyed in any season.

Wilderness regained

The rugged expanse which forms Val
Grande National Park is 'new' in more
than one sense. Formed in 1992, the
park did not become operative until
1994. Many of the plans which the

park board has for Val Grande are yet
to be started. Rebuilding, clearing and
stabilising paths is a priority. More
ambitious plans include visitor and
environmental education centres, and
museums at eleven different locations
around the park.

The park has not always been a
wilderness. Until the middle of the
20th century, the area was home to
several alpine communities living from
agriculture and forestry. For a variety
of reasons, including poverty and war,
the inhabitants eventually abandoned
their homes and nature reclaimed the
land for itself. The encroachment has
been rapid, but this part of the park's
history is still evident in the pastures,
cottages and lime kilns scattered
throughout.

History is also present in the surviving
paths, which were mainly formed by
the people who lived here as they
went about their work. Many of these
are now impassable as nettle, scrub
and wild raspberry bushes have taken
over. Whilst walkers will benefit when
the work is finished and the area can
be fully accessed, there is a certain
charm to be enjoyed in the sense of
ruggedness and abandonment which
the park now holds. For those who
prefer some guidance, many of the
main routes within the park have
been kept open and are well used.

Climbers on Torrione in the park

For those who want a challenge, the other historic routes can still be tackled with a bit of initiative. Alternatively, qualified alpine guides lead walks within the park.

Refuges

Unfortunately there is minimal refuge accommodation available within the park. Many refuges were built in the area by the Italian Alpine Club in the 1880s but most of these were destroyed in the war and have not been restored. Those that have are spartan, with a limited number of beds, although they are well-placed for the longest routes and can be booked in advance. There are plans to renovate more, but in the meantime there are many abandoned dwellings which can serve as emergency shelters.

Monte Faié

A good introductory route to the park, or one for those who are short on time, leads to the top of Monte Faié on the park's southern boundary. With an altitude of only 1,352m and a gradual ascent, the summit is accessible all year round. The view is an unhindered sweep of the park, including the Val Grande valley, Pedum peaks and Lake Mergozzo.

Abandoned stone cottages at Alpe Qua Givi

Rio Fiorina

Premosello traverse

An interesting hike for visitors with more time is the route that crosses the reserve from Colloro, above Premosello in the west, to Malesco in the north-east. Completed over two days, the path gives a taste of all the park's areas: alpine pastures, woodlands, mountain ridges, lakes, waterfalls and streams. The halfway point is Alpe In La Piana, a stunning spot in the heart of the park, with shelter and space to camp.

In places, the route passes crumbling stone cottages, overgrown wells and meadows – remains of the alpine communities. In others, the paved mule tracks which the farmers once used form the path. Now visitors are more likely to encounter wildlife – badgers, hedgehogs, dormice, chamois and roe deer – than the few humans who still live within Val Grande.

Further afield

There is a sufficient variety of both walks and environments within Val Grande to fill a holiday and the park's information and three visitor centres can provide details on suggested itineraries, as well as maps. For those wishing to roam, the Val d'Ossola is another Piemontese walking mecca.

As a tourism centre, the Val d'Ossola and its subsidiaries have clearly marked paths. The environment is also softer, with a wealth of greenery interspersed in summer with fragile orchids. The highest waterfall in Europe, the Toce, runs here. Part of a hydroelectric scheme, it can be completely turned off if necessary. There are more stunning falls in dell'Alpe Veglia e dell'Alpe Devero, the region's prized nature park. Situated on a high plateau, the falls can be reached by cable-car, if the mule track ascent is too daunting.

Val d'Ossola's cuisine is focused on pasta and meat. Raw beef is popular, as thin carpaccio or marinated, as is goat and pork. These dishes, accompanied by the local wine, will provide all the energy a walker needs.

i CONTACT INFORMATION

Val Grande National Park
Villa San Remigio - 28048
Verbania Pallanza (V.C.O.)
Italy
Tel: (00 39) 0323 557960
Fax: (00 39) 0323 556397
Web: www.comunic.it/parks.htlm

Verbania Tourist Information
Corso Zanitello, 8
I-28048 Verbania
Italy
Tel: (00 39) 0323 503249

Walking and Hiking in Liechtenstein

Despite its diminutive size, walkers are never short of routes to choose from in Liechtenstein, whether it be gentle lowland paths or more demanding Alpine hikes.

Schloss Vaduz

Walking weather

Liechtenstein endures the warm, wet summers typical of a mild climate. The autumn too is a temperate time, with the weather softened by the warm *föhn* wind. Autumn is an especially pleasant time of year for walking in the valleys, with the colours on the trees glowing and mellowing. For most of the year, Liechtenstein's climate is sufficiently balanced to yield a fine grape harvest. There is enough rain, sufficient hours of sunlight and suitably calciferous soils to bear a good ripe crop.

Life in the tiny nation state of Liechtenstein, wedged in between Austria and Switzerland, moves at two distinctly different paces. On the one hand it races ahead of most of the rest of the world in its economic expansion. On the other it travels at a pace more akin to the trails that lace the landscape, mulling over and savouring the lowland and highland finery that is well looked after within its borders.

In the Alps, the resorts of Malbun and Steg have seized upon the snow that settles during the colder months, and have become centres for skiing and other winter pursuits. Between three and six feet of powdery snow cover the mountains from December

The resort of Steg

through to March. Making the most of this, the tourist authorities maintain toboggan runs, winter walking paths and skating rinks. In the summer months the same trails, climbs and passes that are skied, scaled and sledded, become rambling routes.

A chance of medals

The hard work of local communities and of the Liechtenstein Alpine Association (LAA) ensures that hiking has a high profile. The recommended routes and the maintained footpaths range from flat tracks along the banks of the Rhine and easy strolls by the northern agricultural towns of Bendern and Ruggell, through to marked hikes up to Malbun. There are around 160km of waymarked trails in alpine Liechtenstein and 240km crossing the valleys. The tourist board and the LAA have gone so far as to reward walkers with bronze, silver or gold pins as they clock up miles on the principality's paths.

forests in the north. Climbing up out of the towns of Triesen and Vaduz are marked ways along the Fläscherberg and the Panoramaweg, both of which are spectacular trips.

Liechtenstein also boasts hiking courses that will challenge the most hardy of alpine walkers. In the highlands, paths lead up to and over Liechtenstein's big names: the Schönberg and the Galinakopf. The Augstenberg Walk, which takes in the Stüba waterfall, manages to combine a strenuous, exposed alpine trek with a well-marked route through a wild landscape peppered with rare orchids.

The Fürstensteig Walk is, again, well maintained, journeying through narrow gorges and steep passes. It travels over the high ridge between the valleys of the Rhine and the Samina. The difficult ascent is rewarded by breathtaking views over the peaks of Garsellikopf and Drei Schwestern.

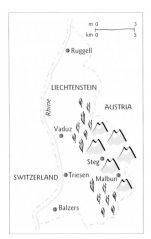

striking outlook onto the lowlands of Liechtenstein running down to the Rhine, and out to the Swiss high country. Excursions to the treasures of the Swiss Alps – Lake Constance, the Walensee, and the cantons of St Gallen and Graubünden – as well as to Vorarlberg in Austria, are popular.

Triesen

Close by the capital city of Vaduz, neighbouring Triesen is an ideal walking base. The town provides access to the lowlands that run down to the banks of the Rhine, as well as to the remoter valleys and the steep trails that lead up the mountainsides.

Many of the country's most attractive nooks are within striking distance of historical Triesen – the ragged gorge up towards the Lawena ravine, the Falknis cliffs, and the pinnacles of the Koraspitz and the Mittagspitz. The size of Liechtenstein and the neat organisation of the walking circuit allow for a flexibility and a freedom that the landscape and the exposure of some of the larger-scale alpine locations rule out.

Climbing Augstenberg (2.359m)

Celebrated routes

Liechtenstein's low country is charted with a good number of walks and nature trails that lead through the woodland and around some of the country's key historic and prehistoric sites. Visitors can walk upon ancient courses and old pilgrims' paths, such as the Wallfahrtsroute and the Salzstrasse. Alternatively, tracks can be taken through the thick fir

Across the border

Liechtenstein's compact size and the location of its towns and resorts encourages border hikes, such as those along ancient smugglers' trails into Austria. These are an opportunity for visitors to step away from the busy Swiss and Austrian resorts, whilst providing a perfect vantage point to look back across to their landscapes. Planken, for example, presents a

ℹ CONTACT INFORMATION

Liechtenstein Tourism
Postfach 139
FL-9490 Vaduz
Lichtenstein
Tel: (00 423) 232 1443
Fax: (00 423) 392 1618
E-mail: touristinfo@lie-net.li

The Deutsche Alpenstrasse

The Deutsche Alpenstrasse provides a tour of the mountains, lakes, traditional pathways and tangible local histories of the Bavarian Alps.

Even dipping into the lands of the Deutsche Alpenstrasse – the German Alpine Highway – there is a lot to absorb. In order to cover all or part of the 500km walking trail it is necessary to allow time for it all to soak in. The towns, monasteries and castles sometimes appear as ancient and otherworldly as the mountains and glacial lakes. Although the mundane business of tourism weighs heavily on some of the resorts, the depth and the dimension of the Bavarian Alps has a mythical quality that remains undiminished.

Bavaria's tradition

Bavaria is a land well acquainted with pilgrimage. Branching out from or crossing over the Alpenstrasse are various historical paths that bear witness to this. The Alpenstrasse itself is an agglomeration of long-established routes that pass through Germany's Alps: the Rossfeldstrasse, the Tatzelwurmstrasse, the Achenpass and the Kehlsteinstrasse.

Rowing on the Hintersee

Bavaria is also well known for the way its people hold on with particular determination to their traditions and heritage. Visitors are likely to see a surprising amount of traditional dress, and will be able to enjoy a folk culture of festivals and processions that remains an animated part of local life.

Walking the Alpenstrasse

The Deutsche Alpenstrasse has been developed and polished since 1933. Starting near Lake Constance the path moves through the Allgäu Alps, up across the Bavarian Alps and onto Berchtesgaden. Although there are countless detours and diversions that allow adventurous walkers to head for high country, the central path of the Alpenstrasse remains at a fairly tolerable incline all along its length.

Bavaria is characterised by its alpine conditions, its mountain lakes, crude peaks and high meadows. Nevertheless, in the summer months it is temperate, with plenty of sunshine. The landscape is dramatic and engaging, and walks look on to a kaleidoscope of chiselled mountain ranges, striking lakeland, and Baroque, Romantic and Gothic architecture.

The Allgäu Alps

Anticipating the drama and the diversity of the high peaks to come, the Allgäu Alps of the Alpine foreland are an attractive diversion. They are home to a number of the great lakes of Bavaria, whilst the many walking trails take in meadows and woodland, moors and villages, and ridges and crests. Along the bottom of the Allgäu Alps lie the remains of Stone Age settlements, revealed by recent archaeological finds. Wangen im Allgäu also provides an insight into times past, as the entire old town, which is a protected national monument, stands largely intact.

Garmisch-Partenkirchen

Looking up to Germany's highest mountain, the Zugspitze, the town of Garmisch-Partenkirchen is a busy tourist resort and a focal point for competitive and recreational winter sports. The town has recently been building on the celebrity that came from its hosting the 1936 Winter Olympic Games and the International

The view from Lockstein across to Berchtesgaden

Alpine Skiing Championship in 1978. The mountains rise up to encompass the town, and cable-cars travel up to the Hausberghöhe, Osterfelderkopf and Hochalm. Beginning in Garmisch-Partenkirchen, a mountain railway takes visitors up towards the top of the Zugspitze. A cable-car scales the final section, terminating at the eastern summit which is topped with a precarious, gilded iron cross. Other cable-cars ascend from Eibsee and from the Tirol region in Austria.

The towns around the Zugspitze lay unofficial claim to being home of the first conquerors of the great mountain: two surveyors were known to have climbed the mountain in 1820 and registered the feat, but received wisdom has it that it was local people that first made it to the top. The Zugspitze represents a pinnacle of the Bavarian Alps' tourist attractions, and the views from the peak, a breathtaking panorama that takes in the breadth of the Central Alps, should be seen.

St Bartolomä on the Königsee

Ettal

In the high valley of Ammergebirge, at an altitude that befits a winter sports resort, the town of Ettal is laden with vivid history. Its ancient Benedictine monastery stands contentedly still, the monks distilling *Ettaler Klosterlikör*, their delicious herb liquor. Ettal is also home to one of the idiosyncratic residences of King Lugwig II. Schloss Linderhof is one of the less extravagant examples, a more subdued private residence than the towering, tottering castle of Neuschwanstein. Having said that, the reception rooms of the building still manage to incorporate gilded carvings, stucco ornamentation and flowing ermine curtains that frame an ostentatious throne, and the grounds accommodate a Wagnerian grotto complete with illuminated lake.

Oberammergau

In Oberammergau, visitors have to be willing to look past the tourist throngs to see the vibrant and enduring cultural heritage. Since a plague retreated from the town in 1633 its inhabitants have assembled every ten years to enact a Passion Play. The impact of what might have slipped into complacent ritual is considerable. Nowadays a cast of some 1,400 people are involved in fulfilling the long-standing obligation.

Off the back of the hospitality and the traditional heritage that the town has to offer, there is good access to the nearby valleys and mountains for walks of all types, be they short strolls or more involved hikes. Guided walks are also regularly organised.

Berchtesgaden

The Deutsche Alpenstrasse ends in Berchtesgaden – the most popular part of the Bavarian Alps, full of spectacular landscapes and varied walking. Both the landscape and the tourist authorities cater for those experienced in outdoor activities as well as those new to hiking. Demanding trails are well signposted and lead up mountains and through canyons. Alternatively, nature ways and accessible footpaths, such as one near the Königsee, are usually no more than a stroll.

ⓘ CONTACT INFORMATION

Oberammergau Tourist Office
Eugen-Papst-Strasse 9A
82487 Oberammergau
Germany
Tel: (00 49) 8822 1021

Berchtesgaden National Park
National Park House
Franziskanerplatz 7
83471 Berchtesgaden
Germany
Tel: (00 49) 8652 64343
Fax: (00 49) 8652 69434
Web: www.nationalpark-berchtesgaden.de/

The Austrian Tirol

*Regional variation and specialist facilities add interest to
the dramatic Alpine walking routes of the Austrian Tirol.*

The Tirol forms the western arm of
Austria, stretching between Germany
and Italy towards Switzerland. Two
sets of Alps run west to east through
the region; the Northern Limestone
Alps which follow the border with
Germany, and the High or Central
Alps in the south. The two ranges are
separated by the Inn river which is
punctuated half way along by
Innsbruck, the provincial capital.
The Tirol's current boundaries are the
result of the Treaty of St Germain
which, after the Second World War,
saw South Tirol becoming part of Italy.
The Austrian Tirol now consists of the
main Tirol province and a second area
known as Östtirol to the south-east.

Outdoor attractions

Tourism is the backbone industry
of the Tirol. The province receives
substantially more visitors than any
other area of Austria – over twice as
many as neighbouring Salzburgerland,
the next most popular region – and it
is unsurprising that the mountains are
the magnet.

Most of the peaks in the Central Alps
are over 3,000m and the majority of
them are glaciated. In winter, the
main activities are snowboarding and
skiing, a focus which, for some
visitors, persists into the summer as
they venture to extreme heights for
glacial skiing. In summer the Tirol is
transformed. Not only is it quieter but
the verdure of the flora – dense green
fields and jewel-hued wildflowers – is
all the more stunning when compared
with the ice-white blanket which
covers it for much of the year.

Walking

The Austrian Tirol is divided into
five regions: in the west, remote
Ausserfern and below it the Oberland
with the frozen expanse of the
Ötztaler Alps; in the centre, historic
Innsbruck and its surrounds; and in
the east, the Unterland and the
separate Tirolean enclave of Östtirol.
To an extent these regions vary,
giving walkers an opportunity to
choose the flavour of excursions.
For wildlife, Östtirol with its portion
of the Hohe Tauern National Park is
best; for culture, Innsbruck has the
greatest variety; for Bavarian influence,
Ausserfern; for glaciers, the Oberland.

Whichever area is chosen, all have
well-marked trails with opportunities
both for low-level river, forest and
valley walks or for high-altitude
options. Even among the alpine trails
there is variation. A walk in the
rugged Zillertal in the Central Alps
will differ both in scenery and
difficulty from one in the limestone
mountains of the Ausserfern.

Another interesting type of route offered in the Tirol is the *Tiroler Ausstellungsstrassen*, or exhibition trails. Trails focus on periods of art and architecture – Baroque, Rococo and Gothic – and lead visitors between pieces held in varied settings within the province. Brochures describe the items, their location and the 'art walks' which connect them.

A further exhibition trail focuses upon Maximilian I, a member of the powerful Habsburg dynasty, who ruled as Holy Roman Emperor from 1493 to 1519. Maximilian was fond of Innsbruck and used it as his base from which to pursue policies of western expansionism. He spent much time and money beautifying the city with buildings and art patronage. Highlights of Maxmilian's exhibition trail include his Renaissance sarcophagus in the Imperial church, and the Golden Roof tower. Made from thousands of gilded copper tiles, the Golden Roof was built as a symbol of Maximilian's power and now houses a museum with exhibits from his reign.

Specialities

The Tirol offers the usual services of mountain guides and schools common within the Alpine regions. In addition it offers fixed-rope climbs. Also known as *vie ferrate*, or iron routes, fixed-rope climbs are challenging mountain routes which have been made more accessible by affixing ladders, ropes and permanent belays. They are graded from 'easy', which are accessible to hikers of moderate fitness, to 'very difficult' for experienced mountaineers only. The abundance of fixed-rope routes within Tirol may be a legacy from one of its more famous 19th century climbers, Hermann von Barth. He proclaimed that 'none of the huge mountains will remain untouched by my irons', and proceeded in one summer to climb eighty eight of the mountains in the Karwendel range which rises behind Innsbruck. It was following this, at the end of the 19th century, that development of the vie ferrate began.

Maximilian's Golden Roof, Innsbruck

Zillertaler Alps

The Zillertaler Alps are part of the Central Alps and lie in the south of the Unterland, along the Italian border. The Ziller river valley which runs from the base of the Zillertaler Alps to Jenbach is one of the most populated and popular areas in the Unterland. This is due to the picture-book scenery – alpine meadows and cows, sparkling rivers, traditional villages – but for walkers it also has the Zillertaler Höhestrasse. Like the Alpine Pass route in Switzerland this is a 'classic' alpine walk, but unlike its neighbour it is made up of a series of trails within one region which can be completed as day walks.

A good base for excursions is the striking upper Zemmgrund valley which extends into the heart of the Zillertal. Zsigmondy Spitze (3,089m) is an accessible peak from the valley but its exposed ridge requires climbing and scrambling experience. An easier summit is Schönbichler Horn, whose 3,133m top can be reached in three to four hours from the valley along a sheltered path. Further into the Zillertaler Alps, Schwarzenstein (3,368m) and Grosser Möseler (3,478m) offer a series of glacier crossings, as they lead southwards to Hochfeller which at 3,509m is the group's tallest peak.

Ausserfern

The Ausserfern region covers the north-west corner of the Tirol, following the diagonal slant of the Lechtal valley. Ausserfern means 'beyond the Fern', a reference to the Fern pass, whose use dates from Roman times. The Fern remains one of

the few means of gaining access to the region, which by Austrian standards is remote. The Lechtal valley lies between the parallel ranges of the Allgäuer and Lechtaler Alps, but their limestone composition means that the valley is softer and greener than those in the Central Alps. The Lech river, which runs along the valley from Vorarlberg in the west, is surrounded by broad water meadows.

Although few of the peaks of the Lechtaler Alps exceed 3,000m, a six day trek across the southern tail of the range enables visitors to enjoy walking in Alpine scenery as well through pastures and forests. The route starts in Pettneu and passes from hut to hut at altitudes around 2,000m before dropping over the range to end at Landeck in the Oberland. It has the benefit that walking times on several days are quite short and no specialist equipment or skills are required.

Cable-cars increase accessibility in places, and panoramas incorporate the four western ranges – Allgäu, Lechtal, Verwall and Samnaun.

In the north of Ausserfern, scenic day walks revolve around the alpine lakes. The smaller ones – Vilsalpsee and Haldensee – are ideal for summer swimming, while the larger Plansee has a steamer in summer and ice-skating in winter. From Reutte it is only 15km over the German border to Füssen, famous for the fairytale castle of Neuschwanstein. Built by King Ludwig II of Bavaria in the 19th century, the castle was immortalised by Walt Disney in the 20th.

Other possibilities for walking in Ausserfern are provided by the E5 European Long Distance and the 01 Central Alpine trails. In the Tirol the E5 traverses both the Allgäuer and Lechtaler Alps before heading south over the Ötztaler Alps to Italy. In Ausserfern the 01 follows the Lechtaler Alps from north to south before passing into Vorarlberg where it ends at the Swiss border.

 **CONTACT INFORMATION**

Tirol Information
Maria-Theresien-Strasse 55
A-6010 Innsbruck
Austria
Tel: (00 43) 512 7272
Fax: (00 43) 512 72727
E-mail: tirol.info@tirolwerbung.at
Web: www.tiscover.com/tyrol

AUSTRIA

Walking in Carinthia

Three main Alpine ranges, two national parks, over 1,000 lakes and plenty of sunshine ensure pleasurable and varied walking in the south of Austria.

It is common for the land-locked countries of central Europe to claim that their southern regions have a Mediterranean feel. Austria is no exception and Carinthia, or Kärnten as it is alternatively known, is promoted as the country's sunniest province. It is true that Carinthia's summers can be very hot and the constant presence of water from the province's 1,270 lakes, combined with the plazas, Renaissance courtyards and patrician villas of its capital Klagenfurt, add to the illusion of being in more southern climes.

Alpine environment

Despite its claims, Carinthia remains an Alpine region. In addition to the Central Alps, the province is home to the crystalline Nockberge range and the dramatic limestone peaks of the Karawanken and Carnic Alps. Unlike the rest of Austria however, it is the lakes and not the Alps which are the tourism draw-card, making summer Carinthia's busiest season. Lake Wörthersee near Klagenfurt is particularly popular as its waters are heated by natural thermal springs. In summer the lake maintains an average temperature of 21°C.

However, the environment is causing concerns in Carinthia and The World Wide Fund for Nature has identified both of the province's national parks as vulnerable to adverse effects from climate change. Warmer temperatures

The Nockberge National Park

will force species from the alpine zones to move higher, leading to crowded habitats and potential extinction. A pilot scheme in the Nockberge has introduced *Tälerbusse*, or 'valley buses' as an intermediate step to banning private transport. The buses aim to access every destination worth visiting and timetables cater for walkers wishing to hike between valleys.

The Nockberge

The Nockberge area lies in the north of Carinthia and is popular with walkers. Its name derives from *Nocken*, the Austrian name for dumplings, and is a reference to the shape of its mountains, which are

gently rounded. The Nockberge range is relatively low by Austrian standards with average heights of around 2,200m, although the proximity of the Central Alps ensures that the scenery is still truly alpine.

The 34km Nockalm Trail leads along the Schiestlscharte and Eisentalhöhe ridges, and offers some of the region's best views of summits, forests and corrie lakes. Other walks include a forest path around the Grundalm reservoir, cultural routes through villages, and family nature trails. The gem of the region is the Nockberge National Park, which covers 186 sq km, all at altitudes over 1,300m. Sixty six species of bird breed within the park, including the dotterel, with its distinctive stop-start run.

The Carnic Alps

The Carnic Alps are part of the Southern Limestone Alps and cover Carinthia's border with Italy. These Alps were formed millions of years ago when the floor of a shallow sea was pushed upwards as the African continent encroached northwards. More recent trauma was suffered here during the First World War, when the Alps formed the front line between Austria and Italy.

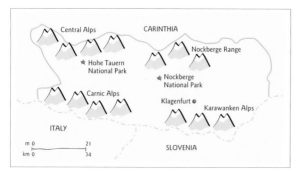

164

These events now form the basis for walking trails. The Geo Trail covers 20km in five sections, giving walkers the opportunity to see fossilised seashells at 2,000m and providing information on the geological history of the Alps. The Carnic Summit Trail leads along the Austrian–Italian border, once the scene of prolonged and bitter fighting but now part of the Friedensweg, or Path of Peace. The path was developed in the 1980s and stretches for hundreds of kilometres along the border and down into Italy.

The Hohe Tauern

Carinthia's second national park, the Hohe Tauern, is situated in the Central Alps, and is shared between Carinthia, Salzburgerland and Tirol. The park provides numerous hiking options and within Carinthia alone there are around thirty specific trails which are detailed in a national park brochure. This does not take into account the multitude of general trails and the routes which fall within the Salzburgerland and Tirol portions but are accessible from paths in Carinthia.

Also of particular interest are the paths in the Tauern valley which follow historical Roman routes. Carinthia came under Roman rule for nearly 500 years from 15 BC as part of the province of Noricum.

The Austrian Central Alps formed a natural boundary for the Romans between their older, southern dominions and their newer ones in the north. The Romans were nervous of the Alps, and myths of monsters abounded. However, passage over them was crucial to trade – spices, silks, glass and wine to the north, and furs, salt and iron to the south.

One of the main pass routes in Carinthia was via the Hohe Tauern pass at the head of the Tauern valley. The use of pack-animals continued into the 16th century, but because of their distrust of the Alps few Roman settlements were established. Instead rest stops sprang up along the routes providing food and shelter to the traders and their surefooted horses.

In the Tauern valley walkers can follow the Römerstrasse, or Roman road, up to the 2,460m pass, visiting en route the historic stone-built Niederer rest house. Paths take in spruce, larch and Arolla pine forest, before climbing past tranquil Kleiner Tauernsee lake at 2,289m, shortly before the pass.

The route creates an impression of the difficulties faced by the merchants, especially as business did not halt with the winter storms. The hardest work fell to the pack-horses, of which the most common breed was the Haflinger. Originally from South Tirol, these sturdy horses are now bred in the park, although they are now only used for trekking excursions.

ℹ CONTACT INFORMATION

Carinthia Tourist Information
Casinoplatz 1
A-9220 Velden
Austria
Tel: (00 43) 4274 52100
Fax: (00 43) 4274 521 0050
E-mail: hotline@carinthia.com
Web: www.tiscover.com/carinthia

Nockberge National Park Information
Nationalparkverwaltung Kärnten
Zweigstelle Nockberge
Austria
Tel: (00 43) 4275 665
Fax: (00 43) 4275 789
E-mail: nationalpark.NO@net4you.co.at

Lake Weissensee

The Arnoweg

*Fortresses, cathedrals, mountains, gorges, mines, caves, bone forges –
the Arnoweg links the historical and natural highlights of
the Salzburgerland.*

In AD 798 the Pope, acting on the instructions of the Holy Roman Emperor Charlemagne, made St Arno the first archbishop of Salzburg. In 1998, to celebrate 1,200 years of the Salzburg archbishopric, the Arnoweg was created. The route covers a corresponding 1,200km within the Salzburgerland province in west Austria. In most places the Arnoweg uses established walking trails, linking them to create a circuitous route roughly following the province's borders.

```
m 0              14
km 0             23

              ARNOWEG

Salzburg
              Fuschlsee

         Hallein

                 SALZBURGERLAND

    St Martin

         Werfen

       Radstadt

   Salzach

Gastein Valley
    ★ Rauris Valley
```

Archbishopric

In the 7th century AD St Rupert made Salzburg the headquarters for his missionary activities and founded a monastic order. His work was continued by his successor, St Virgil, who built the first cathedral. St Arno succeeded Virgil in 785 and with his elevation in 798 gained jurisdiction over the Bavarian dioceses. St Arno and his successors had the powers of secular princes and were zealous in their duties, extending the dominions under their rule and beautifying the city. Their wealth and influence were such that they were able to remain an archiepiscopal principality, despite the proximity of the powerful Habsburgs, until the end of the Holy Roman Empire in the 19th century. Salzburg was given to Austria in 1816, becoming a province with its own government in 1850.

Salzburg

Today, the beautiful architecture and gardens which the archbishops bestowed on Salzburg make it a popular city with tourists. It is also the birthplace of Mozart. From 1771 the famous composer served as the concertmaster for the last archbishop, Hieronymus Graf von Colloredo, an experience he found stultifying.

The font where Mozart was baptised is now in Salzburg's cathedral and, although there is no official start to the Arnoweg, this majestic building seems an appropriate place. The original cathedral built by St Virgil was destroyed by fire in 1167. The current Baroque cathedral was consecrated in 1628 and again in 1959 following restoration after bomb damage during the Second World War.

Hohensalzburg fortress, Salzburg

A path at the base of the Hochkoenig diverts the Arnoweg to Werfen

Also of interest is the Hohensalzburg fortress, the seat of the archbishop princes. Built in 1077 by Archbishop Gebhard, the fortress sits above the city and is the largest preserved fortress from the Middle Ages in central Europe. Its reputation of impregnability made it a bastion for the archbishops and it was never conquered, although on one occasion Markus Sittikus used it to imprison his predecessor until the latter died and Sittikus became archbishop.

The Arnoweg

Heading north from Salzburg, the Arnoweg traces the upper tip of the province before returning south over the Osterhorn mountains. Then, in the east of Salzburgerland, the trail passes through a string of small resorts in the Salzkammergut region.

Despite their proximity to Salzburg, these villages take pride in promoting their traditional culture. Annual harvest festivals are held between August and October. Music, dancing, cider-roasts, farmers' markets and festival parades make the autumn an interesting time to complete this stage of the route. The Salzkammergut lakes are nearby and, as well as water sports and fishing, walkers can see the protected reedbed habitats.

Tauern

Further south, the route enters the mountainous Tauern region, popular in winter as a skiing area. Radstadt, in the Upper Enns valley, was the only town in the Tauern to belong to the Salzburg archbishopric.

In the 15th and 16th centuries the peasants of the Tauern valleys staged uprisings, protesting against taxes and religious restrictions. In the great revolt of 1525 they stormed Salzburg and in 1526 Radstadt was besieged. The uprisings were crushed but Protestantism prevailed in the Tauern until the 18th century when 22,000 peasants were forced to emigrate to solve the 'problem'.

Saalachtal

Walkers electing to head south from Salzburg will pass through the historic town of Hallein Bad Dürrnberg. Celtic peoples mined salt here from 600 BC and the town later gained prominence as a spa due to its therapeutic waters. Beyond Hallein the route branches and walkers can either continue down the Salzach valley or loop west to the Saalachtal. The latter is characterised by limestone geology, resulting in gorges, waterfalls, strange rock formations and caves. Lamprecht's

cave near St Martin runs for 35km, with paths enabling visitors to penetrate far into the mountain. Nearby in Weissbach, the Seisenberg gorge, which was created by the glaciers of the last Ice Age, is a natural monument and has also been opened to visitors.

Hohe Tauern

The southern part of the Arnoweg runs through the Hohe Tauern National Park, which covers many of the highest peaks of the eastern Alps, including Grossglockner (3,798m). In places the Arnoweg corresponds to the park's Haute Route, taking in passes and summits. It is the only part of the Arnoweg requiring mountain equipment and is potentially impassable in winter.

It is, however, the best section of the route for wildlife, with mountain hares, chamois, lynx, eagles, white-breasted dippers and alpine salamanders among the park's high altitude residents. Walkers who notice piles of bones beside the path will have discovered a vulture's 'bone forge'. Bearded vultures have been successfully reintroduced to the park and break large bones by taking them high into the air and dropping them onto rocks.

In the centre of the park, the path passes the Rauris and Gastein valleys, where in the 16th century more than 3,500 miners were employed extracting gold. It is estimated that about 10% of the world's gold reserves were extracted from here, and the wealth this generated is largely responsible for the power which the archbishops were able to wield. Within the Hohensalzburg fortress in Salzburg both the 'Prince's' and the 'Golden' room are decorated with the spoils of the mines.

ℹ CONTACT INFORMATION

Salzburg Region Tourist Bureau
Postfach 1
A-5300 Hallwang bei Salzburg
Austria
Tel: (00 43) 662 6688
Fax: (00 43) 662 668866
E-mail: info@szgtour.co.at
Web: www.salzburg.com/
salzburgerland

The Julian Alps

Slovenia's high-level hiking, captivating rambles and proud mountain traditions are revealed under the scrutiny of the attentive visitor.

In the middle of the 19th century, in the alpine town of Bled, a Swiss doctor named Arnold Rikli ran a climatic spa. He offered rejuvenation and an injection of health to his patients, prescribing an ascetic course of early mornings, cold showers, sunbathing and walks in the mountains. Nearly 150 years on, and somewhat less clinically, the Julian Alps continue to give visitors a jolt, with their great beauty and their knack of being unassumingly spectacular.

Walking in the mountains

The Julian Alps, largely harboured within the boundaries of Triglav National Park, have routes suitable for extended and demanding treks and climbing, as well as plenty of paths for easy tourism. It can pay to be cautious. The couloir by Mount Jalovec, the peak emblazoned on the Slovenian Alpine Federation's coat of arms, is sometimes cordoned off due to icy slopes and rockfalls. Similarly, the path which makes its way from Planica to Pokljuka is not for the faint hearted or those short of experience. It was mapped out by alpinists, for alpinists, and passes through some tough territory.

At the same time, there are many more accessible routes, such as the pass at Staniceva koca, and the paths leading to the Savica waterfall, where alertness is more about taking in the natural phenomena than personal safety. The ridge of Ticarica and Zelnarica, which rises up behind the Valley of Triglav Lakes, is more remote but is not necessarily just for experienced walkers.

A meeting place

Of all the alpine land that rises up in central Europe, it is the easternmost point, Slovenia's Julian Alps, that catches the first rays of sunshine in the morning. The Julian Alps, clustered in the north-west of the country, line up along the borders with Italy and Austria, and effectively form a juncture, not only between national boundaries, but also between the three European linguistic families: Slavic, Germanic and Romanic. The geography of the Julian Alps has a direct effect on walking conditions in the mountains. The high country provides the first variation to the benign Mediterranean conditions that come from the south. The peaks also form a rain barrier, encouraging the wet weather and lush landscapes that typify the region.

The Soča valley

The River Soča flows southwards out of the Slovenian highlands, and on its way it nourishes the alpine valleys. The Trenta valley and the Bovec basin derive their fertility from the river, and have long prospered agriculturally. Hiking trails, both those that benefit from the company of a guide and those that can be undertaken single-handedly, are plentiful. Particularly popular is the trail that leads through the upper valley to trace the source of the Soča. The size of the river and its bright blue-green waters attract international watersports competitors, and the kayaking and canoeing contests are frequent and frenzied. Much is also made of the fact that the Soča provides a particularly fresh and healthy source of water.

The Soča River

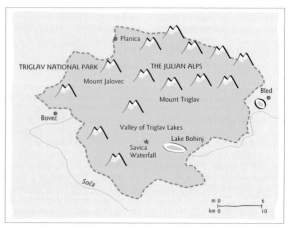

subsequent starvation of many locals. The exquisite Church of St John the Baptist at Ribčev Laz has stood since around the 15th century and has witnessed the Napoleonic Wars, two World Wars, earthquakes and famines.

Alpine traditions

The character of Slovenian alpinism is made of stern stuff, imbuing depth in the experience of walking in the Julian Alps. Historically, the people who have made the mountains accessible have been amateurs and enthusiasts. The first people to make tracks into the highlands were hunters, shepherds, prospectors looking for valuable ores, and herb collectors.

The democratic popularity of the mountains made it all the more difficult to accept the restrictions of German–Austrian control, when, at the end of the 19th century, Slovenians were forbidden to use German paths and huts. The Slovenian Mountaineering Society was at the vanguard of reclaiming the alpine heritage after the wars, and has handed on a legacy of waymarked hiking trails and mountain huts.

Alpine lakeland

The well-marked and comparatively level trails about Lake Bohinj provide another perspective on the way that water complements the mountains. Recommended routes lead walkers around the perimeter of the lake or to points of interest that lie in reach of its shores. In a striking landscape, Lake Bohinj still manages to stand out.

Elsewhere, and in contrast to the fertile areas of the Soča valley, the Valley of Triglav Lakes is noticeably barren. This eerie environment, incorporating a chain of diminished lakes, has taken on a unique role as a habitat for some of the country's more unusual plants and animals.

Hard times

In spite of a sunny aspect, a steady economy and a proud and jovial mountaineering culture, there is little evidence of Slovenia trying to airbrush its history. Along the walks in the Julian Alps there are many statuesque and well-maintained chapels, monuments and museums which concentrate on the losses and the tragedies that have taken place around the territory.

The Church of St Duh, settled on the shores of Lake Bohinj, is an attractive 16th century building, decorated outside with impressive frescoes. Its raison d'être is to commemorate a bad harvest in the Bohinj area and the

In 1895, desperate to hold on to right of way, pride, and to a corner of the mountains in spite of the advance of Austrian–German hegemony, a local priest named Jakob Aljaz bought the land atop Mount Triglav and built a little tower. His tower has since been donated to Slovenia's Mountaineering Society, and has become a symbol of nationhood, independence, and the country's love for its mountains.

ⓘ CONTACT INFORMATION

Slovenia Pursuits
New Barn Farm
Tadlow Road
Tadlow
Royston SG8 0EP
Tel: 01767 631144
Fax: 01767 631166
E-mail: angela.rennie@virgin.net

Slovenian Tourist Board
Dunajska 156
1000 Ljubljana
Slovenia
Tel: (00 386) 61 1891 840
Fax: (00 386) 61 1891 841
E-mail: lucka.letic@
cpts.tradepoint.si
Web: www.slovenia-tourism.si

Triglav National Park

The Postojna Basin and Cerknica

*The paths of the Postojna Basin lead away from busy tourist sites,
taking visitors over and under a complex natural environment.*

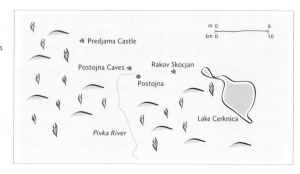

Whilst the province of Notranjska is not subjected to the kind of extremes that characterise Slovenia's high country, its landscapes and conditions are unique and emphatic. The heavy forestation of the countryside, the features of the karst landscape and the penetrating winds all add to the experience. Poljes, sinkholes, swallow holes, blind valleys, dry valleys, caves and abysses – visitors quickly become aware of the close relationship between features below the surface and features above it. As a result, it has recently been proposed that the area around Lake Cerknica, Planinsko polje, the Polojna Cave and Rakov Škocjan be linked, protected and presented as a regional park.

Limestone landscape

The karst landscape and natural phenomena of Slovenia are definitive. Laid out in between Trieste, Nova Gorics and Postojna, the limestone plateau has enthralled speleologists and geologists since the 19th century. But whatever the scientific fascination, to the walker in the midst of the countryside it means that the Postojna basin is a land full of holes.

Torrential rains and the spring melt disappear into the earth. Although Lake Cerknica fills up during winter to a size of 10km long and 5km wide, by June it has vanished. There is something very engaging about this shifting environment. The glacial country of the Alps demands a sense of awe with its vast glaciers which crawl across millennia, but in Postojna there is the feeling of something more magical and mischievous.

The wind in the trees

The bora wind beats Notranjska from the north-east in the winter. It travels across Trnovski gozd to the Bay of Trieste, and has been known to bring with it gusts of 180km/h.
Unperturbed by the fact that the bora has been known to pull roofs off

houses and trees from the ground, the Slovenians use the wind to cure pork leg and produce the local delicacy, *prsut*. The area's thick forests provide some shelter from these winter winds. Historically, the indigenous forests of the karst region were lopped to provide materials for the construction of Venice, but reforestation of the area is well established. Since the 19th century Austrian pines have been planted, and as the farming of livestock waned, pastures were taken over by trees. The forests which now cover over half the Slovenian countryside are recognised as providing environmental, recreational and touristic benefits, and an ideal setting for diverse outdoor pursuits.

The walker's standpoint

There are 9,000km of waymarked trails across Slovenia, maintained by the country's proud walking societies. Paths tend to be set away from roads, and many are organised into networks that follow a cultural, geographical or thematic route.

Because the province of Notranjska has often been seen as a difficult landscape, it is relatively untouched. The region's towns harbour few diversions, and the principal tourist attractions are ancient. Nevertheless, established walking routes abound in Slovenia. The E7 long distance path passes along the Julian Alps and on

Beneath the surface of Postojna

through the karst country to Hodos. The E6 passes by Mount Snežnik, and the Cerknica mountain trail tours the forests and peaks around Rakov Škocjan, Slivnica and Veliki Javornik.

Castles and caves

The handful of tourist attractions that have flourished in the Postojna area are organic, buried into or growing out of the land itself.

Predjama castle, to the north-west of the town of Postojna, has been home to the Patriarch of Aquilieia, the Hapsburgs and Ivan Kobenzl. The surviving 16th century structure and other 12th century remnants are impressive. There are plentiful anecdotes about Erazem Lueger, one-time owner of the castle, whose heroics and untimely end on the toilet have passed into folklore. The castle perches in the middle of a 123m cliff face and looms over a largely inaccessible network of caves.

The popularity of the karst caves of Postojna and their associated tourist trappings (colourful lighting, 26 million visitors, tacky souvenirs, seven centuries' worth of graffiti) cannot destroy their grandeur. Chiselled by the Pivka river, there are 27km of subterranean byways to explore. Reaching down to depths of 1,300m, 6,500 caves have been mapped whilst a further 1,000 remain uncharted. The bizarre dripping stones in the Lepe Jame caves are the result of underground rivers and the surface water that drains through the karst. The Russian Bridge, built in the caves

Predjama castle

by prisoners of war in 1916, offers an eerie reflection of the hardships that were endured on the surface. The Koncertna Dvorana, the concert hall cave, accommodates 10,000 people. Its ceiling is 40m high, and its acoustics are impressive. An echo resounds around the chamber for up to six seconds.

CONTACT INFORMATION

Slovenia Pursuits
New Barn Farm
Tadlow Road
Tadlow
Royston
SG8 0EP
Tel: 01767 631144
Fax: 01767 631166
E-mail: angela.rennie@virgin.net

Slovenian Tourist Board
Dunajska 156
1000 Ljubljana
Slovenia
Tel: (00 386) 61 1891 840
Fax: (00 386) 61 1891 841
E-mail: lucka.letic@
cpts.tradepoint.si
Web: www.slovenia-tourism.si

Lake Cerknica

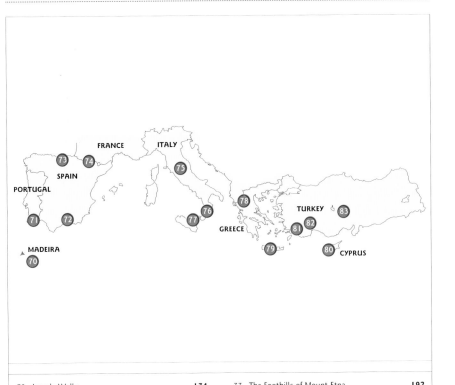

i CONTACT INFORMATION

Cyprus Tourist Organisation
17 Hanover Street
London W1R 0AA
Tel: 020 7569 8800
Fax: 020 7499 4935

Greek National Tourist Office
4 Conduit Street
London W1R 0DJ
Tel: 020 7734 5997
Fax: 020 7287 1369

Maison de la France
178 Piccadilly
London W1V 0AL
Tel: 0891 244123
Fax: 020 7493 6594
E-mail: info@mdlf.co.uk
Web: www.franceguide.com

Italian State Tourist Board
1 Princes Street
London W1R 8AY
Tel: 020 7408 1254
Fax: 020 7493 6695
E-mail: enitlond@globalnet.co.uk
Web: www.enit.it

**Portuguese National
Tourist Office**
22-25A Sackville Street
London W1X 2LY
Tel: 020 7494 1441
Fax: 020 7494 1868
E-mail: iceplond@dircon.co.uk

Spanish National Tourist Office
22-23 Manchester Square
London W1M 5AP
Tel: 020 7486 8077
Fax: 020 7486 8034
E-mail: info.londres@tourspain.es
Web: www.tourspain.co.uk

Turkish Tourist Office
1st Floor
170-173 Piccadilly
London W1V 9DD
Tel: 020 7629 7771
Fax: 020 7491 0773
E-mail: tto@turkishtourism.
demon.co.uk
Web: www.tourist-
offices.org.uk/turkey

Levada Walks

Already famed for its pleasant climate and abundant flora, Madeira's lush interior is becoming increasingly known for its challenging levada walks.

Now known as the pearl of the Atlantic, Madeira was discovered accidentally in 1419 by Portuguese sailors. Situated 1,000km south-west of Lisbon and 800km from the African coast, Madeira and its northern neighbour Porto Santo are the only inhabited islands of a volcanic archipelago – Madeira being the largest at 741 sq km with a population of about 300,000 people. Two groups of uninhabited islands lie to the south of Madeira: the Islas Desertas, a designated nature reserve, and the Selvagens, a bird sanctuary dedicated to scientific research.

Santana, northern Madeira

Climate

With its warm subtropical climate and lush vegetation, Madeira is often referred to as an exotic garden or paradise. North-easterly trade winds bring clouds of moisture across the central mountain range that fall as rain on the northern slopes. Generally, the south is drier and a little more sheltered than the north, although conditions vary according to the seasons. Temperatures are always fairly warm, even through the winter months, and are moderated by a permanent cool breeze.

Levada walks

Levadas are ingenious waterways that were initially constructed in the 15th century for agricultural purposes. Serving as narrow irrigation channels, the levadas diverted excess rainfall to farmers' terraced plots on the lower slopes. Later they were extended to provide water for hydroelectric power.

Rain falling on the mountains seeps down into the volcanic soil, but returns to the surface when it reaches impermeable rock. Forming springs and cascades, the water rushes towards the sea through steep ravines only to be caught in tanks. 2,150km of channels, 40km of which are made up of tunnels, criss-cross an island that itself is only 57km long by 22km wide.

With their narrow maintenance paths on either side, the levadas were built by the first settlers who came from the Algarve region of Portugal. Most of the real work, however, was fearlessly carried out by colonised islanders and imported convicts and slaves, who used crude implements and dangerous methods to hack the channels out of the bare rock face. During the 1940s, newer levadas that are more like mini-canals were constructed as a result of combined agricultural and industrial development plans commissioned by the Portuguese government.

Paths have always existed alongside the levadas to provide access for the *levaderio*, who manages and maintains the waterways and directs each farmer's allocation of water to his plot. These paths have recently been developed as walking trails and have become very popular with visitors to the island, as they offer an interesting alternative to the usual mountain walks. However, the trails are notorious for being rather hair-raising in parts and are not for the vertiginous or the faint-hearted.

The waters of the older levadas plunge wildly through narrow gorges on a steep descent from the mountain heights, with clumps of wildflowers fringing their banks. These provide the more dramatic and challenging routes for the walker: thin strips of slippery path follow the levadas as they skirt tall cliffs of cascading water on one side with nothing but a sheer vertical

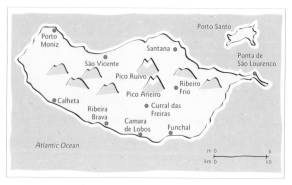

Life on the island

In the last twenty years Madeira has grown rapidly. In the past the island was popular with passengers from the many cruise liners who disembarked here. Its warm climate and attractive landscape, coupled with a conspicuous lack of sandy beaches, soon made the island a favourite of the more discerning visitor. Consequently, the predominant mood on Madeira is more relaxed, and less frantic than other 'sun and fun' destinations, although its capital – Funchal – is a lively town.

Whilst the island's coastal roads are spectacular, they are also precipitous, and one of the best ways of getting around in safety, while remaining free to enjoy the views, is to use the efficient local bus services, taxis and tour guides. These can take visitors to fascinating villages, where many of the levada walks begin. Other walks in the interior traverse Madeira's central mountain range. Recommended trips include the climb to Pico do Arieiro, the island's second tallest peak at 1,816m. It is reached on slightly more accessible paths than Pico Ruivo (1,862m), Madeira's highest summit which is a further 10km away, along a far more treacherous trail. The two peaks shadow the island's deepest valley,

drop on the other. It is always a good idea to negotiate the more difficult routes with a guide.

The ancient laurisilva forest, combining lichen-covered laurel, bay, yew, cedar and heather trees is indigenous to Madeira, and a thick carpet covers the valley floors and overhangs the levadas. The newer canals run parallel to their predecessors across the island, and are perfect for easier lower level walks. They have a more controlled flow of water in their wide channels and their generous banks on either side are deliberately planted with lilies and hydrangea.

which is in fact the crater of an extinct volcano. It hides the village of Curral das Freiras; its 16th century convent was where the nuns of Funchal hid during frequent pirate attacks on the island.

Outside the towns, agriculture is the main activity on Madeira owing to the fertile, well-irrigated soils, and a surprising variety of crops are grown along the terraced hills. On the lowest levels, produce such as figs and grapes, and cereals including wheat, maize, rye and barley are planted. Higher up the slopes, bananas, mango and passion fruit are grown, while the valleys are dense with orchards of apples, cherries and plums.

The sea provides the main ingredients for many of Madeira's typical dishes: thick tuna steaks fried in garlic are delicious, and *Bacalhau* – dried and salted cod cooked with garlic and potatoes – is popular on the island.

[i] CONTACT INFORMATION

Madeira Tourist Office
Avenida Arriaga, 18
9000 Funchal
Madeira
Tel: (00 351) 291 229057
Fax: (00 351) 291 232151
Web: www.madeiratourism.org

Madeira's dramatic coastline

The Algarve

Although better known for its beaches and tourist centres, the Algarve region of southern Portugal amply rewards those who take the time to explore the countryside's fascinating coastal, hill and riverbank routes.

Bordered by the Atlantic on two sides, and separated from Spain by the broad Guadiana river to the east, the Algarve region stretches across the south of Portugal. Over the past twenty years, the greatest change has taken place along the coastal belt, with the development of fishing villages into busy tourist centres. However the sprawl has been upward rather than outward, and the majority of land is under protection. Some of it provides valuable wildlife environments such as the salt marshes of the Rio Formosa National Park and the Castro Marim Reserve.

Beyond the coast

While there are no designated long-distance routes in the Algarve, almost all of the region is suitable for walking. Certain parts of the coast are still only accessible on foot and subsequently are not much visited by the average tourist. The intrepid hiker can experience uplifting views from high cliff walks and discover isolated beaches and sheltered coves, as well as sand spits and fertile lagoons.

Heading inland, a series of low mountain ranges – the Serra de Monchique in the west and the Serra Caldeirão further east – distinguish the

Woman shelling corn

northern Algarve from the flat open plains of the neighbouring Alentejo province. In quieter areas, the traditions and pace of life seem hardly to have changed over the past few centuries. These hills and valleys are host to a myriad of landscapes, and their unspoilt villages display a rich cultural heritage. The infrastructure is underdeveloped with farming, fishing and traditional crafts still predominant sources of income for locals.

Landscapes of the Algarve

The warm climate of the Algarve, with its short winters and long summers, is the main reason for the region's popularity with foreign visitors. The months of July and August are the hottest, although temperatures are moderated by light Atlantic breezes. For walkers, April and May and the cool autumnal months are the optimum times to visit.

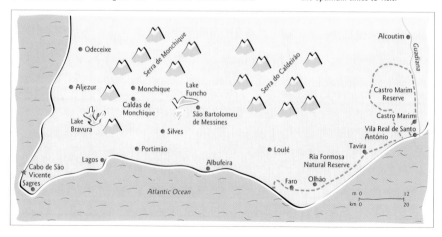

Spring sunshine prompts groves of blossoming fruit trees all over the region and an eruption of wildflowers along riverbanks and on the hillsides. The mainly schistose hills of the northern Algarve are covered in mediterranean scrub or *matos* made up of scented rosemary and the gum cistus rock rose, while fig trees, locust trees and dwarf palm trees are found both around the coast and inland.

The taller granite range of the Serra de Monchique in the west supports a wider variety of flora including purple-leaved satin flowers, red peonies, blue scillas and wild orchids. Pine and eucalyptus woods grow here, and later in the season oak leaves cloak the landscape in an autumnal explosion of colour. The pink-flowered oleander seeks moisture in ravines, and clumps of mimosa grow along the roadsides. Wildflowers such as the Bermuda buttercup mix with bougainvillea and bright begonias in the towns and villages, adding colour to whitewashed village houses.

The Barrocal region, known as the garden of the Algarve, stretches from Cape St Vincent in the west across the Algarve to Tavira and forms a fertile strip between the coast and the hills. Limestone ridges divide valleys of rich red soil where farmers cultivate vines, citrus fruits, and almond and avocado trees, as well as evergreen plantations of carob, olive and arbutus trees.

Piles of drying bark from cork oak trees can be seen around the countryside. This harvest forms an important part of the rural economy, as cork products are one of Portugal's major exports.

People, history and culture

The number and variety of archaeological sites dotted around the Algarve reflects the influence of successive occupying civilisations. The first Ibero-Celtic tribes were followed by Phoenician, Carthagian and Roman invaders. After the decline of the Roman empire, Visigoths from the north dominated until the Islamic Moors seized control in the 8th century. Their rule lasted for over 500 years until the Christian reconquest of Spain and Portugal. During the 15th century, the Algarve, with its strategic coastal towns of Cape St Vincent, Sagres and Lagos, was the centre of Portuguese exploration and the colonisation of new territories under Prince Henry the Navigator.

The many beautiful churches in the villages and towns date from the 8th to the 19th centuries, and there are some fine examples of domestic architecture incorporating colourful tiling and mosaics, and a range of unique architectural features. In the country villages, the small low houses are simply constructed with walls of schist or baked mud. Their sparkling lime exteriors are enlivened by bright touches of paint, picking out doorways or windows.

Older members of the village community still practice traditional skills, often sitting in relaxed groups, working and chatting outside their front doors. Local materials are used to fashion small decorative items from jute, corn husks and wood, and baskets from reeds and coarse rope, as well as woven blankets, fine lace, linen and crochet work.

i CONTACT INFORMATION

Algarve Region Tourism
Av. 5 de Outubro, 18
8000 Faro
Portugal
Tel: (00 351) 289 800400

Cork oak drying in the sun

Andalusia

Only half an hour away from the bustle of the Costa del Sol, on the southern side of Granada, the mountains of the Sierra Nevada and the green valleys of Las Alpujarras are an oasis of rural beauty and peace.

In southern Andalusia, the snow-capped peaks of the Sierra Nevada rise to the south of Granada, providing a dramatic backdrop to the ancient Moorish city. On the southern slopes of the range, the lush valleys of Las Alpujarras are dotted with rivers and springs, smallholdings and pretty villages. The climate, scenery and rugged terrain make the Alpujarras popular with walkers. The high mountains of the Sierra Nevada offer more challenging trekking routes, as well as skiing from November to May.

Local history

Over the years, mountain rivers have deposited rich alluvial silt along their banks, fertilising the soils of the valleys. Farming communities have thrived ever since the Ibero-Celts settled the region over 2,000 years ago. Their remains have been found at Capileira, and the intricate terraced plots constructed on the slopes are a valuable part of their legacy. The influence of the Berber tribes who settled here in the 12th century is still apparent in the low flat-roofed stone houses of the Alpujarras.

The Moors were later exiled to this far corner of Spain and promised freedom from persecution. They adapted and modified the terraces by contributing a complex system of irrigation channels. After a series of half-hearted Moorish revolts, the Spanish Christians reneged on their agreement, finally expelling the Moors in the 1560s. Peasants were brought in to repopulate the land and two Moorish families were allowed to remain in each village to demonstrate the agricultural techniques. The lands were then controlled by a few powerful families, with most of the population poverty-stricken. The situation was worsened by the Franco regime, and the area still suffers from high unemployment and low literacy levels. However, fruit and crop cultivation thrives and tourism is beginning to create opportunities for improvement.

The Alhambra, Granada

The Sierra Nevada

To the south-east of Granada, the ski resort of Solynieve provides access to the higher slopes. A 25km route over the mountains from Solynieve to Capileira includes the summit of Veleta (3,470m), and passes Mulhacén (3,482m), the tallest peak in the range. Although the route is walkable, the southerly approaches to these summits are more favourable and more rewarding in terms of scenery.

Trevélez (1,476m), a village on the southern side of the range, claims to be the highest permanent settlement in Spain, although some Pyrennean villages could easily challenge it. Trevélez marks the end of walks based around the High Alpujarras village itinerary, and the start of tougher paths to the high peaks. From here, the ascent of Mulhacén takes about six hours, but allow extra time for rests and diversions.

The Rura Integral de los Tres Mil traverses all the summits of the Sierra Nevada over 3,000m. A gruelling three to four day walk, it starts in Jerez del Marquesado on the south side of the Sierra and finishes at Lanjarón in the Alpujarras. Not recommended for the inexperienced or the faint-hearted, certain sections of the route however can be linked with other lower paths.

The sub-alpine slopes of the Sierra Nevada harbour a diversity of mountain plants. Up to fifty varieties are endemic to the region, including the fragrant honeysuckle *Lonicra arborea* which grows to 10m in height. However, walking in the Sierras themselves can be disappointing as there seems to be a frustrating lack of surprise or suspense along the paths. Despite the fact that the massif is the highest in continental Spain, spectacular views comparable to other ranges are infrequent or obscured by other peaks.

Winter in the Sierra Nevada

The High Alpujarras

The paths in the High Alpujarras derive from the Camino Real (the Royal Way), an ancient mule track which up to recently provided the only access to the steep villages. The loveliest sections cross green wooded hills and floral meadows, the dry air freshened by cool springs and streams. However, several of the paths have been turned into pitted tractor trails and forestry tracks, with many unappealing firebreaks. Some even terminate abruptly in dead ends and often the walker must undertake a little road-walking. Despite this, the roads and paths are quiet and peaceful, used only by farmers, their livestock and intermittent ramblers.

View south from Bubion over the Poqueira gorge to Las Alpujarras

Most frequently accessed from Lanjarón, on the western edge of the valleys, the High Alpujarran villages are intrinsic to the walking experience. The lively market town of Orjiva marks the start of walks into the valleys and a winding road climbs north through several settlements before reaching the striking Poqueira gorge. With its source near Mulhacén, the Rio Poqueira cuts out a steep ravine from the shale and mica of the upper mountains, widening as it trickles down to the valleys.

Three of the most popular Alpujarran villages are positioned at precipitous heights along the gorge. Perched on steep terraced ledges amongst dense vegetation and scattered stone farmhouses or *cortijos*, they exude an almost cosmopolitan atmosphere. Pampaneira has a yoga and Buddhist centre, a sign of the region's popularity with a growing New Age community. The highest of the three villages, Capileira can be used as a base for walks around the gorge and treks south to Pampaneira, the pretty village of Carataunas, and Orjiva.

Local food and drink

Andalusia's cuisine has inherited the styles of the many cultures that have influenced the region. The fertile lower Alpujarran valleys harbour citrus and almond groves and olive trees, while chestnuts, avocados and bananas thrive in the warm, dry climate. Most wine growing takes place on the southern Alpujarran slopes and it is cheap, plentiful and flavoursome across the region.

Winter stews are a staple and the pork of the area is renowned, particularly the cold cured hams of Trevélez. A classic Andalusian recipe is *gazpacho*, a cold, refreshing soup of tomatoes, cucumber and green pepper in olive oil, garlic and vinegar, often served with croutons. Cooking in the Mediterranean style is a feature of the Andalusian coast and a localised emphasis on confectionery, sweets and pastries shows a distinct Arab influence.

ℹ CONTACT INFORMATION

Andalusian Mountain Federation
Camino de Ronda
101 Edifico Atalya 10, of.7G
18003 Granada
Spain
Tel & Fax: (00 34) 958 291340

Andalusian Tourist Information
Edificio Corral del Carbón
18009 Granada
Spain
Tel: (00 34) 958 225990
Fax: (00 34) 958 223927
Web: www.andalucia.org

m 0   2.5
km 0   4

Veleta   Mulhacén

⬥ Granada

SIERRA NEVADA

Jeres del Marquesado

Poqueira

Lanjarón

Trevélez ●

Trevélez

● Capileira

Portugos

Pampaneira ●   ● Busquistar

Pitres

Poqueira
Gorge

● Lanjarón

Órjiva   LAS
ALPUJARRAS

Picos de Europa

The jutting limestone peaks of the Picos de Europa face out from the Cantabrian mountains to the Atlantic coast and are a favourite destination for walkers, climbers and cavers.

The Picos de Europa is a collection of tall peaks, some reaching over 2,600m, that runs parallel to the Atlantic coast of northern Spain. Fabled as the last point of land on view to Spanish sailors on their way out to sea, the range forms a high curving massif, 40km long and 20km wide. It straddles the provinces of Oviedo in the north, León in the west and Santander to the east.

Three massifs

The spread of the mountains roughly forms a triangle pointing inland, with its base at the northern towns of Cangas de Onis (west) and Panes (east). Four main rivers, the Sella, Cares, Duje and Deva, divide the Picos into three massifs, known as the Cornión (western); Urriello (central); and Andara (eastern) regions.

The highest peaks are concentrated in a complex knot in the central region – which consequently receives more visitors – whilst the Covadonga National Park makes up most of the green, more vegetated western zone. The arid lands of the east have been heavily mined for their rich minerals and although less popular than other parts of the range, the Andara is still worth visiting, with good spots for caving and walking, such as the Morra de Lechugales ridge (2,441m).

Geology and landscape

Only 25km inland from the coast, the outline of the Picos has been shaped largely by glacial factors and moisture from the sea. Split by narrow gorges, the irregular limestone peaks display cirques and alpine lakes, as well as the deep caves, columns, sinkholes and underground rivers and streams expected of a karst landscape. In fact the hard limestone pinnacles are somewhat atypical as they form part of the eastern end of the Cordillera Cantábrica mountain chain, which is composed mainly of slate and granite. Mostly green and pastoral, the lower

valleys of the Picos are scattered with picturesque villages and farms. Rural activities dominate: goats and sheep graze thin vegetation and agriculture is still small-scale, although tourism is gradually beginning to take hold as a potentially viable local enterprise.

Walking routes

The subdivision of the Picos de Europa into interconnecting valleys and canyons offers diverse opportunities for walkers. The towns and villages that encircle the range provide a nearby base or starting off point for short day or half day walks. Longer itineraries through the massifs can also be planned, stopping at the many mountain refuges for shelter.

Some brown bears remain in the Picos' wilderness

Covadonga National Park

Cangas de Onis is the main town of the western region. It has several historic buildings of note and a 12th century Romanesque bridge that arches over the Río Sella. The entrance to the Covadonga National Park lies 7km from Cangas at the village of the same name. It is most famous for the Covadonga shrine, located in a cave on a rocky overhang, that marks the site of the Christian victory over the Moors in 722. Uphill from here is the Mirador de la Reina, with views out to sea on one side and over the park and lakes on the other.

From the Vega Redonda refuge further on, many routes can be taken through the park: the Mirador de Ordiales is a relatively easy hike with terrific views, whilst a much tougher day-long, high-level walk exists along the ridge of the Cornión massif to the Vega Huerta refuge (1,970m).

Urriello – the central massif

Famous for its cheese, made from a mixture of cow's, sheep's and goat's milk, Arenas de Cabrales is another town which borders the central Urriello region. From Arenas, a side road following the Cares river leads south to the village of Puente Poncebos. Walks from here include the route east through the Río Duje gorge to the villages of Tielve and Sotres, and treks into the heart of the Picos massif.

Although only accessible by foot or on horseback along narrow dirt tracks, the nearby villages of Camarmeña and Bulnes on either side of the Cares river, are quiet outposts of mountain life and both are worth a detour. Bulnes is a good base for excursions to the mountains; the striking landmark of Naranjo de Bulnes (2,519m) which is notoriously difficult to climb, and Torre de Cerredo – at 2,648m, the tallest peak in the Picos range.

Cares gorge

From Posada de Valdeón in the southern valley of Valdeón, a trail follows the route of the Río Cares to the quiet village of Cordiñañes, and on to the even more isolated hamlet of Caín. This is the starting point for the classic Picos walk – the Cares gorge or Garganta Divina, a breathtaking ravine with steep walls 1,000m high, that stretches for 12km from Caín to Poncebos in the Cabrales valley. Separating the central and western massifs, the gorge is negotiated by a narrow path along the cliff-face, created by the water authorities to service hydroelectric schemes powered by the Cares river.

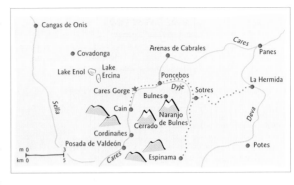

Wildlife

The wildlife of the Picos is possibly its second most important attraction, and the mountains, valleys and forests are important habitats for bird, mammal and insect life. Although the chances of wolf or bear sightings are unlikely these days, it may be possible to spot the rare Pyrenean desman, a timid vole-like creature known to frequent the riverbanks of the Covadonga National Park, whilst a population of 'wild' horses still graze near the Covadonga lakes. Ever present atop the mountain plateaux, chamois share the peaks and narrow gorges with golden eagles, booted and short-toed eagles, and griffon and Egyptian vultures. Beech forests cover the mountain slopes up to 1,300m, and with the craggy lower cliffs, are host to alpine choughs and smaller raptors such as goshawks, kestrels, peregrines, sparrowhawks and eagle owls. Wild cats traverse both environments, whilst mixed deciduous woodlands shelter black and middle spotted woodpeckers, red squirrels, wild boar and deer.

Owing to the lack of intensive agriculture, the valleys and fields of the Picos de Europa still benefit from relatively low levels of pesticide use, helping to maintain specimens of native flora. Man-made hay meadows, originally hundreds of years old, are home to over forty species of orchid, as well as narcissus, monkshood, fritillaries, jonquils, and the tiny dog's tooth violet. They are also a natural feeding ground for butterflies and small songbirds such as the black redstart, rock thrush and wallcreeper.

Conditions

In winter, walking below the snow line in the lower valleys is possible, however many higher mountain paths are snow-covered from October to late spring. May and June often bring frequent storms and later in summer the humidity is high, although when mist and cloud clears the sun can be scorchingly hot. Late summer or early autumn is recommended as the best time to visit, although temperatures can still be quite high.

[i] **CONTACT INFORMATION**

Cantabrian Tourist Office
Plaza de Velarde, 5, Bajo.
39001 Santander
Spain
Tel: (00 34) 901 111112

León Tourist Office
Plaza de la Regla, 4.
24003 León
Spain
Tel: (00 34) 987 237082

Asturias Tourist Office
Plaza de la Catedral, 6
33003 Oviedo
Spain
Tel: (00 34) 985 213385

The Pyrenees

Forming a natural frontier between France and Spain, the spectacular mountains of the Pyrenees stretch for 480km from the Atlantic across to the Mediterranean coast.

The Pyrenees are said to differ from other European ranges, and the Alps in particular, in that they still retain an element of wilderness and isolation, and have so far escaped widespread damage from over-development. This narrow border of peaks encompasses several separate massifs: the rivers that flow from the mountains spilt the range into distinct regions, each with their own landscape, climate, ecosystem, language and culture.

If the regions that make up the Pyrenees can be said to share a feature, it must be that of diversity; from the folklore, art and architecture to be found in the French region of Ariège, to Catalonia's wealth of Romanesque churches and picturesque villages, or the lakes and peaks that form Aigüestortes Sant-Maurici National Park's glacial landscape.

The rolling mountains of the eastern Pyrenees are covered by deciduous forests that sweep towards Mediterranean beaches. Here, steep foothills dictate a rough and rocky coast on both sides of the border. On the French side, the river valleys of the Tech and Têt flow east from the Cerdagne region to the sea, whilst in Spain, the Garrotxa region boasts a natural park of extinct volcanoes, and the medieval town of Besalú.

Walking in the Pyrenees

The mixed terrain of the Pyrenees is suited to all levels of walkers: the peaks are lower than those of the Alps, with Pico de Aneto the highest summit at 3,404m. Too vast to experience in one short visit, the range's individual regions can be used as a base from which to explore.

Circuitous walking trips and looping trailheads are well-established, covering the valleys, gorges and lower reaches of the range. Venturing off the main routes is amply rewarded by the discovery of lesser-known side routes and higher, more isolated ridges and mountain paths.

Long-distance routes

Three main routes traverse the range: the Grande Randonnée 10, the Haute Randonnée Pyrénéene, and the Gran Recorrido 11. Although these paths sometimes run parallel to each other and may often cross and interlink, they are in fact very different.

Located wholly in France, the GR 10 is a low-level, well-marked route, covering relatively easy terrain. It is ideal for the less ambitious walker. In contrast, the HRP skirts the watershed of the taller peaks and is a higher, more challenging path, with many variations. It stays mainly on the French side, only occasionally crossing over into Spain. During the 1980s, the GR 11 was developed through stunning Pyrenean landscapes as the Spanish equivalent to the GR 10. There are also many other shorter GR and local routes which sometimes trace part of the main long-distance walks.

The national parks

Two national parks adjoin each other for 15km along the Pyrenean frontier. The Spanish Parque Nacional de Ordesa y Monte Perdido (Ordesa National Park) was established in 1918 as Spain's first protected area, initially to preserve the Ordesa canyon. It was later extended to include a number of high peaks, the Valle d'Añisclo and the sources of the Cinca and Tella rivers.

At 3,355m, Monte Perdido is the highest mountain in the park. Four main valleys drain from it, each forming dramatic limestone canyons: the most famous of these being the Valle de Ordesa. Lying parallel to the mountains it is one of the few valleys to run east to west. Ordesa's colourful banded limestone palisades were first carved out by glacial action. Rising over 1,000m along each side of the gorge, they tower above the fast flowing Arazos, a tributary of the Ara.

On the French side, the Parc National des Pyrénées (the Pyrenees National Park) commands a narrow strip along the border. Its widest point is near the Pic du Midi d'Ossau (2,884m) and across the Vallée du Marcadau, between the town of Cauterets and Mt Vignemale (3,298m), the highest point of the French Pyrenees. Hikes from here lead to the stupendous Cirque de Gavarnie, a glaciated semicircle of staggered walls rising 1,400m into the sky. A natural gap in the wall of the cirque, the Brèche de Roland, provides a gateway to the Ordesa National Park and Alto Aragón.

Climate

Steeper on the French side, and more populated, the mountains here have an alpine climate and are often shrouded in mist and rain. On the Spanish side, the weather is drier and warmer, the villages and valleys more desolate and rural.

In high summer the combination of hot dry air from the southern slopes and cool damp air from the north creates unpredictable weather and frequent thunderstorms on taller summits. Mid June to late September is the summer season, the best time for walkers, although snow may linger on higher ground. A trip in July or August however should be avoided as it can be uncomfortably hot and busy.

Butterflies are as plentiful as the meadow flowers

Plants and wildlife

The mix of mediterranean and alpine climates produces a broad variation in plant and animal life in the Pyrenees. Over 3,000 species of flora can be found, some of which are confined to limited parts of the range. The rock jasmine, for example, is found only

Bearded vulture

around Gavarnie and Monte Perdido. The variety of plants in bloom peaks in June and July, but from early spring the lower foothills are carpeted with irises, yellow rattle, gentian, narcissus and the Pyrenean ramonde. The abundance of small plants, as well as olive and almond groves, heather and aromatic herbs, makes the mountains highly attractive to butterflies, notably swallowtails, apollos and skippers.

The high mountains are particularly rewarding for bird-watchers: raptors such as the lammergeier (or bearded vulture), the griffon and the Egyptian vulture roam the skies, while golden, booted and short-toed eagles, red and black kites and alpine choughs can also be spotted.

The chamois population flourishes across the range, with marmots, wild boar, deer and red squirrels inhabiting the forested areas. Sadly, the small Pyrenean brown bear is close to extinction, whilst the native Pyrenean ibex survives only in small numbers in Ordesa National Park.

ℹ CONTACT INFORMATION

Pyrenees National Park Office
59 Route de Pau
F 65000 Tarbes
France
Tel: (00 33) 5 6244 3660
Fax: (00 33) 5 6244 3670

Ordesa National Park
Plaza de Cervantes
5 - 4 Planta
22071 Huesca
Spain
Tel: (00 34) 974 243361
Fax: (00 34) 974 242725

**FEEC: Federacio d'Entitats
Excursionistes de Catalunya**
Rambla 61
1r., 08002 Barcelona
Spain
Tel: (00 34) 93 302 6416

Ordesa National Park

An Art Lover's Tour of Eastern Tuscany

The birthplace of artists and the inspiration for writers and poets, eastern Tuscany's rich heritage can be discovered in its villages and towns, while its valleys and forests are a delight to explore on foot.

The quiet wooded landscape of eastern Tuscany and the Casentino region has long been a place of peace and sanctuary for monks and hermits. Its hills, valleys and streams lie along the western side of the Apennines, Italy's spine, and north of the A1 Autostrada which connects Florence and Arezzo on its way to Rome. The sources of two of Italy's great rivers can be found here; the Arno, which flows west to Florence and beyond, and the Tiber, growing and widening through the Tuscan countryside to Rome.

Changing seasons are reflected in the foliage of Casentinesi National Park's forests

In contrast to more populous and industrialised parts of Tuscany, the eastern area is quieter and less built up. Although it boasts many fine churches, monuments and medieval sanctuaries, as well as examples of ancient Etruscan and Renaissance art and architecture, tourism has not spoilt the area. Its dense forests of silver fir have for centuries been harvested by local communities for charcoal and building materials, and to supply Italy's shipping and naval fleets. Now they are mostly preserved as a vital wildlife and ecological resource.

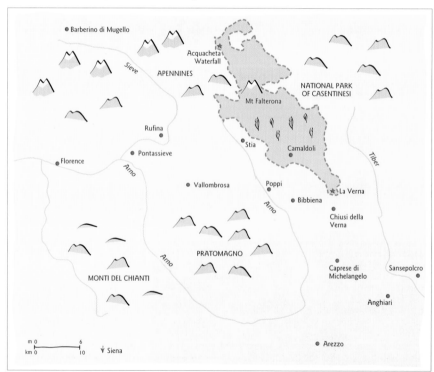

Giacomini falls in Casentinesi National Park

Golden light

A visit to this part of Italy is best undertaken during spring or autumn, to avoid the intense heat of high summer. Wildflowers put on a stunning final burst of blooms during the early autumn and the famous Tuscan light is at its most golden, catching the turning colours of beech, hazel, oak and sweet chestnut woods that blanket the hills.

Established country trails and mule tracks cross pasture and woodland, passing farms and ruined sawmills; elsewhere the walker must tread tarmac to get from town to town. These back country roads are mostly narrow and winding with little traffic, and still offer rewarding vistas over the Tuscan landscape.

Mugello

Leading north-east out of Florence, the S67 state road closely follows the course of the River Sieve through Pontassieve and the Chianti-producing town of Rufina. This scenic valley cuts through the mountains to Mugello, a forested basin sheltering cultural gems such as the Franciscan monastery of Bosco del Frati, with its wooden crucifix said to be by Donatello, and the 15th century Villa di Cafaggiolo of the Medicis at Barberino di Mugello.

From Pontassieve it is worth making a small detour to Vallombrosa, with its interesting walled abbey and small community of monks. Set in deep woodland, the surroundings inspired the poet John Milton when he visited here in 1638.

The rich green colours of Lama forest in Casentinesi National Park

Foreste Casentinesi

From the S67, walkers can take either of the two minor roads that cross over the Pratomagno ridge (1,000m) into the Casentino plain. Here, primeval forests of giant silver firs and ancient beech trees thickly swathe the land, relieved only by the numerous streams and torrents that run down from the Apennine ridge.

Stia, Poppi and Bibbiena are part of a chain of villages that border the Arno as it winds southwards across the plain towards Arezzo. With the Arno on one side and the National Park of Foreste Casentinesi, Monte Falterona and Campigna on the other, these towns are perfect bases from which to explore the depths of the park. Various waymarked trails – some forming part of the Apennine GEA long-distance walking route – traverse the park's 360 sq km. Dante enjoyed this area while in exile, and commemorated the Acquacheta waterfall in the north of the park.

Bibbiena and La Verna

Bibbiena is Casentino's commercial centre. Its 12th century church, the Pieve di Santi Ippolito e Donato, has an altarpiece by Bicci di Lorenzo and holds paintings by artists of the Siena school. A road climbs over the Casentino range to one of the pilgrimage sites within the park: famous for its association with St Francis, the monastery of Chiusi della Verna also holds a large collection of terracotta sculptures by Andrea della Robbia. A track leads north from Chiusi to the La Verna sanctuary. Dramatically located on a rocky outcrop on the southern slope of Monte Penna (1,283m), it is the site of the hermitage of St Francis, who is said to have received his stigmata here in 1224.

Artists' inspiration

Situated quite close to each other in the Tiber valley, a network of towns are worth visiting for their wealth of artistic treasures, modestly contained in unassuming local buildings, and as the birthplaces of two of the most important artists of the Renaissance.

With excellent views over the surrounding countryside, Caprese Michelangelo is the birthplace of Michelangelo Buonarroti. As well as changing its name to reflect its prestigious association, the village has converted the town hall (where Michelangelo's father served as governor) to the Museo Michelangelo, with photographs, memorabilia and reproductions of the artist's works.

Heading further into the Tiber valley, the busy commercial town of Sansepolcro is the birthplace of the fresco artist Piero della Francesca. A collection of his work is on display in the Museo Civico, the most famous being *The Resurrection* (1463); an intense depiction of a triumphant Christ, eerily rising out of his tomb, unnoticed by the sleeping soldiers. The *Madonna della Misericordia*

(1462), is one of several other works here by Piero. This altarpiece depicts an outsized Madonna sheltering those who commissioned the picture under her outspread cloak.

Lucca Signorelli's 15th century *Crucifixion* is also in the Museo Civico, as well as works by Pontormo and Matteo di Giovanni, with further examples from the Siennese and Florentine school in the town's Romanesque duomo and the San Lorenzo church. South of Sansepolcro, at the cemetery chapel of Monterch, is another example of Piero's work. The iconographic *Madonna del Parto* conveys the conflicting emotions of the expectant Virgin Mary.

The historic town of Anghiari is the site of the famous battle of 1440 between Florence and Milan. Located on a hilltop overlooking the fields of the upper Tiber valley, Anghiari's russet-hued buildings are a typical example of a medieval walled town. Its museum houses examples of local crafts and a 1420 Madonna carved in wood by Jacobo della Quercia. The Santa Maria delle Grazie church has a high altar and tabernacle from the Andrea della Robbia workshops and Matteo di Giovanni's 15th century *Madonna and Child*.

Arezzo

Once one of the wealthiest cities in Tuscany, and for a long time a rival to Florence, Arezzo's glory has faded a little. It is the birthplace of both Petrarch – the 14th century poet and humanist – and Giorgio Vasari, painter, architect and art historian, whose house, Casa Vasari, can be visited. Because of damage during the war, its medieval streets have been replaced with wide avenues and the town's urban character can consequently be a little hard to define. Among its many interesting architectural, archaeological and artistic treasures, the 13th century church of San Francesco can claim to be the jewel in Arezzo's crown. The site of Piero della Francesca's magnificent fresco cycle *The Legend of the True Cross* (1452–56), the painted walls tell the story of the origins of the cross upon which Christ was crucified, and display the artist's ambitious experiments with perspective and colour.

ℹ CONTACT INFORMATION

Foreste Casentinesi National Park
via G. Brocchi7 – 52015
Pratovecchio (AR)
Italy
Tel: (00 39) 0575 50301
Fax: (00 39) 0575 504497
E-mail: parco@technet.it

Bibbiena Tourist Information
Via Berni, 25 – 52011
Bibbiena (AR)
Italy
Tel & Fax: (00 39) 0575 593098

The Church of San Paolo in Alpe

Walking in Calabria

Forming the southern 'toe' of Italy, the rough and ready Calabria region is defined by wild mountain areas and long stretches of beach around its 800km coastline.

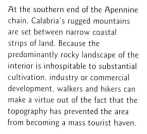

At the southern end of the Apennine chain, Calabria's rugged mountains are set between narrow coastal strips of land. Because the predominantly rocky landscape of the interior is inhospitable to substantial cultivation, industry or commercial development, walkers and hikers can make a virtue out of the fact that the topography has prevented the area from becoming a mass tourist haven.

A number of national parks have been established and these offer some of the most rewarding walks to be had in Calabria's wilderness. Pollino National Park – Italy's largest and least visited national park – is in the north of the region; Calabria National Park is located in the east of Italy's 'toe'; and the remote Aspromonte National Park is in the extreme southern tip of Italy. They have been set up to preserve some of the area's last remaining endemic species such as the primeval Calabrian or loricato pine, the wolf, the wildcat and rare

raptors. In the centre of Calabria, between the mountain areas, are open plains covered in dense woodland. The Sila forests are important wildlife reserves and are host to some attractive walks.

Climate

The optimum months for visiting Calabria are during spring and autumn. At high altitudes, warm spring sunshine finally arrives in late April or early May and begins to melt the deep winter snows that blanket the hills and mountains. The coastal plains facing west to the Tyrrhenian Sea and east to the Ionian Sea hardly ever endure snow or cloud and are popular with holidaymakers.

Jasmine plantations and abundant citrus groves of orange, lemon and bergamot trees are bathed in warmth and sunshine for most of the year. In September the number of summer visitors abates somewhat, leaving the

narrow roads and long beaches relatively uncongested. The coastal waters are still warm enough for swimming and the woods inland yield a varied mushroom crop as well as displaying glorious seasonal colours.

Past empires

With a troubled and turbulent past, Calabria's fortunes have been closely associated with the ancient empires of Greece and Rome. However, since the region's glory days, the important cities and strategic military positions that once dominated the landscape have been systematically ravaged by a series of damaging events including the Punic Wars, frequent foreign invasions and various natural disasters.

Over the centuries, Calabria's high mountainous landscape has provided a refuge from persecution for ethnic and linguistic minorities. The influence of Greeks, Waldensians (or Provençals) and Albanians is very

La Cattolica, Stilo

Girotte cave

The summits of the calcareous–dolomitic Pollino massif – Monte Pollino (2,248m) and Serra Dolcedorme (2,267m) – offer high-level hikes and climbs for experienced walkers. Towns and villages, churches and monuments, as well as geographical features share both Italian and Albanian names, due to the Balkan descent of Pollino's mountain communities.

One of the more dramatic expeditions within the park involves a day-long round trip that begins and ends at the village of Civita and explores the 910m deep Raganello gorge which cuts through the park in a north–south direction. The path heads north from the village through the wooded slopes of the Raganello Natural

obvious in the language, cooking, dress and customs of the area. Greek, Roman, Byzantine and Norman remains abound at sites such as Maratea, Metaponto and Sibari; elsewhere the earth has yielded many archaeological finds. Some of these are housed in the Museo of Magna Grecia in Reggio, and in both civic and provincial museums in towns such as Vibo Valentia, Crotone and Sibari.

After the Second World War, a programme of development known as the *Casa per il Mezzogiorno* was instituted by the Italian government. New roads, irrigation projects and developments in infrastructure improved conditions for local communities who had suffered seriously from poverty, de-population and high levels of emigration. As part of this initiative, tourism projects attempted to exploit Calabria's wonderful beaches but, luckily for the walker, most visitors focus mainly on the resorts of the Ionian coast.

Pollino National Park

Waymarked walking trails through Pollino National Park utilise forestry paths and old farm and mule tracks. These cross lower valleys and rolling pastures that lie in the shelter of the mountains. Higher spots, such as the landmark peak of La Falconara (1,643m), provide panoramic views of valleys and meadows covered in wild grasses and flowers.

The port of Scilla on the Veduta coast in southern Calabria

Reserve, curving round to a viewing point sited above a dramatic drop down into the chasm. The walk then proceeds south, and follows a low-level route through the rough terrain of the gorge. The trail is closely bordered by high overhanging walls and is scattered with rocks, boulders and pools. The Roman 'Devil's bridge' or Ponte del Diavolo crosses the (sometimes raging) Raganello torrent which signifies a return to civilisation and the last leg back to Civita.

The sentinels of Pollino

Originally a native of the Balkan peninsula, the loricato or Calabrian pines – nicknamed 'the sentinels of Pollino' – have been adopted as the logo of the national park. These silver-barked trees can now only be found in a few restricted zones, and the 2,000 that fall within the territory of the park are strictly protected. Some of these ancient giants are over 2,000 years old – their gnarled trunks locked deep in the rocky landscape, and their branches fanning out on either side in a distinctive wide shape. Lower slopes are host to olive groves and Turkey oaks. Beech trees appear next, which give way to tall pines and juniper scrub further up.

Bird species outnumber mammals: eagle owls, goshawks, kestrels and peregrines hunt and nest between the crags and the thick forests. Small numbers of wolves hide in the remote parts of the park whilst other mammals such as foxes, roe deer, badgers, pole cats, porcupines and pine martens are more numerous.

The combination of mountain and marine environments encourages a rich variety of species within the park. Wildflowers such as daisy, crocus, cyclamen, bluebell and violet swathe the lower meadows whilst alpines such as periwinkles, the alpine pasque flower and spring gentians nestle between the rocks higher up.

The Sila forests

Lying to the east of Pollino are the forests of the high-level limestone and schistose Sila plain. Separated by mountains, they fall into three zones, each with slightly varying characteristics in terms of landscape, fauna and vegetation. The largest single area is the Sila Grande, sandwiched between the Sila Greca to the north and the Sila Piccolo to the south. Eastern zones of the Sila Grande and Sila Piccolo make up a large portion of the Calabria National Park while to the south the sugar-loaf massif of Aspromonte has also been designated a protected reserve.

The Sila's extensive forests are made up largely of beech, oak, ash, maple, alder and chestnut woods. Calabrian and Sila pine fringe several large artificial lakes, such as Lake Arvo and Lake Cecita in the Sila Grande. Initially created for hydroelectric schemes, these lakes have contributed a further environment for birds, mammals and fish. It is possible that wolves still roam in some more impenetrable parts of the Sila forests, whilst golden eagles favour the skies over the peaks.

ⓘ CONTACT INFORMATION

Pollino National Park
Palazzo Amato
Via Mordini 20
85048 Rotonda (PZ)
Italy
Tel: (00 39) 0973 661692
Fax: (00 39) 0973 661671

Aspromonte National Park
Via Aurora – 89050
Gambariedi S. Stefano in
Aspromonte (RC)
Italy
Tel: (00 39) 0965 743060
Fax: (00 39) 0965 743026

Detail of the Fontana Largo Mercato, Tropea

ITALY

The Foothills of Mount Etna

On the largest island in the Mediterranean, smouldering Mount Etna towers above cultivated foothills and Sicilian country villages.

Sicily's strategic position between Europe and Africa, together with its fertile soil and natural resources have led to a long history of colonisation. From a sequence of Greek, Roman, Arab, Norman and Spanish invaders to its absorption into Italy in 1861, the island has been a melting pot of cultures, people, art and architecture.

With the majority of Sicily's 6 million inhabitants living in its cities and market towns, the villages around Mount Etna on Sicily's north-eastern edge are peaceful, and undamaged by the growth in tourism that has affected some of the towns along the coast. A regional park has been established to protect the area that

reaches from the circle of communities at the base of Mount Etna to the main crater at its 3,300m summit. This territory is a perfect location for walks of all levels in a variety of exhilarating landscapes.

Walks around Mount Etna

Walking in the foothills of the world's tallest and most active volcano is not as ludicrous or dangerous as it first sounds. In fact, considering its proximity to such an unpredictable neighbour, the landscape around Mount Etna is surprisingly populated. Villages thrive on the fertile volcanic earth that can be transformed by farmers from molten lava and ash into rich black soil within twenty years.

Etna is made up of three craters whose eruptions and deposits contribute to the fluctuating height of the mountain. The climb to Etna's summit was famously undertaken in antiquity by the Emperor Hadrian. Today, access to the main crater is restricted for safety reasons but this is usually no longer a main objective,

Walking excursions across lava

The impact of the lava flows can be seen in the volcanic terrain of irregular slabs and spikes, with striking rope-like formations known as *pahoehoe* (after solidified lavas typical of Hawaii). The eruption that formed the Dammusi pass on the northern side of Etna lasted from 1614 to 1624 and had a major effect on this part of the volcano. The Valle de Bove was created by the collapse of parts of the ancient crater on Etna's eastern side between 1991 and 1993, forming a vast basin spanning 35 sq km.

Scattered around Etna are tubular underground caves formed by channels of lava. Used for centuries by local people for shelter, burial places and as ice chambers, these fascinating grottoes can now be visited by the public.

Taormina

The medieval town of Taormina is an interesting base from which to discover the area. Dramatically positioned high above the sea with Etna at its back, it offers spectacular vistas across the Mediterranean to Calabria on the Italian mainland. The town has become a busy tourist centre and for those who wish to get even further away from it all, the remote villages of Etna's lower slopes offer a more secluded base. It is perhaps the popularity of Taormina's beaches, bars and boutiques, and its growing reputation as a resort, that makes the mule tracks and paths in the outlying countryside so solitary.

as the mountainside is covered with walking trails past fascinating volcanic features. Although Etna and its secondary volcanoes intermittently spew lava and ash, the last major eruption was in the 1980s. An observatory monitors the cones and tourist visits are cancelled at the smallest signs of activity.

Routes that fall within the confines of the regional park are marked with signposts, with maps and itineraries available from park information offices. Outside the park zone, old dirt roads and farm tracks form a network of trails connecting farmsteads and villages, and linking up with the official park routes. Locals have acted on the abundance of lava, using it as building material for houses, architectural features and paving slabs. Examples can be seen along the numerous mule tracks (some lava-paved) that pass low walls, farmhouses and outbuildings, leading walkers to the higher mountain trails and various viewing points and geological sites of the Etna Regional Park.

The major eruptions and lava flows over the last few centuries have created the huge variety of lava formations that make up Etna's unique topography. Eruptions from volcanic vents on the east side of the mountain have melted a destructive trail through any communities that lay in their path towards their ultimate destination – the sea.

Pahoehoe lava formations

Taormina still makes an excellent day trip however, with its scenic setting, cosmopolitan atmosphere and the several important monuments sheltered within its narrow streets. One of its most famous sites is a Greek temple. Originally dating from the Hellenistic period (3rd century BC), it was expanded by the Romans in the 2nd century AD. Set into a hill 214m above the town, it is remarkably well preserved, to the extent that open air plays are still staged here on summer evenings. Its semicircular rows of seating form a wide curve, with clear views out over the town below, the bay, and solemn, sleeping Etna.

Etna's vegetation

Leaving behind the attractions of Taormina and the other coastal resorts, the tracks that surround Etna's profile climb through three levels of vegetation. Once covered by oak woods, but now comprised of vineyards, citrus groves and fruit trees, the lower levels are planted with the man-made terrace systems first introduced to the island by Arab settlers. Hardy hazelnut, pistachio and pear trees persist even to heights of 1,500m.

From this point on, however, wooded areas of chestnut, beech and birch trees cloak the higher slopes. Birch and beech continue to grow above 2,000m, the southernmost extent of these European species. On the north-eastern side of the mountain, beautiful woods of Corsican pine and oak are found around the towns of Castiglione di Sicilia and Linguaglossa.

Giant trees include a huge holm-oak that is 30m high and 10m wide at its base, and the famous 'Chestnut of One Hundred Horses' whose branches are believed to have been wide enough to shelter Queen Jeanne d'Anjou and her one hundred knights. In spring, the bright yellow flowers of the Etna broom colonise the lower hillsides and contrast with the black soil.

An ice cave about 2,050m above sea level on Mount Etna

Above the tree line, hardy mountain plants such as milk-vetch and groundsel survive alongside plants endemic to Etna such as the holy pulvino thorn, whose cushion-like clumps serve to shelter the tiny Etna violet and other less sturdy specimens. Above 2,500m, most vegetation peters out, as recent lava flows and a newer layer of encrusted ash form a desert topography.

Etna's wildlife

Wolves, wild boar and deer once roamed the thickly forested slopes of Etna until hunting, deforestation and road building saw the destruction of their habitat. Smaller mammals however, such as wildcats, martens, foxes, porcupines, hedgehogs, hares, dormice and bats have survived. The rich variety of flora that abounds in the area attracts an array of beautiful insects and butterflies. Although the establishment of a regional park and the recognition of the area's ecological importance have increased protection and awareness, these species are still under severe threat. Numerous bird species include many varieties of owl, plus golden eagles, sparrowhawks, peregrines and kestrels. Quails, wild doves and cuckoos inhabit the forests along with a multitude of small songbirds. Lake Gurrida to the north-west of Etna provides a natural wetland environment for waterfowl including herons, little egrets and mallards.

Etna's climate

Around the territory of Etna itself, a range of climatic zones exist according to altitude. There can be a 20°C drop in temperature in the short distance from the sunny beaches of the coast to the higher slopes. The best seasons for walking in the park are spring and autumn, as extreme temperatures dominate winter and summer. In April, the air is warm; the snows melt from Etna's summit and woodland plants bloom. By May, peonies, orchids and narcissi have created an explosion of their own in the form of bright swathes of colour cloaking the pastures. By September, after a long hot summer, the sea has warmed up and the harvest fruits are ripe and ready to fall. Winter comes late, with good weather lasting until mid November.

ⓘ CONTACT INFORMATION

Etna Natural Park
Via Etnea, 107/A
95030 Nicolosi (CT)
Sicily
Italy
Tel: (00 39) 095 914588
Fax: (00 39) 095 914738
E-mail: fruizione@parcoetna.ct.it
Web: www.parcoetna.ct.it

Walking in the Píndhos Mountains

Looping trails and old shepherds' paths traverse the high forest-clad mountains of the northern Píndhos and weave amongst the valleys and villages of the unique Zagóri region.

Walking in the Pindhos

Closely bordering Albania, the wild landscape of Zagóri is set in the northern province of Epirus and has as its regional capital the lakeside town of Ioánnina. Byzantine churches, medieval monasteries and ancient stone-arched 'packhorse' bridges are scattered throughout the countryside.

Traces of the (once numerous) Vlach or Roumaní population of shepherds still graze their sheep in these border regions, and shelter in the crumbling remains of shepherd huts and sheepfolds. The area is best explored on foot, along old paths and fragments of the 03 and E6 trails.

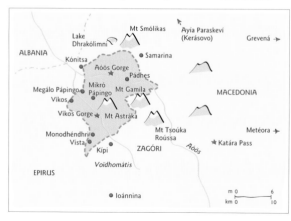

The Zagóri villages

The forty six small villages of the Zagóri region – known collectively as the Zagorokhória – comprise a cluster of traditional mountain settlements. Their distinctive houses, squares, and municipal and farm buildings are solidly constructed from local grey slate hewn from the mountains. Dating from the 14th century, the houses in particular display an architectural style unique to the area.

The people of the Zagorokhória have traditionally sustained their living from agriculture, as well as artisan crafts such as gold and silversmithing, weaving and woodcarving. Arable farming is impossible on the rugged, infertile slopes of the Píndhos, and most engage in stock raising and the cultivation of fruit and vegetables. Delicious milk, butter and cheese, as well as wine and honey are produced in the region, with supplies of nuts and wood gleaned from the forests.

Histories

The territory of Epirus has long been an area of dispute, witnessing a succession of invasions from the Ancient Greeks and Romans, to Slavic, Gothic and Norman tribes. Surrounded by the high massifs of the Píndhos, the northern communities of Zagóri have always maintained a seige-like approach to threatening forces, even enjoying a relative amount of independence and control over their affairs during Ottoman rule.

During the Second World War, the mountain settlements were an important stronghold of the Resistance movement. These same villages, however, sadly proved to be the centre of bloody fighting between the communist core and occupying forces during the subsequent Greek Civil War of the 1940s.

With changes and improvements only beginning to take place in the last decade, the effects of war and deprivation can still be seen in depopulated Zagorokhória villages with their mix of new and old buildings, and a proud but ravaged community who are only now beginning to recover from the turbulent events of their past.

Walking in central Zagóri

One of a number of separate ranges which make up the northern Píndhos, the Timfi massif dominates central Zagóri and also falls into the territory of the Víkos-Aóös National Park. Dividing the Aóös river and its famed gorge in the north from the River Voïdhomátis and the Víkos gorge in the south-west of the park are several interesting limestone summits.

These include Mt Astráka (2,436m), near the village of Megálo Pápingo and its smaller, prettier twin, Mikró Pápingo; the central peak of Mt Gamíla (2,497m); and Mt Tsoúka Roússa to the east of the park. Winding roads and tracks connect the peaks and the villages. The 03 walking trail continues further north into the mountains past Mt Smólikas – at 2,637m, the second highest peak in Greece.

The Pápingo villages are a good starting point for more strenuous walks into the mountains towards Mt Astráka (and its mountain refuge); the high-level Lake Dhrakólimni; and the Karterós pass between Mt Gamíla and the eastern Zagóri. The 03 route varies in difficulty with the terrain, but the beauty of walking in the area

is that the trails loop and twist around each other. Remote paths regularly connect with other sections, often affording a change in scenery, attractive detours and a relief from the more taxing stretches.

Two high-level trails lead from Paleosélli and its neighbouring village Pádhes, towards the Náneh refuge and Mt Smólikas. The mountain dominates the isolated northern reaches of Zagóri and a number of challenging hikes can be explored between Smólikas and its nearby lake, with an option to descend from the summit into the village of Ayía Paraskeví (Kerásovo), or continue on a longer seven hour trail east to Samarina, reputed to be the highest village in Greece.

The Víkos gorge

The breathtaking Víkos gorge can be approached from the south by Monodhéndhri, one of the best preserved of the Zagóri villages, or from the Pápingo villages to the north. It takes about half a day of walking and scrambling to complete its 12km length, but is one of the highlights of a visit to the Zagóri region. In the general area of the Víkos gorge are several interesting detours. North of Monodhéndhri, the hamlet of Oxiá has a special viewing point that offers wonderful views looking out across the gorge.

'Packhorse' bridges

The countryside around Zagóri is littered with unusual architectural features in the form of stone-arched or 'packhorse' bridges. These simple but charming structures gracefully span the rivers, ranging in length from single to triple arches. Beautifully constructed and engineered, with paved or cobbled surfaces, they are believed to have been built in the 19th century, and are often located at the end of old tracks that were once the main routes through the mountains between the villages.

The best examples of these bridges are found near Monodhéndhri around the southern Zagóri villages; between Vísta, Tsepélovo, Koukoúli and Kípi (a splendid triple-arched model).

One of the Zagóri villages

Metéora

Across the mountains in the province of Macedonia, the monasteries of Metéora – the word literally means 'monasteries in the air' – rise up suddenly out of the plain of Thessaly. With the Pindhos as a backdrop, a series of sheer-sided rocky pinnacles pierce the sky, bizarrely topped by Byzantine monasteries and convents. Reached from Ioánnina and the western side of the Pindhos range by the dramatic Katára pass, the strange formations and their man-made additions are a spectacular feat both of natural geological forces and human ingenuity and imagination.

Although some have fallen into disuse and routes are not waymarked, ancient paths that were originally constructed by the inhabitants to link the settlements still exist. With the aid of a local map, walkers can explore remoter parts of Metéora on foot, thus avoiding the hordes of tourists that crowd the area in high season.

ℹ CONTACT INFORMATION

Forest Directorate of Ioánnina
6 Averof Str
45221 Ioánnina Perfecture
Greece
Tel & Fax: (00 301) 651 26591

Ministry of Agriculture
General Directorate of Friends
and Forest Environment
3-5 Ypokratous Str
10164 Athens
Greece
Tel: (00 301) 362 8327
Fax: (00 301) 361 2710

Stone-arched 'packhorse' bridge

The White Mountains and the Samariá Gorge

Crete's White Mountains are best discovered on foot: walks range from the surprisingly verdant and precipitous Samariá Gorge to the solitude of cross-mountain trails and sea-freshened coastal routes.

Formed as a result of geological activity several million years ago, Crete's three main massifs are comprised of closely packed, tall limestone peaks. Each with their own characteristics, they are full of steep ravines running north to south from the mountains to the sea. The massifs, which are dotted with caves once used as sacred sites as well as hiding places during war, are divided by high open plateaux stretching between the ranges. Some – such as those of Omalós lying at 700m in the White Mountains of western Crete – are empty, inhabited only by grazing stock, while the more fertile plains are heavily farmed and populated.

Rising out of a baked Cretan landscape, the limestone crags of the Lefká Óri, or White Mountains, sparkle in the sun against a blue sky. On the western side of the island, the range presents a formidable barrier between the more developed north and the quieter southern coast. The mountains are penetrated by a single official road, but hold several hugely satisfying walks. A network of traditional paths – some paved, some rough – form a series of trails through the mountains. These exist alongside road upgrades and development but are still used by shepherds and goatherds, donkey-borne elderly peasants and children.

Interspersed with the sights and sounds of the Cretan countryside is the rich cultural and architectural heritage of the island. Churches and chapels, monasteries and shrines, often with internal and external frescoes, bear witness to a dominant Byzantine and Venetian influence.

Navigation

Opportunities for walking begin as early as March in a good spring (although it is still too cold for camping at this time), and last through to November. However, visitors will get the most out of a trip at either end of the main summer season – April, May and early June, or September and October – as the temperatures will be cooler and crowds will have diminished.

For political and military reasons, accurate and up to date maps of the region are non-existent. Some of the walks form part of the Cretan section of the European Rambler Association's E4 trail that crosses the island, and are, as such, waymarked by black and yellow flags. These, however, are often hijacked for target-practice by bored shepherds. Red, blue or yellow paint daubed on rocks helps to signify other routes, but walkers are advised not to rely on these too heavily.

Samariá gorge

Along with the ancient Minoan palace at Knossos, the impressive Samariá gorge and its surrounding national park ranks as one of Crete's most popular tourist attractions. The gorge deserves its reputation as an awe-inspiring (as well as strenuous) walk, and although the busy pathway can be off-putting, numbers do dwindle outside the high summer months. Famed as Europe's longest gorge, this 5-6 hour, 18km walk remains an exhilarating experience. Because of dangerous conditions during winter, the park is only open from May to mid-October.

The steep walls of the Samariá gorge

At the crack of dawn, bus-loads of tourists leave the town of Khaniá on the northern side of the island for the village and high plain of Omalós. The nearest settlement to the start of the gorge, some people disembark here for facilities and refreshments. For independent walkers, it is advisable to stay in the village overnight, rising extremely early in the morning in order to get on the trail before the crowds. A more isolated alternative is to book a night at the Kallergi hut, further to the east, which is also a good base for longer hikes into the White Mountains.

From Omalós, the road continues a short distance until at 1,200m above sea level, it reaches a tourist pavilion and the Xilóskala – a wooden staircase made from reclaimed tree trunks. From here, the 1,000m descent from the top of the plain into the upper gorge begins. To the right of the path looms Mount Gíngilos, a wall of scree and rock.

The Tarraios river that cuts through the gorge – a trickle in summer, a torrent in winter – has contributed to the verdant, alpine-like scenery for which Samariá is famous. Fragrant pines, cypresses and wildflowers cloak the slopes. The park that surrounds the gorge is one of the last mainland refuges of the Cretan wild goat or ibex, the *kri-kri*. The beasts remain

sensibly out of sight of visitors, preferring to graze on the ridges and mountains alongside the gorge.

The small plain church of Áyios Nikólaos, set beside the river amongst chestnut and eucalyptus trees, precedes the abandoned village of Samariá which marks the halfway stage of the walk. After this, the path steepens as the gorge cuts deeper into the rock. Its tall sides lean closer and closer together, their narrowest point being at the Sideropórtes or 'Iron Gates'. Here the walls rise up 325m and, only 3m apart, almost meet overhead.

The last few kilometres descend down to the fishing village of Ayía Rouméli. From here, hikers can walk east along the coast to Loutró, or, like most others, catch the boat to the ferry ports of Soúyia to the west and Hóra Sfakíon (Sfakiá) to the east, where bus services take passengers back to Khaniá or on to other destinations.

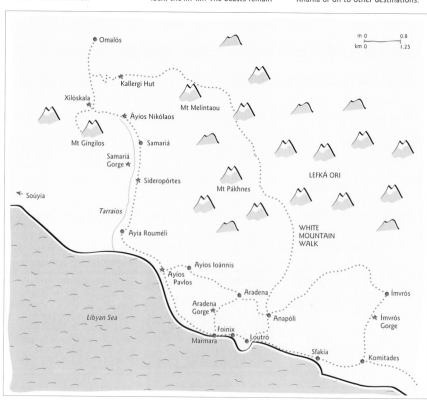

The Lefká Óri, or White Mountains, of western Crete

Mountain and coastal walks

Just before the tourist lodge at the head of the Samariá gorge, a path to the east twists and turns in a northerly direction for an hour and a half until reaching the sanctuary of the Greek Mountaineering Club hut at Kallergi. From here, the E4 route leads further north-east into the Lefká Óri, crossing a jagged landscape over barren grey rocks and passing beneath the towering height of Melíntaou (2,133m). Golden eagles soar in the thin cold air of these high regions, and true isolation is shared only by a cutting wind and the goats and sheep that graze the sparse mountainsides.

The central massif of the Lefká Óri spans 500 sq km and rises to Crete's second highest mountain, Mount Pákhnes (2,453m) – an almost inaccessible peak set in the heart of the range. From around this central core, rugged trails negotiate steep climbs over rough scree and provide several days of potentially tough but rewarding walking. Tracks often follow the routes still-used by shepherds.

The thyme-scented paths of the south-western coast skirt rocky coves and quiet beaches – less popular with tourists and developers because of their mostly pebbly shores and small size. Undulating trails along the cliffs

pass through sleepy fishing villages and provide soothing views out across the Libyan Sea. A circular walk from the village of Loutró leads north along switchback paths to the foothill village of Anapóli (from where other ways can be followed further into the mountains). From here it curves west to Aradena and south back towards the sea through the steep descent of the Aradena gorge. A 15km walk in all, it can be extended to the remote village of Ayios Ioánnis, sweeping south past the church of Ayios Pavlos overlooking the sea, and then heading west to Ayia Rouméli or east back along the coast through Marmara and the ancient port of Foinix to Loutró.

Ímvrós gorge

Ímvrós gorge is reached by walking or bussing the 3km from Sfakia via the town of Komitades. The gorge begins just after Komitades, a trail picking its way between the rocks and leading walkers inland towards the mountains. Alternatively, a bus can be taken up to Imvrós and the walk completed in a downhill direction from there to the coast. Though not as dramatic as Samariá, Ímvrós is less crowded and therefore more peaceful, although walkers are still recommended to set off early to get the most from this three hour, 8km walk.

The path follows the course of a twisting river, its rough, stony banks passing dark caves hidden deep within the hillsides. As the trail climbs higher, looking back there are fine views of the glittering sea from elevated rocky points on either side of the path. Soft pines, wild fig trees and scrubby heath waft their scents across the clear air, and give shelter to small songbirds such as the blue rock thrush.

The easy-going pebbly path becomes paved with rock slabs as the pass closes in on the gorge, its black walls creating a hollow chamber reaching up to a narrowing chink of blue sky. Towards the top of the climb, the walls widen again and open up to a high plateau topped by the village of Ímvrós and its surrounding white peaks.

CONTACT INFORMATION

Greek National Tourist Office
Pantheon Building
40 Kriari St
Khaniá
Greece
Tel: (00 301) 821 92943 / 92624

Forest Directorate of Khaniá
Chrysopygi
Khaniá
Greece
Tel: (00 301) 821 22287
Fax: (00 301) 821 21295

Walking in the Troodos Mountains

Deep in the high Troodos mountains, the attractions of clear air, tall forests and aromatic nature walks vie with Byzantine monasteries and churches, traditional mountain villages and isolated retreats.

The five domes of the 10th century Agia Paraskevi basilica

The mountains of the Troodos massif dominate the south-western side of Cyprus. The area's peaceful villages, rich wildlife and striking scenery provide a haven for visitors who wish to escape the busy coastal tourist resorts that have so transformed the island in the past few decades.

The mountain communities – each with their own particular speciality or handicraft – are welcoming and friendly, and the pace of life is relaxed. Historians, pilgrims and lovers of art and architecture all flock to the Troodos to explore the Greek and Roman remains, Byzantine churches and monasteries, and medieval fortresses that dot the countryside and the coasts.

Others are attracted by the beauty and environmental importance of a unique physical landscape, and the forests, valleys and rivers that characterise the mountain zones. Here, pine-scented paths cut through ancient forests that cover the steep slopes of hard igneous rock. The massif offers one of the best preserved and most intensively researched sequences of the Earth's crust in the world.

Although the Troodos mountains stretch across the island, the Troodos area itself refers only to the territory enclosed within a 4–5km radius of the mountain resort of the same name. Low-level forests of Calabrian pine, and plantations of black pine at

altitudes over 1,200m, form the forests that cover the area around Mt Olympus – at 1,951m, the tallest of the peaks. The Cypriot government has collectively classified the forests as a National Forest Park, with special areas of environmental sensitivity singled out as nature reserves. Designated paths are a good way of exploring Mt Olympus and the settlement of Troodos, with the wider reaches of the range also crossed by walking trails.

History

Owing to its strategic position between the African, Asian and European continents, Cyprus has witnessed an eventful and turbulent history and its location, once vast pine forests and rich mineral resources have always attracted outside interest. Its 9,000 year old civilisation has seen the arrival of the first Greek settlers in the 12th and 11th centuries BC; followed by invasions from Phoenicians, Egyptians and Romans; as well as the glories of the Byzantine era.

Crusader, Gothic and Venetian oppressors left their mark in the form of castles, churches and maritime fortifications, with British occupation following the opening of the Suez canal in the late 19th century. Under Italian and German forces, Cyprus's Jewish population was decimated during the Second World War and it was not until 1960 that the island became an independent republic. Although Cyprus has been divided since Turkey's invasion of the northern half of the island in 1974, today it is a peaceful destination.

Churches and monasteries

The Troodos region is known for its concentration of specially preserved Byzantine monasteries and churches, nine of which are included in the UNESCO world heritage list. Nestled between valleys or perched halfway

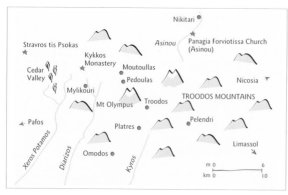

The interior frescoes of Asinou church

up inaccessible peaks, these secret jewels were hidden away to avoid the threat of foreign attack and the looting of valuable collections of relics, art and artefacts held by the priests and monks. Ranging from the tiniest mountain church to some of the larger, more prestigious monasteries, the simple rural architecture of these buildings belies the glittering Byzantine frescoes and mosaics that so richly adorn the doorways and walls of their interiors.

Trails of the Troodos

On the north-western side of the Troodos range, in the fertile cherry-growing Marathasa valley, the village of Pedoulas with its listed 15th century church is a good base for day walks leading into the heart of the mountains. Possible excursions include trails leading north to the chapel at Moutoullas; west through the green Platy valley to the village of Mylikouri; and north-west to Kykkos monastery and on to the forests of Cedar valley.

The tiny 13th century chapel at Moutoullas displays frescoes dating from 1280 and is one of the earliest examples of steep-pitched wooden roofs typical of Troodos' churches.

Lying on the northern side of the Troodos massif, the valley of Solea boasts a wealth of Byzantine churches and picturesque villages. South of Nikitari village, is the early 12th century Church of Panagia Forviotissa of Asinou. It contains extremely beautiful and important frescoes which date from the 12th century onwards. Images from the Bible and scenes depicting the Virgin Mary cover the interior walls and ceiling in vibrant blues, reds and golds.

Kykkos and Cedar valley

Kykkos monastery, the largest and most famous in Cyprus, was founded in 1100. Dedicated to the Virgin Mary, it has an ecclesiastical museum that houses a number of art treasures, including a gilt icon of the Virgin which is attributed to St Luke and is enclosed in a shrine of mother-of-pearl and tortoiseshell. The monastic community at Kykkos is also known for the production of a locally distilled spirit called *zivania*.

From Kykkos, walking trails lead south-west to the majestic natural forests of Cedar valley. The valley contains over 200,000 indigenous Cyprus cedar trees that are unique to the island.

This territory of ancient trees rising gracefully into the sky provides an important refuge for the rare Cyprus moufflon. Found only on the island, this wild sheep with huge curving horns has been adopted as the country's national animal. The forestry station at Stavros tis Psokas maintains a national reserve for the moufflon, with numerous popular nature trails of the area also starting from here.

Fragrant vegetation

The aromatic trees, shrubs and flowers of Troodos blend with the mountains, rivers and sky to create a wonderful aroma-filled environment that continually stimulates the senses. High levels of rainfall and long hours of sunshine, combined with the altitude and geology of the region, have created a special ecological niche – home to just over half of the plant species that are endemic to the island. Of these, St John's wort, Troodos cat mint and Troodos sage (from which tea is made), are endemic to these mountains, with other Mediterranean species such as orchid, cyclamen, peony, alyssum and lavender also commonly found.

ⓘ CONTACT INFORMATION

Cyprus Tourism Organisation
Leoforos Lemesou 19
PO Box 24535
CY -1390
Lefkosia (Nicosia)
Cyprus
Tel: (00 357) 2 337715
Fax: (00 357) 2 331644
E-mail: cytour@cto.org.cy
Web: www.cyprustourism.org

Cedar valley

The Lycian Way

A spectacular route through the mountains and along the coastline of south-west Turkey, following the line of Roman and Ottoman roads, mule tracks and nomad trails.

The Lycian Way is Turkey's only long-distance footpath, stretching over 400km from the popular resort of Ovacik to near the Mediterranean city of Antalya, passing through the seaside towns of Kalkan, Kaş and Finike, as well as many ancient sites.

Mount Olympos as seen from the Lycian Way

Walking the way

The Lycian peninsula which gives the route its name is a land of soaring limestone peaks, sheer cliffs, deep valleys and secluded coves; a dramatic landscape softened in places by fertile stretches of coastal plain and sandy beach. The path is waymarked to French 'Grande Randonnée' standards and there is a guidebook so navigation should not be too difficult, but this is an innovative path and some sections are remote. Although it takes in excess of forty days to complete the entire route, walkers can choose much shorter sections. Pensions and hotels can be found along the trail but in isolated areas the walker must rely on village houses or camping.

Spring is the best time to walk, as the weather is pleasantly warm, the flowers profuse and the peaks still snow capped, but short spells of wet weather cannot be ruled out. Autumn has the advantage of warm, but not hot, days, while winter brings short days but sunny weather. Remember though, with a low of sea level and a high of 1,800m, several seasons can be encountered in one day.

Mediterranean scenes

The wildflowers are stunning, especially in late winter and spring, with cyclamen, grape hyacinth, orchids and anemones in abundance. Strawberry and bay trees are common low down, while magnificent stands of cedar of Lebanon guard the high passes. The coastal strip is immensely fertile, with villagers cultivating every kind of crop from oranges and olives to aubergines and artichokes.

Hunting has reduced wildlife, but boars are numerous in forested areas and tortoises, terrapins and lizards ubiquitous. Turtles breed on some of the beaches along the route, and birds range from the rare Smyrna kingfisher to the common buzzard.

Long histories

A walk through Lycia is a walk through both landscape and history. The tombs left by the native Lycian civilisation, both free-standing sarcophagi and those carved from sheer cliffs, are unique. The area also boasts some of the best-preserved and most spectacularly situated classical sites in the Mediterranean, including the beachside Roman remains at Patara and the massive theatre at Myra. Remote Byzantine churches hide away in the valleys of Lycia, and villagers still use the Ottoman domed cisterns which dot the landscape.

On the Lycian Way near Kekova

Anemones

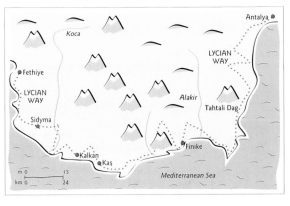

Lycian peninsula, and affording wonderful views over the sea and Taurus range, the summit can be reached with relative ease from the Lycian Way's highest point of 1,800m.

Other active ideas

If walking the Lycian Way, sunbathing, and visiting the fishing towns, villages and ancient sites in the region do not suffice, activities on and around the route include sailing and windsurfing, swimming and diving, sea kayaking and paragliding, rock climbing, canyoning and, in season, downhill and touring skiing.

[i] CONTACT INFORMATION

Upcountry (Turkey) Ltd
24 St John's Road
Buxton SK17 6XQ
Tel & Fax: 01298 71050
E-mail: upcountryturkey@
hotmail.com
Web: www.upcountry.freeserve.co.uk

Upcountry (Turkey) Ltd
Antalya P.K. 528
Turkey
Tel & Fax: (00 90) 242 243 1148
E-mail: kateclow@garanti.net.tr

Ways of life

Although many locals now derive much of their income from tourism, in the villages life continues much as it has done for centuries. The phrase used by villagers to describe travellers, *tanri misafir* (guests of God), still rings true, and it is often hard to pass through a village without being offered tea, fruit, a meal or even a bed for the night. The semi-nomadic Yörük people of the area still take their flocks of sheep and goats to the *yayla* (high pastures) in the spring, only returning to the village in autumn, and families of woodcutters carry on a traditional itinerant lifestyle in the region's many forests.

Sidyma

A couple of days from the western end of the way, the site of ancient Sidyma is one of the few places where the visitor can view a classical site much as one of the Victorian gentlemen travellers would have found it. Here, the village of Dodurga has been built amongst the ruins of the ancient city, and the pillars and blocks from Roman public buildings have been used to great effect in the locals houses and chicken coops.

Kaş and Kalkan

Once a Greek fishing village, Kaş is now a booming tourist resort with a wide range of accommodation, restaurants and shops. A good base for exploring the southernmost sections of the Lycian Way, Kaş, with its safe harbour, is used by the cruise yachts which ply the Lycian coast. Nearby, Kalkan clings to a steep cliff above a beautiful bay, a smaller, slightly upmarket version of Kaş.

Mount Olympos

Known to the Turks as Tahtali Dağ (meaning wooded mountain) this 2,366m peak is one of the many Mount Olymposes dotted around the Mediterranean world. Dominating the skyline on the eastern seaboard of the

The view across to Cirali

Turkey's Lakeland

A little known but easily accessible region of beautiful freshwater and saline lakes, high peaks, deep gorges and dark caves where the Taurus mountains meet the Anatolian plateau.

The mountains ringing the region's lakes are an extension of the Taurus mountain chain, which runs from east to west along Turkey's southern coast. At an altitude of a little over 900m, these shallow highland lakes perfectly mirror the peaks and hills rising from their shores. The largest and most beautiful are Eğirdir and Beyşehir, freshwater lakes holding carp, pike-perch and crayfish. The highest peak in the region, Dedegül, is just under the 3,000m mark, and is partially snow covered in even the hottest summer, the meltwater from which feeds into the massive cave system which riddles the massif.

The region is semi-arid, with most of the precipitation occurring in winter and early spring. Winters are cold, with snow falling heavily on the mountains. When the northerly *poyraz* wind blows down from Russia, the wind chill factor is telling, and in exceptional years Lake Eğirdir has frozen. Spring is generally temperate, with warm days and cold evenings, giving way to a dry, hot summer, though daytime highs seldom exceed 30°C and nights are pleasantly cool.

Wildflowers and rare birds

Much of the forest and vegetation has fallen prey to woodcutters and goats, but pine and cedar trees still clad the lower slopes of the mountains. There are also spectacular displays of spring flowers when the winter snows begin their annual recession, with wild tulips and crocuses in profusion.

The Kaşnak forest near Kovada lake is famous for a unique type of oak tree that was once prized for barrel making, and is also home to a variety of butterflies. Wild boar roam the forested mountains to the south of Eğirdir, and foxes and badgers are fairly common.

Lammergeier vultures, lesser spotted eagles and alpine choughs circle the higher peaks. Turkey's lakeland is also on a very important bird migration route, and bird-watchers from all over the world are attracted to the region in May, hoping to see passing rarities, as well as indigenous species like the golden oriole and crag martin.

The town of Eğirdir

The most attractive lakeland town, and the only one to have adequate facilities for large numbers of visitors, Eğirdir is built on a peninsula jutting out into the lake of the same name. Hittites, Phrygians and Byzantines all once controlled the town, but its major monuments, the mosque of Hızır Bey and the Islamic religious school of Dündar Bey, were built by the Selçuk Turks in 13th century. Perhaps the most attractive feature is Yeşilada, a tiny offshore island now linked to the town by a causeway. The many comfortable pensions and small hotels on this peaceful island retreat make a natural base for organising day walks or longer treks in the surrounding mountains.

The Angel's Pastures below Dedegül

Dedegül and the mountains

Many of the lakeland peaks are easily within the range of the averagely fit and experienced hillwalker, but three in particular stand out. The highest of these is 2,992m Dedegül, a bulky giant that is surprisingly easy to climb, and can be done in one long day. The usual starting point is Melekler Yaylasi (Angel's Pastures) at 1,700m, which is a lovely alpine meadow set in pine forest. The views over Lake Beyşehir from the summit are superb.

Closer to Eğirdir, 2,635m Davraz can also be scaled in a day, but camping on the mountain will make it a more memorable experience. With views to the north over Lake Eğirdir and the Isparta plain and to the south over the Taurus range, the ridge walk along Davraz's 'spine' is recommended.

Mt Barla has a more rounded profile than Davraz or Dedegül, and its whale-back ridge dominates the western shore of Eğirdir lake. Beneath the mountain sits the village of Barla, a cluster of wooden houses huddled together at the foot of a dramatic rock spur, surrounded by orchards of walnut, apricot and cherry trees. The remains of an old Greek church perch on a hillside above the village, and a massive plane tree shades a house where an important and controversial Moslem saint once lived and preached.

Yörük nomads on Mt Barla

Ways of life

Fishermen using small wooden boats and nets still eke a precarious living from the Eğirdir and Beyşehir lakes. Tourism is becoming more important, but the mainstay of the economy is agriculture, particularly fruit farming, and autumn is a riot of apple blossom. Isparta has a traditional carpet industry, and also distils the rosewater used in soap and perfumes from the petals of the rosebushes that grow on the surrounding plain.

Of most interest to the walker are the Yörük people, nomads whose black goat hair tents dot the mountain slopes in spring and summer, and who will often invite the walker in to share a glass of sweet black tea or *ayran* (a salted yoghurt drink). Beware, though, of their fierce dogs guarding the flocks against predators.

ℹ CONTACT INFORMATION

Upcountry (Turkey) Ltd
24 St John's Road
Buxton SK17 6XQ
Tel & Fax: 01298 71050
E-mail: upcountryturkey@hotmail.com
Web: www.upcountry.freeserve.co.uk

Upcountry (Turkey) Ltd
Antalya P.K. 528
Turkey
Tel & Fax: (00 90) 242 243 1148
E-mail: kateclow@garanti.net.tr

Fishermen on Lake Eğirdir

The Aladağlar Mountains

A lofty group of limestone peaks, the Aladağlar mountains are the highest of the mighty Taurus chain, and are often compared by climbers and trekkers to the Italian Dolomites.

![The Aladağlar range]

The Aladağlar range

A number of impressive peaks are squeezed into the 1,000 sq km covered by this compact range, the highest of which is Mt Demirkazik at 3,756m. The uplands are dotted with several permanent and many seasonal lakes, despite the porous nature of the limestone rock, and there are some very impressive waterfalls to the east of the range. *Ala* means speckled in Turkish, and *dağlar* translates as mountains, the name 'speckled mountains' coming from the fantastic contrasts of colour, light and shade in

this rugged range, where the white limestone is stained red and black in places, and the peaks glow pink and cream in the sunset.

June and early July are good months to visit, as the weather is generally stable, warm and sunny, the high passes are negotiable and there is plenty of drinking water. Later in the summer, temperatures get very hot in the day, even at altitude, and the streams and lakes dry up. October is much cooler and pleasant for walking but the first snows usually begin to fall. Winter brings a lot of snow, with avalanches presenting a real risk in March, April and even May.

Hidden inhabitants

Bird-watchers visit the Aladağlar in numbers, partly because it is on a major autumn migration route, partly because of the birds who live in these mountains year round. Species they particularly seek out are the grouse-like Caspian snow cock, the wallcreeper and the alpine accentor, as well as many types of birds of prey. Alpine flowers stud the meadows in spring and early summer. Pine forests cloak the lower slopes of some peaks,

whilst around the villages, mulberry and walnut trees are ubiquitous, and apple orchards a sea of blossom in spring. Ibex and possibly even wolves still inhabit the range, although the casual walker is very unlikely to come across either. However, foxes and marmots are more common.

A way of life

In summer the alpine meadows of the mountains are alive with the sound of bleating flocks of sheep and goats, and the black wool tents of the

Map labels:
- Demirkazik
- Mt Demirkazik
- Niğde
- Mt Embler
- Yedigöller
- Mt Kizilkaya
- Mt Cebel
- Mt Kaldi

nomadic Yörük people sit clustered around water sources. Shepherds wander high up the mountainsides in search of fresh grass for their charges, whilst the women back at camp milk the flocks, churn butter and make cheese and yoghurt. The women are also highly skilled in weaving, and produce beautiful flatweave carpets *(kilims)* to traditional designs.

Trekking and walking

The most popular route is a traverse of the range, starting in the north at the *Dağ evi* (mountain hut) just above Demirkazik village and in the shadow of Mt Demirkazik. The hut is an excellent base for day walkers, offering comfortable accommodation, and access to both the highest peak and several interesting valleys.

It takes several days to reach the easterly exit point, the village of Ulupinar, below which are the Kapus falls, where a number of underground streams burst with spectacular force from a dramatic cliff-face. En route the walker will pass beneath the faces of several lofty peaks, negotiate a 3,450m pass and spend some time around the Yörük encampments on the Yedigöller (Seven Lakes) plateau.

Walkers with a rope and experience can ascend some of the peaks without too much difficulty, including the

Celikbuyduran pass in May

classic south-east face of Mt Demirkazik. However, the peak most easily accessible to the trekker as opposed to mountaineer is the impressively high Mt Embler. At 3,723m, it is the second highest peak in the range but only a two hour round trip from the head of the 3,450m Çelikbuyduran pass.

Central Turkey

The density of the imposing peaks and relative ease of access from Ankara or the Mediterranean coast at Adana make this the most popular mountain range in Turkey. Trekking, walking and technical mountaineering are the most obvious activities in the region, along with ski mountaineering and touring in winter, and bird-watching in spring and autumn.

The surreally eroded landscape of Cappadocia and its warrens of rock dwellings and churches lies just to the north; indeed the town of Niğde, on the southernmost rim of Cappadocia, is the natural starting point for trips in the Aladağlar. The Mediterranean coast directly south of the range is disappointingly flat and industrialised, although it gets spectacularly better west of Mersin.

ℹ CONTACT INFORMATION

Upcountry (Turkey) Ltd
24 St John's Road
Buxton SK17 6XQ
Tel & Fax: 01298 71050
E-mail: upcountryturkey@hotmail.com
Web: www.upcountry.freeserve.co.uk

Upcountry (Turkey) Ltd
Antalya P.K. 528
Turkey
Tel & Fax: (00 90) 242 243 1148
E-mail: kateclow@garanti.net.tr

Mule and muleteer, with Mt Demirkazik behind

CONTACT INFORMATION

Bulgaria –
BAAT (Bulgarian Association
for Special Interest Travel)
20-V Stamboliiski Blvd
Sofia 1000
Bulgaria
Tel: (00 359) 2 989 0538
Fax: (00 359) 2 980 3200
E-mail: odysseia@omega.bg
Web: www.newtravel.com

Croatian National Tourist Office
2 The Lanchesters
162-164 Fulham Palace Road
London W6 9ER
Tel: 020 8563 7979
Fax: 020 8563 2616
E-mail: info@cnto.freeserve.co.uk
Web: www.htz.hr

Czech Tourist Authority
Czech Centre
95 Great Portland Street
London WIN 5RA
Tel: 020 7291 9920
Fax: 020 7436 8300
Web: www.czech-tourinfo.cz

Estonian Tourist Board
Mündi 2
10146 Tallinn
Estonia
Tel: (00 372) 641 1420
Fax: (00 372) 641 1432
E-mail: info@tourism.ee
Web: www.tourism.ee

Hungarian National Tourist Office
46 Eaton Place
London SWIX 8AL
Tel: 020 7823 1032
Fax: 020 7823 1459
E-mail: htlondon@hungarytourism.hu
Web-site: www.hungarytourism.hu

Latvian Tourist Board
4 Pils Square
LV1050 Riga
Latvia
Tel & Fax: (00 371) 722 9945
E-mail: ltboard@latnet.lv
Web: www.latviatravel.com

Lithuanian State Department
of Tourism
Vilniaus g. 4/35
2600 Vilnius
Lithuania
Tel: (00 370) 2 622610
Fax: (00 370) 2 226819
E-mail: tb@tourism.lt
Web: www.tourism.lt

Polish National Tourist Office
Remo House
310-312 Regent Street
London WIR 5AY
Tel: 020 7580 8811
Fax: 020 7580 8866
E-mail: pnto@dial.pipex.com
Web: www.pnto.dial.pipex.com

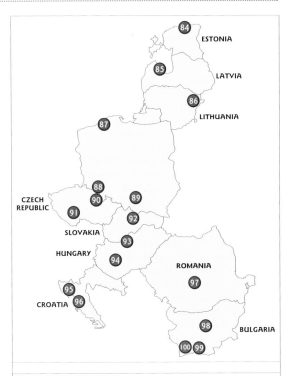

Romanian National
Tourist Office
83a Marylebone High Street
London WIM 3DE
Tel: 020 7224 3692
Fax: 020 7935 6435

Slovakia –
Czech & Slovak Tourist Centre
16 Frognal Parade
Finchley Road
London NW3 5HH
Tel: 0800 026 7943
Fax: 020 7794 3265
Web: www.czech-slovak-tourist.co.uk

ESTONIA

The North Estonian Glint

Following the Glint, as it traverses the most Westernised of the new Baltic states, reveals a complex and enthralling cross section of the country's environment and history

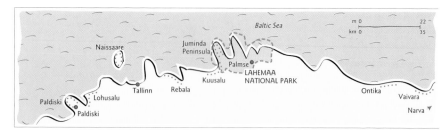

Estonia is rightly proud of the quality and diversity of its jagged peninsulas, deep-cut bays, mixed forests, rushing rivers and naturally acidic peat bogs, and is keen to promote itself as a centre for ecotourism. To the east of the capital city, Tallinn, is Lahemaa National Park, whilst along the coast are several short sections of Euroroute 9, the transcontinental route from the French Atlantic to St Petersburg. But don't presume that northern Estonia is always pristine. Its other allure is the ebb and flow of human history; of endeavour and opulence in medieval trading ports set against the turbulence and oppression of the 20th century.

Summer sunsets

Winter is cold, dark and short; ideal for sitting in the warmth of a café or cellar bar in Tallinn, but not for exploring the wind-whipped coastline. The summer months are warm and breezy. June is a time of short nights, as the sun dips just below the horizon, bathing the sky in shades of pink rather than bringing darkness.

The North Estonian Glint

The Glint provides a theme of physical continuity as it threads its way for over 200km across this part of Estonia. Stand at the edge of the sea

and turn to face south; the Glint is the limestone plateau that rises up sharply from the lower lying coastal plains. The break point is marked by a banked wall, often eroded to present a gentle slope, but sometimes still a high limestone cliff of browns, greys, yellows and mottled whites.

The North Estonian Glint is a small part of the Baltic Glint that sweeps from Öland, near Sweden, across the Baltic seabed to Lake Ladoga in Russia. Limestone and dolomite rocks form the top layers, overhanging the softer clay and shale which are eroded at a faster rate. To the west of Tallinn, at Türisalu and Rannamõisa, the sea still

The sandy seashore at Lahemaa

The nature trail through the Viru raised peat bog in Lahemaa

meets the cliff and the waves keep the face clean, revealing the intricacies of the geological layers. East of Tallinn, the Glint is fronted by a wide coastal plain. Here the face is often hidden by rock debris, but Lahemaa's Valgejõgi valley has open sections.

Tallinn

Tallinn is an atmospheric city of narrow backstreets breaking out into open squares. Whilst the architecture is medieval Germanic – townhouses with tall, thin windows and colourful facades – the town is now influenced by the West, in particular Helsinki which is only 80km north. Everyone recommends exploring Tallinn on foot. From the thick stone and cone-topped watchtowers of the outer walls, visitors wind their way through the

A forest nature trail in Lahemaa

213

Graveyard Gate on Naissaare island, a 19th century memorial to English sailors

Maarja church on Naissaare, first built in 1856

main square. Here, Old Thomas, a weather vane, sits on the town hall keeping a protective lookout. The trail ends at Toompea, where the elaborate arches and green domes of the Alexander Nevsky cathedral sit opposite the pink castle, now home to Estonia's new parliament. Alternatively, take a ferry to the nearby island of Naissaare and follow the waymarked route around the southern coast.

Lahemaa National Park

Lahemaa (the Land of Bays) is a peaceful slice of rural Estonia, full of varied landscapes interspersed with snippets of the country's history. The coast has a serrated outline with pointed peninsulas undercut by wide bays. The Glint lies further inland, so flat plains roll right down to the Baltic's edge. Seabirds are uncommon as the level ground provides little protection, although gulls, mallards and swans are found at Eru Bay.

Nearly 70% of the park is covered in forest. Swathes of dry pine on sandy soils mix with smaller areas of deciduous woodland containing elm, ash and alder. The trees echo with the chirping of songbirds and the insistent tap of woodpeckers. Undergrowth and clearings are the habitat of birch mice and red squirrels, as well as prowling wolves, lumbering brown bears and browsing moose. Although tracks may be evident, especially in winter, the animals are usually difficult to spot.

The other important ecosystem in Lahemaa is bogland. Surrounded by pine and willow, the acidic waters of the mires support a few hardy plants, whilst bog pines grow in the better drained areas. Where the excess water accumulates in pools there is no vegetation. The brown water, far from being polluted, is very pure but too acidic to support even algae. The bogs' solitude makes them a haven for birds. Cranes arrive every autumn on their way south, whilst rare species include red-throated divers.

Lahemaa's trails

The park authorities have developed a series of routes that introduce visitors to the different landscapes. The Viru explores the quiet stillness of a raised peat bog; the Nõmmevseki follows the River Valgejõgi as it crosses the Glint's cliff face; the Käsmu combines pine forests with glacial deposits on the coastal plain; and the Majakivi leads walkers around the Juminda peninsula to one of the largest erratic boulders in Estonia.

The eastern side of Naissaare island

Just to the south-west of the park, the 23km Kuusalu Path is an introduction to the area's folklore and early history. Starting from the village of the same name, the first stop is the site of a 9th century willow stronghold built on log rafts in the middle of a bog. From here, travel further back in time to a group of Bronze Age stone-chest barrows at Hundikangrud and pitted sacrificial stones at Alliku. The final site is the former Muuksi stronghold, a 2,000 year old fortress protected on two sides by steep cliffs and on a third by a now ruined stone wall. Locals used to gather here to light bonfires on Midsummer's Night.

Paldiski

Paldiski graphically illustrates Estonia's 20th century. Originally established as a naval stronghold by Peter the Great in the early 1700s, the port was off limits to all except the military following the Soviet occupation. It was home to a submarine training school, as well as facilities that produced nuclear fuel. Paldiski has not yet recovered from this legacy; depopulated with the Soviet withdrawal, it remains a stark, forlorn reminder of the recent past.

However, the town is the starting point of a 26km hike that explores the impressive Pakri Cape Landscape Reserve. The Glint's cliffs are in evidence all around the coast, rising from the sea and reaching a height of 25m at the tip of the peninsula. The 19th century lighthouse still operates, flashing its warning lights over the water. On the eastern side, the streams that drain the grasslands and woods tumble over the bank, forming mini waterfalls with the spring melt, before drying in the heat of summer. Off the coast at Leetse, a glacial boulder 17m in circumference sits alone in the sea. Nearby are the ruins of a 17th century manor, and the remains of a Soviet missile base.

The eastern landscape

The landscape changes east of Lahemaa. The scattered remnants of postwar open-cast mining and smokestacks linger. The clearance of this industrial detritus is a mammoth task and will take many years.

The North Estonian Glint

Narva is the point at which Estonia ends. More Russian than Estonian in character, the city is a shadow of its former self. The historic wealth of this ancient trading port was reduced to rubble after the Second World War and only a few original buildings remain. One of them, Narva castle, sits squarely on the river's edge confronting the Ivanogrod fortress on the Russian banks, reminding visitors that present animosities are not new.

Between Lahemaa and Narva another section of the E9 has been established. The Vaivara Path passes through forests and climbs hills, continually testifying to the conflicts that have plagued Estonia. From Vaivara, twice destroyed by war, the path reveals a litany of graveyards, bunkers, trenches and fortifications from the First World War, Wars of Independence (1918-20) and the Second World War. This walk reveals why Estonia is so proud of its independence.

CONTACT INFORMATION

Estonian Tourist Board
Mündi 2
10146 Tallinn
Estonia
Tel: (00 372) 641 1420
Fax: (00 372) 641 1432
Web: www.tourism.ee

Lahemaa National Park Visitor Centre
Palmse
EE45202 Viitna
Estonia
Tel: (00 372) 32 34196
E-mail: i-palmse@lahemaa.neti.ee

From Riga to Cape Kolka

Scratch the surface and Latvia reveals fragments of different worlds – the Art Nouveau architecture, the fields where the corncrake thrives, and the last of the Livs.

Latvia is a new nation, rightly proud of gaining its independence in 1991. As the country emerges from its cocoon, it is the reassertion of a long-held and distinctive national identity that is most likely to interest visitors. Latvia does much more than mimic the late 20th century West; instead there are opportunities to weave a slow path through the country's varied histories. For walkers it is a chance to amble and explore rather than stride out on a long trek.

Whilst Riga has the bustle and sophistication of any capital city, there is still the chance to step away into a quiet street or pause in the shadows of a church in the old city. To the west, along the coast, life moves at a slower pace again. Here there is solitude: circuitous journeys through spacious parks and forests; paddling in the sea as the waves lap onto the long, sandy beaches; or pottering in small museums and fishing villages, recreating images of past people and communities.

Riga's history

Riga will celebrate its octocentenary in 2001 and is keen to reawaken interest in itself; it was only in the 1930s that Riga's glitzy combination of contemporary architecture and fashionable social scene saw it labelled 'the Paris of the North'.

Back in the the 13th century, shortly after its establishment by the German Knights of the Sword, the archbishops of Riga gained ascendancy in the city. As a member of the Hanseatic League, Riga was the funnel for all the trade along the River Daugava between Russia to the east and the Baltic to the west. The wealth of the city is reflected in its houses and churches. One day Riga will possibly become as popular as Prague; however, whilst the city remains just a little unknown, there is still the chance to absorb a Latvian atmosphere, rather than an international one.

Kemeri National Park

Riga's heritage

A stroll through the streets of the city centre reveals the built legacy of each generation, with Romanesque, Gothic, Baroque, Neoclassical and Art Nouveau styles, as well as variations in between, clashing enthusiastically. One of the best examples of this is the Dome cathedral. A vast red-bricked edifice dominating the main square, it was begun in the 1200s; various reconstructions through the centuries have made a heady mixture of styles. Today it houses the world's fourth largest organ and hosts regular concerts. The spire on top of St Peter's church is a good place to look over

Black stork chicks

the rest of the old city; the narrow streets, the castle, the medieval guild houses, the squat Swedish Gate and the Powder Tower, the last remaining of the eighteen towers that once guarded the perimeter wall.

To the east, beyond the tight knit old quarter, is the spread of 19th and 20th century Riga. Elizabetes and Alberta Streets contain some of the best examples of German Art Nouveau architecture in Europe. On Brivibas Boulevard stands the Latvian version of the Statue of Liberty, built in 1935 as a symbol of national independence. North of the monument is Bastion Hill and a memorial to the five people killed in 1991 by Soviet troops. Latvia's history is never simply old.

Latvia's riviera

Sandwiched between the sea and the Lielupe river, Jūrmala is a calm, tranquil stretch of sandy beaches, sweet smelling pine forests and wooden summerhouses sitting quietly on empty streets. With its sulphurous waters and curative muds, the fifteen separate villages that comprise the resort originally developed as a series of health spas in the 18th century. The western end of Jūrmala is included in Kemeri National Park which was established in 1997.

The focal point of this part of Kemeri is a large landscape park which intertwines the natural and the man-made; artificial islands sit in lakes and canals connect streams. Wandering the 15km of paths or boating the waterways reveals more of the human influence on the park. There is a grand five storey hotel, its Classical portico reminiscent of a fine English country house, as well as a rotunda on the 'Isle of Love' and a hermitage deliberately lost in the woods.

The beach is a popular destination with Latvians

Kemeri National Park

Beyond Jūrmala, Kemeri is more of what is normally expected of a national park. Inland is a sweep of forests criss-crossed with paths that ford streams and skirt marshes. In summer people pick blueberries, cranberries, cloudberries and raspberries, or hunt for mushrooms under the trees. A rustle of leaves may be the passing of a shy red deer and the footprints in the mud evidence of wild boar. Three-toed and

white-backed woodpeckers tap insistently, whilst eagles hunt on high. The mires are home to rare orchids – Baltic marsh, flecked marsh, fen and Lady's slipper – as well as solitary elk. In hayfields there is a good chance of hearing the distinctive *crex crex* cry of a corncrake. Declining drastically throughout Europe as intensive agriculture envelopes more farmland, corncrakes are a regular summer visitor to Latvia and their presence has been celebrated in song, on stamps and on coins.

The Livs

Before the arrival of the German invaders before the 13th century, it was the Livs, a Finno-Ugric people, who were the sole inhabitants of what is now Latvia. Now their language and culture are nearly extinct; fourteen fishing villages on the rugged

coastline of the north-west have been made protected areas but this may be too late as there are only ten native speakers left. At Cape Kolka, walking through the dunes and forests reveals an isolation and wildness not really found at Kemeri. Here it is easy to understand the plain colouring of the Liv flag: green for the forests, white for the beach and blue for the sea.

ℹ CONTACT INFORMATION

Latvian Tourist Board
4 Pils Square
LV1050 Riga
Latvia
Tel & Fax: (00 371) 722 9945
Web: www.latviatravel.com

Kemeri National Park
'Meza Maja'
LV2012 Kemeri -Jūrmala
Latvia
Tel: (00 371) 776 5386
Fax: (00 371) 776 5040

Lady's-slipper orchid

Aukštaitija National Park

*Travelling through Aukštaitija in a small boat creates an intimacy with
this fascinating landscape as visitors are saturated with the noises and
colours of the lakes and forests.*

Aukštaitija is a park of lakes. There are
126 of them – some several hundred
hectares in size, many much smaller –
linked by rivers and streams, and it is
this network of water that makes it
difficult to walk within the park.
Away from the small roads that snake
between villages, most paths soon
peter out at a bank edge. The best
way to travel is by boat, moving at
the pace of the current, stopping off
to climb hills and peer into forests,
and camping under the night sky.

In eastern Lithuania, away from the
milder influence of the Baltic Sea, the
climate exhibits some continental
characteristics. Only the brave should
attempt a winter visit. Frosts sharpen
the morning air as early as September
and can linger to May, whilst thick
snows cover the ground from
December to March. Most visitors,
however, come between June and
September. Temperatures are in the
high teens in July, although the daily
weather is described euphemistically
as 'changeable', so be prepared.

Aukštaitija National Park

Established as Lithuania's first
national park in 1974, Aukštaitija has
traditionally been a popular location
for holidays. The capital city, Vilnius,
is only 100km to the south.
The area's protected status helps to
promote the sustainable use of an

important landscape: shelter for the
rare plants and forest animals, better
recreational facilities for visitors, and
the continuation of rural occupations.

Standing on top of Ladakalnis Hill
(175m) provides a good impression of
the 405 sq km park. Moulded during
the last Ice Age, the landscape is full
of soft undulations. Ridges of glacial
material and hills are given blurred
green outlines by the sweep of dense
coniferous trees, whilst the lower
ground is covered with clean blue
water. The lakes lie next to each other
forming a chain, with wooded
moraines or slight rises in the bedrock
acting as separating strips.

The green and the blue

Forests cover nearly two thirds of the
park. The majority are old pine stands
– the one at Ažvinčiai being around
200 years old – although there is also
a substantial amount of spruce and
birch, as well as a juniper grove at
Pabaluose which is rare so far north.

The bee-keeping museum at Stripeikiai

The depths of the forests are inhabited by elk, red and roe deer, wild boar, foxes and the occasional wolf. Rare plant species thrive in the darkest nooks. A single specimen of the ghost orchid, with its translucent pale pink flowers, grows in a reserve. It is the only example in Lithuania.

Along the lake edges feed black-throated divers, black storks, curlews and snipes. In wet pastures a small splash of crimson could be a Siberian iris; yellow marsh saxifrage prosper in the marshes around Lake Gilūtas in the south; whilst white water lilies, with their bright white petals and yellow stamen, float languorously on the water's surface in secluded coves.

Starting from Palūšė

There are over one hundred settlements scattered throughout the park. Often consisting of no more than a few farming families they are home to only 2,000 inhabitants in total. Most visitors will spend some time in Palūšė. As well as being the location of the park's administrative centre, most of the tours and paths branch out from the village.

A botanical trail loops to the north, an introduction to the forests, the lakes, the meadows and the wetlands, whilst a 5km fitness trail attracts the energetic. An old church is the main feature of Palūšė itself. Built in the 1750s, the small Baroque building displays parchment-yellow timber topped with a silver-grey pitched roof. Next to it is a freestanding bell-tower. The bell, which still rings, dates from 18th century, as do artefacts in the church itself.

A passage through the park

Most boat trips go west into Lake Lušiai where a sculpture trail through the forest runs along the north shore. People have lived in Aukštaitija for over 2,000 years and during this time each lake and hill has gained a name and a story. The trail builds on this theme, with carved totems depicting scenes from folk tales or drawing inspiration from the environment.

On the southern edge of Lake Baluošas, where in Russian doll style one of the five islands has its own lake, is Trainiškis. Near the village is a solitary oak tree, 23m high and 800

Ghost orchid

years old, once reputedly the site of pagan sacrifices. Just to the south is the Balčio strict wildlife reserve and several kilometres to the north is Ažvinčiai forest, although entry to either fragile environment is not permitted without a park guide.

Apiculturists, or beekeepers, have always had a distinctive role in Lithuania. As far back as the early 16th century their duties and rights were written in law. The history of the art is documented at Stripeikiai's bee-keeping museum and visitors are encouraged to taste the final product.

The Ginučiai mound sits between Lake Ūkojas and Lake Linkmenas. Evidence of a moat and ramparts suggest it may have been the site of Linkmenas castle, a defensive position protecting Lithuania's border in the Middle Ages. Close by is Ladakalnis Hill. As the hill is a good starting point for a visit to the park it can be worth walking the 10km trail from Palūšė before going on a boat trip.

CONTACT INFORMATION

Aukštaitija National Park
Tourism Centre
4759 Palūšė
Ignalinos District
Lithuania
Tel: (00 370) 29 52891
Fax: (00 370) 29 53135
E-mail: anp@is.lt

The watery Aukštaitija landscape

Poland's Baltic Coast

The Baltic coast has a pleasant, bracing climate – a perfect encouragement to march briskly along the endless shoreline and explore the back streets of the old ports.

Poland's Baltic coast is an undulating landscape of sandy beaches, rolling dunes and small coastal lakes with the flat expanse of the blue-grey Baltic Sea merging into the horizon. Outside of July and August, the coast is quiet with the resorts returning to their usual peaceful existence as sleepy fishing towns and villages. Inland lies the Pomeranian Lakelands, with their swathe of primeval forest filled with rushing streams and dotted with hundreds of small lakes.

Spring comes late to the coast and is generally followed by short, cool summers. Occasional summer highs are the best time for swimming in the Baltic. Not being a warm sea, only the brave will venture in at other times. Autumn tends to be warmer than in central Poland, whilst winters are short with only a smattering of snow.

The shifting dunes in Słowiński National Park

PTTK

The Polish Tourist Country Lovers' Society (PTTK) is one of the oldest outdoor organisations in Europe. As well as actively being involved in protecting and preserving Poland's ecological heritage, the PTTK has marked thousands of miles of walking, cycling, riding and kayaking routes throughout the country. Their hostels provide a useful network of accommodation, especially in the depths of the countryside.

Euroroute 9

The Baltic Coast makes up a section of E9, one of the long distance walking routes across the continent. The Polish portion starts at Świnoujście on the Polish–German border and finishes 537km later at Braniewo near to the Russian enclave of Kaliningrad. The route takes walkers through Poland's two coastal national parks and the Hanseatic trading ports.

Wolin National Park

The Island of Wolin rests on top of Szczecin Bay in the north-west corner of Poland. The core of the island is now a national park with 40km of walking trails. On the exposed Baltic side of the island the 95m high cliffs are being severely eroded by the sea and the wind, and are retreating nearly a metre a year. On the opposite side, protected by the bay, there are wide sandy beaches and dunes with thick clumps of sea holly. Inland, the hills are covered with mixed and deciduous forest, including ancient beech stands.

Gdańsk's medieval river frontage

Each route is no more than a day ramble, but there is always plenty to see; an ecology centre at Międzyzdroje provides a good introduction to the area; a climb up the very small Zielonka Hill gives clear views over the river marshes; whilst the crystal clear lakes in the east of the park are bewitching. Over 230 species of bird have been recorded in the park, including the white-tailed sea eagle with its majestic 2.5m wing span.

Słowiński National Park

Słowiński protects Europe's most active area of shifting dunes. Two large coastal lakes – Łebsko and Gardno – are separated from the sea by a 35km long sand bar. The stable 'grey' dunes are overgrown with lyme grass, beach grass and pine, whilst the 'white' dunes are constantly being shifted by the winds. These latter dunes are presently moving inland at a rate of 10m per year, burying pine trees and encroaching on coastal lakes.

As well as a trail along the length of the sand bar, there is an inland route of similar length past the silted lake edges and across the peatlands that form the other part of Słowiński. The park is an important staging post on annual bird migration routes and walkers may also spot rare Polish species such as king eider, Richard's pipit and white-winged lark.

Gdańsk

The major Baltic port of the Hanseatic League, Gdańsk developed rapidly from the 14th century as a independent and prosperous trading

city protected by the Polish kings. The German merchants celebrated their wealth with richly decorated churches, fine 16th century town houses, wide streets and impressive archways. Tragically the city was destroyed towards the end of the Second World War, but the historic core has since been painstakingly and magnificently restored. North of the Gdańsk lies the Hel peninsula, a sand bar which stretches out protectively into the Gulf of Gdańsk. Only 500m wide, the sand bar sits 20m above the sea, the dunes stabilised by pine

trees. Boats run regularly from Gdańsk, and away from the small summer resorts the beaches are empty and quiet with only the whistling wind for company.

Pomeranian Lakeland

Drawa National Park is at the heart of the Pomeranian Lakeland. The area is characterised by ancient forests and ribbon lakes interspersed with flat peat bogs, whilst the absence of industry and limited agricultural development means that this environment is largely untainted. The PTTK has marked several walks around the lakes and through the villages.

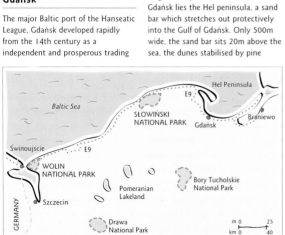

CONTACT INFORMATION

Słowiński National Park
Bohaterów Warsawy 1A
76-214 Smołdzino
Poland
Tel : (00 48) 59 811 7204
Fax: (00 48) 59 811 7509
E-mail: spn_park@sl.onet.pl

Wolin National Park
ul. Niepodległości 3
72-510 Międzyzdroje
Poland
Tel: (00 48) 91 328 0737

Silesia and the Sudeten Mountains

*In the south-west of Poland the historical heritage of the lowlands
is combined with the remote beauty of the mountains.*

The sandstone rocks of Góry Stołowe

The Silesian Lowlands are flat and densely populated. Having been won and lost in battle and traded in diplomatic treaties over the centuries, the towns and cities display Austrian, Bohemian, Prussian, Russian and Polish influences. The wars are reflected in the imposing castles, the wealth of the medieval traders in the resplendent architecture, and the importance of religion in the fine churches and pilgrimage routes.

The Sudeten mountains lie to the south, lining the Polish border with the Czech Republic. Lower in altitude than their Carpathian counterparts to the east, the mountains are older and more rounded. Here the landscape is distinctly rural with farms, small resorts and spa towns nestling in valleys beneath forested slopes.

This part of Poland offers a mixture of routes. As well as exploring individual local areas, walkers can follow several long trails which link the lowlands with the mountains and their national parks. Both short and long routes are well marked by the Polish Tourist Country Lovers' Society (PTTK), which also operates hostels and tourist accommodation across the country.

Long distance trails

International routes I-21 and I-22 start in the lowlands, the I-21 on the River Odra at Wrocław and the I-22 to the west in Legnica. Both routes head south, passing through the Góry Stołowe region at the centre of the Sudeten range before arriving at the Czech border. The E3 is part of the trans-European network running from the French Atlantic across to the Black Sea. Poland's Sudeten section starts to the west of the town of Jelenia Góra and runs along the foothills of the Karkonosze mountains before sweeping south through the Góry Złote to the Czech Republic.

Wrocław to the mountains

Wrocław is Poland's fourth largest city and the main tourist attraction of the lowlands. Prior to the Second World War, Wrocław was the German city of Breslau. The city was largely destroyed and abandoned during the final stages of the war, before being repopulated in the post-war years by Poles who were displaced by the Soviet Union's westward shift. Restoration has been a slow process and is not as complete

as in other cities. However Wrocław is still very impressive with its central marketplace and numerous museums, as well as houses, churches and bridges in Gothic, Renaissance and Baroque styles.

South of Wrocław the main points of interest are Sobótka and Świdnica. At Sobótka, Mt Ślęża rises sharply from the surrounding plain. The mountain was an important centre of pagan worship until the 11th century and rough granite sculptures are still scattered over the slopes. Further south-west is Świdnica, a town that rivalled Wrocław for economic dominance in the 14th and 15th centuries. Swidnica's mercantile wealth, as usual, found expression in the sumptuous architecture of the core of the city.

Legnica to the mountains

To the south of the industrial town of Legnica is Legnica Field, where in 1241 the Tartar army, sweeping westwards across Europe, defeated the Silesians in battle, beheading their leader. However, the events of the day slowed and weakened the Tartars and they were subsequently unable to

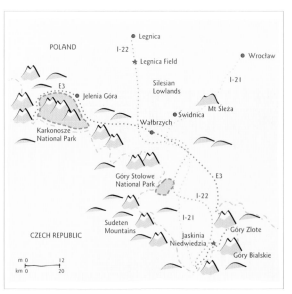

forests on the lower slopes through to peat bogs and rocky summits. The best trip is the exhilarating ridge walk between Mt Szrenica (1,362m) and Mt Śnieżka (1,602m).

Góry Złote

To the east of Wałbrzych, the E3 route swings southwards through Góry Złote which lies just across the Kłodzko valley from Góry Stołowe. Miedzygórze is a pleasant base to start from and there are several paths leading to the highest point at Mt Śnieżnik (1,425m). However, the best sight is actually hidden down in the valley near Kletno. Here is Jaskinia Niedźwiedzia (Bear cave). Named after its Ice Age inhabitants, the cave is now home to several species of rare bat. Visitors explore the upper level corridors and rooms with their beautiful stalactites and stalagmites.

take Legnica itself. A church now commemorates the site of the execution. The route continues south, passing through pleasant countryside until Wałbrzych appears on the horizon. The city is a dirty, industrial centre which is best avoided. However, don't miss Ksiaz castle – an eclectic collection of architectural styles, with each new wing or tower seemingly built with a general disregard for the aesthetics of the existing structure.

Góry Stołowe

Both I-21 and I-22 wind their way through Góry Stołowe National Park. Góry Stołowe means 'table mountains' and consists of a weathered sandstone plateau topped by rock formations shaped by wind and water erosion. Szczeliniec (919m) is a geological reserve with 'the giant's head' and 'the camel' amongst its outcrops. Nearby at Bledne Skały, sandstone boulders form a giant rock labyrinth.

A day or two can easily be spent wandering about the park, exploring all its nooks and crannies and enjoying the glorious views from the plateau cliff tops. After resting weary legs in one of the local spa towns, it is worth paying a visit to the macabre Chapel of the Skulls at Czermna or the pilgrimage church at Wambierzyce.

The Karkonosze mountains

The E3 skirts the Karkonosze and walkers are often diverted from the valley floors by the allure of the mountains. The highest part of the massif forms the Karkonosze National Park and is a popular Polish hiking destination. Paths at Karpacz and Szklarska Poręba, or chairlifts if preferred, take hikers from the spruce

[i] CONTACT INFORMATION

Karkonosze National Park
ul Chalubinskiego 23
58-570 Jelenia Góra
Poland
Tel & Fax: (00 48) 75 53726

Góry Stołowe National Park
Sloneczna 31
57-250 Kudowa Zdroj
Poland
Tel: (00 48) 74 661436

Wrocław town hall

The Trail of the Eagles' Nests

*The trail winds its way over pitted hills, between the now ruined
castles that defended Poland's southern borders in the Middle Ages.*

The Kraków-Częstochowa Upland is
a band of gentle hills stretching
between these two historic cities. It is
predominately a limestone landscape
of stumpy peaks and weathered
outcrops, with steep ravines
separating hills riddled with caves. As
well as the Trail of the Eagles' Nests,
which weaves its way leisurely over
the Upland for 165km, there are many
shorter waymarked routes. Kraków is
also an ideal base from which to head
into the Tatra mountains.

The castles of the trail

In the 14th and 15th centuries the
Kraków-Częstochowa Upland was the
natural border between the kingdoms
of Bohemia and Poland. Anxious to
preserve their territorial interests, the
Polish kings built a series of imposing
defensive strongholds on the hilltops.
All the castles were destroyed in the
17th century during the Swedish
Wars and the Trail of the Eagles'
Nests weaves its way past these
picturesque ruins. The most
spectacular is at Ogrodzieniec where
the castle is embedded into the top of
the hill, with the rock itself forming
part of the external walls.

Częstochowa

Częstochowa lies at the northern end
of the trail with the fortified Jasna
Góra monastery a potent symbol of
Polish Catholicism. The centre of the
country's most important pilgrimage,
several million visitors a year journey
to the site from around the world.
The focus of veneration is the icon of
the Black Madonna, to which many
miracles have been attributed.

The monastery was established in the
14th century. Substantial fortification,
with the proceeds of the 16th and
17th century trading boom, ensured
that the monastery withstood the
Swedish sieges of 1655. Inside, there
are rich Baroque decorations with an
exquisite ebony and silver altar and
much priceless goldwork.

The Chapel of Blessed Kinga, Wieliczka salt mine

Ojców National Park

Just to the north of Kraków, the trail
passes through Ojców National Park.
Ojców covers 19 sq km of the Pradnik
and Saspowska valleys and is a

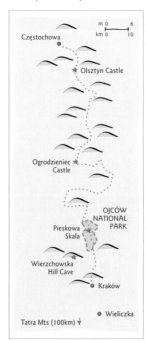

microcosm of the Upland region.
Again a limestone landscape, its
canyons and cliffs are filled with rocks
eroded over time to form strange
shapes. Hercules' Club is an 18m high
freestanding limestone column, whilst
the Krakowska Gate is a natural arch
at the entrance to the park. Hidden in
the cliff-faces there are over 200
caves, of which Ciemna and Lokietek
are the only two open to the public.
To the south-west is Wierzchowska
Hill cave, which at 1,000m in length
is the longest cave in the Upland.

Ojców's caves are home to seventeen
species of bats (there are only twenty
one in the whole of Poland), a
proliferation that has made the bat
the Upland's symbol. The mixed
forests of fir, pine, beech and oak
provide habitats for small predators,
such as marten and fox, whilst over
600 species of butterfly flit across the
meadows on the ravine floors.

Pieskowa Skala is the exception on a
trail of otherwise ruined castles.
Sitting on the slopes behind Hercules'
Club and surrounded by a sea of
trees, the original 14th century Gothic
structure building was transformed
into a Renaissance fortress in the
mid 16th century. Although it did
not escape the Swedish Wars, careful
restoration has returned it to its
former glory.

Kraków

Kraków, the jewel in the crown of
Poland's cities, marks the southern
end of the trail. Its role as the
commercial and political capital of
Poland until the late 16th century is
captured in the outstanding Baroque
architecture of the city's historic core.
The huge central *Rynek* (market
square), the royal castle and cathedral
on the Wavel Hill complex form a
UNESCO site of world cultural
heritage. Kraków boasts over 6,000
historic buildings, and remains a
vibrant cultural centre with a host of
festivals throughout the year.

Jasna Góra monastery, Częstochowa

Tatra mountains

The Tatras, the only alpine mountains in Poland, are within easy reach of Kraków. The best place to walk is the national park where there is an extensive network of paths. In the western half of the park, where it is quieter, walkers will find a landscape of rounded tops and long valleys. The Chocholowska valley leads up to Mount Wolowiec and the Koscieliska valley to Lake Smerczynski.

In the High Tatras, in the east of the park, the granitic rocks have been formed into a classic glacial landscape of pyramidal peaks, high cirques and U-shaped valleys. Two popular starting points are the cable-car up to Mount Kasprowy Wierch and the road up to the spectacular Morskie Oko glacial lake at the base of Mount Rysy.

Wieliczka salt mine

It may seem unusual for a salt mine to have gained UNESCO recognition, but Wieliczka is a little different. Mining has been continuous here since the 13th century, and the workings now stretch for over 320km and down to 327m below the surface.

The public can tour 3.5km of the passages, walking through large natural rock chambers and visiting three chapels carved entirely from salt. The Chapel of Blessed Kinga lies 100m underground. 50m long and 12m high, it is richly decorated with a salt altar, salt sculpture, salt reliefs and salt chandeliers.

🛈 CONTACT INFORMATION

Ojców National Park
32-047 Ojców
Poland
Tel: (00 48) 12 389 2005

Tatra National Park
ul Chalubinskiego 42a
34-500 Zakopane
Poland
Tel: (00 48) 165 63203
Fax: (00 48) 165 63579

CZECH REPUBLIC

North-East Bohemia

The Český ráj, which translates attractively as 'Bohemian Paradise', is one of finest parts of the Czech Republic. Take the time to clamber up from the pathways and sit on a ledge overlooking the forest's green roof.

The understated trio of the Český ráj, Orlické hory and Broumov are a little different. Visiting them is more akin to opening the pages of a story book than stepping back in time. Here, adventure is not in climbing the highest mountain or walking the furthest distance, but discovering what's hidden behind the strangely shaped rocks or hearing legends of wicked noblemen and ruined castles.

One of the other main attractions of this part of the Czech Republic is that it has not become a mass destination. The crowds are attracted either by the grandeur of Prague or the height of the Krkonoše mountains, leaving a few free to enjoy the calm atmosphere of this part of Bohemia. Long, warm summers mean that the weather is fine from late spring through to early autumn. For the Krkonoše, or for Prague, avoid July and August when both positively heave with tourists.

The Český ráj

The Český ráj is an old sandstone plateau riven with river valleys and stream courses. Its remaining rocky outcrops form densely packed, worn blocks and towers, all imaginatively named to reflect the objects or people they could represent. Within the bulk of the plateau, volcanic rocks have forced themselves to the surface, producing isolated hills rich in agates, ameythsts and other precious stones.

All of the Český ráj is heavily forested, with pine trees growing on top of even the most inaccessible pinnacles. There is the rich, sweet scent of needles, which fall to produce a soft carpet underfoot. Relatively unknown outside of the country, walkers can enjoy the shadowed quiet of the sandstone 'rock cities' and the fairytale magnificence of the many castles in relaxing solitude.

From Turnov to Jičín

The Český ráj is a compact area with its best features located between Turnov and Jičín. Either town is a pleasant base and the walk between the two is a recommended alternative to travelling between sites by car. The most popular 'rock cities' are Hrubá Skála, near to Turnov, and Prachovské Skály, closer to Jičín. The latter impresses for the sheer size of its massed outcrops, whilst the former has the more intricate features, its shaped needles and columns standing close together to produce a labyrinthine network of paths.

Other sites are close by. Near to the village of Malá Skála are the Suché rocks, a sandstone spine of white fingers protruding through the greenery. North of Turnov is Postojná, the largest sandstone cavern in the region. North again are the Bozkov caves and their subterranean lakes.

Castles & fortresses

The ruined fortress of Trosky is the most famous landmark of the Český ráj. Sitting precipitously on an outcrop, its two Gothic towers, named 'the Old Woman' and 'the Maiden', were built high on two separate columns of basalt which rise above the surrounding sandstone. Dominating the plateau, Trosky has a haunting appearance that has long attracted painters, poets and visitors.

Sandstone rock formations in the Český ráj

226

Kost is the best preserved of the castles. Built in typical Gothic style in the 14th century on top of a ridge, Kost survived wars before succumbing to fire in the 16th century. Burnt to the ground, its shell was used as a granary. This inauspicious fate, however, ensured it was ignored during later centuries when other castles were transformed into Baroque or Romantic monuments to opulence. Kost was restored recently to reflect its original architecture.

Broumov

Tucked away in the north-east corner of north-east Bohemia, Broumov is an attractive, forested landscape with similar rock formations to those in the Český ráj. The Broumov walls are a 12km long ridge. Marking the watershed between the Baltic and the North Sea, the walls are composed of blocks of sandstone up to 100m high separated by narrow canyons. There are sweeping views into nearby Poland from the top of the ridge, while the Adršpach and Teplice rocks are to the west. Between the three sites there are over 1,700 pillars, creating sinuous mazes of passageways.

Orlické hory

People flock to the Krkonoše mountains because of their snow-capped ridges, spruce forests and facilities for winter and summer holidays. The climb to the highest point of Sněžka or a walk along the ridge bordering Poland is rewarding, but the paths can be busy.

For secluded, peaceful walking, the Orlické hory to the east is a better alternative. These mountains form a 50km ridge, again adjoining Poland, peaking at Velká Deštná (1,115m). The upper slopes are thick with spruce although some deforestation, due to industrial air pollution, is apparent. The ridge falls away to an upland plateau of oak, beech and flower-filled meadows.

A mountain path traverses the length of the range. Established by a local man named Jirasek in the 1920s, the 90km route is part of a much wider network of day hikes. The 17km ridge section is the best of the high-level walking, whilst there are paths to the mountain peat bogs and the military fortifications dating from the 1930s.

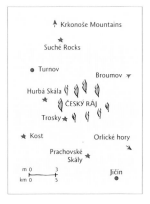

ⓘ CONTACT INFORMATION

Czech Tourist Authority
Czech Centre
95 Great Portland Street
London WIN 5RA
Tel: 020 7291 9920
Fax: 020 7436 8300

Czech & Slovak Tourist Centre
16 Frognal Parade
Finchley Road
London NW3 5HH
Tel: 0800 026 7943
Fax: 020 7794 3265
Web: www.czech-slovak-tourist.co.uk

The ruins of Trosky castle

The Czech Greenways

A wandering, languorous, lowland route that explores the cultural heritage of one of the most picturesque regions in central Europe.

The Czech Greenways runs for 400km south and east between the cities of Prague and Vienna. The route takes walkers through an idyllic landscape of small farms and well-tended fields, rolling hillsides and leafy forests, and past fortified towns and imposing castles lining medieval trade routes. Many of these areas of natural beauty are designated reserves, and each town is steeped in its own individual history of trade, war and religion.

Although the patchwork of local trails that form the route is old, the Greenways is a new phenomenon. Developed and publicised by conservationists in the wake of the 1989 revolution, the Czech Greenways seeks to protect and preserve the intricate, undisturbed landscapes of Bohemia and Moravia from unfettered development.

Prague's bridges across the Vltava river

Freedom to explore

The central and southern parts of the Czech Republic enjoy hot, dry summers with the best time to walk between May and September. The warmth of spring sees the emergence of wildflowers in the meadows; summer's long, hazy days are occasionally interrupted by brief, cooling thunderstorms; whilst in autumn the grapes are picked and crushed to make the year's vintages.

The other attraction of the Greenways is its easy variety. There is no compunction to complete the whole route, leaving walkers free to explore the landscapes that most interest them. As an alternative, it is possible to cycle, following a signposted route along the backroads, or canoe the wide rivers. The route has seven main sections, but each is divided into day walks. Companies offering guided tours often skip between sections, choosing particular points of interest. It is possible to do the same on self-guided or independent holidays and most towns have a Greenways information centre.

Tábor and the Hussites

The town of Tábor is situated south of Prague in the lower Vltava valley. Decades before Martin Luther's reforming activities, the town was a centre of the Táborites, an extreme wing of the 15th century Hussite movement, which advocated religious and social reforms. After defeating Catholic armies, the Taborite community finally succumbed to more moderate Hussite forces. Today, signs of this sleepy town's turbulent history are seen in its maze of streets, designed to disorientate enemy troops, as well as in the exhibits at the Hussite military museum.

Girls in traditional costume, Southern Moravia

Blanský les

Blanský les lies just to the north of the town of Český Krumlov. A managed forest reserve, the land rises to over 1,000m and the remaining primeval beech stands mingle with cultivated spruce and pine. The shady beech form their own ecological niche and are home to rare plants as well as wood pigeon, flycatchers and grouse. There is a path leading from the magnificent castle in the town to the viewing platform at Kleť, the highest point in the area.

The Třeboňsko wetlands

To the east is Třeboňsko. Between the 14th and 16th centuries, settlers on this marshy plateau built a series of canals to drain and fill over 400 artificial carp ponds. The ponds remain in use today and form an important part of the mosaic of wetland ecosystems that characterise this newly protected landscape area. There are floodplain forests adjacent to the meandering sweep of the River Lužnice and its network of pools and oxbow lakes, together with alder and willow marshes, wet meadows and vast, flat peat bogs. Třeboňsko is an important site for birds, with ducks, geese, swans, herons and bitterns nesting amongst the wetlands.

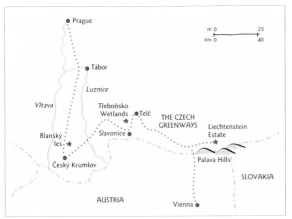

Pálava & the Liechtensteins

Southern Moravia offers one of the strangest combinations of the Greenways. The ancient landscape of the rugged Pálava hills sits incongruously next to a 19th century forest and garden complex which stretches for 12km between châteaux at Lednice and Valtice. The hills are gentle treeless chunks of white limestone rich in wildflowers, with forest and wet meadows along the floodplain of the River Dyje.

The Liechtenstein family was not one to be overly impressed by nature itself and in the 19th century thought they could do better. The result was the planning and planting of the Bořĺ les to celebrate both ancestral memories and the continuing wealth of the dynasty. The forest is 200 sq km and in between the fields and fish ponds are dotted assorted temples, archways and even a 60m high minaret.

i CONTACT INFORMATION

Czech Tourist Authority
Czech Centre
95 Great Portland Street
London W1N 5RA
Tel: 020 7291 9920
Fax: 020 7436 8300
Web: www.czech-tourinfo.cz

Medieval trade routes

The Bohemian–Moravian border was an important junction for the medieval salt, silver and gold caravans that passed between northern and southern Europe. Landštejn castle and the towns of Telč and Slavonice had a symbiotic relationship with the travelling merchants, protecting the routes and providing secure shelter behind fortified walls in return for tolls. By accident of history, neither town has ever really been developed and both are now acclaimed as the country's finest Renaissance towns.

Telč's Gothic buildings were destroyed in a fire in the early 16th century, but the residents' ample wealth funded an immediate rebuilding of the townhouses, market square and château in the contemporary style.

Slavonice has suffered a sadder, slower fate with its population drained by war, disease, economic isolation and, most recently, the politics of the Cold War. Today, the town has the appearance of an old museum, and only slowly is a feeling of colour and movement beginning to return to the streets and squares.

Telč in Southern Moravia

Walking amongst Slovakia's Mountains

With alpine peaks rising decisively over precipitous ridges and plunging glacial valleys, Slovakia's mountains are a haven for walkers.

Popradské Pleso at the bottom of Mengusovská valley in the High Tatras

Slovakia defines itself by its mountains. The east and west of the country is flat, but the central regions are distinguished by the sweep of the Carpathians. The mountains – the High Tatras, the Low Tatras, the Malá Fatra and the Veľká Fatra – have a potent symbolism. Historically they have been identified by Slovaks as guarantors of freedom. This high regard is reflected in the composition of the national flag: across the central blue band is a red Gothic shield, a double cross rising from the middle peak of a chain of three mountains.

Vysoké Tatry – High Tatras

The High Tatras are affectionately and aptly known as the 'Little Giant Mountains'. 'Little' as the range is squeezed into a surprisingly compact area – the main ridge, which stretches from Ľaliové Sedlo in the east to Kopské Sedlo in the north-west, is only 27km in length. 'Giant' as the mountains, six of which are over 2,500m in height, were created in the same epoch as the Alps and the Himalayas. Seeing the High Tatras

for the first time, visitors cannot help but be struck by their grandeur. On a clear day the transition from lowlands to foothills to mountains is breathtaking.

In the hilly lowlands, green pastures rise leisurely towards the north. The gentle ascent is punctured by the streams that, having plunged from the mountains, merge, widen and deepen to become small rivers which mould their own shallow valleys. These wend their way into a network which eventually drains into the Black Sea far to the south-east. Within this landscape, partially hidden behind clumps of evergreens, are hamlets with timber churches and farmsteads with steep triangular roofs.

Ahead, at the foot of the peaks, there is a noticeable change in the colour and angle of the slopes. These are the dark foothills where the bright summer sun is absorbed by thick swathes of Norway spruce and Scots pine. In these forests, away from the intruding paths, prosper brown bears, lynx, wolves and deer.

Capercaillie and woodcock blend into the damp undergrowth, their natural camouflage ensuring they are rarely seen. Amongst the trees, hawks and owls hunt small mammals, including the shy forest dormouse and the Tatran shrew. In the few open spaces, identifiable from a distance by the glint of sunlight on metal, are the ski resorts which act as bases for walkers in the summer and early autumn.

From the lowlands the tree line is clearly visible. Above it, with only scrub and dwarf pine able to survive the poor soils and harsh climate, the true nature of the mountains is unmasked. Steep valleys reach back into the heart of the massif. Each begins high up in a separate glacial corrie at the base of a pyramidal peak. Ridges separate the valleys, their thick flanks strewn with boulder fields, individual rocks detached from the granitic mass by a continuous cycle of freezing and thawing. Between each snow-capped peak is strung a connecting arête, the narrow path and steep sides providing a thrilling hike if the route is passable.

The Tatry National Park

With snow covering the mountains for over 200 days a year, many paths are closed in winter and spring. Late spring can be a good time to visit, as long as the snow has melted. Even then streams are full and fast flowing, making them difficult to cross. Summers are busy, so early autumn is probably the best time to walk. It is important to note that conditions defy the tag of 'littleness'; many of the routes are arduous, whilst above the forests, the mountains are exposed, temperatures low and the weather subject to rapid change.

Walking routes

Red daubs of paint mark the Magistrála, the longest route in the High Tatras. Starting at Podbanské, the trail traverses the southern slopes of the range, flitting either side of the tree line as the terrain permits. It finishes at a chalet on the other side of Skalnaté Pleso, one of over one hundred small lakes perched in glacial hollows or behind moraine deposits. Over 45km in length, few walkers will tramp from end to end, but many will use parts of it to access the valleys and the peaks that sit above.

The resort of Štrbské Pleso lies towards the west of the range, next to a lake of the same name and beneath Solisko (2,404m). The Magistrála skirts the town before climbing up Mengusovská

valley and out of the forests. Two of the main peaks are within a hard day's walk from Štrbské Pleso. A marked path tackles Kriváň (2,494m) across its south-west slopes, the difficult ascent rewarded by spectacular views of the Western Tatras, east over the packed peaks of the High Tatras and south to the broad ridge of the Low Tatras. Alternatively, leave the Magistrála at Popradské Pleso and climb to Rysy (2,499m) which straddles the border with Poland. The view to the north is of the Polish Tatras, themselves protected within a national park.

Further along the foothills to the east, the funicular railway from Starý Smokovec to Hrebienok is a pleasant and gentle start to a day's walking. The snouts of two valleys meet just above the terminal. A marked trail snakes up the Veľká studená valley, passing twenty seven tarns on its way to the Zbojnícka chalet. The chalet sits at the head of the valley, idyllically situated under the penetrating gaze of four mountains.

Much more than a mountain hut, Zbojnícka, as with the other chalets in the High Tatras, provides comfortable accommodation and hot meals for tired walkers. It is possible to return the same way, but crossing over into adjacent valleys provides for a more varied trip. It is also worth a brief detour to the north to look west to Gerlachovský štít (2,665m).

Nízke Tatry – Low Tatras

The Low Tatras are an interesting alternative to their counterparts to the north. Away from a few focal chairlifts, these mountains, although part of another national park, have a desolate emptiness not always associated with a managed landscape. Walkers get a real sense of solitude, especially in the east of the 90km range where the paths are quiet.

Although lower in height, the Low Tatras have the same characteristics as the High Tatras. On the main granitic mass, above the tree line, grows Austrian leopard's bane with its big yellow flowers, whilst alpine aster and edelweiss flourish on the isolated limestone outcrops. Marmots populate the meadows, whilst chamois were reintroduced twenty years ago.

[i] CONTACT INFORMATION

High Tatras National Park
TANAP Administration
Vila Zorka 10
059 60 Tatranská Lomnica
Slovakia
Tel & Fax:(00 421) 969 446 7195
E-mail: tanap@sazp.sk

Low Tatras National Park
Správa NAPANT
Internátna 2
974 01 Banská Bystrica
Slovakia
Tel: (00 421) 88 4130 888
Fax: (00 421) 88 4130 820
E-mail: napant@sazp.sk

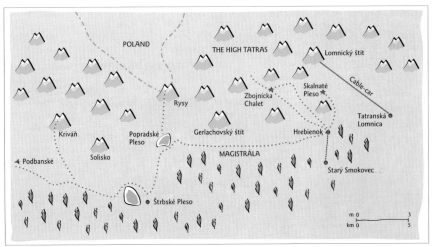

The Danube Bend

Nestling in the bend of the Danube are some of the best hiking routes in the country, winding across empty hills and skirting the historic towns of Hungary's past.

That Budapest collects plaudits with a remarkable ease should be no surprise, for it is a beautiful, vibrant city. On the west bank of the Danube is Buda, with its winding streets, imposing castle complex and sense of history. On the east side is Pest, the younger, more cosmopolitan sibling, concentrating on future opportunities rather than the lessons of the past.

The area also has many caves. Fractures in the rocks, originally caused by movements in the Earth's crust, have been expanded and shaped by the mixing of underground thermal waters and colder surface water that has seeped into the ground. Pálvölgy and Szemlőhegy are good examples, with their stalactite structures and shaped aragonite and gypsum crystal deposits.

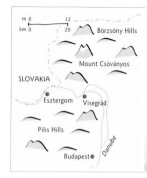

A scarce swallowtail

For walkers, the first hills actually lie within the city boundaries. The Buda Valley Landscape Protection Reserve, a 100 sq km swathe of forested hills, is a popular weekend destination for hikers. Take the small railway and then climb the final metres to the highest point for panoramic views over the city. Alternatively follow one of the paths which scatter throughout the reserve and enjoy the silence in contrast to the bustle of the streets half an hour away.

Esztergom

If Budapest is the 'Pearl of the Danube' then Esztergom is rightly called the 'Pearl of the Danube Bend'. Sitting on the southern banks of the river, the town's small size belies its historical importance. Hungary's patron saint, Stephen, was born in Esztergom and after unifying the Magyars under Roman Catholicism was crowned king there on Christmas Day in the year AD 1000. Shortly after his death he was canonised. The town retained its position as the royal seat for several centuries until the court moved to the defensive stronghold of Buda. However, Esztergom held onto its religious role and today remains the seat of the primate of Hungary.

The huge 19th century basilica, consecrated in 1856 with Franz Liszt conducting his own *Esztergom Mass*, dominates the skyline. The church houses an extensive collection of

ecclesiastical art and ornament, but it is the tomb of Cardinal József Mindszenty that is the focal point for many Hungarian visitors. The cardinal, who died in 1975, spent many years in prison or exile because of his vehement opposition to the Communist authorities. His will decreed that his body should never be returned to Hungary whilst the Communists were still in power. He was buried in Esztergom in 1991.

Pilis and Börzsöny hills

To the south of Esztergom rises the white limestone massif of the Pilis hills. Easily accessible from Budapest, the walking centre is Dobógokő. From here the two main routes are up to the high point of Pilis-tető (756m) or north through the forested hills to

Buda hills

Pálvölgy cave

the town of Dömös. The latter route runs along the ferociously named Rám precipice before ending with sweeping views of the Danube. As in the Buda hills, the other places to explore are underground, although at Vaskapu there is a rather confusing exception. Here, the cave ceiling and walls have collapsed, leaving an isolated, freestanding entrance rock.

On the other side of the river, abutting the Slovakian border, are the secluded Börzsöny hills. Wet, cool and quiet, the slopes are a haven for protected plants and birds. Diósjenő, in the east, or Kismaros, in the south, are both good starting points for a journey into the heart of the area and Mount Csóványos (929m).

Other marked trails connect the smaller peaks and the surrounding villages. One of the best routes is from Nagy Hideg Hill west to Nagybörzsöny. A mining centre in the Middle Ages, the village's past wealth is reflected in its churches. The 13th century Church of St Stephen is one of the finest examples of the Romanesque style in rural Hungary.

Visegrád

To the east of Esztergom, just as the Danube turns decisively southwards, sits Visegrád, another of the settlements in the Bend with a long and turbulent history. Behind the town rise the slopes of the Visegrád hills with plenty of paths for a day's wandering. Walkers may stumble on the rather incongruous summer bobsleigh track or the naturally warm outdoor bathing pools at Lepence.

The Visegrád citadel sits atop crags overlooking the Danube, commanding magnificent views of the river below and the Börzsöny hills beyond. Now slowly being restored after years of neglect, the citadel was built in the 13th century in response to the destruction wrought by the Mongol armies in previous decades. In the 14th century, aware of increasing hostility within Buda, the kings briefly moved their power base to the safety of the citadel.

Below the citadel, by the river, are the remains of the royal palace, established by Robert of Anjou and extended to a lavish size by Matthias Corvinus in the 15th century. It disappeared in the face of Turkish invasion and mudslides, and was increasingly presumed never to have existed, until discovered by accident in the 1930s. It remains only partially excavated and largely unrestored.

Further or faster

If the Danube Bend sounds a little too compact and relaxing then there are some exhilarating alternatives. The National Blue Trail, which crosses the northern part of Hungary from west to east, runs through the Bend. It takes walkers from the Danube at the Slovakian border, south through the Pilis range to Budapest, then north up the eastern bank, past Szentendre Island, and into the Börzsöny hills. The trail is part of Euroroute 4, the Mediterranean Arc, which starts in Gibraltar and arches up into central Europe before descending down through Romania and Bulgaria to the southern tip of the Greek mainland.

An exhausting option is to take part in what can only be described as Hungarian speed marches. These organised hikes involve walkers covering long distances, perhaps 50 or 100km, in a set time period. The most arduous is the 110km tramp from the Börzsöny hills to Budapest, to be completed in a mere 27 hours.

[i] CONTACT INFORMATION

Duna-Ipoly National Park
Hűvösvölgyi út 52
1021 Budapest
Hungary
Tel: (00 36) 1 200 4033
Fax: (00 36) 1 200 1168

The Danube Bend

233

Lake Balaton

The weathered volcanic hills and the mild climate have produced a landscape of quiet, green beauty along the northern shores of Hungary's Lake Balaton.

Located 100km to the south-west of Budapest, Balaton is the largest lake in central Europe. The southern shore is Hungary's most popular tourist destination and is lined with old towns and newer summer resorts that are crowded during the heat of July and August. Water temperatures rise quickly in the spring, reaching 26°C at the height of the summer, making swimming, sailing and windsurfing popular activities.

On the northern side, there is much less development. Landscape reserve status has historically protected the hills, forests and marshes away from the immediate shoreline, but the reed beds that line the lake edge and play an important balancing role in the aquatic ecosystem have only recently been safeguarded by conservationists.

New growth

Different parts of the northern shore are revealed throughout the seasons. Winter is cold and crisp: everywhere is snow covered and the lake freezes. In spring, the first growth returns, transforming in summer into shaded beech woods and wildflower meadows. By autumn, when the colours turn and the ground is carpeted in reds, oranges and purples, the grapes are ripe and ready to be harvested.

A white egret, symbol of Hungarian conservation

Balaton National Park

Balaton Uplands National Park was established in 1997, drawing together the landscape reserves and nature conservation areas situated on the northern edge of the lake. The Balaton Uplands cover 570 sq km, from the deciduous forests of the Koloska valley in the north-east to the wetlands and bird haven of Kis Balaton in the south-west.

As well as protecting the area's many unique geological and botanical sites, the park authorities promote the continuation of traditional agricultural practices, including viticulture.

Walking in the Káli basin

The secluded nature of the basin has long been appreciated: Roman soldiers were the first to settle within the protective envelope of hills. With Rome's decline the area was populated by the Káli tribe who founded the basis of the seven villages that still exist. Salföld, in the south-west, is a typical example with its whitewashed houses and proud church spire. Nearby are the ruins of a 13th century monastery dedicated to Mary Magdalen. Outside the village is the park's conservation farm which acts as an educational centre.

The basin is criss-crossed with a network of precisely signposted routes. The Káli basin round trip is a three day hike which takes in all the villages and the major sights. The look-out tower on top of Fekete Hill provides good views across the area, with its sweeping panorama of oak and beech forests, bog meadows, pasturelands and small, silted lakes.

Stone seas

The Káli basin is a geological mélange of red sandstone, limestone and dolomitic bedrock, interspersed with basalt cones. Having forced itself to the surface, the basalt cooled quickly, shrinking and splitting to form tall hexagonal columns that rear up above the surrounding weaker rocks. The best examples are at Hegyestű, Király and Ördöggátja.

The fields around Szentbékkálla contain one of the few remaining examples of a stone sea. The huge boulders which lie strangely scattered across the slopes mark the remnants of the petrified dunes from the ancient Pannonian Sea.

Basalt rock columns at Hegyestű

The Badacsony

The Badacsony

The Badacsony is to the south-west of the Káli basin. Volcanic in origin, this isolated hill rises from the shoreline of Lake Balaton to a high point of 437m. Having been quarried for basalt over many years, the Badacsony is now a protected landscape. Not as pillared as at Hegyestú, the basalt columns are known as 'stone stacks'. Loose rock eroded from around the column bases partially collapses them, producing thick scree.

The hill's fertile soils are protected from erosion by a hornbeam–oak forest on the plateau, ash–beech groves on the rockier slopes and lime trees on the scree. These soils, along with various microclimates and the heat retentive properties of the dark rock, support colonies of rare sub-Mediterranean plants, including eleven protected species. Black bryony, red cotoneaster, hollyfern, sweet alyssum, yellow stonecrop and variegated iris can all be found.

Badacsony's productive conditions were recognised by early settlers who initiated a long history of wine making. Evidence of Roman vineyards can be found in frescoes decorating nearby villas, as well as implements unearthed in excavations.

Tihany

The Tihany peninsula juts out into Lake Balaton from the northern shore. Smaller in area than the other parts of the national park, Tihany nonetheless still displays the rich geological and floral variety that characterises the Káli basin and the Badacsony. The hillsides are covered in vineyards and oak–ash forests, whilst the grass pastures are rich in plants and insects. Over 800 species of butterfly have been documented.

As well as providing sweeping views of the lake, the high point of Csúcs Hill reveals the extent of the peninsula's two closed lakes. Belsó lies 25m above the level of Balaton. It is surrounded by fifty geyserite and hydroquartzite cones, the minerals deposited by thermal water that periodically gushed to the surface once the initial phase of volcanic activity had ceased.

The peninsula also has a long history of settlement. The village of Tihany is a patchwork of old houses and fishing boats nestling on the lakeside. The dominant feature is an 11th century monastery and its thatched church. For a time the monks lived in shelters carved into the side of Óvár Hill.

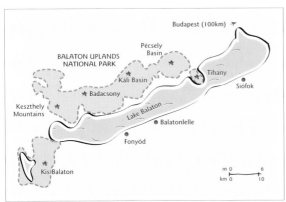

[i] CONTACT INFORMATION

Balaton Uplands National Park
Vár u. 31
8200 Veszprém
Hungary
Tel: (00 36) 88 427855
Fax: (00 36) 88 427056

CROATIA

Istria, Cres and Risnjak

Istria is much more than a resort. And beyond the peninusla lie the islands of the Adriatic and the mountains of the mainland.

The north-west is not a specific administrative region of Croatia. However in this corner of the country three very different landscapes offer a variety of active holidays to those who wish to get out of the hotel and into Croatia itself. The undulating, wooded hillsides of Istria surround the riviera resorts; the islands of the Adriatic are framed by the clear, blue sea; and the region of Gorski Kotar boasts high plateaux, mountain peaks and thick forests.

Istria and the islands enjoy a typical Mediterranean climate with hot summers and mild winters. The winds from the Adriatic are a pleasant cooling influence, as is the sea itself. Inland at Gorski Kotar the summers are shorter and throughout the winter and there is a lot of snow.

The Istrian paradox

Istria is a major Croatian and European tourist destination with over 2 million visitors seeking out the summer sun on the peninsula's western coast each year. Yet, despite this influx, Istria does not have the

Rovinj

depressing characteristics of many Mediterranean resorts. The riviera is a pleasant place in which to enjoy the sun and the sea, and a good base from which to leisurely explore the the beauty of the landscape and the rich cultural heritage of the area.

There is much to see on the coast beyond the main riviera. As well as the bigger beaches, there are hidden bays, secluded coves and small islands to discover. At the south-west corner of the peninsula is Brijuni National Park, an archipelago of fourteen islands. The mild Mediterranean climate has encouraged thick forests of pine, cypress, oak, bay and cedar to flourish. The coastal seas are rich with fish and molluscs, whilst inland, deer and moufflon roam. Veli Brijun, the largest island, has 74km of paths and roads to explore.

Beyond the coastal fringe, the Istrian interior is a green landscape of rolling hills and swathes of deciduous woodland interspersed with vineyards, small farms and old villages. Typical of the latter are the settlements of Buje and Grožnjan, perched on hilltops overlooking the

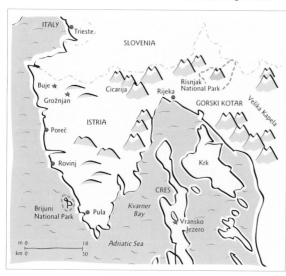

A mosaic in the Basilica of St Euphrasius, Poreč

farms below, and protected by thick defensive walls and sentry towers. This is a good place to rediscover cycling legs. Hire a bike and enjoy the gentler pace of life on the back roads and the many marked trails.

Istria's past

Istria has been enriched over the past thousand years by the ebb and flow of different civilisations and their archaeological legacies. In Brijuni the remains of a 1st century Roman villa rustica stretches around a bay on the main island. The buildings, which include three temples, residential quarters for the priests and commercial premises, are highly decorated with painted interior walls.

Poreč was originally a small Roman military base but is known primarily for the Byzantine Basilica of St Euphrasius. Dating back to the 6th century, the complex centres on a church, atrium, octagonal baptistery and palace. Well preserved and richly

decorated, the floor mosaics are compared to those found in Ravenna and the basilica has been listed by UNESCO. Rovinj is one of the nicest towns on the riviera, easily combining its traditional and modern roles as local fishing port and resort, against a background of a long and interesting

history. The present three-nave Church of St Euphemia was built in the early 18th century on the site of two early Byzantine churches. Inside you can see a 6th century classical sarcophagus of St Euphemia, as well as paintings of the Last Supper and Christ in the Garden of Gethsemane.

Motuvun – one of the hill towns on the Istrian peninsula

Cres

Kvarner presents itself as the region of shores, highlands and islands directly to the east of Istria. Cres and Krk are the biggest islands in Kvarner Bay and visitors are attracted to the former in particular by the plants and animals, the indented coast, the sea and the solitude. There are places to bike, walk, climb, swim and sail.

Cres is the second largest island in the Adriatic. Limestone and dolomite dominate, creating a contrasting littoral karst landscape of occasionally snow-clad peaks and lowland plateaux; gently sloping shorelines and steep cliffs; lush Mediterannean forest and sparse maquis. One feature that deserves a specific mention is Vransko lake. Sitting in the centre of the island, the lake is a natural reservoir fed by rainwater from surface and subterranean channels. The surface of the lake is above sea level, but its bottom is 74m below.

The island is rich in plant life. In the northern part, with cold, dry winds gusting south in winter, the flora is typically sub-Mediterannean with oak and sweet chestnut woods. In the south, which is protected by the hills, are evergreen coniferous forests. Everywhere there are wild herbs that give the local food its distinctive taste, wildflowers in the pastures and, as a reminder of the human influence, thousands of olive trees.

The islands of Brijuni National Park

Over ninety species of bird nest on the island. As well as eagles, falcons and owls, there is a dedicated ornithological reserve for the white-headed griffon vultures which nest, unusually, on rocks next to the sea.

Risnjak National Park

The other side of Kvarner is the highlands on the mainland. Gorski Kotar is a wide, heavily forested, karst plateau rising to jagged peaks. Easily accessible, owing to the proximity of the main Zagreb–Rijeka road, the area is a popular destination with Croats for walking, climbing and mountaineering. Risnjak National Park is at the northern end of the plateau and covers over 30 sq km rising from the tableland at 620m to the main peak, Risnjak, at 1,528m.

The park's varied climatic influences – the sea from the south-west, the Dinaric mountains from the south-east, the continent from the north-east and the Alps from the north-west – have enabled over 4,000 plant species to prosper. Accompanying these are over a hundred brown bears, lynx (*ris* in Croatian and after which the park is named), wolves, wild cats, wild boar, deer and chamois, as well as 500 species of butterfly.

There are also notable sights outside of the park itself. Lokvarska is one of several caves open to visitors in the summer. Over 1,000m long and dropping 140m in depth, the cave features an impressive array of stalactites, stalagmites and calcified columns. Vražji Prolaz (the Devil's Passage) at Skrad is a narrow gorge with a precipitous path winding its way through it to the 90m Zeleni vir waterfall at the far end. The Ćićarija mountains are just to the west of Gorski Kotar. A 40km long barrier that blocks Istria off from the rest of Croatia, the chain peaks at Platnik

Gorski Kotar

The rocky coast of the island of Cres

(1,273m). Being nearer to the sea the climate is considerably milder than at Risnjak, although there is often still snow on the summits in May.

For the serious walker there are four major long-distance routes in the area. One of them, the Rijeka mountain traverse, is a six to seven day walk taking in all the important peaks. Starting from near the Ćićarija mountains in the west, the route passes through Risnjak and then turns south over Velika Kapela to finish at Crikvenica on the coast. Paths are well marked and mountain huts provide overnight accommodation. An authorised guide is recommended.

CONTACT INFORMATION

Croatian National Tourist Office
2 The Lanchesters
162-164 Fulham Palace Road
London W6 9ER
Tel: 020 8563 7979
Fax: 020 8563 2616
Web: www.htz.hr

Velebit and Paklenica National Park

Whether high on a wild ridge, deep in a verdant woodland or wandering the streets of an ancient town, there are many ways to enjoy this part of the Adriatic.

Velebit is an untamed mountainous ridge which looms as large in the Croatian mentality as it does on the ground. Lying adjacent to the Adriatic and occupying over 2,000 sq km in a belt 145km long and up to 30km wide, this limestone mass is a designated UNESCO biosphere reserve. Velebit is perfect for those wanting to explore a fascinating area in solitude. It is possible to hike the whole length of the ridge, following Premuzic's path and staying in mountain huts, whilst the more compact Paklenica National Park also offers excellent walking opportunities.

On the ridge

Despite its proximity to the coast and the pleasant climate of nearby island archipelagos, Velebit's size ensures that only on the coastal slopes is it typically Mediterranean. On the top of the ridge the climate is consistently continental, with intense summers exacerbated by the scarcity of surface water and then followed by cold, harsh winters. The peaks of Velebit endure temperatures below 0°C on 160 days in a year. July to September are thus the best months to visit.

Velebit's landscape

Velebit combines sheer size with the jagged intricacies of karst landforms. From afar it has an impressive bulk, with the ridge being untouched by any major transverse passes. On both sides steep slopes sweep downwards, to sea level at the coast and inland to the Lika plateau. Thus, Velebit stands isolated and aloof as a long barrier separating the sea from the interior. The ridge's limestone has been weathered over thousands of years to create a landscape of deep gorges, sheer cliffs, dark sinkholes, caves and subterranean drainage systems.

As with the climate, the flora of Velebit varies with altitude and location. The coastal slopes are rocky, with a thin covering of maquis and scrub. Inland there is considerably more variety, with broad, leafy woods developing into denser, wilder beech, juniper and pine forests towards the peaks. Just below the ridge, the flora becomes sub-alpine with meadows filled with wildflowers. Bears are the most famous residents of the reserve, but wolves, martens, wildcats, deer, snakes, golden eagles, griffon vultures and long-eared owls can also be found.

Sculpted limestone rock in Velebit

Limestone crags rising above the pine forests in Velebit

Paklenica National Park

Paklenica, the area surrounding Vaganski (1,757m), was designated a national park in 1949. One of the more accessible areas of Velebit, the 36 sq km park offers an impressive array of karst phenomena. Paklenica is based within the catchment area of two rivers, centring on a long, forested valley with cliffs rising to 400m. Isolated peaks, such as Anića kuk, are favourites with climbers, whilst Manita pec and Jama vodarica are two subterranean formations for potholers to explore.

Caves

Croatia has many complex cave systems but few are open to visitors. However, in the Cerovac caves, south of the town of Gračac, 900m of both Gorna Spilja (1,290m) and Donja Spilja (2,510m) are accessible to the public. Amongst the stalactites and caverns, highlights include the 'Wishing Well of Life' and the 'Crystal Hall', as well as a rock profile said to resemble Djed Mraz (Santa Claus).

Wandering the wilderness

For the adventurous, Hajdučki and Rožanski kukovi represent Velebit at its wildest and most inhospitable. Covering an area of 20 sq km in the north of the park, these imposing, white peaks are separated from each other by seemingly endless ravines.

One of these, Lukina Jama, descends for 1,353m, making it one of the world's deepest holes. Elsewhere the landscape is characterised by strangely shaped rocks, vertical cliffs and stunted, windblown trees.

Velebit's variety

Part of the attraction of Velebit is the variety of different landscapes hidden in small niches of the reserve. On the Podorje coast, deep river gorges have been flooded by the Adriatic, creating long sheltered coves. Nearly 1km long and around 100m wide, Zaratnica Bay would be termed a fjord in Norway.

The Stirovaca valley has been called a romantic corner in the wilderness. Like an enchanted kingdom, the secluded valley floor with its dense spruce forest and fresh water springs offers solitude and peace.

Baske Oštarije is one of the few places in Velebit where the different climatic regimes meet. Separating the central and southern sections of the reserve, the plateau is known as the Mountain Pass of Wind and Sun. Cold continental winds whipping over the peaks meet the warmth of the Mediterranean sun under clear skies.

Zadar

Zadar is the administrative, commercial and cultural centre of the Velebit area. The town has had a turbulent history having been occupied by or defended from the Romans, Croat-Hungarians, Venetians and Turks at different points, resulting in a variety of architectural styles and a mosaic of city walls. It is best known for its ecclesiastical architecture. The 9th century St Donat's church is a fine example of a pre-Romanesque building, and the Cathedral of St Stosija is a 12th century Romanesque church built on an early Christian basilica. Zadar's museums also house a collection of paintings by Carpaccia, Lotha and Banic.

[i] CONTACT INFORMATION

Croatian National Tourist Office
2 The Lanchesters
162-164 Fulham Palace Road
London W6 9ER
Tel: (020) 8563 7979
Fax: (020) 8563 2616
Web: www.htz.hr

The Transylvanian Alps

Escape from the legacy of Dracula into an exhilarating world of rugged peaks, alpine panoramas, sparkling lakes and bottomless gorges, where even the cruellest of vampires would tremble in awe.

Transylvania. Few relatively unvisited parts of the world have acquired as fixed a reputation as has this area of Romania. The region's mystique as a land of rural tranquillity shadowed by foreboding mountains is an image that is constantly recycled by the legend of Dracula.

Here the fertile valleys are filled with villages and wooden churches, girls in colourful costumes and shepherds driving flocks of sheep. Looming close are the mountains' steepled peaks. Dark nights are illuminated by the flash of lightning, and the sound of horses' hooves echo as a lone rider enters the castle forecourt . . . Stop, it's not really like this!

Southern Carpathians

The Carpathians cover one third of Romania. The Southern Carpathians, which are also known as the Transylvanian Alps, branch off from the main Carpathian range near the city of Brașov and sweep south-west to the Serbian border. Rather than suggesting a pastoral utopia, the Transylvanian villages and small towns on the northern flank have an air of slight neglect. Romania has had a difficult time economically since the revolution in 1989 and facilities for both locals and visitors are limited. The mountains, however, do possess a thrilling wildness. High, rocky, exposed and empty, the Transylvanian Alps are a final bastion of untamed nature in central Europe.

Mountain conditions

In the mountains, winter lasts from November through to May or June, with heavy snows obliterating paths and winds taking temperatures well below freezing. Under these conditions the Transylvanian Alps are the preserve of well-equipped alpine mountaineers. Skiing is restricted to the eastern slopes of the Bucegi massif. When the snow begins to melt, walkers return. However, the

Brașov

weather is changeable even in the height of summer, with mist or rain always a possibility. Paths are marked by daubs of paint on rocks or trees, but a map (unfortunately, accurate ones are hard to find) or local guide is essential. Accommodation is provided by chalets, which range from hotels with restaurants to basic facilities.

The Bucegi massif

The main road from Brașov south to Bucharest, Romania's capital city, passes through the Prahova valley which forms the eastern border of the Bucegi massif. Not surprisingly, ease of access makes the massif a popular

The old town in Brașov

destination for weekenders and holidaymakers. The valley caters for all tastes from grand hotels at Sinaia and Bușteni to spartan campsites. Two cable-cars serve the massif, although walkers will probably prefer to tramp one of the three main routes through the thick forests to the plateau. Once on the plateau the terrain is relatively easy. A network of paths link the chalets, passing by wind-carved stones, along rocky precipices, through alpine meadows and eventually up Mount Omu, the highest peak at 2,505m.

Piatra Craiului

The Piatra Craiului ridge is squeezed between Bucegi to the east and the Fagaras mountains to the west. Only 18km in length, this compact sliver of white limestone peaks is regarded as one of the most beautiful sights in the Alps. The two-day north–south ridge trail is both challenging and rewarding. Starting at either Plaiul Foii in the north-west or Curmatura in the north-east, walkers climb up to the ridge before following a somewhat precarious path along the narrow spine. The descent at the southern end leads into a karst landscape of deep gorges and pitted slopes where water penetrating the rock has carved a series of caves.

Fagaras mountains

The Fagaras are the heart of the Transylvanian Alps. Despite being close to the resorts of the Prahova valley, the mountains' inaccessibility has preserved them as a haven for both wildlife and dedicated outdoor enthusiasts. The railway line and road to the northern side are around 10km from the central ridge and 2,000m below it. From the southern side, it is a two or three day hike from the nearest village to the main peaks. Once the effort has been made to reach the ridge, most people walk part or all of it, sleeping in the chalets or camping. It can take between five and

Domogled mountain

In the far south-west, the spa town of Bàile Herculane is 10km north of the River Danube, which marks the border with Bulgaria. The town traces its history back to Roman times when tired legionnaires bathed in the hot springs. The soldiers erected statues in praise of the god Hercules, from which the town's name was later derived. Above the spa rise the beech- and pine-clad sides of Domogled mountain. Under the influence of a more Mediterranean climate than Retezat and the Fagaras, the flora in this protected reserve is noticeably different to that found further east along the Alps. The marked path to the peak (1,106m) is a full day's trek.

Dracula

Bran castle, near to Braşov, claims to have been the home of Prince Vlad Ţepeş, or Vlad the Impaler, upon whom Bram Stoker based his Dracula character. Commanding a pass between the mountains, Bran's thick white walls rise out of the surrounding forest, but although it looks the part, documentary evidence favours a remote castle at Poienari as the Prince's original residence.

ten days to cover the 75km between Sebesul de Sus (to the west) and Plaiul Foii (to the east). For most of the distance the ridge stays above 2,000m and includes Moldoveanu (2,553m) and Negoiu (2,535m).

Retezat National Park

Retezat was first designated a national park in 1935 and has since been expanded to cover 560 sq km at the western end of the Alps. After the sinuous ridges to the east, Retezat's bulky massif has a certain solidity to it. Intense glaciation has played an important role in the landscape.

Retezat is characterised by chiselled peaks, deep corries, sparkling lakes and rounded valleys. The lower slopes are a mixture of beech, oak and fir forests, whilst above the tree line the alpine meadows are filled with flowers in spring. Walkers will often see marmots, occasionally chamois or deer, but rarely, if ever, shy brown bears, wolves or lynx. Eagles command the open skies whilst treecreepers, woodpeckers, wagtails and dippers prefer the hush of the forest and the mountain streams. The chalet at Pietrele is a good base, as most of the park is within a day's walk from here.

ⓘ CONTACT INFORMATION

Romanian National Tourist Office
83a Marylebone High Street
London W1M 3DE
Tel: 020 7224 3692
Fax: 020 7935 6435

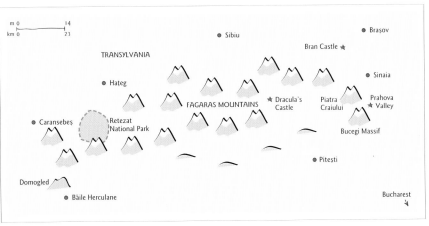

Kom-Emine

Alternating between ancient forests, high mountain meadows and ragged outcrops of rock, an enchanting assortment of scenery rich in human and natural history is encountered along the Kom-Emine.

Known to local people simply as 'Kom-Emine', the Bulgarian section of the European Rambler Association's E3 trail runs for nearly 700km along the ridge of the Stara Planina, crossing the length of the country from the Serbian border in the west to the Black Sea in the east.

Any journey along the E3 trail gives a fascinating insight into Bulgaria's past, for these mountains are studded with numerous monuments and historic sites. There is also a succession of reserves and protected localities scattered along the entire length of the range, making the route an extremely rewarding one for naturalists. Although none of the individual stages are particularly difficult in themselves, the undulating character of the trail makes some sections fairly tiring, particularly along the western half of the route which leads over many of the range's highest peaks, several of them with altitudes over 2,000m.

Iskŭr river gorge

Practicalities

With very few settlements lying on the line of the trail, walkers planning an extended journey along the route need to give careful thought to provisioning. In general, the choice is either between carrying a heavy well-stocked pack, or else travelling light and detouring more often to pick up supplies. However, with a major trunk road and railway line running along the foot of the mountains to the south, the route can easily be split up into separate sections.

Because of its geographic location, the Stara Planina represents a meeting place between cooler continental winds from the north and warmer Mediterranean air masses from the south. This produces a fairly fickle climate with the possibility of clouds suddenly unleashing a heavy shower at any time. Spring tends to be worse in this respect, with summer and

autumn generally much warmer and more settled. Winter on the other hand is often quite severe with heavy snows and biting winds making the mountains somewhat less hospitable.

Klisurski monastery

The north-western corner of Bulgaria is one of the most peaceful and unspoilt regions of the country, an idyllic rural backwater that is almost unvisited by tourists but which hides a host of treasures. Not only are there many reserves and protected natural sites, there are also several exquisite monasteries tucked away here in the forested folds of the mountains. Lying just off the E3 trail, and accessible by a marked path which breaks off from Mt Todorini Kukli (1,785m), the

Klisurski monastery is one such example, a medieval foundation that was ransacked several times during the Ottoman occupation, but which has subsequently been restored and now offers fine accommodation.

The Vrachanski Balkan

Close to its western end, the Stara Planina is cut by the mighty River Iskŭr. This has created a deep gorge which is both the lowest point along the trail and also one of the most dramatic. The sheer rock walls and bristling crags make this a popular site for climbers, as well as a favoured haunt for eagles and falcons. There is a very rich flora, and for this reason, a large area of the bordering Vrachanski massif is a specially protected reserve.

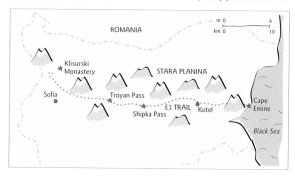

full of roses, and the nearby Etûra Ethnographic complex. Here, along the banks of a bubbling stream, is a picturesque cluster of rustic workshops where a variety of artisans can still be observed practising their traditional handicrafts and skills.

Kotel

One of the best starting points from which to explore the eastern section of the trail is Kotel, a small sleepy town which lies serene and half-forgotten in the green heart of the mountains. Despite a terrible fire in the 19th century, it still preserves many fine examples of timber-framed houses from the National Revival Period. Famed as the birthplace of several national heroes, Kotel is also known for its attractive carpets and goat-hair blankets.

Rock climbing at Lakatnik in the Vrachanski Balkan

The Troyan pass

The Troyan pass (1,565m) offers convenient access to the E3 trail and to the surrounding Central Balkan National Park. It is named after the Roman emperor Trajan Augustus who made it a major link route between the provinces of Dacia to the south and Moesia to the north, setting up several guard-posts and watchtowers in the region. Later, during the Ottoman occupation, the Turks established their own series of fortifications around the pass, which became the scene of heavy fighting during the 1877-78 Russo–Turkish War. Today a massive triumphal arch commemorates those felled in battle.

Etûra Ethnographic complex

Along a marked path that breaks off from the pass and drops down the northern flank is the Sokolski monastery, with its pretty courtyard

Cape Emine

The most easterly tip of the Stara Planina, Cape Emine marks an abrupt end to the E3 trail. Here the mountains terminate with a high crumbling cliff falling sheer towards the sea. For walkers having completed either the whole or even just a section of the route, the refreshing blue water below is a tempting sight.

Because the cape is also an important landmark for the many birds which migrate every spring and autumn along the western shore of the Black Sea, ornithologists coming here at times of passage are usually well rewarded by frequent sightings.

ℹ CONTACT INFORMATION

BAAT (Bulgarian Association for Special Interest Travel)
Odysseia-IN Ltd (activity / special interest tour operator)
20-V Stamboliiski Blvd
Sofia 1000
Bulgaria
Tel: (00 359) 2 989 0538
Fax: (00 359) 2 980 3200
E-mail: odysseia@omega.bg
Web: www.newtravel.com

Perelik Guiding Services
31a Canterbury Road
Herne Bay
Kent CT6 5DQ
Tel: 01227 373046
Fax: 01227 373727
E-mail: perelik2000@yahoo.com

Drianovo monastery

BULGARIA

The E8 Trail

The route traced out by the Bulgarian section of the E8 trail is exceptionally varied, offering something for every taste.

Opened in 1993, the Bulgarian section of the European Rambler Association's E8 trail runs for about 600km across the southern part of the country. Travelling circuitously south-east, an ever-changing succession of landscapes unrolls.

The trail starts in the Rila mountains, a region of breathtaking beauty with high alpine peaks and sparkling glacial lakes. Having traversed the Rila's easternmost massif and the highest mountain in south-eastern Europe, walkers enter the Rodopi range, where the landscape immediately changes. These mountains form the most extensive range in the country – a sea of rippling ridges that cover a vast part of southern Bulgaria and are hauntingly beautiful and mysterious.

Walking in the Rodopi mountains

'Mushroom' rock formations

Old roads and bridges, fortresses and churches all serve as reminders to the long-standing economic, cultural and strategic significance of these mountains. In many places, time seems to have stood still, and the visitor encounters a rural way of life which appears to have changed little over the past few hundred years. Many of the hamlets and villages have preserved their unique stone and timber houses. The local people maintain a traditional rural existence working the fields by hand and grazing livestock in the meadows.

The natural history of the region is equally as rich as its cultural legacies. The Rodopi is a remote refuge for many plants and animals that are now either extinct or exceptionally rare elsewhere. Here, brown bears, wolves and wildcats still find a safe haven amongst ancient coniferous forests that are some of the most extensive and pristine in Europe.

Seasons

For ordinary hikers, the highest parts of the Rila are inaccessible during the winter, and are best left to well-equipped alpinists until the start of summer. Many western parts of the Rodopi also experience heavy snowfalls, and here too drifts can often be found lying late into April or even early May.

When the snow finally melts, spring and early summer are extremely green and beautiful, with wildflowers decorating the woodland glades and meadows. It is mostly warm and sunny, but there are often short, sudden downpours accompanied by thunder and lightning. During summer and autumn the weather tends to be more stable, and later in the year the forests start to change colour, and a bountiful supply of wild mushrooms, fruits and nuts are found growing alongside the trail.

Musala

Starting from Borovets, one of Bulgaria's largest skiing resorts, the E8 trail begins abruptly, leading up through the forests and out into the alpine zone on the very first day. The focus of the Rila section of the route is undoubtedly the ascent of Mt Musala (2,925m), the highest peak in south-eastern Europe, a proud 8m higher than its nearest rival, Mt Mitikas in Greece's Olympos range. The summit area may be somewhat scruffy, but the panorama it offers over a vast swathe of the Balkan peninsula is superb.

Forests and reservoirs

The Rodopi mountains are rich in natural resources. The eastern part harbours a varied assortment of rocks and minerals, whilst the western part is a land blessed with timber and water. This is a striking feature of the trail, particularly during the first few stages where there is a series of reservoirs used for hydroelectric power. Dominating the opening sections, however, are the forests. The Rodopi mountains account for over three quarters of the total area of Bulgaria's coniferous forests, providing high quality timber to the state, and a secure home for many birds and animals.

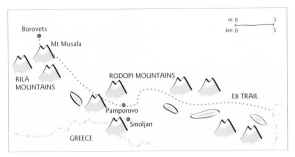

Caves and gorges

South of Devin, the character of the trail changes abruptly, and walkers reach a striking karst region where the grey limestone rocks have been deeply scored by rivers and fissured by caves. The rocks are a refuge for several rare and endemic flowers, as well as a nesting site for birds like the wallcreeper. The numerous caves and caverns make the region a favourite with speleologists. Between the villages of Yagodina, Trigrad and Mogilitsa two major systems are now open to the general public.

Land of Orpheus

Tucked away in a valley at the northern foot of the Perelik massif is the small village of Shiroka Lŭka, a cluster of white-washed cottages built in traditional Rodopi style. An architectural reserve and ethnographic centre, the villagers still preserve many of their old folk customs and festivals. Shiroka Lŭka also boasts one of the most famous folk music schools in the country, thus keeping alive the legacy of Orpheus who, according to legend, roamed this part of the Rodopi in his youth.

Pamporovo

Set amidst coniferous forests and striking rock outcrops, the Pamporovo region has steadily developed into a popular mountain resort. Most visitors come here to enjoy some of the most reliable skiing conditions the country has to offer. In summer, it is an ideal starting point for an array of hiking trails that fan out into the surrounding mountains.

Bachkovski monastery

Beyond Pamporovo, the trail wends its way north through the Prespa and Dobrostan massifs. Here, it is well worth making a detour down into the valley of the Chepelarska Reka to visit the monastery near the village of Bachkovo. The second largest in the country, and one of the most atmospheric, it was founded during the 11th century. The monastery was destroyed during the Ottoman occupation, and most of the structure had to be rebuilt, but it still remains a beautiful architectural complex with some outstanding frescoes on the walls of its churches and refectory.

ℹ CONTACT INFORMATION

BAAT (Bulgarian Association for Special Interest Travel)
Odysseia-IN Ltd (activity / special interest tour operator)
20-V Stamboliiski Blvd
Sofia 1000
Bulgaria
Tel: (00 359) 2 989 0538
Fax: (00 359) 2 980 3200
E-mail: odysseia@omega.bg
Web: www.newtravel.com

Perelik Guiding Services
31a Canterbury Road
Herne Bay
Kent CT6 5DQ
Tel: 01227 373046
Fax: 01227 373727
E-mail: perelik2000@yahoo.com

The stone bridge at Mogilitsa village

The Four Mountain Traverse

The Four Mountain Traverse, the Bulgarian section of the European Rambler Association's E4 trail, is a challenging high-level route that passes through some of the most spectacular scenery in south-eastern Europe.

The Four Mountain Traverse starts from the outskirts of the Bulgarian capital Sofia, and runs south for some 240km across the Vitosha, Verila, Rila and Pirin mountains. With much of the trail running through reserves and national parks, camping is rarely an option. However, there are many mountain huts along the route offering basic accommodation. To complete the whole traverse would take several weeks, but it is simple to split it up into sections, and there are plenty of connecting paths that enable walkers to plan a variety of shorter tours.

For naturalists, the E4 provides an ideal means of visiting the protected areas in the region. The route explores deciduous and coniferous forests, sub-alpine scrub, high mountain meadows, and scree and rock habitats. The extremely varied flora includes a mix of central European and more typically southern species, along with a generous sprinkling of local endemics. There is also interesting fauna, ranging from rarely seen brown bears and wolves, to an assortment of grasshoppers and butterflies that enliven every meadow.

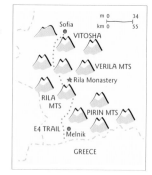

Times of year

During the winter, the mountains of south-western Bulgaria are usually under a deep blanket of snow. This has led to the development of several ski-resorts in the region. There are also plenty of possibilities for winter walking, and although many of the higher peaks and ridges are only accessible to experienced alpinists, hikers equipped with snow-shoes can still explore several sections of the trail. It is always advisable to join an organised trek, since avalanches are a threat in several parts of the Rila and

Pirin. With improved chances of sunshine and settled weather, the period from July to September is recommended as the best time to undertake extended hikes along the E4 trail. Even at the end of summer, there are still many beautiful flowers to be seen blooming between the rocks and in the alpine meadows.

The playground of Sofia

Rising directly up to the south of the Bulgarian capital, the great dome of the Vitosha massif has long been a welcome retreat for local people as they try to escape from the smog and bustle of the city. Easily reached by public transport, and studded with hotels and huts, at weekends Vitosha has the appearance of a giant park. Despite this, there is a surprising amount of unspoilt nature here and botanists in particular will find much of interest, with many unusual species growing directly alongside the trail as it crosses Vitosha's peaty high-level plateau.

Verila

Beyond Vitosha, the trail crosses the Verila massif, one of Bulgaria's more modest and less visited ranges. Low and rounded, with the highest summit only reaching a little over 1,400m, the Verila provides a gentle respite before tackling the mighty mountains to come. Although not as spectacular as the other sections, the walking is nonetheless pleasant. Routes pass through forests of beech, hornbeam and oak, where there is always the chance of catching sight of a red squirrel or roe deer.

The Sedemte Ezera cirque

On entering the Rila mountains, the trail quickly leads into the Sedemte Ezera cirque, so called on account of its seven sparkling lakes that lie clustered high on the mountainside like a horde of scattered jewels. This is one of the most beautiful and

Hiking in the snow in Vitosha

frequently visited places in the range, particularly in August when members of a religious group known as the White Brotherhood gather here to praise God and nature, welcoming the sunrise with songs and dances.

Malyovitsa

Having threaded its way between the Seven Lakes, the trail climbs up onto the ridge above, and undulates steadily along towards Mt Malyovitsa – at 2,729m, the second highest summit in this section of the Rila. As well as being a magnet for walkers, this region also attracts many climbers, for both Malyovitsa and the neighbouring peaks offer some of the most challenging climbing routes in the country.

Rila monastery

Traversing the Malyovitsa ridge, the view south over the valley of the Rilska Reka encompasses Rila monastery, which nestles far below in some of the Rila's most beautiful

View from the top of Mt Musala, Rila National Park

Sand pyramids near Melnik in the Pirin mountains

forests. The extra effort needed to detour there from the trail is well rewarded, for this is one of the most stunning architectural complexes in Bulgaria, and an important religious and cultural centre that has justifiably been declared a UNESCO world heritage site.

Northern Pirin

The final section of the trail runs through the Pirin mountains, the legendary home of the Slavic thunder god, and a mountain range that is even more rugged and wild than the neighbouring Rila. The northern part of the Pirin is particularly spectacular, and the first couple of days walking are some of the most challenging along the whole trail, especially the traverse of the Koncheto ridge.

Here, at an altitude of over 2,800m, the marble crest narrows to little more than 50cm, and with sheer drops on either side, passage over the slippery smooth rocks is assisted by a metal cable. Having overcome this, walkers are then confronted by the imposing northern face of Mt Vihren – at 2,914m, the highest peak in the Pirin. In fact the ascent is not as difficult as it looks, and with a little easy scrambling the summit can be reached.

Melnik

Although lying off the E4 trail, the town of Melnik makes a fitting alternative end to the walk. It is one of the most beautiful towns in Bulgaria and is an architectural reserve protecting a unique collection of dazzlingly white houses from the National Revival Period. The setting is equally spectacular, for Melnik lies nestled into a deep-cut gorge surrounded by weird and wonderful sandstone pinnacles. Melnik is also famed for its fruity red wine which is matured in cool cellars that have been tunnelled into the flanks of the gorge.

ℹ CONTACT INFORMATION

BAAT (Bulgarian Association for Special Interest Travel)
Odysseia-IN Ltd (activity / special interest tour operator)
20-V Stamboliiski Blvd
Sofia 1000
Bulgaria
Tel: (00 359) 2 989 0538
Fax: (00 359) 2 980 3200
E-mail: odysseia@omega.bg
Web: www.newtravel.com

Perelik Guiding Services
31a Canterbury Road
Herne Bay
Kent CT6 5DQ
Tel: 01227 373046
Fax: 01227 373727
E-mail: perelik2000@yahoo.com

CREDITS

Thank you to all those individuals and organisations who contributed material for the Activity Series.

■ Text credits

Julian Perry	Bulgaria
Benedikte Ranum	Norway
Terry Richardson	Turkey

■ Picture credits

Pictures are credited from top to bottom on each relevant page. Every effort has been made to ensure that these are correct. If there are any unintentional errors or omissions we would be pleased to update the information in future editions.

4a   Photo SVZ / W. Storto
4b   The Highlands of Scotland
        Tourist Board
4c   Luxembourg National Tourist Office
4d   Finnish Tourist Board
4e   Vilsandi National Park
4f   Algarve Tourist Board
8a   Den Norske Turistforening
8b   Destination Bornholm
8c   Faroe Islands Tourist Board
8d   Finnish Tourist Board
8e   Nordland Reiseliv a/s
8f   Faroe Islands Tourist Board
10   Photo: Timo Hentilä
11   Finnish Tourist Board
12a   Lieska Tourist Service
12b   Lieska Tourist Service
13   Lieska Tourist Service
14   Finnish Tourist Board
15a   Seitseminen National Park
15b   Finnish Tourist Board
16a   Seitseminen National Park
16b   Seitseminen National Park
18   Swedish Travel & Tourism Council
19   Photo: Pelle Anderson
20   Swedish Travel & Tourism Council
21a   Swedish Travel & Tourism Council
21b   Photo: Pelle Anderson
22   Swedish Travel & Tourism Council
23a   Swedish Travel & Tourism Council
23b   Vidmark i Värmland
24   Skånes Tourist Board
25a   Skånes Tourist Board
25b   Swedish Travel & Tourism Council
26   Nordland Reiseliv a/s
27a   Nordland Reiseliv a/s
27b   Nordland Reiseliv a/s
28a   ©Trond Emblemsvåg
        (Karstein Telstad Speisalen,
        Photo: Schrøder Trondheim)
28b   ©Trond Emblemsvåg
        (Photo: Jonny Remmereit)
29   ©Trond Emblemsvåg
        (Photo: Jonny Remmereit)
30   Photo: Hanne Sundbø,
        Reisemål Ryfylke as
31a   Reisemål Ryfylke as
31b   Reisemål Ryfylke as
32a   Holmsland Klit Turistforening
32b   Holmsland Klit Turistforening
33   Holmsland Klit Turistforening
34   Photo: W. Ferchland, The Danish
        Tourist Board, Copenhagen, Denmark
35a   Ebeltoft/Mols Turistbureau
35b   Ebeltoft/Mols Turistbureau
37a   Photo: J. Sommer, The Danish Tourist
        Board, Copenhagen, Denmark
37b   Lars Espersen
38a   Lars Espersen
38b   Lars Espersen

39   Lars Espersen
40a   Iceland Travel Group Ltd
40b   Iceland Travel Group Ltd
41a   Iceland Travel Group Ltd
41b   Iceland Travel Group Ltd
42   Faroe Islands Tourist Board
43   Faroe Islands Tourist Board
44a   Copyright: Kevin O'Hara
44b   Greenland Tourism
45   Greenland Tourism
46a   Greenland Tourism
46b   Location Greenland
46c   Greenland Tourism
47   Greenland Tourism
48a   North Yorkshire Moors National Park
48b   The Highlands of Scotland
        Tourist Board
48c   Bord-Failte / Brian Lynch
48d   The Highlands of Scotland
        Tourist Board
48e   ©ENPA
48f   ©ENPA
50   Bord-Failte – Irish Tourist Board,
        Photo: Pat O'Dea
51   Bord-Failte – Irish Tourist Board,
        Photo: Pat O'Dea
52a   Bord-Failte – Irish Tourist Board
52b   Bord-Failte – Irish Tourist Board
53   Bord-Failte – Irish Tourist Board
54a   Mayo Naturally Ltd
54b   Mayo Naturally Ltd
55   Mayo Naturally Ltd
57a   Bord-Failte / Brian Lynch
57b   Bord-Failte / Brian Lynch
58   Northern Ireland Tourist Board
59a   Northern Ireland Tourist Board
59b   Northern Ireland Tourist Board
60   Aberdeen and Grampian Tourist Board
61a   Aberdeen and Grampian Tourist Board
61b   Aberdeen and Grampian Tourist Board
62a   Argyll, the Isles, Loch Lomond,
        Stirling & Trossachs Tourist Board
62b   The Highlands of Scotland
        Tourist Board
63a   Paul Tomkins – Scottish Tourist Board
63b   The Highlands of Scotland
        Tourist Board
64   Richard Mearns
65a   Richard Mearns
65b   Keith Kirk
66a   Keith Kirk
66b   Richard Mearns
67   Richard Mearns
68a   Ron Shaw
68b   Ron Shaw
69a   Scottish Borders Tourist Board
69b   Scottish Borders Tourist Board
70   The Countryside Agency,
        North East Region
71   Department of Leisure and Tourism
72a   The Countryside Agency,
        North East Region
72b   Department of Leisure and Tourism
73a   Yorkshire Tourist Board
73b   Yorkshire Tourist Board
74   North Yorkshire Moors National Park
75a   Yorkshire Tourist Board
75b   Yorkshire Tourist Board
76a   Trans Pennine Trail Office
76b   Trans Pennine Trail Office
77   Trans Pennine Trail Office
78a   Photo: Maureen Sandford
78b   Photo: Maureen Sandford
79   Photo: Maureen Sandford
80a   Photo: Maureen Sandford
80b   Photo: Maureen Sandford
81a   Countryside Agency – Jos Joslin,
        The Ridgeway National Trail
81b   Countryside Agency – Jos Joslin,

        The Ridgeway National Trail
82   Roy Westlake / Cornwall Tourist Board
83a   Cornwall Tourist Board
83b   ©ENPA
84   Wales Tourist Board
85a   Wales Tourist Board
85b   Wales Tourist Board
86a   Gwynedd Council
86b   Wales Tourist Board Photo Library
87   Wales Tourist Board Photo Library
89   Gwynedd Council
90a   Photo: Nardin
90b   Netherlands Board of Tourism
90c   Touristik Nördlicher Schwarzwald e.V.
90d   Luxembourg National Tourist Office
90e   Fremdenverkehrsverein Regensburg,
        Ferstl
90f   Parc Naturel Régional
        Normandie-Maine
92a   CDT Finistère
92b   CDT Finistère
93   CDT Finistère
94a   Photo: D Maraux
94b   Photo: D Rondot
95   Photo: A.M.B.
96   CDT Lot-et-Garonne, D. Jacquard
97a   CDT Lot-et-Garonne, M. de Vos
97b   Tourisme d'Aquitaine
98a   CRT Riviera / Palomba / Image du Sud
98b   Office de Tourisme Municipal
        de Breil sur Roya
99   CRT Riviera / D. Martin / Image du Sud
100a Office de Tourisme de Florac
100b Office de Tourisme de Florac
101   Office de Tourisme de Florac
102   Office de Tourisme de Florac
103a Luxembourg National Tourist Office
103b Luxembourg National Tourist Office
104   Luxembourg National Tourist Office
105   Luxembourg National Tourist Office
106   Belgian Tourist Office
        Brussels & Ardennes
107a Belgian Tourist Office
107b Document OPT & K. Van Lidth
108   Belgian Tourist Office
        Brussels & Ardennes
109a Vlaanderen Tourist Office
109b Vlaanderen Tourist Office
111a Netherlands Board of Tourism
111b Netherlands Board of Tourism
112a Netherlands Board of Tourism
112b Photo: Staatbosbeheer / Freek Zwart
113   Photo: VVV Texel
114   Landkreis Emsland – Amt für Wifo
115   Marketing und Tourismus GmbH
        Osnabrück
116   Städt Verkehrsamt Lahnstein
117   Städt Verkehrsamt Lahnstein
118a Braunfelser Kur GmbH
118b Marburg Tourism and Marketing GmbH
119   Tourist Information, Wetzlar
120   ©Tourismuszentrale
        Fränkische Schweiz
121   ©Tourismuszentrale
        Fränkische Schweiz
122a FVV Ostbayern
122b Oberpfälzer Waldverein
123   Tourismusverband Ostbayern e.V.
125a Kurverwaltung Schluchsee /
        Hochschwarzwald
125b Touristik Nördlicher Schwarzwald e.V.
126a Kurverwaltung Schluchsee /
        Hochschwarzwald
126b Tourist-Information Titisee Neustadt:
        Erich Speigelhalter
127   Touristik Nördlicher Schwarzwald e.V.
128a Parco Nazionale Dolomiti Bellunesi
128b Kärnten Werburg Marketing and
        Innovations

250

128c Photo SVZ / W. Storto
128d O.T. Chamonix Mont-Blanc France,
    Photo: T. Barnett
128e Mario de Biasi: Südtirol Tourismus
    Werburg
128f Foto-archiv Tirol Werbung
130 Parc National de la Vanoise,
    Photo: Philippe Benoit
131a Parc National de la Vanoise,
    Photo: Philippe Benoit
131b Parc National de la Vanoise,
    Photo: Patrick Folliet
132 O.T Chamonix Mont-Blanc France,
    Photo: Tim Barnett
133 O.T Chamonix Mont-Blanc France,
    Photo: Tim Barnett
134a O.T Chamonix Mont-Blanc France,
    Photo: Tim Barnett
134b O.T Chamonix Mont-Blanc France,
    Photo: F Leclaire
135 O.T Chamonix Mont-Blanc France,
    Photo: Tim Barnett
136a Photo: Denis Fiat
136b Photo: Jean Pierre Nicollet
137a Photo: Jean Pierre Nicollet
137b Photo: Robert Chevalier
138a Photo SVZ / W. Storto
138b Bernese Oberland Tourism
139a Bernese Oberland Tourism
139b Bernese Oberland Tourism
140a Zentral Schweiz – tourismus
140b Zentral Schweiz – tourismus
141 Zentral Schweiz – tourismus
142a Archivio fotografico, Ticino Turismo
142b Archivio fotografico, Ticino Turismo
143a Tourist Board, Switzerland
143b Archivio fotografico, Ticino Turismo
144 Tourist Board, Switzerland
145a Tourist Board, Switzerland
145b Tourist Board, Switzerland
146a Tourist Board, Switzerland
146b Tourist Board, Switzerland
147a Tourist Board, Switzerland
147b Valais Tourism
148 Photo SVZ / Ph. Geigel
149a Mario de Biasi: Südtirol Tourismus
    Werburg
149b F Milanesio: Südtirol Tourismus
    Werburg
150 Reiseol: Südtirol Tourismus Werburg
151 Andergassen: Südtirol Tourismus
    Werburg
152a Parco Nazionale Dolomiti Bellunesi,
    Photo: E. Canal
152b Parco Nazionale Dolomiti Bellunesi
152c Parco Nazionale Dolomiti Bellunesi
153 Parco Nazionale Dolomiti Bellunesi,
    Photo: G Poloniato
154 Parco Nazionale Val Grande
155a Parco Nazionale Val Grande
155b Parco Nazionale Val Grande
156a Liechtenstein National Tourist Office
156b Liechtenstein National Tourist Office
157 Liechtenstein National Tourist Office
158a Photo: Liedtke & Kern
158b Photo: Ammon
159 Photo: Ammon
160 Foto-archiv Tirol Werbung
161 Foto-archiv Tirol Werbung
162 Foto-archiv Tirol Werbung
163a Foto-archiv Tirol Werbung
163b Foto-archiv Tirol Werbung
164 Kärnten Werburg Marketing &
    Innovations Management
165a Kärnten Werburg Marketing &
    Innovations Management
165b Kärnten Werburg Marketing &
    Innovations Management
166 Austrian National Tourist Office

167 Austrian National Tourist Office
168 ©Slovenian Tourist Board
169a Slovenia Pursuits
169b ©Slovenian Tourist Board
170 ©Iris Kürschner
171a Slovenian Pursuits
171b ©Iris Kürschner
172a Terry Richardson,
    Upcountry (Turkey) Ltd
172b Cyprus Tourism Organisation
172c Algarve Tourist Board
172d Parc National d´Aiguestortes-
    Sant Maurici
172e Cyprus Tourism Organisation
172f Parco dell'Etna
174 Madeira Tourist Office
175a Madeira Tourist Office
175b Madeira Tourist Office
176 Algarve Tourist Board
177a Algarve Tourist Board
177b Algarve Tourist Board
178a Sean Harper
178b Granada Tourism Office
179 Sean Harper
180a CENEAM – O.A. Parques Nacionales,
    España
180b CENEAM – O.A. Parques Nacionales,
    España
181 Spanish Tourist Office, London,
    Photo: M Brossa
182 Tourisme d´Aquitaine
183a CENEAM – O.A. Parques Nacionales,
    España
183b Parc National Des Pyrénées
183c CENEAM – O.A. Parques Nacionales,
    España
184 National Park of Foreste Casentinesi
185 National Park of Foreste Casentinesi
186 National Park of Foreste Casentinesi
187 National Park of Foreste Casentinesi
188 Italian State Tourist Board
    (E.N.I.T.), London
189 Italian State Tourist Board
    (E.N.I.T.), London
190 Italian State Tourist Board
    (E.N.I.T.), London
191 Italian State Tourist Board
    (E.N.I.T.), London
192a Parco dell'Etna
192b Parco dell'Etna
193 Parco dell'Etna
194a Parco dell'Etna
194b Parco dell'Etna
195 Parco dell'Etna
196 Global Scenes, Tunbridge Wells
197 Global Scenes, Tunbridge Wells
198 Global Scenes, Tunbridge Wells
199 Balis
200 Hellenic Tourism Organisation
201 Hellenic Tourism Organisation
202 Cyprus Tourism Organisation
203a Cyprus Tourism Organisation
203b Cyprus Tourism Organisation
204a Terry Richardson,
    Upcountry (Turkey) Ltd
204b Terry Richardson,
    Upcountry (Turkey) Ltd
204c Terry Richardson,
    Upcountry (Turkey) Ltd
205 Terry Richardson,
    Upcountry (Turkey) Ltd
206 Terry Richardson,
    Upcountry (Turkey) Ltd
207a Terry Richardson,
    Upcountry (Turkey) Ltd
207b Terry Richardson,
    Upcountry (Turkey) Ltd
208a Terry Richardson,
    Upcountry (Turkey) Ltd

208b Terry Richardson,
    Upcountry (Turkey) Ltd
209a Terry Richardson,
    Upcountry (Turkey) Ltd
209b Terry Richardson,
    Upcountry (Turkey) Ltd
210a Polish National Tourist Office
210b Czech Tourist Authority
210c Lubomir Popiordanov / Odysseia-in
210d Vilsandi National Park
210e Hungarian National Tourist Board
210f Czech Tourist Authority
212 Laheema National Park,
    Mr Arne Kaasik
213a Laheema National Park,
    Mr Arne Kaasik
213b Laheema National Park,
    Mr Arne Kaasik
214a Guido Leibur
214b Guido Leibur
214c Guido Leibur
215 Estonian Tourist Board
216a Photo: Andis Liepa
216b Photo: Andis Liepa
217a Photo: Andis Liepa
217b Photo: Andis Liepa
218 Aukštaitija National Park
219a Aukštaitija National Park
219b Aukštaitija National Park
220a Polish National Tourist Office
220b Polish National Tourist Office
221 Polish National Tourist Office
222 Polish National Tourist Office
223 Polish National Tourist Office
224 Polish National Tourist Office
225a Polish National Tourist Office
225b Polish National Tourist Office
226a Czech Tourist Authority
226b K plus servis – IT services
227 Czech Tourist Authority
228a Czech Tourist Authority
228b Czech Tourist Authority
229 Czech Tourist Authority
230 Czech and Slovak Tourist Centre
232a Duna-Ipoly Nemzeti Park Igazgatóság
232b Duna-Ipoly Nemzeti Park Igazgatóság
233a Duna-Ipoly Nemzeti Park Igazgatóság
233b Hungarian National Tourist Board
234a Balaton-felvidéki Nemzeti Park
234b Balaton-felvidéki Nemzeti Park
235 Hungarian National Tourist Board
236 Croatian National Tourist Board
237a Croatian National Tourist Board
237b Croatian National Tourist Board
238a Croatian National Tourist Board
238b Croatian National Tourist Board
239 Croatian National Tourist Board
240 Croatian National Tourist Board
241a Croatian National Tourist Board
241b Croatian National Tourist Board
242a Romanian Tourist Board
242b Romanian Tourist Board
243 Romanian Tourist Board
244 Lubomir Popiordanov / Odysseia-in
245a Lubomir Popiordanov / Odysseia-in
245b Lubomir Popiordanov / Odysseia-in
246a Lubomir Popiordanov / Odysseia-in
246b Lubomir Popiordanov / Odysseia-in
247 Lubomir Popiordanov / Odysseia-in
248 Lubomir Popiordanov / Odysseia-in
249a Lubomir Popiordanov / Odysseia-in
249b Lubomir Popiordanov / Odysseia-in
256a Dawn Runnals / Cornwall Tourist
    Board
256b Faroe Islands Tourist Board
256c Photo: Joomas Trapido
256d Bernese Oberland Tourism
256e Circeo National Park
257f Photo: D Maraux

INDEX

INDEX